Treated Like a Child

Stockholm Studies in Child Law and Children's Rights

VOLUME 8

The titles published in this series are listed at *brill.com/sscl*

Treated Like a Child

Age Discrimination and Children's Rights

Edited by

Aoife Daly, Pernilla Leviner and Rebecca Thorburn Stern

BRILL | NIJHOFF

LEIDEN | BOSTON

This work and its open access publication were supported by Ragnar Söderberg's Foundation, Sweden.

The Library of Congress Cataloging-in-Publication Data is available online at https://catalog.loc.gov
LC record available at https://lccn.loc.gov/2025027167

Typeface for the Latin, Greek, and Cyrillic scripts: "Brill". See and download: brill.com/brill-typeface.

ISSN 2405-8343
ISBN 978-90-04-70842-6 (hardback)
ISBN 978-90-04-70843-3 (e-book)
DOI 10.1163/9789004708433

This book is printed on acid-free paper and produced in a sustainable manner.

Contents

Notes on Contributors

Priscilla Alderson
is professor Emerita of Childhood Studies at the Social Research Institute, University College London. She has conducted sociology research for over forty years, and her most recent research concerns children's and parents' consent to heart surgery. She also writes and lectures on critical realism.

Claire Breen
professor of Law at the Faculty of Law, University of Waikato. She has published extensively on children's rights law. Key publications include *The Standard of the Best Interests of the Child* and *Age Discrimination and Children's Rights*, and articles in the *Human Rights Quarterly*, *International Journal of Children's Rights*, and *Harvard Human Rights Journal*. She has received research grants from the Royal Society Te Apārangi Marsden Fund, as well as the New Zealand Law Foundation.

Aoife Daly
is professor of Law at University College Cork (Ireland) and specializes in human rights law at the School of Law. Her research focuses on children's environmental rights, climate action, and access to justice. She is author of *Children, Autonomy and the Courts* (Brill, 2018) and *Child/Youth Climate Action and Human Rights Law* (forthcoming 2025 with Routledge). She is an award-winning university teacher and also enjoys teaching children about human rights through art. In 2023, she secured a European Research Council Consolidator Grant to build a team to carry out a large-scale research study on child/youth climate justice – inside and outside the courts – around the world. She is a member of the Global Network of Human Rights and the Environment and UCC's Environmental Research Institute.

Pernilla Leviner
is professor of Public Law at the Faculty of Law and connected to the Stockholm Centre for the Rights of the Child at Stockholm University. Her research interests lie within and across the fields of public and family law – more specifically, child law and social welfare law. Her work addresses different aspects of the relationship between the state, the family, and the individual, including children's rights, often focusing on the responsibility and role of public authorities.

Manfred Liebel

Ph.D., is professor Emeritus of Sociology at the Technical University of Berlin and Honorary Professor of Intercultural Studies on Childhood and Children's Rights at the University of Applied Sciences Potsdam, Germany. His research involves working-class and Indigenous children and youth. He collaborates with and consults for movements of working children and adolescents in Latin America, Africa, and India. Recent publications include *Decolonizing Childhoods* (2020) and *Childhoods of the Global South* (2023).

Michael George Marcondes Smith

is a Ph.D. candidate in International Human Rights Law at the Faculty of Law, University of Antwerp, and a member of the Law and Development Research Group. He holds an LL.M. in international human rights law from Lund University and a Bachelor of Law from the Presbyterian University Mackenzie. He is a qualified lawyer registered with the São Paulo branch of the Brazilian Bar (OAB-SP). His doctoral research centers on the limits of interpreting the principle of equality and non-discrimination as a norm of international law and its application to socio-economic inequality.

Lucia Rabello de Castro

is professor of Childhood and Youth at the Instituto de Psicologia, Federal University of Rio de Janeiro, Brazil. She was Co-founder and Director (1998–2013) of the Interdisciplinary Research Centre on Childhood and Youth of this university. Since 2013, she has served as Chief Editor of the Latin American journal *DESIDADES – Scientific Journal on Childhood, Adolescence and Youth.* She is also Past Elected President of Research Committee 53 (Sociology of Childhood) of the International Sociological Association (ISA).

Rebecca Thorburn Stern

is professor of Public International Law at the Faculty of Law, Uppsala University, and Visiting Professor of Human Rights at the Faculty of Law, Lund University (2024–2027). Her research interests include asylum and migration law, children's human rights, and the relationship between national and international law. Recent projects include multidisciplinary studies of the use of medical evidence in asylum cases and the significance of time in asylum and citizenship law.

Wouter Vandenhole
is full professor of Human Rights and Children's Rights and directs the Law and Development Research Group at the Faculty of Law, University of Antwerp. His research interests include children's rights, economic, social, and cultural rights, the relationship between human rights law and sustainable development, and thicker human rights accountability. Recent topics include a post-territorial and post-state human rights paradigm, transformative equality, early marriage, and intercountry adoption.

John Wall
is distinguished professor of Philosophy, Religion, and Childhood Studies and Founding Director of the Childism Institute at Rutgers University–Camden, United States. He is author or editor of nine books and dozens of articles and chapters on the intersection of political philosophy and children's rights. He is best known for developing the critical theory of childism and for advocating for children's suffrage.

CHAPTER 1

Introduction

Aoife Daly, Rebecca Thorburn Stern and Pernilla Leviner

1 Equality, Non-discrimination, and Children

Equality and non-discrimination are essential foundations of the rule of law, as well as fundamental moral principles. Article 1 of the Universal Declaration of Human Rights[1] proclaims that "all human beings are born free and equal in dignity and rights", and all core human rights treaties at both global and regional levels stipulate that States have an obligation to uphold the principle of non-discrimination. This includes the UN Convention on the Rights of the Child[2] (CRC). Although definitions and understandings may differ when it comes to equality and non-discrimination, it is useful to note that the CRC monitoring body, the UN Committee on the Rights of the Child (the CRC Committee) outlines that: "the general principle of non-discrimination in the Convention prohibits differences in treatment on grounds that are arbitrary and objectively unjustifiable".[3] It can also be said that [e]quality is the positive face of non-discrimination.[4]

The prevalence of the principle of non-discrimination does not, however, guarantee that differential treatment with negative consequences for specific individuals or groups does not occur. Nor do they mean that such treatment is questioned or even perceived as problematic. A case in point is children. Children – commonly defined as individuals under the age of 18 years – are often subject to differential treatment compared with adults. Although such differentiation is often intended to be in the best interests of the child, motivated by children's vulnerability and evolving capacities – compulsory schooling and minimum age requirements for criminal responsibility, consent, and marriage being a few examples – there are also numerous instances where differential

1 UN General Assembly, Resolution 217A (III), Universal Declaration of Human Rights, A/RES/217(III) (December 10, 1948).

2 UN Convention on the Rights of the Child (1989).

3 UN Committee on the Rights of the Child (CRC), *Consideration of reports submitted by states parties under article 44 of the Convention. Concluding observations of the Committee on the Rights of the Child: Belgium*, (2002) CRC/C/15/Add.178, 13 June 2002, para. 6.

4 D. Moeckli, 'Equality and Non-discrimination', In S. Farrior (ed.), *Equality and Non-discrimination under International Law*, Vol. II (Routledge, London, 2015) pp. 53–70.

 | DOI:10.1163/9789004708433_002

treatment may have adverse effects. Examples include the lack of protection against corporal punishment,[5] the criminalization of certain acts only when committed by a child (status offences),[6] limitations of political participation,[7] restricted access to healthcare in matters concerning reproductive health,[8] and the increasing exclusion of children from urban public spaces.[9]

When age or childhood serves as the primary basis for treating children less favourably than adults, this raises the question of whether such treatment is justifiable, legitimate, and proportionate or whether it constitutes discrimination on the grounds of age – in other words, whether children are being discriminated against for being children. This question is the starting point for this book, which originates in the research project *Treated Like a Child: Children and Age Discrimination Law in Sweden and the UK*.[10] The aim of the project is to bring children's rights analysis to the topic of non-discrimination from the perspective of the treatment of children as a distinct group. It seeks to draw attention to the largely ignored potential to progress children's rights in the framework of non-discrimination in relation to children as a group. It is argued in this project that attention to the ways in which we treat children differently – and whether various instances of differential treatment are justifiable or not – will benefit the realization and respect for children's rights, and develop children's rights studies. As children require protection, it is sometimes necessary to treat them differently, but it is argued that in the legal context (and, indeed, other contexts) greater reflection must be made of whether excluding children from non-discrimination frameworks is justifiable.

5 B. J. Saunders et al. (eds.), *Corporal Punishment of Children – Comparative Legal and Social Developments Towards Prohibition and Beyond*, Stockholm Studies in Child Law and Children's Rights, Vol. 4 (Brill Nijhoff Publishers, Leiden, 2018).

6 CRIN, *Discrimination and Disenfranchisement: A Global Report of Status Offences*, third edition, 2016. Examples may include violating local curfew laws, underage drinking, and truancy.

7 *See e.g.* L. Beckman, 'Children and the Right to Vote', In A. Gheaus et al. (eds.), *The Routledge Handbook of the Philosophy of Childhood and Children* (Routledge, Abingdon/New York, 2018).

8 A. Daly et al., 'The UN Convention on the Rights of the Child, Article 2 and Discrimination on the Basis of Childhood', 91:3 *Nordic Journal of International Law* (2022) pp. 419–452.

9 J. Bourke, "No Messing Allowed": The Enactment of Childhood in Urban Public Space from the Perspective of the Child', 24:1 *Children, Youth and Environments* (2014), pp. 25–52.

10 The project has received funding from the Ragnar Söderberg Foundation, Grant ID R20/18.

That children are a distinct group is demonstrated not least by the fact that there is an international treaty dedicated specifically to their rights. Besson and Kleber point to the centrality of the prohibition of discrimination in the context of children's rights, noting how "historically [...] the struggle against child discrimination has been a central driving force in the development of the rights of the child".[11] The non-discrimination clause in the CRC's Article 2 plays a key role as one of the four general principles in light of which the CRC and its individual provisions should be interpreted and implemented.[12] Article 2.1 requires State Parties to "respect and ensure the rights set forth in the present Convention to each child within their jurisdiction without discrimination of any kind, irrespective of the child's or his or her parent's or legal guardian's race, colour, sex, language, religion, political or other opinion, national, ethnic or social origin, property, disability, birth or other status". The second paragraph (Article 2.2) obliges State Parties to take all appropriate measures to ensure that children are protected from discrimination or punishment on the basis of status, actions, activities, opinions, or beliefs of parents, legal guardians, or family members. Article 2 moreover requires States actively to identify individual children and groups of children the recognition and realization of whose rights may demand special measures[13] and to gather data necessary to identify discrimination taking place. The article thus creates both positive and negative obligations for State Parties, requiring that they not only refrain from discrimination of children but also actively address and counteract measures directly or indirectly discriminating against children. The non-discrimination clause of Article 2 is, in other words, essential for all children's equal enjoyment of the rights established by the CRC.

As can be seen above, the wording of Article 2.1 clearly relates to discrimination against children in disadvantaged groups such as ethnic or religious minorities or children with disabilities.[14] What it does not do is refer explicitly to the essential characteristic of any child – that is, being underage, of young age, in a state of childhood. Part of the explanation for this might be

11 S. Besson and E. Kleber, 'Article 2: The Right to Non-Discrimination', In J. Tobin (ed.), *The UN Convention on the Rights of the Child. A Commentary* (Oxford University Press, Oxford, 2019), p. 42.

12 Committee on the Rights of the Child, General Comment No. 5 (2003): General measures of implementation of the Convention on the Rights of the Child, CRC/GC/2003/5, para. 12.

13 Ibid.

14 *See e.g.* M. Skivenes and K. H. Søvig (eds.), *Child Rights and International Discrimination Law: Implementing Article 2 of the United Nations Convention on the Rights of the Child* (Routledge, New York, 2019).

the fact that neither age nor childhood are explicitly mentioned among the protected grounds in other core human rights treaties at the global or regional levels – for a long time it was, more or less, a non-issue. However, the non-discrimination clauses are open-ended in the sense that they are not limited to the grounds enumerated but also include a reference to 'other status'. 'Other status' has in recent years increasingly been recognized by human rights treaty bodies as also covering age, including young age.[15] In international jurisprudence, however, application of young age as a discrimination ground has thus far been limited,[16] perhaps partly for reasons of the (mis)understanding that (young) age discrimination should be treated differently – more strictly – than discrimination on other grounds; what Vandenhole refers to as "age discrimination exceptionalism".[17]

Even considering the fact that it is only relatively recently that age has been recognized as a protected ground in human rights jurisprudence, it is surprising how limited attention has thus far been paid, in the literature and in practice, to the potential of CRC Article 2 to protect under-18s from any discrimination they may experience because of their status as children.[18] There is literature which examines children and discrimination in depth, but it is either in need of more modern examination[19] or discrimination on

15 W. Vandenhole et al., *Children's Rights: A Commentary on the Convention on the Rights of the Child and its Protocols* (Edward Elgar Publishing, Cheltenham, 2019), p. 56; C. Breen, 'The Ageing of Article 2(1): The Child's Right to be Free from Age-based Discrimination', In M. Skivenes and K. H. Søvig (eds.), *Child Rights and International Discrimination Law: Implementing Article 2 of the United Nations Convention on the Rights of the Child* (Routledge, New York, 2019) p. 63; Besson and Kleber, *supra* note 11, p. 42; Daly et al., *supra* note 8; G.L. Neuman and A.M. Ibrahim, 'When is age discrimination a human rights violation?', 36:2 *Harvard Human Rights Journal* (2023) pp. 223–246; B. D. Mezmur, 'Based Solely on Their Date of Birth? Rethinking Age Discrimination Against Children under the Convention on the Rights of the Child', 36:2 *Harvard Human Rights Journal* (2023) pp. 261–281. *Cf* also A. Bruce, *Which Entitlements and for Whom? The Convention on the Rights of Persons with Disabilities and its Ideological Antecedents* (Lund University, Lund, 2014) p. 332, n. 837.

16 H. Hejny, 'Justifying age discrimination in Europe: A case law analysis', 13:2 *The Journal of Aging and Social Change* (2023), pp. 15–28, Daly et al., *supra* note 6.

17 *See* W. Vandenhole, 'Age discrimination exceptionalism?', *Harvard Human Rights Journal online* (2022). https://journals.law.harvard.edu/hrj/2022/12/age-discrimination-exceptionalism/, last visited 20 February 2025.

18 Besson and Kleber, *supra* note 11; Breen, *supra* note 15; M. Liebel, 'Adultism and Age-based Discrimination against Children', In D. Kutsar and H. Warming (eds.), *Children and non-discrimination* (CREAN, 2014); Skivenes and Søvig, *supra* note 14; Mezmur, *supra* note 15.

19 *See e.g.* C. Breen, *Age Discrimination and Children's Rights: Ensuring Equality and Acknowledging Difference* (Martinus Nijhoff, Leiden, 2006).

the basis of age or childhood is one of many discrimination topics covered along with characteristics such as gender and ethnicity.[20] Although literature focusing specifically on age-based discrimination of children is scarce, there is a growing interest in the field, indicating a growing awareness of the need to address differential treatment of children in relation to adults within the framework of discrimination, including in the legal sense. As already indicated, the aim of this edited volume is to contribute to this development by bringing much-needed analysis to the topic of non-discrimination and children's rights from the perspective of the treatment of children as a distinct group, and to draw attention to the largely ignored potential to progress children's rights in the framework of non-discrimination – CRC Article 2 in particular.

The fact that the CRC Article 2 does not explicitly include 'age' among the discrimination grounds has, as Lundy observes, sparked criticism of the treaty for being 'adultist'.[21] This term is defined by Wall as referring to "the historically normative marginalization of children by age".[22] The same phenomenon is referred to by other authors as 'childism', a term used by Young-Bruehl to describe prejudice against children leading to oppression and structural discrimination of children.[23] Wall uses the term 'childism' to describe a lens or prism for critiquing the deeply engrained adultism he holds pervades societies and scholarship.[24] In spite of differing language, this literature can be seen as united in its aim to highlight that the framing of children as inferior permeates societies. We believe that this phenomenon influences how children are perceived as rights holders, and even as humans.[25] This approach, discussed in

20 Skivenes and Søvig, *supra* note 14.

21 L. Lundy, 'Children's Rights from an International Perspective', In R. Adami et al. (eds.), *The Rights of the Child. Legal, Political and Ethical Challenges* (Brill, Stockholm, 2023), p. 4.

22 J. Wall, 'Adultism and Voting Age Discrimination', 36:2 *Harvard Human Rights Journal* (2023), pp. 329–340, 329.

23 E. Young-Bruehl, *Childism: Confronting Prejudice against Children* (Yale University Press, New Haven, 2012). *See also* R. Adami, 'Childism – on Adult Resistance to Children's Rights', In R. Adami et al. (eds.), *The Rights of the Child. Legal, Political and Ethical Challenges* (Brill, Stockholm, 2023).

24 J. Wall, 'From childhood studies to childism: reconstructing the scholarly and social imaginations' 20:3 *Children's Geographies* (2019), pp. 257–270.

25 Research shows that States regularly cite poor attitudes to children as a barrier to their enjoyment of their rights, *see e.g.* R. Thorburn Stern, *Implementing Article 12 of the UN Convention on the Rights of the Child: Participation, Power and Attitudes* (Brill/Nijhoff, Leiden, 2017).

the contributions to this book, has bearing on to what extent children may be discriminated against in relation to adults without the differential treatment in fact being recognized as 'discrimination'.

In the initial phase of the research project which this anthology is part of, the young advisory group (YAG) at the European children's rights unit at the University of Liverpool (where Aoife Daly then worked) was consulted. The YAG brings together local children and young people from Liverpool to provide input into research projects related to children and young people. We wished to engage directly with children's views about the potential relevance and impact of our project. We presented the ideas related to children and equality/nondiscrimination to them and had a fruitful discussion. They expressed that the main area of concern for them was difference of treatment of children in relation to work. As editors of this anthology we therefore endeavoured to ensure that we included a chapter relating to children and work.[26]

2 Contributions to This Volume

The contributions in this volume seek to explore a variety of aspects of age-based discrimination of children and analyse the concept of age-based discrimination as such in relation to children. Although the starting point of the book can be described as legal, the context and methodological approach are interdisciplinary. The authors come from a range of scholarly disciplines, including law, childhood studies, philosophy, and sociology.[27] Detrimental treatment of children is an everyday issue and therefore transcends the discipline of law. Article 2 of the CRC is clearly key when discussing children's legal rights. However, if children's legal rights are the only framework engaged, we may well overlook broader elements and valuable aspects of equality and non-discrimination for children. Work across disciplines is therefore needed to illustrate how the field of children's rights and discrimination can be understood and analysed from different angles and perspectives.

The first contribution looks specifically at the position on age-based discrimination thus far taken by the CRC Committee. In this chapter, *Aoife Daly, Rebecca Thorburn Stern,* and *Pernilla Leviner* examine the jurispru-

26 See https://www.liverpool.ac.uk/humanities-and-social-sciences/research/research-themes/children-childhood/ypag.

27 The authors in this book met and discussed draft papers at a workshop in Stockholm in June 2024.

dence of the CRC Committee with a view to understanding its approach to discrimination on the basis of age or childhood.[28] It is established that even though child-specific discriminatory practices such as corporal punishment are criticized by the CRC Committee, they are seldom labelled 'discrimination' as such. The Committee generally reserves consideration of the non-discrimination clause expressed in CRC Article 2 for traditionally disadvantaged groups of children such as girls, ethnic minorities, and children with disabilities. Article 2 is rarely used to protect children from discrimination on the basis of childhood, with Daly, Thorburn Stern, and Leviner noting that "there appears to exist an assumption across most societies that this is unproblematic".[29] It is concluded that Article 2 has much potential for drawing attention to detrimental treatment for being young/under 18 years, but that more attention must be paid to the phenomenon in law, practice, and scholarship. The authors in their final comments point to how a CRC Committee General Comment on discrimination on the basis of childhood under Article 2 would be an important step in this direction.

The four subsequent chapters all take a predominantly theoretical approach to the issue of age discrimination of children. One issue when discussing differential treatment of children compared with adults is whether it can be considered discrimination in the legal sense. *Michael G. Marcondes Smith* and *Wouter Vandenhole* in their chapter explore how disadvantage on the grounds of childhood can best be addressed conceptually. They ask which is the better frame: the principle of best interests of the child, which is what has traditionally been mobilized in child law and human rights law, or the prohibition of discrimination? Using voting rights as an illustration, Marcondes Smith and Vandenhole argue that non-discrimination in combination with the best interests principle may point to an avenue for a more coherent argumentation regarding the discriminatory nature of childism. However, Marcondes Smith and Vandenhole stress that this holds true only if discrimination law is 'handled with care', meaning that its technical intricacies are thoroughly considered: the identification of a comparator, a prohibited ground of discrimination, and an assessment of whether the differential treatment can be considered reasonable and justified. They also point to one of the

28 The chapter was previously published as an article in the *Nordic Journal of International Law* in 2022 (Vol. 91, Issue 3, pp. 419–452). It is published in this volume with the kind permission of the Journal.

29 A. Daly, R. Thorburn Stern, and P. Leviner, 'The UN Convention on the Rights of the Child, Article 2 and Discrimination on the basis of Childhood: The CRC Paradox?', in this volume.

main challenges when addressing differential treatment of children and adults in a legal perspective, namely the way in which childhood is constructed and understood.

Claire Breen in her contribution discusses the inertia around recognizing age discrimination and its profound implications for the implementation of children's rights. Although recognizing that age-based distinctions may have an important role in navigating the (sometimes contradictory) complexities that come with being a child, Breen holds that to prevent uninterrogated age-based distinctions from masking age discrimination, the child's right to be free from discrimination must include discrimination based on age. It is argued that CRC Article 2 must play a key role in this regard. The chapter aims to offer a nuanced understanding of age-based distinctions that seek to ensure equality and avoid age discrimination so as to navigate such complexities in a more meaningful way. Breen also suggests that age discrimination raises important questions for our understandings of discrimination more generally.

'Childism' and 'adultism' are key concepts in many contributions to this volume. In his chapter, *John Wall* argues that age discrimination against children is not only a denial of their rights, but also a manifestation of historically entrenched systems of adultism. Therefore, he contends, age discrimination must be addressed as both a normative issue and a legal problem, and critiqued through the lens of childism in a similar vein with feminism, decolonialism, and the like. Illustrating his argument with the issue of age discrimination in the right to vote in national and international law, Wall shows that the problem lies not only in the law itself, but equally in attitudes to normative power, and argues that age discrimination against children raises profound questions about what appears normal and settled in society and law.

Lucia Rabello de Castro in her contribution discusses how discrimination against children is couched in the CRC and national laws created as a consequence of the CRC, in terms of an age episteme which naturalizes and essentializes age power differentials between adults and children. The age episteme plays an important role in developmental paradigms which have underpinned claims to civilize and subordinate children. Rabello de Castro argues that a normalization of social positions based on age ensures the superiority of adults over children, thereby legitimizing intergenerational relations of domination and discrimination against children. She offers a critique of the age episteme with the aim to deconstruct the underpinnings of age classifications and to argue in favour of other possible ways to conceptualize the child and the adult in intergenerational relationships.

The subsequent five contributions focus more specifically on particular fields or situations in which children may be, directly or indirectly, overtly or covertly, discriminated against on the basis of age or childhood. *Aoife Daly* in her chapter puts the spotlight on the climate crisis. Although one of the groups that will suffer disproportionally due to the climate crisis is children, their possibilities to influence climate policy are limited as they cannot influence policy by using the power of the vote in general elections. Children are thus forced to find alternative ways to contribute to combating climate change. One option is climate litigation, in which arguments drawing on the principles of non-discrimination and equality can play an important role. Daly argues that although there are a number of difficulties with positioning children and youth in the non-discrimination/equality framework, including the fact that under-18s are frequently excluded from frameworks prohibiting unfair discrimination, there is considerable potential in using non-discrimination clauses such as CRC Article 2 in climate litigation. Although these cases are not always legally successful, Daly argues that relying on the principle of non-discrimination has the effect of drawing attention to the effects of the climate crisis on children in particular. It also demonstrates that we can and should use the framework of non-discrimination and equality when it comes to detrimental treatment of children.

Working children are the focus of *Manfred Liebel*'s chapter. Liebel argues that working children are discriminated against both due to age and because they work, and therefore live in a way that is not foreseen in the prevailing pattern of childhood in the Global North. Their discrimination is expressed, Liebel holds, for example by the fact that their work is not recognized, that they are more economically exploited than adults, and that they are denied labour rights, including participation in decision making in matters that affect them as working children. Liebel in his chapter explores the forms of adultism and discrimination that affect working children, describes the specific ways in which they experience and resist them, and argues that to counteract discrimination of working children, 'childhood' as well as 'work' must be understood differently than they currently are.

In migration law and policy, numerous measures have been taken to ensure that children's 'double vulnerability' as both children and migrants is taken into account, preventing children in the context of migration from being at a disadvantage compared with adults. *Rebecca Thorburn Stern,* drawing on examples related to the child's right to be heard, the assessment of asylum claims, and access to family reunification, argues that – despite such measures – children are still at risk of being treated more unfavourably than adults due to age or childhood. Thorburn Stern in her contribution explores the potential of the principle of non-discrimination as expressed in Article 2 of the CRC to address adverse differential treatment of children relative to adults in migration contexts. She makes the argument that systematically invoking Article 2 to identify unequal treatment based on age may contribute both to strengthening the rights of children in a migration context and to challenging prevailing assumptions regarding the legitimacy of according children fewer or more limited rights than adults solely on the basis of age.

A central human right, highly valued by adults, is respect for each person's autonomy and bodily integrity. In many national jurisdictions, a person's body may be touched only after the person concerned has given explicit or at least tacit informed consent. The major exception to this protection is legal minors. For them, parents' or guardians' consent is required, but not their own consent. *Priscilla Alderson* in her chapter draws on her decades-long research into parents' and children's consent when discussing age-based discrimination against children in the context of medical treatment, specifically surgery. Alderson discusses the advantages and disadvantages of legalizing consent and explores reasons and supporting pressures behind the long-held ageist views that undermine respect for children's consent.

In the last chapter of this book, *Pernilla Leviner* discusses children in the context of fighting gang crime in Sweden, asking whether these children are considered bearers of rights or of problems. Taking as her starting point recent shifts and contradictions in the Swedish child protection and welfare system, Leviner analyses how certain children – often second-generation migrants living in disadvantaged areas – in the context of the fight against gang criminality are on the one hand subjected to 'adultification' and 'over-responsibilization', making them responsible in the same way as adults, while on the other hand being perceived as 'different' and therefore in need of more control than adults – being 'treated like children' and thus at risk of being subject to age-based discrimination. Leviner describes this as an exclusionary mechanism of the welfare state, concluding her chapter with the reminder that the CRC applies fully to all children, not only those fitting into certain norms, and that treating certain children differently for political purposes, such as adhering to a 'tough on crime discourse', risks weakening the understanding of what it means to be a rights holder.

3 Common Themes

There are a number of common themes arising from the chapters. One such theme is social practice. Rabello de Castro's chapter refers to the everyday life of children in school, and the ease with which play can be disregarded in the interests of adult needs and ideas. Alderson's paper considers how helping the child (in the health law context) also means helping the entire family, and social practice therefore means that the family must be supported in order to help the child. The concept of power and how power plays into the dynamic between adults and children is another important theme which emerges from the chapters, Breen's and Liebel's contributions being two examples. Part of 'adultism' and resistance to equality for children is the fear that adults have of losing control. Control is something adults, parenthood, and institution want to maintain. This is related to the theme of conservatism and a reluctance to think differently about children even when confronted with clear evidence that we need to do so. Note for example the struggle of working children to have rights to suit the realities of their lives (Liebel). Daly's chapter points to the fact that it took an existential crisis – the climate crisis – to finally break through barriers and have non-discrimination for children brought as an argument in an international application.

It is emphasized in many of the chapters that we should be careful about unduly excluding age from our analysis of treatment of children. Leviner points out that there is a risk of adultification of children, whereby their special characteristics are not acknowledged. There is a particular risk of this occurring when an issue becomes politicized, with gang violence being one example. The chapters of both Leviner and Liebel highlight that some people under the age of 18 years are deemed deserving of the label 'children with rights'; experiencing both benefits and disadvantages, whereas others are excluded from being labelled as 'children' and consequently lack access to certain rights, particularly when they are from racial minorities or seeking asylum (see Thorburn Stern's chapter). This raises questions which relate to children's vulnerability on the one hand and their agency on the other. It is crucial to understand that positioning children in the framework of equality and non-discrimination does not always mean treating them identical to adults. Equality sometimes means taking adequate steps to recognize the unique circumstances of children where necessary – examples of that include when children are in conflict with the law or when they are seeking asylum.

Children's exclusion from political participation also emerges as a key issue in relation to equality and non-discrimination. Daly outlines how litigation is an option for children and youths to influence states' decision-making. Marcondes Smith and Vandenhole ask if and how the best interests principle assists in accounting for children's vulnerability, and argue for a well-defined articulation of childhood as a category that stands to benefit from democratic participation.

It is important to consider the terminology and definitions in this area at this point in the volume. This is not least because of the diversity of the literature when it comes to children's rights and equality/non-discrimination. Note above, for example, the fact that the term 'childism' is used by Young-Bruehl to describe prejudice against children,[30] but by Wall as akin to feminism (i.e., an empowering term).[31] Likewise authors may decide in this volume to adopt definitions of terms such as equality and non-discrimination which are different across the chapters. As editors, we opted to ensure freedom for authors in this regard for a number of reasons, including different understandings of terms across different disciplines (for example inside and outside of the discipline of law). We simply asked that authors define their terminology in their own chapter.

This volume aims to provide analyses of existing literature in the area, as well as analyses of law and jurisprudence. It is set in a context where there are fundamental shifts at both the national and the international level in relation to children, as a result of global disruptions. For example, the principle of non-discrimination was for the first time (in 2020) relied upon by child applicants in an international human rights law application – the *Duarte Agostinho* application (European Court of Human Rights).[32] This was in the context of State obligations to children and youths in the climate crisis. In 2022, the Supreme Court in New Zealand agreed that children from 16 years old should gain the right to vote – an argument made using the principle of non-discrimination.[33] It is time to consider children's rights in relation to said principle. We hope that the chapters of this book, and this volume as a whole, will benefit the rights framework more broadly by drawing attention to our common humanity and the need to see all humans as equals.

30 Young-Bruehl, *supra* note 23; Adami, *supra* note 23.

31 Wall, *supra* note 24.

32 ECtHR, *Duarte Agostinho and Others* v *Portugal and 32 Others*, Appl. No. 39371/20, decision on admissibility 9 April 2024.

33 New Zealand Supreme Court, *Make It 16 Incorporated v Attorney-General* [2022] NZSC 134.

CHAPTER 2

The UN Convention on the Rights of the Child, Article 2, and Discrimination on the Basis of Childhood: The CRC Paradox?

Aoife Daly, Rebecca Thorburn Stern and Pernilla Leviner

Abstract[1]

The CRC as an instrument calls attention to children as a group. Yet paradoxically it has not resulted in explicit consideration of discrimination against children on the basis of childhood (i.e. detrimental treatment for being young/under 18) in the same way that has happened for other groups like women and ethnic minorities. Children are more likely to suffer poverty and violence than adults, and under-18s are largely excluded from national legislation prohibiting unfair discrimination. In this article the jurisprudence of the Committee on the Rights of the Child is examined and it is established that even though child-specific discriminatory practices such as corporal punishment are criticised by the Committee, they are seldom labelled 'discrimination' as such. The Committee reserves consideration of Article 2, which enshrines the principle of non-discrimination, for traditionally disadvantaged groups of children such as girls and ethnic minorities. It is concluded that Article 2 has great potential for drawing attention to detrimental treatment for being young/under 18, but that the phenomenon must be more explicitly referenced with greater frequency in law, practice, and scholarship.

1 Introduction

Equality and non-discrimination are the keystone principles of international human rights law, enshrined in every international and regional international human rights instrument, including the United Nations Convention on the Rights of the Child ('CRC'). Article 2 of the CRC stipulates that states will ensure that children enjoy their CRC rights "without discrimination of any kind".

1 This chapter was previously published by the same authors in 2022 in the *Nordic Journal of International Law* (Vol. 91:3, pp. 419–452). It is published in this volume with the kind permission of the Journal.

Attention has been provided in law, practice and academia to discrimination against children on the basis that they belong to particular minority groups such as racial or ethnic minorities; those with disabilities; or due to gender or legal status.[2] However, there is still limited explicit recognition at national and international level that children face discrimination because they are children, which we will refer to here as discrimination 'on the basis of childhood'. How Article 2 can be used as a tool to counteract such discrimination is also largely unexplored. The fact that we have the CRC at all calls attention to children and to the rights they hold as a group (as well as rights they have as individuals). This, however, is not necessarily the same as recognising that children as a group may face discrimination like other minorities or vulnerable groups.

The limited acknowledgment of age and/or childhood as grounds for discrimination against children is somewhat surprising. The principle of non-discrimination is of key importance in the general human rights context. Added to this, states regularly cite poor attitudes to children as a barrier to the enjoyment by children of their rights.[3] Furthermore, there are many concrete examples of children facing exclusion and unfair treatment because of the low status accorded to childhood compared to adulthood in most societies. Examples considered in this article range from disadvantageous legal protections (e.g. protection from assault) to status offences (such as curfew violations targeted solely at under-18s). It is also now increasingly accepted that children are affected disproportionately by emergencies such as the covid pandemic[4] and by the climate crisis.[5]

After considering examples of how children can be subject to discrimination because of age and childhood, the main focus of this article is to examine and analyse the ways in which the Committee on the Rights of the Child (hereafter 'CRC Committee' or 'Committee') has considered discrimination of children in its jurisprudence. We have focused in particular on Concluding Observations on state party reports, conducting both qualitative and quantitative analysis. It is concluded that the CRC Committee generally only consid-

2 *See e.g.* M. Skivenes and K. H. Søvig (eds.), *Child rights and international discrimination law. Implementing article 2 of the United Nations Convention on the Rights of the Child* (Routledge, New York, 2019).

3 R. Thorburn Stern, *Implementing Article 12 of the UN Convention on the Rights of the Child: Participation, Power and Attitudes* (Brill/Nijhoff, Leiden, 2017).

4 European Network of Ombudspersons for Children, *Position Statement on "COVID-19: learning for the future"* Adopted by the ENOC 25th General Assembly, 29 September 2021.

5 A. Daly, 'Climate Competence: The impact of youth climate activism on international human rights law', 32 *Human Rights Law Review* (2022).

ers discrimination in the context of children belonging to particular minority groups such as racial or ethnic minorities; those with disabilities; or due to gender or legal status (from here referred to as 'traditionally disadvantaged groups'). There is little explicit consideration given by the Committee to the fact that children can face discrimination because they are children. We highlight that many of the issues examined by the Committee could be said to represent instances of discrimination on the basis of childhood, though the Committee does not explicitly frame them as such.

This article argues for greater recognition that children as a group belong in the framework of equality and non-discrimination. It also aims to underline how important Committee comments could be for tackling detrimental state laws and practices in relation to children. It also seeks to encourage the Committee, academics and non-governmental organisations (e.g. in shadow reports) to consider the possibility of framing issues such as poor attitudes to children under Article 2, so that equality and non-discrimination issues relating to children can be better understood as such. Section 2 reflects on examples of discrimination against children on the basis of childhood. Section 3 briefly considers the text of CRC Article 2. Section 4 involves in-depth examination of the jurisprudence of the Committee from the perspective of discrimination against children on the basis of childhood. Sections 5–7 provide reflection on the jurisprudence of the Committee relating to traditionally disadvantaged groups. Final conclusions are then drawn on the jurisprudence of the Committee in this area, and the potential for progressing children's rights by being more explicit about instances of discrimination against them on the basis of childhood.

2 Recognising Discrimination against Children and Young: Examples of Unfair Treatment

The terms *non-discrimination* and *equality* are complex concepts, from a legal as well as linguistic perspective. The concepts constitute fundamental moral principles as well as key constitutional principles in democratic societies, and are – as mentioned above – included in all major international human rights treaties.[6] The UN Committee on the Rights of Persons with Disabilities for example emphasises the link between the prohibition of discrimination,

6 S. Besson and E. Kleber, 'Article 2: The Right to Non-discrimination', in J. Tobin (ed.), *The UN Convention on the Rights of the Child: A Commentary* (Oxford University Press, Oxford, 2019) p. 43.

equality and human dignity, describing them as the cornerstones of human rights.[7] 'Equality' and 'discrimination' are often referred to as different sides of the same coin (with equality' and 'non-discrimination' sometimes used interchangeably).[8] Equality is the positive statement of the principle – a person is treated equally with others – and discrimination is the negative statement, as in a person is discriminated against when not treated equally.[9]

There is relatively little analysis in legal scholarship of discrimination on the basis of childhood. This is the case both in relation to other elements of international law, and also in relation to national level. In short, there is little knowledge about how children may suffer discrimination on the basis of childhood. As Webb points out in this context; "we have hardly begun to understand how discrimination against children affects their life and welfare".[10] Yet there is ample evidence that children suffer such discrimination. In this section we will consider examples of situations in which children face discrimination on the basis of childhood both directly and indirectly.

2.1 *Direct Discrimination*

Discrimination can be either direct or indirect. *Direct* discrimination means that a person is treated unfairly compared to another person in a similar situation as a result of special attributes of that person, such as age. Direct discrimination against disadvantaged groups is often prohibited at national and international level through the principle of non-discrimination/equality. Equality laws – legal frameworks which advance equality of opportunity for all – exist in many states. Frequently, discrimination is only recognised at national level in these frameworks on the basis of a particular 'protected char-

7 UN Committee on the Rights of persons with Disabilities, *General Comment No. 6 (2018) on equality and non-discrimination*, CRPD/C/GC/6, 26 April 2018, para. 4–7.

8 *See e.g.* UN Committee on the Rights of the Child, *General comment No. 14 (2013) on the right of the child to have his or her best interests taken as a primary consideration (art. 3, para. 1)*, CRC/C/GC/14, 14 January – 1 February 2013, para 41; UN Committee on the Rights of the Child, *Concluding observations on the sixth periodic report of Hungary*, CRC/C/HUN/CO/6, 3 March 2020, para. 16(a). Some authors feel that there is some nuance to this however, *see e.g.* G. MacNaughton, 'Untangling Equality and Non-discrimination to Promote the Right to Health Care for All', 11 *Health and Human Rights* (2009), pp. 47–63.

9 Besson and Kleber *supra* note 6, p. 57; S. Besson, 'The Principle of Non-discrimination in the Convention on the Rights of the Child', 13 *International Journal of Children's Rights* (2005), pp. 433–461.

10 E. Webb, 'An Exploration of the Discrimination-Rights Dynamic in Relation to Children', in A. Invernizzi and J. Williams (eds.) *The Human Rights of Children. From Visions to Implementation* (Ashgate, 2011), pp. 286–306, 290.

acteristic'.[11] Yet childhood as a protected characteristic is rarely included in national jurisdictions. The UK is an example of a jurisdiction where under-18s as a group are largely excluded from protection. At the time of the passage of the bill which would become the UK's Equality Act 2010 (which came into force in 2012), NGOs such as the Children's Rights Alliance for England (CRAE) pointed to instances of discrimination on the basis of childhood in the UK.[12] Nevertheless being under the age of 18 was ultimately not included as a protected characteristic (with the exception of some provisions relating to work).[13] Harriet Harman, then Leader of the House of Commons, told members of the UK Parliament: "The provisions will not cover people under 18. It is right to treat children and young people differently ... and there is little evidence of harmful age discrimination against young people".[14] This was in spite of the submission of CRAE detailing numerous instances of discriminatory practices in relation to children, some of them seemingly dangerous. Cases were reported for example of ambulance operators refusing to help emergency callers who appeared to be adolescents.[15]

In Sweden, conversely, under-18s were included in equality law, yet with little difference in practice as compared with the UK example. In Sweden, age as a discrimination ground was introduced with the 2008 Discrimination Act.[16] The focus at this point was primarily on discrimination against older individuals in the context of employment.[17] The Act was amended in 2013 to, among other things, broaden the scope of the prohibition of age-based discrimination (it had previously been limited to education and

11 *See e.g.* M. Campbell, 'CEDAW and Women's Intersecting Identities: A pioneering new approach to intersectional discrimination', 11 *Revista Direito GV* (2015), pp. 479–504.

12 Children's Rights Alliance for England, *Making the Case: Why children should be protected from age discrimination and how it can be done: Proposals for the Equality Bill, 2009*, Children's Rights Alliance for England, 2009. <https://archive.crin.org/en/library/publications/united-kingdom-making-case-why-children-should-be-protected-age-discrimination.html>, accessed 26 April 2022. *See also* Equality Commission Northern Ireland, *Strengthening Protection for all Ages Ending Age Discrimination in the Provision of Goods and Services Proposals for Reform – Full Report*, April 2012. <www.equalityni.org/ecni/media/ecni/Addressing%20inequalities%20Policy/StrengtheningProtectionAllAgesFullReport.pdf>, accessed 26 April 2022.

13 *See further* S. Flacks, 'Is Childhood a Disability: Exploring the Exclusion of Children from Age Discrimination Provisions in the Equality Act 2010', 26:4 *Child and Family Law Quarterly* (2014), p. 421–438.

14 *See* C. Davies, 'Discrimination "a fact of life for British children"', *The Guardian*, 29 March 2009.

15 Children's Rights Alliance for England, *supra* note 12, p. 9.

16 *See* Discrimination Act (Diskrimineringslagen [2008:567]), Chapter 1, Section 1.

17 Prop. 2007/08:95 *Ett starkare skydd mot diskriminering*.

working life). It is emphasized in the government bill preceding the amendment of the Act that age as a discrimination ground applies to all ages, including children.[18] Yet the law seems to have had limited effect so far on age-based discrimination in relation to children. At the time of writing, no cases on age-based discrimination of children have been tried in Swedish courts.

Apart from these examples of how children and childhood are being excluded from discrimination laws, there are also many other examples where *direct discrimination* against children due to age is accepted with few if any objections. One example of this is that under-18s are generally not permitted to vote, in spite of the fact that the arguments put forward to justify this are highly questionable at best. Some refer to a perceived disinterest on the part of under-18s in relation to politics, for example, yet children have great capacity for political activity.[19] The disenfranchisement of under-18s is particularly paradoxical considering many work and pay taxes, thus contributing to society's resources without being allowed to exercise influence over how resources are allocated.[20]

A second example of direct discrimination of children due to age is the practice in some jurisdictions (e.g. the UK and the US) of subjecting under-18s to curfews whereby they are legally not permitted outside at particular times. In the UK, children can also be banned from areas such as streets and shops, and special devices are even used by business people to cause auditory discomfort to younger ears (which can hear at higher frequencies). These measures are supposedly aimed at reducing 'anti-social behaviour'.[21] The same kind of curfews, increased use of emergency care orders, and an overall 'tough-on-crime-agenda' are now also discussed in politics in Sweden in the context of combatting gang criminality and violence, without consideration of how this might limit children's fundamental rights illegitimately.[22]

18 Prop. 2011/12:159 *Ett utvidgat skydd mot åldersdiskriminering*.

19 *See e.g.* L. Beckman, *Frontiers of Democracy. The Right to Vote and its Limits* (Palgrave Macmillan, London 2009); J. Wall, *Give Children the Vote: On Democratizing Democracy* (Bloomsbury Publishing, New York, 2021).

20 *See e.g.* A. Daly, *A Commentary on the United Nations Convention on the Rights of the Child, Article 15: The Right to Freedom of Association and Peaceful Assembly* (Martinus Nijhoff, Leiden, 2016).

21 Children's Rights Alliance for England, *supra* note 12.

22 *See* for example newly introduced possibility to monitor young offenders, Prop. 2019/20:118, *Ungdomsövervakning* and several proposals by the second largest political party, Moderaterna, https://moderaterna.se/nyhet/10-monsterbrytande-reformer-att-stoppa-gangen/ from September 2020 last visited 29 May 2021.

Corporal punishment is another prime example of legal discrimination against children. Despite the proven negative effects on children's wellbeing, in many countries (including England), laws protecting adults from violence exclude children in circumstances where a parent delivers 'physical punishment'.[23] Such issues are rarely framed as a matter of discrimination against children, nor are they considered in the context of higher rates of homicide for children compared to adults, though physical punishment and homicide are likely linked.[24]

2.2 *Indirect Discrimination*

Indirect discrimination results when a policy or rule applies to everyone, but has an inadvertent but unfair impact on people in a particular group. This is particularly important for children as seemingly neutral policies can detrimentally affect them. It is accepted for some purposes that children have special vulnerabilities which must be catered for and which justify differential treatment. Nevertheless, these special needs are routinely ignored, leading to disadvantage for children. Children may find it difficult to access justice as compared with adults, for example, due to lack of knowledge of the legal system or lack of resources.[25] It is also little known that children are more likely than adults to be poor. Globally, children represent half of those struggling to survive on less than $1.90 a day.[26]

As children generally do not have the right to vote, they do not have the political power to mitigate such policies. The best interests principle is incorporated in the national laws of many jurisdictions and could be argued to combat indirect discrimination by ensuring decisions are made with children in mind. However, this does not always happen in practice, particularly where the CRC has not been incorporated into domestic law. Courts often remain

23 B. Saunders et al., *Corporal Punishment of Children: comparative legal and social developments towards prohibition and beyond* (Brill/Nijhoff, Leiden, 2018). *See* information on countries having banned corporal punishment on the website of the organisation Global Initiative to End Corporal Punishment. <https://endcorporalpunishment.org/countdown/>. In February 2022, 63 countries have full prohibition of corporal punishment.

24 *See* UK House of Commons Health Committee, *The Victoria Climbié Inquiry Report Sixth Report of Session 2002–03* (UK House of Commons Health Committee, 2003), para. 55. Available <https://publications.parliament.uk/pa/cm200203/cmselect/cmhealth/570/570.pdf>, last visited 8 July 2022.

25 *See e.g.* A. Daly, *Children, Autonomy and the Courts: Beyond the Right to be Heard* (Brill/Nijhoff, Leiden, 2018); Child Rights International Network, *Access to Justice for Children: Challenging Violations of Children's Rights* (Child Rights International Network, 2016).

26 UNICEF, *Child Poverty*, <www.unicef.org/social-policy/child-poverty>, last visited 1 June 2022.

resistant to the claim that states have an obligation to implement this CRC principle in policy-making, as happened in 2021 where the UK Supreme Court emphasised the viewpoint that it would be undemocratic to give undue weight to 'unincorporated international treaties' such as the CRC. The case in question dealt with a policy capping child benefit to only two children per family,[27] which disproportionately affected mothers and children.

Recent crises have also led to recognition that children as a group can face indirect discrimination. Covid measures during the pandemic for example have been acknowledged to have disproportionately affected children. Research of the European Network of Ombudspersons for Children (ENOC) reveals that "children as a population and specific groups of children ... were more likely to be adversely affected by Emergency Measures in response to Covid-19".[28] These had an impact on rights relating to children's mental health, freedom of assembly, and other rights. ENOC stated in 2021 that, where future crises hit, measures limiting children's rights "should only be introduced where these are: necessary, proportionate, non-discriminatory and time limited".[29]

Another important phenomenon which has brought indirect discrimination to the fore at international level is climate change.[30] An application was made to the European Court of Human Rights in 2020 which argued that climate policies of states are placing most of the economic and environmental burden on the younger generation. The child and youth litigants argue that insufficient attention is being given to how to share the burden of the consequences of carbon emissions. They argue that there is inadequate reduction of carbon emissions in the present which will disproportionately affect the younger generation. This ground breaking application to the European Court of Human Rights appears to be the first time such a provision is being used to protect 'youth' from discrimination.[31]

There are therefore many situations in which children are subject to direct as well as indirect discrimination. It is surprising that the UN framework has

---

27 *SC, CB and 8 children, R. (on the application of)* v *Secretary of State for Work and Pensions & Ors* [2021] UKSC 26 (9 July 2021).

28 European Network of Ombudspersons for Children, *Synthesis Report: Mapping the impact of emergency measures introduced in response to the COVID-19 pandemic on children's rights in ENOC member states* (European Network of Ombudspersons for Children, 2021) <https://enoc.eu/?p=4262>, last visited 29 May 2022.

29 European Network of Ombudspersons for Children, *ibid.*

30 Daly, *supra* note 5.

31 *See* petition at Global Legal Action Network website: <https://youth4climatejustice.org/>, last accessed 3 June 2021.

not been well utilised when it comes to protecting children from discrimination on the basis of childhood in the way that it has for women, ethnic minorities and others. Children are a significantly vulnerable group, particularly considering the fact that they are more likely than adults to experience a host of dangers and risks such as violence and poverty. There is also much evidence that there are poor attitudes to children, and that they are affected by discriminatory policies. There are clear arguments therefore that childhood should be recognized as a protected characteristic, as is the case for other groups such as women, ethnic and racial minorities, and people with disabilities. This would have a number of potential benefits for children as a group. It would have the effect of drawing explicit attention to discrimination against children, and making it clear that it is unacceptable. It would obligate law makers and other to explicitly outline differential treatment that is proportionate and necessary on the one hand, and detrimental treatment that is arbitrary on the other. It would likely encourage research into the links between negative attitudes to children, and the dangers and risks that they face as a group. It would also likely increase research and reflection in relation to the need for more specific legal distinctions amongst children themselves – the differences in status between a baby and a teenager and so on.

The jurisprudence from the CRC Committee is examined in Section 4 to ascertain how discrimination is addressed. Section 3 first provides a short description of the meaning of Article 2 of the CRC as interpreted in various legal sources and literature, as well as a brief reflection on discrimination under the CRC as opposed to other UN human rights treaties such as the Convention on the Elimination of Discrimination Against Women (CEDAW).

3 The Text of CRC Article 2

Article 2 of the CRC provides that all rights in the instrument pertain to every individual child without exception. Article 2.1 of the CRC essentially mirrors Article 2.1. of the International Covenant on Civil and Political Rights (ICCPR) on non-discrimination. It reads as follows:

> States Parties shall respect and ensure the rights set forth in the present Convention to each child within their jurisdiction without discrimination of any kind, irrespective of the child's or his or her parent's or legal guardian's race, colour, sex, language, religion, political or other opinion, national, ethnic or social origin, property, disability, birth or other status.

Article 2.2 refers to the extension of the protections of 2.1 to discrimination which children may face on the basis of the characteristics of parents or guardians; acknowledging the significance of the child-parent/guardian relationship, and the consequences that this may have for discrimination against the child herself.

The principle of non-discrimination is a particularly crucial one within the CRC, which makes it all the more important to provide thorough elaboration. Together with the best interest principle (Article 3), the right to life, survival and development (Article 6) and the right of children to be heard (Article 12), the CRC Committee emphasises that it is one of the principles which must guide interpretation and implementation of all articles of the treaty.[32] The fact that the CRC Committee saw fit to include it amongst the most key provisions of the Convention highlights the vital importance of the principle of non-discrimination in international human rights law generally, as well as its importance for children.

It may be noted that the language of CRC Article 2 does not refer to 'equality', but only to 'discrimination'; though this does not seem to have any particular consequences for the interpretation of the article.[33] The word 'discrimination' is not explicitly defined in the CRC. In a much-cited definition of discrimination in its General Comment on non-discrimination, the Human Rights Committee stated that for the purpose of the ICCPR, the term:

> ...[S]hould be understood to imply any distinction, exclusion, restriction or preference which is based on any ground such as race, colour, sex, language, religion, political or other opinion, national or social origin, property, birth or other status, and which has the purpose or effect of nullifying or impairing the recognition, enjoyment or exercise by all persons, on an equal footing, of all rights and freedoms.[34]

The Committee on the Rights of the Child made a comment in its concluding observations in relation to Belgium which reinforces this particular definition,

---

32 UN Committee on the Rights of the Child, *General Comment No. 5: General measures on the implementation of the Convention on the Rights of the Child*, CRC/GC/2003/5, 27 November 2003, para. 12.

33 Besson and Kleber, *supra* note 6, pp. 57–58.

34 UN Human Rights Committee, *CCPR General Comment No. 18 Non-discrimination*, 10 November 1989, para. 7.

outlining that: "the general principle of non-discrimination in the Convention prohibits differences in treatment on grounds that are arbitrary and objectively unjustifiable".[35]

The fact that age is not explicitly referenced in CRC Article 2 is of course notable, although the argument can be made that it is to fall under the heading of "other status".[36] The same can be said in relation to the ICCPR, which also refers to "other status". Yet discrimination on the basis of childhood has so far not been a discussed extensively in legal scholarship and the focus has mainly been on issues of discrimination against certain groups of children, that is 'traditionally disadvantaged groups'.

Some commentators have argued that Article 2 protects against discrimination on the basis of childhood. Breen's 2006 monograph *Age Discrimination and Children's Rights* was ground-breaking because she considers children in the context of the equality and non-discrimination provisions of international human rights law, arguing that every differential treatment of children should be proportionate and justifiable.[37] She makes the point that detrimental treatment of children is due to structural inequalities.[38] She opines that Article 2 frames discrimination in terms of differences between adults and children (while also pointing out that age-based discrimination can take place within the category of children itself).[39] She argues that failure to identify childhood/age as a site of discrimination has serious consequences – it makes it difficult for those using the law to "access, explore and embrace the differences between children and adults"[40] and, also, to move away from "liberal rights theory's view of children's difference as being less than adults".[41] Sutherland also points to childhood as a source of discrimination. She argues that the

35 UN Committee on the Rights of the Child, *Concluding Observations of the Committee on the Rights of the Child, Belgium*, CRC/C/15/Add.178, 13 June 2002, para. 6.

36 *See e.g.* W. Vandenhole et al., *Children's Rights: A Commentary on the Convention on the Rights of the Child and its Protocols* (Edward Elgar Publishing, Cheltenham, 2019), para. 2.14.

37 C. Breen, *Age Discrimination and Children's Rights* (Martinus Nijhoff Publishers, Leiden, 2006).

38 C. Breen, 'The Ageing of Article 2(1): The child's right to be free from age-based discrimination', in M. Skivenes and K. H. Søvig (eds.), *Child Rights and International Discrimination Law: Implementing Article 2 of the United Nations Convention on the Rights of the Child* (Routledge, New York, 2019).

39 Ibid, pp. 64 and 66.

40 Ibid, p. 67.

41 Ibid.

inferior status accorded to children and young people and the effects of negative societal attitudes towards under-18s.[42]

There is however some divergence from arguments that CRC Article 2 contains a right of children to be free from discrimination on the basis of childhood. Abramson in his 2008 commentary on Article 2 does not explicitly consider discrimination on the basis of childhood.[43] Archard considers the issue of age-related discrimination from a philosophical perspective, and takes the position that while it is indeed possible for children as a group to be discriminated against in relation to adults, this is not what is covered by CRC Article 2. Instead, he holds that it is "about the discriminatory treatment of some children by comparison with other children"[44] (i.e. traditionally disadvantaged groups). Archard however also emphasises that the discussion on Article 2 leads to a broader discussion on what it means to discriminate as such, and discriminate against children in particular.[45]

When considering the principle of non-discrimination, it is useful to consider the CRC as compared with other UN human rights treaties. One may well ask the question as to whether the CRC as an international human rights instrument is different to other treaties tailored to individual groups when it comes to non-discrimination. CEDAW and the UN Convention for the Elimination of Racial Discrimination (CERD) for example both explicitly have the word 'discrimination' in their very names. This may raise the question as to whether these instruments are different from the CRC on the basis that they are particularly designed to tackle discrimination against women and on the basis of race. Unlike CEDAW and CERD however the UN Convention on the Rights of People with Disabilities (CRPD) does not contain a direct reference to discrimination in its title, and it is clearly aimed at protecting people with disabilities from discrimination. It does explicitly state in Article 5 that "States Parties shall prohibit all discrimination on the basis of disability and guaran-

42 E. Sutherland, 'Article 2 of the United Nations Convention on the Rights of the Child: Non-discrimination and Children's Rights', in M. Skivenes and K. H. Søvig (eds.), *Child Rights and International Discrimination Law: Implementing Article 2 of the United Nations Convention on the Rights of the Child* (Routledge, New York, 2019), pp. 28, 30.

43 *See* B. Abramson, 'Article 2: The Right of Non-discrimination', in A. Alen et al. (eds), *A Commentary on the United Nations Convention on the Rights of the Child* (Martinus Nijhoff Publishers, Leiden, 2005).

44 D. Archard, 'Respecting Age: Discrimination against the Young and the Old', in M. Skivenes and K. H. Søvig (eds.), *Child rights and international discrimination law: Implementing Article 2 of the Convention on the Rights of the Child* (Routledge, New York, 2019), pp. 44–45, 52.

45 Archard, *supra* note 44, pp. 52–53.

tee to persons with disabilities equal and effective legal protection against discrimination on all grounds". This points of course to a much clearer emphasis on protecting from discrimination on the basis of disability as a characteristic, when compared with the approach to childhood as a characteristic in the CRC. In any case, it is difficult to establish whether these instruments are directly comparable, considering a number of factors, including the fact that they were drafted in different decades (the CRC in the 1980s and the CRPD in the 2000s).

Intersectionality is another important concept to consider in relation to discrimination on the basis of childhood. Intersectionality, a term coined by Kimberlé Crenshaw in 1989,[46] recognises that individuals can experience discrimination in relation to multiple and intersecting identities.[47] Sutherland emphasises that though childhood itself may be a source of discrimination, some groups of children face intersectional discrimination, in that they face discrimination on multiple grounds, for example being "a poor, female child with disabilities from an ethnic minority" may be discriminated against via policies harming teenage, single mothers.[48] It could be argued that the work of the CRC Committee relating to discrimination against traditionally disadvantaged groups is inherently work on intersectional discrimination. This is because the work relates to discrimination against people who are both children (the primary recipients of CRC rights), and also people from traditionally disadvantaged groups such as girls and ethnic minorities.

The Committee on the Elimination of Discrimination against Women has acknowledged intersectionality as part of the scope of state obligations under CEDAW.[49] Campbell points out that, although CEDAW has been criticised for being "based on a monolithic woman" (i.e. taking a single characteristic approach), the Committee "is praised for addressing women's different identities".[50] There is great potential then for the CRC to do the same. It is beyond the scope of this article to examine the issue of intersectionality in-depth. However if CEDAW can have the effect of explicitly drawing attention to the treatment of individuals both because they are women, *and* because they are from traditionally disadvantaged groups, then the CRC can do the same for

46 K. Crenshaw, 'Demarginalising the Intersection of Race and Sex', 1 *University of Chicago Legal Forum* (1989), p. 139.

47 *See e.g.* Campbell, *supra* note 11.

48 Sutherland, *supra* note 42, p. 30.

49 *See further* P. Chow, 'Has Intersectionality Reached its Limits? Intersectionality in the UN human rights treaty body practice and the issue of ambivalence', 16 *Human Rights Law Review* (2016), pp. 453–481.

50 Campbell, *supra* note 11, p. 483.

children. The data outlined below indicates that at present this is not being done explicitly.

It has been opined that recent developments in CRC Committee jurisprudence indicates "an evolving recognition that children may be subject to age-based discrimination".[51] In the next section we will turn to analysis of this jurisprudence in an attempt to demonstrate how the Committee approaches equality and non-discrimination in relation to children as a group, and whether the Committee has in fact moved towards recognition of discrimination on the basis of childhood.

4 CRC Committee Jurisprudence and Discrimination against Children on the Basis of Childhood

4.1 *Methodology*

For the purpose of this research, we examined all the concluding observations of the CRC Committee since the beginning of 2005 until the end of 2020. We aimed to ascertain the extent to which the Committee considers and makes recommendations in relation to discrimination against children because they are children. This research exercise involved examination of a total of 494 concluding observations and recommendations of the Committee. A quantitative analysis of references by the Committee to the words 'discrimination' and 'equality' was conducted. These terms of course also help identify the words non-discrimination and inequality as they are contained within them (as in non-*discrimination* and in*equality*).

It must be acknowledged that there are limitations to this exercise, considering there are many other words which can be used to highlight issues of non-discrimination/equality, and there are other ways in which discriminatory laws and practices can be described – consider the example of physical punishment outlined below. It is intended however that this word search would simply provide insight into the use of these terms by the Committee over time, and therefore further our knowledge of how the concepts of discrimination and inequality are treated in relation to the CRC. It would also have been ideal to examine all Committee jurisprudence including concluding observations from the beginning of Committee jurisprudence. Although it would have been desirable to examine more words and a longer time-frame, our parameters were what was feasible in the course of the exercise.

51 Breen, *supra* note 38, p. 64.

It would also have been useful to examine all of the state reports and shadow reports to the Committee, as this will determine much of what the Committee has to say in its concluding observations on state reports. Again, this exercise was beyond the scope of this study, but it is an area in which further research is needed.

4.2 *Use of the Terms 'Discrimination' and 'Equality' in Committee Jurisprudence*

Table 2.1 provides an overview of the number of concluding observations documents produced by the Committee in each year, and the number of

TABLE 2.1 Annual frequency of the committee's use of "discrimination" and "equality" in concluding observations

Year	Number of C.O. documents created by the CRC in each respective year	Mention of *Discrimination* in each respective year	Mention of *Equality* in each respective year
2020	9	9	8
2019	22	19	9
2018	26	22	15
2017	36	21	17
2016	36	26	22
2015	44	30	19
2014	34	25	14
2013	36	26	15
2012	41	30	23
2011	23	18	13
2010	30	19	13
2009	1	1	0
2008	33	17	13
2007	36	21	10
2006	51	28	21
2005	36	30	30
Total:	494	342	235

times the words discrimination and equality were mentioned in those documents.

A quantitative analysis can only tell us so much, however presenting the number of times the Committee uses the words discrimination/equality does provide an important snapshot. The first point to observe is that the word discrimination is used much more than the word equality. The focus on non-discrimination rather than equality is perhaps unsurprising considering the wording of Article 2 refers to discrimination rather than equality. The second point is that in general there does appear to be growing consideration of the theme of discrimination, albeit in terms of characteristics beyond childhood (gender, race etc.), in the Committee's concluding observations. Committee references to discrimination can in some ways seem to lack a discernable pattern however. In 2005 for example, the Committee used the word discrimination 30 times over 36 documents (so in almost all documents). However, just a year later in 2006 the Committee considered the word discrimination in a (proportionately) much lower number of documents – only 28 times in 51 documents (just over half of documents). In 2009 it seems that only one concluding observations/recommendations document (relating to Tunisia[52]) was produced by the Committee.

The term discrimination arises in roughly half of documents until 2011 where the Committee used the word discrimination 18 times over 23 documents – a significant increase. It seems that the word discrimination was used with greater frequency from that point. In 2019 for example the word discrimination was used 19 times over 22 documents, so in almost all. 2020 was of course a highly unusual year with the advent of the global pandemic. There were only nine concluding observations documents produced by the Committee in 2020. It is of note however that there were the same number of discrimination references and documents that year. Overall it is safe to say that there has been an increasing rate of reference to discrimination in Committee jurisprudence since its advent. The term equality is used a little more sporadically, however it can be said that, particularly in recent years, it appears in most Committee concluding observations.

In the next section, there will be a substantive analysis and overview of the main themes regarding non-discrimination which were identified in Committee concluding observations in the course of this study. We will begin by considering what are arguably the most important and clear references by the Committee to instances of discrimination on the basis of childhood.

52 UN Committee on the Rights of the Child, *Concluding Observations on the Fiftieth Periodic Report of Tunisia*, CRC/C/OPAC/TUN/CO/1, 6 February 2009.

4.3 *Discrimination against Children on the Basis of Childhood*

As noted above, the principle of non-discrimination is a general principle of the CRC, in that all other rights have to be considered in light of the principle. For this reason it appears that there generally is a 'non-discrimination' section in each concluding observation document. In some instances, discrimination arises as a particular problem for a state, as was the case for Italy in 2019:

> The Committee reminds the State party of the indivisibility and interdependence of all the rights enshrined in the Convention and emphasizes the importance of all the recommendations contained in the present concluding observations. The Committee would like to draw the State party's attention to the recommendations concerning the following areas, in respect of which urgent measures must be taken: allocation of resources (para. 8); non-discrimination (para. 15); education (para. 32); asylum-seeking and refugee children (para. 34); and children in situations of migration (para. 36).[53]

The Committee will sometimes simply make a blanket recommendation that a particular state ensures that all children enjoy the right to be free from discrimination. For example in the Committee's concluding observations on Lebanon from 2017, the Committee "recommends that the State party … Ensure that all children enjoy equal rights under the Convention, in law and practice, without discrimination".[54] It appears here that the Committee is not referring to discrimination against children as a group, but rather to children from particular groups which are vulnerable to discrimination, such as ethnic minorities or children with disabilities.

In its concluding observations, there are a number of references by the Committee to problematic attitudes to children, detrimental treatment of children, and other situations that could be framed as discrimination on the basis of childhood. However there appears to be only one clear example of the Committee explicitly referring to discrimination against children on this basis, and this is in relation to the state reports of the UK. The 2016 concluding observations (on the UK's fifth report) reads as follows:

---

53 UN Committee on the Rights of the Child, *Concluding observations on the combined fifth and sixth periodic reports of Italy*, CRC/C/ITA/CO/5-6, 28 February 2019, para. 4.

54 UN Committee on the Rights of the Child, *Concluding observations on the combined fourth and fifth periodic report of Lebanon*, CRC/C/LBN/CO/4-5, 22 June 2017, para. 14.

> **Non-discrimination**
> 21. The Committee is concerned that:
> (a) A number of provisions under the Equality Act (2010) exempt children from the protection against age discrimination and, in Northern Ireland, the proposed legislation on age discrimination excludes children under 16 years of age;
> 22. The Committee recommends that the State party:
> (a) Consider the possibility of expanding legislation to provide protection of all children under 18 years of age against discrimination on the grounds of their age;[55]

Looking at the history of Committee comments to the UK, it is quite possible that this represents an evolution in the approach of the Committee. In the 2002 concluding observations in relation to the UK, for example, the Committee does not reference discrimination on the basis of childhood. Rather it simply lists discrimination against traditionally disadvantaged groups of children such as those with disabilities and ethnic minority status.[56]

By 2008 however the Committee appears to have become more explicit about issues relating to discrimination against children on the basis of childhood. In its 2008 concluding observations (on the UK's combined third and fourth report) the Committee welcomes the forthcoming Equality Act, and notes the risk of discrimination faced by children from traditionally disadvantaged groups. Then the Committee further notes concern: "at the general climate of intolerance and negative public attitudes towards children, especially adolescents, which appears to exist in the State party, including in the media, and may be often the underlying cause of further infringements of their rights".[57]

Significantly, the Committee continued in its 2008 concluding observations to recommend that the UK implement "urgent measures to address the intolerance and inappropriate characterization of children, especially adolescents, within the society, including in the media".[58] This is a bold statement in relation to negative attitudes in a States Party. It likely came about because of the

55 UN Committee on the Rights of the Child, *Concluding observations on the fifth periodic report of United Kingdom of Great Britain and Northern Ireland*, CRC/C/GBR/CO/5, 12 July 2016, paras. 21–22.

56 UN Committee on the Rights of the Child, *Concluding observations: United Kingdom of Great Britain and Northern Ireland*, 9 October 2002, CRC/C/15/Add.188, paras. 22–23.

57 UN Committee on the Rights of the Child, *Concluding observations: United Kingdom of Great Britain and Northern Ireland*, 3 October 2008, CRC/C/GBR/4, para. 24.

58 Ibid, para. 25.

approach of the NGO shadow report of the Children's Rights Alliance for England (CRAE).[59] CRAE decided to explicitly refer to 'age discrimination' in their report, outlining discriminatory treatment that under-18s may face on the grounds of age. CRAE referenced examples such as dispersal by police, and detrimental treatment on "public transport, access to emergency services, shops and leisure facilities and the availability of health and social care services to vulnerable teenagers".[60] As noted above, CRAE used these same arguments to lobby for inclusion of being under-18 as a protected characteristic in the UK's then-forthcoming Equality Act. This example perhaps demonstrates the extent to which NGOs can have a major impact on the pronouncements of the Committee in its concluding observations, and the extent to which civil society has the potential to shape CRC jurisprudence on Article 2. In this case, it resulted in one of the very few instances where the Committee has recommended that the state directly address negative attitudes to children on the basis of childhood, rather than on the basis of their membership of traditionally disadvantaged groups.

In recent years, there appears to have been increasing reference to discrimination on the basis of childhood in activities of the Committee outside of the concluding observations process. In 2019, the CRC Committee together with the Committee on the Elimination of All Forms of Discrimination against Women drafted a Joint General Comment on harmful practices emphasising that such practices are, amongst other things, grounded in discrimination based on age.[61] The CRC Committee in 2017 co-ordinated with the Committee on Migrant Workers in drafting two joint General Comments, emphasising that children in migratory situations are entitled to the enjoyment and upholding of their rights, regardless of their age and their legal status.[62] In joint

59 CRAE, *NGO alternative report to the Committee on the Rights of the Child – ENGLAND* (CRAE, 2008), Available at http://www.crae.org.uk/publications-resources/ngo-shadow-report-to-the-un-committee-on-the-rights-of-the-child-2008/ (last visited 5 May 2022).

60 Ibid, p.5.

61 UN Committee on the Rights of the Child/UN Committee on the Elimination of All Forms of Discrimination against Women, *Joint general recommendation No. 31 of the Committee on the Elimination of Discrimination against Women/general comment and No. 18 of the Committee on the Rights of the Child on harmful practices*, CEDAW/C/GC/31/Rev.1–CRC/C/GC/18/Rev.1, 14 November 2014.

62 UN Committee on the Protection of the Rights of All Migrant Workers and Members of Their Families, *Joint general comment No. 3 (2017) of the Committee on the Protection of the Rights of All Migrant Workers and Members of Their Families and No. 22 (2017) of the Committee on the Rights of the Child on the general principles regarding the human rights of children in the context of international migration*, CMW/C/GC/3-CRC/C/GC/22,16 November 2017, para. 21–26.

General Comment no. 4, it is underscored that older children (between 15 and 18 years of age) tend to be provided with lower levels of protection than younger children or sometimes be considered as adults or accorded an ambiguous migration status until they turn 18.[63] In recent general comments, the Committee has also been making groundbreaking statements in relation to the status of children. The Committee's 2016 general comment on adolescents for example makes reference to discriminatory attitudes against adolescents, stating:

> Adolescence itself can be a source of discrimination. During this period, adolescents may be treated as dangerous or hostile, incarcerated, exploited or exposed to violence as a direct consequence of their status. Paradoxically, they are also often treated as incompetent and incapable of making decisions about their lives.[64]

The general comment on children in street situations[65] is also important. There is extensive attention paid to the devastating effects of discrimination on children in street situations – as members of ethnic minorities, as vulnerable people who are not taken seriously by police when they must complain about crimes committed against them, and so on. Nevertheless, it is very noticeable that even though the entire thrust of the general comment relates to the vulnerability of children as opposed to adults in street situations, and the vulnerability of children in street situations to mistreatment and abuse by adults, there is no explicit reference to discrimination on the basis of childhood. For example the Committee lists the type of discrimination faced by children in this situation: "Children can face multiple and intersecting forms of discrimination, for example, on the basis of gender, sexual orientation and gender identity/expression, disability, race, ethnicity, indigenous status."[66] Yet childhood itself is not listed. It is perhaps assumed that being a child is a major risk factor – perhaps *the* major risk factor – for discrimination. Yet it is omitted from the list.

---

63 Ibid, para 3.

64 UN Committee on the Rights of the Child (CRC), *General comment No. 20 (2016) on the implementation of the rights of the child during adolescence*, CRC/C/GC/20, 6 December 2016, para. 21.

65 UN Committee on the Rights of the Child, *General comment No. 21 (2017) on children in street situations*, CRC/C/GC/21, 21 June 2017.

66 Ibid, para. 26.

4.4 *Discrimination against Children "under the Radar"*

There are however issues which constitute discrimination against children which may not always be framed by the Committee as such. These issues therefore can be said to go under the radar in a search for discrimination on the basis of childhood in Committee jurisprudence.

Hitting or otherwise harming children for punishment, often known as physical punishment or corporal punishment is one such issue. There are often different assault laws in place for children and adults to account for corporal punishment. As this is detrimental treatment of children on the basis of childhood, this can certainly be described as discrimination. In the Committee's report on the concluding observations of the Cook Islands in 2020 for example, it expresses concern that corporal punishment is permitted at home and in some care settings: "The Committee is concerned in particular that section 32 of the draft crimes bill elaborated in 2017 provides for the so-called "lawful correction of a child", as does the Crimes Act."[67] The Committee urges the state to repeal relevant laws and conduct awareness-raising programmes.[68] This reference to the children's rights violation of corporal punishment is positioned under the heading of 'violence against children' in the Committee's concluding observations. On the one hand this is unsurprising as this is a phenomenon of permission to adults in certain circumstances to assault children. On the other hand, given that in the Cook Islands (as in many other countries) it remains possible for adults in some certain circumstances to assault children in this way lawfully, this could certainly be framed as a discrimination issue. It need not necessarily be considered solely under Article 2, as this may distract from serious issues of violence against children. However there is great potential for both considering it as violence *and* discrimination. Doing so – emphasising that corporal punishment in this context is an issue of unfair discrimination, enshrined in and mandated by the legal system in the Cook Islands – would help draw attention to the issue of discriminatory practices against children as a group, and the links between this discrimination and violations of other rights such as freedom from violence.

Another issue which is covered by the Committee extensively in its concluding observations is cultural attitudes. The Committee has repeatedly made the important point that what it refers to as "cultural attitudes" whereby there is a lack of respect for children, or an underestimation of children, can

---

67 UN Committee on the Rights of the Child, *Concluding Observations on the combined second to Fifth Periodic Reports of the Cook Islands*, CRC/C/COK/CO/2-5, 2 April 2020, para. 25.

68 Ibid, para. 26.

pose barriers to children's participation rights. The Committee does not specifically reference discrimination here, but it is quite clear that the cultural attitudes in question constitute prejudicial attitudes to children, and therefore discrimination.[69] Such attitudes and tradition can have negative effects on children being seen as rights holders in the first place; see e.g. concluding observations on Japan where the Committee expresses concern that "traditional views which fail to respect the child as a human being with rights severely limit the weight given to children's views".[70] The Committee has also emphasized that States are obliged to "take adequate measures to raise awareness and educate the society about the negative impact of such attitudes and practices and to encourage attitudinal changes in order to achieve full implementation of the rights of every child under the Convention".[71] This is very similar to the Committee comments on negative attitudes in the UK,[72] however unlike those UK comments, the Committee has not made the connection between negative attitudes and Article 2 in its concluding observations on Japan. These comments generally appear to be made under the heading of Article 12, the right of children to be heard and to have due weight given to their views.

Another indirect pronouncement by the Committee on discriminatory attitudes that was in the case of Australia in its 2019 concluding observations on that state. Commentators including the Prime Minister made derogatory statements about young climate protestors in the course of that year. The Committee went on to express "its concern and disappointment that a protest led by children calling on government to protect the environment received a strongly worded negative response from those in authority, which demonstrates disrespect for the right of children to express their views on this important issue".[73] The word 'discrimination' was not directly used, although discriminatory attitudes is what the Committee appears to be strongly pointing to. This appears to be another instance in which the Committee could have explicitly considered discrimination against children (under Article 2) but instead considered it to be an issue under Article 12, the right to be heard.

69 Thorburn Stern *supra* note 3, pp. 109–110.

70 UN Committee on the Rights of the Child, *Concluding observations: Japan*, CRC//C/JPN/CO/3, 20 June 2010, para. 43.

71 UN Committee on the Rights of the Child, *General Comment No. 12 The right of the child to be heard*, CRC/C/GC/12, 1 July 2009, para. 76.

72 UN Committee on the Rights of the Child, *Concluding Observations on the fifth periodic report of United Kingdom of Great Britain and Northern Ireland, supra* note 56.

73 UN Committee on the Rights of the Child, *Concluding observations on the combined Fifth and Sixth Periodic Reports of Australia*, CRC/C/AUS/CO/5-6, 1 November 2019, para. 40.

Another point of importance is the fact that children of different ages within childhood may experience discrimination differently. The Committee frequently criticises detrimental treatment of 'younger children'. In its comments on the 2019 report of Italy, the Committee references "the right of the child to be heard without any discrimination due to age".[74] There is no context as to why the Committee makes this point, but it seems to relate to the Committee having been provided with information that younger children are unheard more frequently than older children. The Committee is clearly inclining towards making a point about age discrimination here, although it could have been much more explicit about whether it is pointing to discrimination between younger and older children, or discrimination between adults and children.

Considering that all these issues could clearly be referred to as discrimination under the heading of Article 2, there is scope here for the Committee to be more explicit. It could directly reference the Article 2 principle of non-discrimination. The Committee could be more vocal on the matter of how these issues are equality/non-discrimination issues, and therefore progress CRC Article 2 in the process.

5 Traditionally Disadvantaged Groups of Children Noted by the Committee as Experiencing Discrimination

As mentioned before, the majority of references to discrimination relate to children from 'traditionally disadvantaged groups' which are particularly vulnerable to discrimination. The Committee frequently makes reference to discrimination against children on various grounds such as gender, ethnicity, disability, religion and so on, and has also added numerous other groups such as children in the care of the state, children in street situations and migrant children to its list of children from groups that are particularly vulnerable to discrimination.[75] As this constitutes the bulk of the Committee's references to discrimination, it is important to give these points consideration here. These references clearly can contribute to our understanding of the Committee's approach to discrimination against children on the basis of childhood. This is because the approach taken by the Committee to discrimination against traditionally disadvantaged groups will provide insight into

74 UN Committee on the Rights of the Child, *Concluding observations on the combined fifth and sixth periodic reports of Italy*, *supra* note 53, para 18.

75 *See* Besson and Kleber, *supra* note 6.

possibilities for how it will approach discrimination on the basis of childhood. This is particularly important considering the need for research into how the CRC can deal with intersectional discrimination.

One common approach by the Committee in a concluding observations report is to make reference to the need to tackle discrimination against groups which are particularly experiencing discrimination in a particular country. For example, Hungary's treatment of LGBQTII+ persons in the past few years has been well known. In 2020, the Committee stated that Hungary must in particular tackle discrimination against lesbian, gay, bisexual, transgender and intersex children, and to take measures to educate the public about equality and non-discrimination and to expand its programmes in schools.[76] Much of the time however, the Committee does not make clear why it is singling out particular groups for attention in a state context.

The Committee also lists groups experiencing discrimination in a particular state. Usually it is groups which one would expect, such as girls and people with disabilities. In the case of Tuvalu, however the Committee, in this 'listing' process, included children living in the outer islandsin Tuvalu in its concluding observations on that state, noting "the persistent de facto discrimination against, among others, girls, children with disabilities and children living in the outer islands, especially with regard to access to education, health care and services, and development".[77]

This raises the point that the Committee does make reference to particular groups who may not stereotypically be included for example in protected characteristics and domestic equality law. The Committee for example urged states to tackle discrimination against children affected by HIV/AIDS in the case of Botswana[78] and discrimination against children in alternative care in the case of Bulgaria.[79] In the Committee's concluding observations on Syria, it expressed concern about "discrimination against children based on where they live, particularly regarding access to education, health services and safe water".[80] In its concluding observations on the report of Korea,

76 UN Committee on the Rights of the Child, *Concluding observations on the report of Hungary, supra* note 8, para. 16 (a).

77 UN Committee on the Rights of the Child, *Concluding observations on the combined second to fifth periodic reports of Tuvalu,* CRC/C/TUV/2-5, 31March 2020, para. 16. (b).

78 UN Committee on the Rights of the Child, *Concluding observations on the combined second and third reports of Botswana,* CRC/C/BWA/CO/2-3, 26 June 2019, para. 22. (b).

79 UN Committee on the Rights of the Child, *Concluding observations on the combined third to fifth periodic reports of Bulgaria,* CRC/C/BGR/CO/3-5, 21 November 2016, para. 35.

80 UN Committee on the Rights of the Child, *Concluding observations on the fifth periodic report of the Syrian Arab Republic,* CRC/C/SYR/CO/5, 6 March 2019, para. 17.

the Committee noted discrimination against "rural children, economically disadvantaged children" in access to services for example healthcare and education.[81] Another group which may not traditionally be considered alongside those having protected characteristics is considered by the Committee in relation to Cote d'Ivoire. The Committee expresses deep concern about persistent discrimination against, amongst other groups, children with albinism.[82]

The Committee makes frequent reference to discrimination against girls. In some concluding observations, the Committee notes that whilst there is discrimination against many groups, discrimination against girls is particularly problematic. For example in the case of Korea, the Committee noted that regarding conditions of children held in detention, that there were inappropriate conditions including overcrowding and a lack of access to medical assistance: "especially for girls".[83]

Often, the Committee points to laws concerning sex or healthcare which are gender problematic, noting for example an issue with the definition of rape in the case of Norway:

> The lack of free consent not being at the centre of the definition of rape in section 291 of the Penal Code, which applies to children above 14 years of age, regarding which the Committee on the Elimination of Discrimination against Women and the Human Rights Committee have already raised concerns.[84]

In relation to Norway, the Committee also emphasised "oversexualized representations of girls in the media" and recommended that Norway allocate resources for research into possible connections between this and gender-based

---

81 UN Committee on the Rights of the Child, *Concluding observations on the combined fifth and sixth periodic reports of the Republic of Korea*, CRC/C/KOR/CO/5-6, 24 March 2019, para. 16(a).

82 UN Committee on the Rights of the Child, *Concluding observations on the second periodic report of Côte d'Ivoire*, CRC/C/CIV/CO/2, 12 July 2019, para. 19.

83 UN Committee on the Rights of the Child, *Concluding observations on the combined fifth and sixth periodic reports of the Republic of Korea*, *supra* note 81, para. 46. (f).

84 UN Committee on the Rights of the Child, *Concluding observations on the combined fifth and sixth periodic reports of Norway*, CRC/C/NOR/CO/5-6, 4 July 2018, para. 17 (b) (with reference to: Committee on the Elimination of Discrimination against Women (CEDAW), *Concluding observations on the ninth periodic report of Norway*, CEDAW/C/NOR/CO/9, 22 November 2017, para. 24 (g) and Human Rights Committee, *Concluding observations on the seventh periodic report of Norway*, CCPR/C/NOR/CO/7, para. 15 (b)).

violence.[85] Likewise, in the case of El Salvador, the Committee urges the state to increase efforts to tackle discrimination against girls “particularly regarding their access to education and to sexual and reproductive health services, and in relation to sexual violence, civil unions and teenage pregnancy”.[86]

Children with disabilities are a group which receives a lot of attention from the Committee from the perspective of discrimination. The Committee noted recently that “children with disabilities [are] being subjected to stigmatization, discrimination, abandonment and concealment from society” in its examination of the report of the State of Palestine.[87] The Committee often emphasises inclusive education for children with disabilities in the context of non-discrimination, as was the case in Mozambique’s report, where the Committee also emphasised the need to have human rights-based approaches, as well as strategies to eliminate discrimination when it comes to children with disabilities.[88]

The Committee frequently has detailed familiarity with specific issues affecting children with disabilities in a particular state context. For example, in relation to Botswana, the Committee notes efforts to combat discrimination against children disabilities, although the Committee cites further rights issues with which the state must deal:

> The Committee welcomes the establishment of the Disability Public Education Office to combat the stigmatization of and discrimination against children with disabilities and the steps taken by the State party towards adopting a human rights-based approach to disability. It also notes that a draft national disability framework is pending approval by parliament. It is concerned, however, about the lack of information regarding the situation of children with disabilities and the insufficient progress in ensuring their access to inclusive education.[89]

85 UN Committee on the Rights of the Child, *Concluding observations on the combined fifth and sixth periodic reports of Norway*, CRC/C/NOR/CO/5-6, 4 July 2018, para. 12.

86 UN Committee on the Rights of the Child, *Concluding observations on the combined fifth and sixth periodic reports of El Salvador*, CRC/C/SLV/CO/5-6, 29 November 2018, para. 13.

87 UN Committee on the Rights of the Child, *Concluding observations on the initial report of State of Palestine*, CRC/C/PSE/CO/1, 6 March 2020, para. 48(b).

88 UN Committee on the Rights of the Child, *Concluding observations on the third and fourth periodic reports of Mozambique*, CRC/C/MOZ/CO/3-4, 27 November 2019, para. 31.

89 UN Committee on the Rights of the Child, *Concluding observations on the combined second and third reports of Botswana*, *supra* note 78, para. 43.

The Committee often emphasises the need to ensure equality for Indigenous people (see for example the comments of the Committee on the state report of Bolivia).[90] The Committee states that Australia must "address disparities in access to services by Aboriginal and Torres Strait Islander children…" (as well as other groups).[91]

The Committee also frequently makes reference to discrimination against children who may be non-nationals, for example stating that Denmark should "[e]nsure that all children, including those attending boarding schools, or foreign children … have access to the standard educational system…".[92] In its report on Korea, the Committee comments on discrimination against "multicultural children and refugee children".[93]

6 Age, Discrimination and Domestic Law in Committee Comments

Age does sometimes arise when it comes to discrimination. For example, in its concluding observations on the report of Saint Vincent and the Grenadines the Committee expresses concern about discrimination against lesbian, gay and bisexual children. In particular the Committee calls attention to criminalization of consensual same-sex conduct between men under the Criminal Code (1990). The Committee notes that the relevant law "may penalize boys above 16 years of age for same-sex sexual activity".[94] This type of reference to discrimination is obviously relevant to age, as age limits are noted. However, the age limits appear to be incidental to the issue under consideration. It is not necessarily discrimination against children that is the issue at hand, but rather the characteristic in question such as sexuality. This can however be considered in the framework of intersectionality, when one considers i. the charac-

90 UN Committee on the Rights of the Child, *Concluding observations on the report submitted by the Bolivarian Republic of Venezuela under article 8, paragraph 1, of the Optional Protocol to the Convention on the Rights of the Child on the involvement of children in armed conflict*, CRC/C/OPAC/VEN/CO/1, 3 November 2014.

91 UN Committee on the Rights of the Child, *Concluding observations on the combined fifth and sixth periodic reports of Australia*, CRC/C/AUS/CO/5-6, 1 November 2019, para. 19.

92 UN Committee on the Rights of the Child, *Concluding observations on the fifth periodic report of Denmark*, CRC/C/DNK/CO/5, 26 October 2017, para. 62.

93 UN Committee on the Rights of the Child, *Concluding observations on the combined fifth and sixth periodic reports of the Republic of Korea*, *supra* note 81, para. 16.

94 UN Committee on the Rights of the Child, *Concluding observations on the combined second and third periodic reports of Saint Vincent and the Grenadines*, CRC/C/VCT/CO/2-3, 13 March 2017, para. 22.

teristic of being a child, together with ii. the additional characteristic (such as sexuality) combine to create an enhanced type of discrimination.

The Committee focuses on domestic laws and policies when it comes to issues of discrimination and equality. The Committee sometimes notes where a state has domestic law which prohibits discrimination. This is the case in its concluding observations on the report of Bosnia and Herzegovina: "The Committee notes with appreciation the legislative, institutional and policy measures adopted to implement the Convention, in particular the amendments to the Law on Prohibition of Discrimination in 2016".[95]

The Committee will also emphasise where discrimination is not accounted for in the domestic legal system. For example, in its concluding observations on the report of Sri Lanka, the Committee states that, in order to guarantee that the principle of non-discrimination is observed in law and practice the state should: "Ensure compliance with article 2 of the Convention by incorporating the principle of non-discrimination into its domestic legislation and conduct an in-depth revision of its legislation".[96]

Also, in relation to the report of Micronesia the Committee noted that although the state has protection against discrimination enshrined within its constitution, important grounds are omitted from this protection:

> The Committee welcomes the information provided during the dialogue that the State party has undertaken legislative measures to expand the grounds on which discrimination is prohibited. It notes that the Federal Constitution and state constitutions of the State party provide for equality and equal protection of the law and that discrimination on the grounds of race, sex, language, national, ethnic or social origin and property is prohibited. The Committee is concerned, however, that discrimination on all explicit grounds covered under the Convention, including disability and religion, is not prohibited.[97]

The Committee notes where particular laws are discriminatory in a state, they should be amended. In the case of Tuvalu for example the Committee notes

---

95 UN Committee on the Rights of the Child, *Concluding observations on the combined fifth and sixth periodic reports of Bosnia and Herzegovina*, CRC/C/BIH/CO/5-6, 5 December 2019, para. 3.

96 UN Committee on the Rights of the Child, *Concluding observations on the combined fifth and sixth periodic reports of Sri Lanka*, CRC/C/LKA/CO/5-6, 2 March 2018, para. 16(a).

97 UN Committee on the Rights of the Child, *Concluding observations on the second periodic report of the Federated States of Micronesia*, CRC/C/FSM/CO/2, 3 April 2020, para 23.

that domestic law confers advantages to children of spouses via the Tuvalu Lands Code 1962. The Committee on examining the report of Tuvalu and other discriminatory laws; urging that such laws are changed and recommending that Tuvalu enact anti-discrimination legislation.[98] The Committee also emphasises that implementing laws that prohibit discrimination will include "adequately sanctioning perpetrators and providing child victims of discrimination with appropriate remedies".[99]

In the Committee's efforts to deal with discrimination against children taken together with another characteristic, the Committee sometimes references other relevant international human rights obligations. For example in its response to the state report of Cote d'Ivoire, when highlighting the gender specific harmful practice of marriage under the age of 18 years, the Committee stated: "the Committee urges the State party to expedite the adoption of the draft law on marriage to remove all exceptions that allow marriage under the age of 18 years".[100] This perhaps highlights the potential for progressing into different approaches to discrimination against children – through CEDAW for example – combining the CRC with other instruments which have strong non-discrimination clauses.

When equality frameworks are mentioned by the Committee, it is not in relation to the failure to include childhood as a protected characteristic. The Committee refers e.g. to the lack of legislation on discrimination in its 2019 report on Japan, and urges the state to "[e]nact comprehensive anti-discrimination legislation"[101] but the Committee does not make the point that childhood should be a protected characteristic. The exception to this, as noted above, is in the 2016 concluding observations (on the UK's fifth report), where the Committee recommends that the UK considers the possibility of expanding legislation to ensure protection of all children under 18 years of age against discrimination on the grounds of their age.[102]

98 UN Committee on the Rights of the Child, *Concluding observations on the combined second to fifth periodic reports of Tuvalu*, CRC/C/TUV/2-5, 31 March 2020, para. 17(b).

99 UN Committee on the Rights of the Child, *Concluding observations on the combined fifth and sixth periodic reports of Rwanda*, CRC/C/RWA/CO/5-6, 28 February 2020, para. 15(a).

100 UN Committee on the Rights of the Child, *Concluding observations on the second periodic report of Côte d'Ivoire, supra* note 82, para. 18.

101 UN Commitee on the Rights of the Child, *Concluding observations on the combined fifth and sixth periodic reports of Italy, supra* note 53, para 18.

102 UN Committee on the Rights of the Child, *Concluding observations on the fifth periodic report of the United Kingdom of Great Britain and Northern Ireland*, CRC/C/GBR/CO/5, 12 July 2016.

The Committee often emphasises the importance of the availability of complaints mechanisms for children where they may be experiencing discrimination. For example in the case of Bosnia and Herzegovina the Committee urges the state to:

> Continue efforts to effectively implement the Law at all levels, including by disseminating information on where children can report discrimination and harmonizing the legislation at all levels within the State party, in compliance with the Law.[103]

Similarly, in the concluding observations relating to the report of Montenegro, the Committee recommends when combating discrimination, part of this implementation will involve "adequately sanctioning perpetrators, providing child victims of discrimination with effective and appropriate remedies".[104]

7 Recommendations of the Committee on Combating Discrimination

As with other rights, the committee has made recommendations relating to the principle of non-discrimination which are important to outline here. In General Comment No. 5, the Committee emphasises that the principle of non-discrimination "requires States actively to identify individual children and groups of children the recognition and realisation of whose rights may demand special measures".[105] The Committee also highlighted the "need for data collection to be disaggregated to enable discrimination or potential discrimination to be identified". This could also be interpreted to point to the need of states to gather information on how children as a group are affected by particular phenomena such as violence and homicide. Failing to do this potentially masks the extent of violence against children as a group, which can be argued to constitute a non-discrimination issue.

In its concluding observations, the Committee makes specific recommendations as to how states should tackle various types of discrimination. One such recommendation which is relatively common is awareness-raising cam-

---

103 UN Committee on the Rights of the Child, *Concluding observations on the combined fifth and sixth periodic reports of Bosnia and Herzegovina, supra* note 95.

104 UN Committee on the Rights of the Child, *Concluding observations on Montenegro*, CRC/C/MNE/CO/2-3, 22 June 2018, para. 22(a).

105 General Comment No. 5, *supra* note 32, para. 12.

paigns. For example in its examination of the report of the State of Palestine, the Committee urged that the state:

> Undertake awareness-raising campaigns in order to combat stigmatization, prejudice and multiple forms of discrimination against children with disabilities, promote a positive image of such children and their recognition as rights-holders, with respect for their dignity and evolving capacities on an equal basis with other children.[106]

Likewise, in the case of Portugal, the Committee recommends that the State do more to raise awareness among public and civil servants, as well as law enforcement official:

> … to combat stereotyping, prejudice and discrimination against girls, children with disabilities, children in migration, those of ethnic, religious and racial minorities, including Roma, people of African descent and Muslim children, as well as lesbian, gay, bisexual and transgender adolescents and intersex children.[107]

In the case of Hungary, the Committee particularly expressed that the state should take measures to implement non-discrimination programmes in schools.[108] In countries in which the Committee deems appropriate, reference is made to community and religious leaders as crucial in efforts to eliminate discrimination against particular groups of children. For example in the case of Mauritania, the Committee urges that the state do this: "[I]n close cooperation with civil society, the media and community and religious leaders, through awareness-raising programmes aimed at creating an enabling environment that promotes equality among children".[109] In its report on Austria, the Committee noted with praise the fact that the state had taken measures such as establishing units for investigation of incitement to hatred.[110]

---

106 UN Committee on the Rights of the Child, *Concluding observations on the initial report of Palestine*, *supra* note 87, para. 49. (b).

107 UN Committee on the Rights of the Child, *Concluding observations on the combined fifth and sixth reports of Portugal*, CRC/C/PRT/CO/5-6, 9 December 2019, para. 14.

108 UN Committee on the Rights of the Child, *Concluding observations on the sixth periodic report of Hungary*, CRC/C/HUN/CO/6, 3 March 2020, para 16(a).

109 UN Committee on the Rights of the Child, *Concluding observations on the combined third, fourth and fifth reports of Mauritania*, CRC/C/MRT/CO/3-5, 26 November 2018.

110 UN Committee on the Rights of the Child, *Concluding observations on the combined fifth and sixth reports of Austria*, CRC/C/AUT/CO/5-6, 6 March 2020, para. 16.

Clearly allocating sufficient resources to deal with discrimination will be necessary. In the concluding observations relating to the report of Montenegro, the Committee recommends when combating discrimination, part of this implementation will involve "allocating sufficient human, technical and financial resources for the effective implementation of related national strategies".[111]

8 Conclusion

The CRC outlines the rights to which under-18s are entitled; and it has certainly been successful in drawing attention to the rights and interests of children. Yet its non-discrimination article – Article 2 – is almost without exception applied to traditionally disadvantaged groups such as girls, ethnic and racial minorities and children with disabilities. It is used little, if ever, to protect children from discrimination on the basis of childhood. There appears to exist an assumption that this is unproblematic, and perhaps that; "by reason of age alone, children should be afforded less and lesser legal rights than adults".[112]

There is a lot to be learned from the ways in which the Committee responds to discrimination against particular groups of children. Many of the concluding observations and recommendations which are directed at tackling discrimination against traditionally disadvantaged groups such as girls and children with disabilities will be useful to guide approaches when it comes to children as a group more broadly. For example, as mentioned above, in its examination of the report of the State of Palestine, the Committee urged that the state undertake awareness-raising campaigns in order to combat discrimination against children with disabilities.[113] The same approaches could be taken to combat discrimination against children on the basis of childhood.

Ganty points out (albeit in the context of socio-economic status) that the prohibition of discrimination is an empowering legal tool in the protection of disadvantaged people.[114] It can assist in scrutiny of disadvantage; it can have a

111 UN Committee on the Rights of the Child, *Concluding observations on the combined second and third periodic reports of Montenegro*, CRC/C/MNE/CO/2-3, 22 June 2018, para. 22(a).

112 R. Sandland, 'Lessons for Children's Rights from Disability Rights?', in E. Brems et al. (eds), *Children's Rights Law in the Global Human Rights Landscape. Isolation, Inspiration, Integration?* (Routledge, Abingdon, Oxon, 2017) p. 124.

113 UN Committee on the Rights of the Child, *Concluding observations on the initial report of Palestine*, *supra* note 87, para. 49(b).

114 S. Ganty, 'Poverty as Misrecognition: What Role for Antidiscrimination Law in Europe?', 21:4 *Human Rights Law Review* (2021) pp. 962–1007.

role in combating stereotypes and stigma, and can have "an important cross-cutting function in cases of multiple discrimination". This seems particularly pertinent for children, considering that where there is discrimination on the basis of gender, race and so on; 'multiple discrimination' could well be likely. Being a child will put members of these traditionally disadvantaged groups at greater risk of discrimination, with all of the danger and risk that this brings. It is clear that greater levels of research into the nature of intersectionality, children and the CRC is needed. Intersectional discrimination is cumulative, and it has been argued that "the result is qualitatively different, or synergistic".[115] This means that discrimination on the basis of childhood taken together with other categories under the CRC is an important area for future research.

As noted above, the Committee often lists a number of examples in one section of their concluding observations of children from 'traditionally disadvantaged groups' who are experiencing discrimination. These often include girls, ethnic minorities, children with disabilities and other groups. It is often not made quite clear on what basis these particular groups are being singled out for special attention, and therefore the committee comments sometimes seem somewhat inconsistent.

The Committee's inconsistent approach also means that it has not been made clear that states must refrain from discriminating against children on the basis of childhood. As noted above in Sections 1–2, there is a sense in all societies that children as a group are so different that it is acceptable to simply exclude them from equality frameworks. It must be made clear to states that detrimental treatment of children must be analysed and determined on a case by case basis, and only happen as is necessary and proportionate, as argued by Breen. She considers the special status of children and the need to consider the differences between children and adults: "The actual appropriate response is a question of balance in every case whereby the appropriate administrative or judicial decision-makers assess the legitimacy, proportionality and necessity of the limitation in question."[116]

There is an evolution to be seen in the approach of the Committee to the issue. The quantitative analysis indicates that there is increasing attention being given to discrimination and equality in committee jurisprudence. The UK example demonstrates what can be achieved if NGOs (in this case the Children's Rights Alliance for England) and others give proper attention to classifying the issue of poor treatment of children where appropriate as dis-

115 S. Fredman, *Discrimination Law*, 2nd ed. (Claredon, 2011).

116 Breen, *supra* note 37, p. 12.

crimination against children. The Committee is clearly open to examining issues in this framework.

The emphasis of the Committee that 'cultural attitudes' should not impact on children being heard and taken seriously is an interesting one and intersects greatly with the issue of discrimination against children. It is an area which is ripe for the Committee to explore discrimination themes, rather than replace it with simply reference to 'attitudes'. Discrimination is a factor which likely underlies so many of the human rights issues affecting children and this needs to be made more explicit by the Committee. To emphasise poor attitudes to children as *discrimination on the basis of childhood* would call attention to many other issues e.g. poverty and violence against children.

It is also important that the Committee has, through general comments and other means, increasingly framed issues as discrimination issues. It is quite possible however that the reason that we are seeing discrimination on the basis of childhood referred to by the committee in collaboration with other treaty bodies, is that these treaty bodies are well suited to focus on discrimination itself. The CRC on its own however remains an instrument which does not appear to be inspiring a focus on discrimination against childhood. It is important to note that this does not need to be the case. The CRC Article 2 reference to 'other status' renders it possible to read into the right of children to be free from discrimination on the basis of childhood. Another area of concern, as noted by Besson and Kleber is that the prohibition of discrimination enshrined in Article 2 remains vague and underexamined.[117] A CRC general comment on discrimination on the basis of childhood under Article 2 would be a helpful and important step towards bringing adequate attention to this issue.

The Committee is willing to analyse issues in the discrimination framework in some circumstances, such as through evidence from Children's Rights Alliance for England (CRAE) in the UK context. It does so when collaborating with other treaty bodies.[118] It is important to ascertain the extent to which increased examination of children's rights issues in the framework of non-discrimination/equality will benefit children. Academics, non-governmental organisations, and the Committee itself should therefore give greater attention to non-discrimination/equality when it comes to children as a group.

117 Besson and Kleber, *supra* note 6.

118 *See* UN Committee on the Rights of the Child/UN Committee on the Elimination of All Forms of Discrimination against Women, *Joint general recommendation No. 31 of the Committee on the Elimination of Discrimination against Women/general comment and No. 18 of the Committee on the Rights of the Child on harmful practices*, 14 November 2014, CEDAW/C/GC/31/Rev.1–CRC/C/GC/18/Rev.1.

CHAPTER 3

'Handle with Care': Addressing Disadvantage Based on Childhood through a Non-discrimination Frame

Michael George Marcondes Smith and Wouter Vandenhole

Abstract[1]

Children are exposed to disadvantage (in the broad sense) because they are children: some offences (status offences) are considered crimes if committed by children, but not if committed by adults. Children are excluded from political participation overall and do not enjoy the right to participate in elections. Young people will suffer more than adults from the triple planetary crisis. They are also more likely than adults to be poor. Underlying all those examples of disadvantage on the basis of childhood are several tenets: that of heightened vulnerabilities, dependency, lesser capabilities as well as that of voicelessness.

This chapter explores how disadvantage on grounds of childhood can best be addressed conceptually. What is the better frame? Traditionally, the best interests of the child (BIC) has been mobilised in children's and human rights law. Others have suggested that the prohibition of discrimination may be a more promising frame. We argue that non-discrimination (in combination with BIC) may point to an avenue for a more coherent argumentation regarding the discriminatory nature of childism. But only so if discrimination law is 'handled with care', that is, if its technicality is fully taken into account: this requires the identification of a comparator and a prohibited ground of discrimination, as well as an assessment whether there is a reasonable justification for the differential treatment. Whether the BIC or non-discrimination

1 The description of our respective contributions is based on the Contributor Roles Taxonomy (CRediT) developed by the National Information Standards Organization (<https://credit.niso.org/>, last accessed 6 September 2024). We have in particular identified the conceptualization and writing roles (both original draft and review and editing). The main structure and argument was jointly defined by both authors. The section on best interests of the child and on discrimination under the Convention on the Rights of the Child was drafted by Wouter Vandenhole, the one on discrimination law more generally by Michael G. Marcondes Smith. Both authors reviewed and provided feedback on the text. As such, we take joint responsibility for the entirety of the work presented. We are grateful for the comments received at a workshop held in June 2024 in Stockholm.

DOI:10.1163/9789004708433_004

frame is used in law, they tend to be confronted with the same challenge: the way childhood is constructed.

1 Introduction

In several instances, children are exposed to disadvantage (in the broad sense) on the basis of being a child: status offences are considered crimes if committed by children, but not if committed by adults. Children tend to be excluded from political participation overall and do not enjoy the right to participate in elections. Younger generations will suffer more than adults from the "triple planetary crisis, comprising the climate emergency, the collapse of biodiversity and pervasive pollution".[2] Moreover, "children are more likely than adults to be poor".[3] Underlying all those examples of disadvantage on the basis of childhood are several tenets: that of heightened vulnerabilities, dependency, lesser capabilities as well as that of voicelessness. In Peleg's reading, children are in an "inherent positionality of inferiority".[4]

How can disadvantage on grounds of childhood best be addressed conceptually? What is the better frame? Traditionally, the best interests of the child (BIC) has been mobilized in children's and human rights law. Others have suggested that the prohibition of non-discrimination may be a more promising frame.[5]

In addressing different forms of relative group disadvantage, discrimination law often faces the initial struggle of defining them in the first place, disadvantage on the grounds of childhood being no exception. However, while mentions are made to different conceptualisations of this form of disadvantage, this chapter centres its attention on more technical questions surrounding

2 Committee on the Rights of the Child, 'General Comment No. 26 (2023) on Children's Rights and the Environment, with a Special Focus on Climate Change' para 1 <https://tbinternet.ohchr.org/_layouts/15/treatybodyexternal/Download.aspx?symbolno=CRC%2FC%2FGC%2F26&Lang=en>.

3 A. Daly et al., 'UN Convention on the Rights of the Child, Article 2 and Discrimination on the Basis of Childhood: The CRC Paradox?', 91:3 *Nordic Journal of International Law* (2022) p. 425–426; W. Thiery et al., 'Intergenerational Inequities in Exposure to Climate Extremes', 374 *Science* (2021) pp. 158.

4 N. Peleg, 'A Children's Rights Dilemma – Paternalism versus Autonomy', In R. Adami et al. (eds.), *The Rights of the Child. Legal, Political and Ethical Challenges* (Brill Nijhoff, Leiden, 2023) p. 11.

5 S. Ganty, 'Poverty as Misrecognition: What Role for Antidiscrimination Law in Europe?' 21 *Human Rights Law Review* (2021) p. 962; Daly et al. *supra* note 3, p. 427.

BIC and non-discrimination. Drawing at times from the excellent contributions to this volume that do a better job at exploring these conceptualisations, this chapter employs the term 'childism' as an attempt to introduce disadvantages on the grounds of childhood within the domain of non-discrimination.

In what follows, we first explain how childism is sought to be countered in children's and human rights law by resorting to the best interests of the child. We continue with an assessment of the potential of the prohibition of discrimination to address disadvantage on grounds of childhood and to protect and empower children. We then argue that non-discrimination (in combination with BIC) may point to an avenue for a more coherent argumentation regarding the discriminatory nature of childism. But only so if discrimination law is 'handled with care', that is, if its technicality is fully taken into account: this requires the identification of a comparator and a prohibited ground of differentiation, as well as an assessment whether there is a reasonable justification for the differential treatment.

The chapter's main arguments are illustrated with reference to political participation. This is done for two main reasons. First, the topic of political participation has received significant attention in children's rights literature, and often serves as an example that grounds opposing theorisations in the field. Second, the chapter seeks a didactic approach concerning technical elements of non-discrimination that can benefit from a clear illustration. With this objective, the example of granting voting rights to children on an equal basis serves to outline the technical arguments that such narrative could require. Further theorisation on the debates surrounding political participation, as well as other examples relating to disadvantages on the basis of childhood are explored in other chapters of this volume.

2 Best Interests of the Child[6]

2.1 *Meaning and Prioritisation*

Disadvantage to children may be sought to be addressed by resorting to specific rights: poverty by relying on the right to a standard of living adequate for the child's development (art. 27 CRC) or the effects of the triple planetary crisis by recourse to the right to life, survival and development (art. 6 CRC), the right

6 This section draws on W. Vandenhole and G. Erdem Türkelli, 'The Best Interests of the Child', In J. Todres and S. M. King (eds.), *The Oxford Handbook of Children's Rights Law* (Oxford University Press, 2020).

to health (art. 24 CRC) or the right to enjoy one's own culture (art. 30 CRC).[7] Often, those more specific rights will be invoked in conjunction with the best interests of the child (BIC) (art. 3 CRC).[8] When little or no support can be found in a specific right BIC may even be the main principle to rely on.

BIC is one of the four general principles that inform the CRC; the other three principles are non-discrimination; the right to life, survival and development; and the right to express one's views and to have them taken into account. In the CRC Committee's view, "[t]he concept of the child's best interests is aimed at ensuring both the full and effective enjoyment of all the rights recognized in the Convention and the holistic development of the child".[9] It "requires the development of a rights-based approach, engaging all actors, to secure the holistic physical, psychological, moral and spiritual integrity of the child and promote his or her human dignity."[10]

In accorance with art. 3 CRC, in all actions concerning children, BIC is to be a primary consideration, and in some instances, such as adoption (see art. 21 CRC), even the paramount consideration. The prioritisation of BIC has been justified by the CRC Committee with reference to "the special situation of the child: dependency, maturity, legal status and, often, voicelessness. Children have less possibility than adults to make a strong case for their own interests and those involved in decisions affecting them must be explicitly aware of their interests. If the interests of children are not highlighted, they tend to be overlooked."[11]

2.2 *Challenges*

2.2.1 Meaning

BIC is an elusive concept. The CRC Committee has argued that it is a three-dimensional concept: a substantive right, an interpretative legal principle and a rule of procedure.[12] In the absence of an authoritative definition of the child's best interests, any best interests assessment is case- and child-specific. The CRC Committee has emphasized that the specific circumstances to be taken into account in a best interests assessment relate to individual characteristics and to the "social and cultural context in which the child

7 See in particular the climate change complaint the CRC Committee has examined, *Sacchi et al* v. *Argentina* (Committee on the Rights of the Child).

8 Ibid.

9 CRC Committee, 'General Comment No. 14 (2013) on the Right of the Child to Have His or Her Best Interests Taken as a Primary Consideration (Art. 3, Para. 1)' para 4.

10 Ibid., para 5.

11 Ibid., para 37.

12 Ibid., para 6.

or children find themselves".[13] To facilitate a best interests assessment, it has drawn up a "non-exhaustive and non-hierarchical list of elements" including the child's views; the child's identity; preservation of the family environment and maintaining relations; care, protection and safety of the child; situation of vulnerability; the child's right to health; and the child's rights to education. Those elements must be balanced with each other in each individual case.[14] Notwithstanding those useful elucidations, it remains very difficult to define the BIC in concrete cases. It is even more difficult to draw on those BIC elements to define BIC of children in general. Whereas the CRC Committee has submitted that "[f]or collective decisions – such as by the legislator – the best interests of children in general must be assessed and determined in light of the circumstances of the particular group and/or children in general", how to do such an assessment and determination is unclear. This is also true regarding the right to political participation: is it in children's general best interest to grant them a right to political participation or not?

2.2.2 Weight

A second challenge is which weight is to be given to BIC. In light of art 3(1) CRC, it cannot "be considered on the same level as all other considerations", neither can it be seen as trumping other interests. A balancing or harmonisation of interests is therefore required, albeit that a "larger weight must be attached" to the child's best interests.[15] Vandenhole and Erdem Türkelli have submitted that "the best interests of the child must be considered chronologically prior to other interests but also be seen as hierarchically higher – without taking an absolutist approach."[16] The fact that the best interests of the child do not trump other interests but rather invite a balance with those interests raises the question whether BIC is the most appropriate legal response to disadvantage on grounds of childhood. For our example of political participation, the question of weight may be less relevant, since the exten-

13 Ibid., para 48.

14 Ibid., paras 52–84.

15 Ibid., paras 37–39. Compare UN Committee on the Protection of the Rights of All Migrant Workers and Members of Their Families (UN Committee on Migrant Workers) and CRC Committee, 'Joint General Comment No. 4 (2017) of the Committee on the Protection of the Rights of All Migrant Workers and Members of Their Families and No. 23 (2017) of the Committee on the Rights of the Child on State Obligations Regarding the Human Rights of Children in the Context of International Migration in Countries of Origin, Transit, Destination and Return' (2017) para 28.

16 Vandenhole and Türkelli, *supra* note 6, p. 217.

sion of voting rights to (certain groups of) children does not pitch their best interests necessarily against those of other groups in society. On the other hand, it could be argued that opening up voting rights to children may uproot the power balance and deprive adults from some of their current dominance in politics.

2.2.3 Paternalism

A third challenge with BIC relates to underlying assumptions about childhood. Although the CRC Committee and others have tried to avoid paternalism in their interpretation of BIC, BIC assessments and determinations are often made by adults (judges, medical staff, migration officers) and based on notions of lack of capacity or incompetence, immaturity, ideas of children as becoming. With Peleg it can be argued that the "'best interest of the child" is probably the main area in which paternalism is most prominent [...]."[17] In her rights-based model for assessing children's capacity, Daly equates BIC with protection (as opposed to the right to be heard, which is considered a proxy for autonomy), which is explained as follows: "Children are a group who are in a unique position of relative vulnerability and adults are obliged to offer them protection from harm".[18] Capacity or competence can refer to legal capacity or mental capacity. ""Legal capacity" is used in the legal sphere to denote the standard for someone to make legally effective decisions [...]."[19] Typically, adults are assumed to have capacity, and children to lack it.[20] Whereas art. 5 CRC explicitly accepts the 'evolving capacities' of children and the parallel evolving role of parents as the child matures, paternalistic protection dynamics often seem to overtake a proper assessment of capacity and a thoughtful balancing of capacity and need for protection.

The assumptions about children's lack of capacity go back to underlying assumptions about childhood. In childhood studies, a distinction has been made between children seen as becomings or as beings.[21] It is debatable whether the CRC has managed to introduce a paradigmatic shift from paternalism to the recognition that children are not only 'becomings' but (also)

---

17 Peleg, *supra* note 4, p. 10.

18 A. Daly, 'Assessing Children's Capacity: Reconceptualizing Our Understanding through the UN Convention on the Rights of the Child', 28 *International Journal of Children's Rights* (2020) p. 480.

19 Ibid., p. 474.

20 Ibid.

21 A. James and A. Prout, *Constructing and Reconstructing Childhood : Contemporary Issues in the Sociological Study of Childhood* (Falmer, 1997).

'beings'.[22] The emphasis on children as becomings who are therefore vulnerable is essentialising and ignores children's agency, resilience, self-determination and autonomy.[23] On the other hand, the swing towards the social constructivist approach to childhood and the emphasis on the agency of children may downplay the biological distinctiveness of childhood as well as the 'biosocial nexus'.[24] Agency has been problematised for its lack of a relational and contextual approach, which has led in turn to a neglect of limiting contexts and the risk of foregrounding a liberal perspective.[25] Conceptualisations of childhood as a 'period of relative autonomy' and agency and autonomy in terms of 'circumscribed autonomy' and 'thin' or 'tactical' agency seek to reconcile the coexistence of vulnerability and agency.[26]

As to our example of political participation, the above suggests that the dominant paternalistic reading of BIC would not be particularly helpful in supporting any plea for allowing children to participate politically. As autonomy grounds the right to express one's views,[27] and as children's views are one of the elements to decide on the meaning of BIC, a more sophisticated and children's rights compliant reading of BIC – as advanced by the CRC Committee – may be supportive of political participation for children, to the extent that they express a view in favour of political participation. The critiques on children's full agency in childhood studies and ensuing conceptualisations of childhood as a period of relative autonomy and autonomy in terms of circumscribed autonomy may help to delineate the ways in which political participation of children is shaped.

Notwithstanding the potential to give the BIC principle a rights-based and therefore also emancipatory reading, there seems to be a path dependency in practice to imbue it primarily with protectionist and paternalistic mean-

---

22 N. Peleg, 'Time to Grow Up: The UN Committee on the Rights of the Child's Jurisprudence of the Right to Development', In M.D.A. Freeman (ed.), *Law and childhood studies : current legal issues volume 14* (Oxford University Press, 2012); Peleg, *supra* note 4; A. Barnes, 'CRC's Performance of the Child as Developing', In M.D.A Freeman (ed.), *Law and childhood studies : current legal issues volume 14* (Oxford University Press 2012); D. Bendo, 'Parallel Lines? Childhood Discourses Emphasized by the Children's Rights Movement and the Emerging Field of Children's Rights Studies', 27 *Childhood* (2020) p. 180.

23 W. Vandenhole et al., *Children's Rights. A Commentary on the Convention on the Rights of the Child and Its Protocols* (Elgar 2019) p. 32.

24 A. Canosa and A. Graham, 'Tracing the Contribution of Childhood Studies: Maintaining Momentum While Navigating Tensions', 27 *Childhood* 25 (2020), p. 33.

25 Ibid., p. 34.

26 Vandenhole et al., *supra* note 23, p. 34.

27 Daly, *supra* note 18, p. 481.

ing. It therefore almost seems a *contradictio in terminis* to resort to BIC to address disadvantage imposed on children because they are children, be it called adultism,[28] childism[29] or ageism.[30] Could discrimination law be a more promising avenue?

3 Discrimination Law

3.1 *The Convention on the Rights of the Child*[31]

As mentioned above, non-discrimination is one of four general principles that inform the CRC. Textually, discrimination is prohibited in Art. 2 CRC. That prohibition is circumscribed in at least three ways. First, the prohibition of discrimination in Art. 2 CRC is accessory: it cannot be invoked independently, but only regarding the rights in the CRC. Since the CRC Committee has read into the CRC a general principle of non-discrimination, the accessory status of non-discrimination is to be nuanced. Second, Art. 2 CRC only prohibits discrimination, but it does not introduce a right to equality (before the law or beyond). Here too, the CRC Committee's interpretative practice downplays the importance of this omission. The CRC Committee does pay attention to formal and substantive equality as well as to positive action. Besson and Kleber further differentiate positive action into special protection measures and temporary special measures.[32] A third weakening of the prohibition of discrimination originates not from the text, but from the Committee's interpretative practice. The Committee considers the right to non-discrimination to be a relative right: limitations are possible, provided they can be justified on reasonable and objective grounds that are necessary and proportionate to achieve a legitimate aim.[33] Unlike other human rights monitoring bodies, which require particularly convincing reasons for differentia-

28 J. Wall, 'Adultism and Voting Age Discrimination', 36 *Harvard Human Rights Journal* (2023) p. 327.

29 R. Adami, 'Childism – on Adult Resistance to Children's Rights', In R. Adami et al. (eds.), *The Rights of the Child* (Brill Nijhoff, 2023); E. Young-Bruehl, 'Childism—Prejudice against Children', 45 *Contemporary Psychoanalysis* (2009), p. 251.

30 E. Palmore, *Ageism: Negative and Positive* (Springer, 1999).

31 This section draws on W. Vandenhole, *Non-discrimination and Equality in the View of the UN Human Rights Treaty Bodies* (Intersentia, 2005); Vandenhole et al., *supra* note 23.

32 S. Besson and E. Kleber, 'Article 2. The Right to Non-discrimination', In J. Tobin (ed.), *The UN Convention on the Rights of the Child: A commentary* (Oxford University Press, 2019).

33 *ABA and Others* v. *Spain* (CRC Committee)[10.7].

tion on grounds of race or gender for example, the CRC Committee does not differentiate between the different grounds when it comes to justifying differential treatment.

The list of prohibited grounds in Art. 2 CRC is open-ended, in particular through the reference to 'other status'. Moreover, the CRC Committee has been one of the most liberal in adding new grounds under that heading of 'other status'. What made the CRC for a while unique compared to other United Nations core human rights treaties is that, at the time of adoption, it was the first UN treaty to include disability as a prohibited ground of differentiation.[34]

A second unique characteristic of Art. 2 CRC is that it imposes a positive obligation on States to ensure that the child is protected against discrimination or punishment because of the parents' status, activities, opinions or beliefs.

3.2 *Human Rights Law*

Non-discrimination, along with equality more broadly, is a concept that underlies human rights law in general, appearing in almost all human rights treaties. For some, distinguishing between equality and non-discrimination simply points to a positive and a negative version of the same concept.[35] Another interpretation makes a distinction between equality on the one hand as a broader or general normative expression, and non-discrimination on the other as a negative command, a prohibition aimed at achieving equality.[36] This applies to national jurisdictions in which broader, constitutional notions of equality tend to inform the legal system as principles, while statutory law regulates a more technical approach to the prohibition of discrimination.[37]

A 'technical' description of discrimination refers to the normative, positive prohibition of discrimination, and must also be distinguished from a lay un-

---

34 Subsequently adopted treaties do also include disability as a prohibited ground.

35 A. F. Bayefsky, 'The Principle of Equality or Non-discrimination in International Law', in S. Farrior (ed.), *Equality and Non-discrimination under International Law* (Routledge, 2015); For some, the conflation of both concepts can be detrimental to the potential of legal equality. *See, for instance*, G. MacNaughton, 'Untangling Equality and Non-discrimination to Promote the Right to Health Care for All', 11:2 *Health and Human Rights Journal* (2009).

36 M. Craven, 'Non-discrimination and Equality', In S. Farrior (ed.) *Equality and Non-discrimination under International Law* (Routledge, 2015) 156.

37 See B. Havelková, 'Resistance to Anti-Discrimination Law in Central and Eastern Europe–a Post-Communist Legacy?', 17 *German Law Journal* (2016) p. 627.

derstanding of discrimination. The distinction here is that mere perception that an injustice is an issue of discrimination does not necessarily qualify it as a matter of discrimination *law*.[38] Internalisation within a normative (legal) structure requires, rather, clear enough standards that may direct a coherent and consistent legal assessment of the issue that is addressed. This involves an attempt to identify the generalisable traits of what exactly that legal artefact seeks to address. The search for the normative concept of non-discrimination is captured by the 'central case methodology' of non-discrimination.[39]

Although theorisations vary as to what can be considered a 'central case' in non-discrimination, a legal formulation can be generalised as addressing a relative disadvantage that is based on a socially identifiable ground. In these terms, discrimination is described as a fault in the distribution of social goods that lends itself to an arbitrary exclusion of one or more persons from accessing these goods.

That the exclusion is considered arbitrary depends on the specific circumstances that define it, including the grounds in question, the aim sought and the proportionality of the measure. Although the aim of the distinction is considered, discriminatory intent is not required for finding discrimination. Discrimination can be direct – i.e. an open act of differential treatment – or indirect – verified in the relatively disadvantageous effects of a measure that formally respects equality in treatment. Substantive equality, as opposed to formal equality, extends the reach of non-discrimination to the effects of measures independently from how they are formulated. As not all distinctions result in discrimination, however, the justifiability of an act of differential treatment must be legally verified through a test.

In international human rights law, the practice of non-discrimination has been significantly fragmented between different treaty regimes and jurisdictions. Despite this fragmentation, similarities remain and some conversion in the technical application of non-discrimination can be observed. This has been described as the "widely-used pragmatic definition of discrimination", meaning "differential treatment in a comparable situation without a reasonable and objective justification".[40] In order to evaluate the potential of a

38 On the distinction between a lay and the legal model of non-discrimination, *see* T. Khaitan, *A Theory of Discrimination Law* (Oxford University Press, 2015).

39 S. Atrey, 'On the Central Case Methodology in Discrimination Law', 41 *Oxford Journal of Legal Studies* (2021) p. 776.

40 W. Vandenhole, *Non-discrimination and Equality in the View of the UN Human Rights Treaty Bodies* (Intersentia, 2005); *See also* S. Gurbai, 'Beyond the Pragmatic Definition? The Right to Non-discrimination of Persons with Disabilities in the Context of Coercive Interventions', 22 *Health and Human Rights* (2020) p. 279.

non-discrimination lens to address differential treatment on the ground of childhood, the fitting of 'childism' within the normative structure of non-discrimination must be considered.

3.3 *Treated like a Child*

A distinction in treatment is what legally defines the core of discrimination. It is important to note that this does not result in equating non-discrimination to equal treatment. Substantive equality, as opposed to mere formal equality, requires a consideration of factual inequalities in addition to inequalities in treatment. The focus on treatment nevertheless remains, as it may be the case that differential treatment may be required at times to correct factual inequalities. Some highlight, however, that a mere distinction (or lack thereof) is not enough to qualify as discriminatory, also requiring the identification of a disadvantage to a particular group.[41] For Tarunabh Khaitan, "[d]iscrimination law seeks to reduce (and ultimately remove) any significant advantage gap between a protected group and its cognate groups".[42] In developing a multidimensional framework of discrimination, Sandra Fredman identifies 'redressing disadvantage' as a core objective of substantive equality.[43] While a sole focus on equal treatment fails to capture the complexities of inequalities as social phenomena, a substantive view of disadvantage gives character to the issue of inequality by identifying the detrimental instance of 'disadvantage' as a problem to be addressed. The complexity of a substantive view of equality has prompted multiple elaborations which place varying concepts in the centre of the prohibition of discrimination, be it human dignity,[44] freedom,[45] a good life,[46] or that centre attention on concepts such as vulnerability.[47] For Khaitan, however, justifying discrimination law and theorising on its norma-

41 *See, for instance*, K. Lippert-Rasmussen, *Born Free and Equal?: A Philosophical Inquiry into the Nature of Discrimination* (Oxford University Press, 2013) p. 18.

42 Khaitan, *supra* note 38, p. 121.

43 Substantive equality expresses an observation of factual circumstances of inequality as opposed to 'formal equality' whereby the focus is placed on the sameness of treatment. *See* S. Fredman, 'Substantive Equality Revisited'. 14 *International Journal of Constitutional Law* (2016) p. 712.

44 D. Réaume, 'Dignity, Equality, and Comparison', In D. Hellman and S. Moreau (eds.), *Philosophical Foundations of Discrimination Law* (Oxford University Press, 2013).

45 S. Fredman, *Discrimination Law* (Second Edition, Oxford University Press, 2011).

46 Khaitan, *supra* note 38.

47 *See* M. Fineman, 'The Vulnerable Subject: Anchoring Equality in the Human Condition' 20:1 *Yale Journal of Law & Feminism* (2008).

tive content are separate (albeit related) exercises. Independently from the moral objectives of discrimination law, its normativity has been widely defined, including within international law, through a technically delimited conception of non-discrimination. Within this established conception, the legal object of non-discrimination can be largely pinned down to the correction of relative group disadvantages in the access to social goods (i.e. a right or entitlement). Non-discrimination differs from a broader notion of equality in that it does not seek to guarantee the equal distribution of a certain good, but merely prevent and remedy arbitrary disadvantages in the *entitlement* to that good.[48] This arbitrariness, meanwhile, stems from the fact that a particular disadvantage is grounded on the individual's membership to an identifiable social group. These groups are represented in the prohibited grounds of discrimination. The application of non-discrimination will therefore presuppose a relative group disadvantage arising from differential treatment in the access to a public good.

Children may indeed be seen to form an identifiable group.[49] The very existence of a Convention devoted to the specific rights of children points to an assumed specificity of children as opposed to adults. What qualifies this difference between children and adults may be inferred from the definition of 'child' present in Article 1 of the CRC. Archard describes a distinction between rights accorded only to children, rights accorded only to adults, and those that apply to both groups.[50] There is little that may raise reasonable doubts as to a possible characterisation of 'children' as a social group, and consequently as a ground of discrimination. At least in what are termed 'open-ended lists' of discrimination grounds, in which mere examples of statuses are outlined, no necessary obstacle is evident for potentially characterising such distinction as discrimination on the ground of childhood. Alternatively, a framework of age discrimination is also applied to distinctions between children and adults and even between children or between adults, all often encompassed by the term 'age-ism'.[51]

---

48 Atrey, *supra* note 39, p. 795.

49 Daly et al., *supra* note 3.

50 D. Archard, 'Respecting Age: Discrimination against the Young and the Old', In M. Skivenes and K.H. Søvig (eds.), *Child Rights and International Discrimination Law* (Routledge, 2019) pp. 45–46.

51 *See* C. Breen, 'The Ageing of Article 2(1): The Child's Right to Be Free from Age-Based Discrimination', In M. Skivenes and K.H. Søvig (eds.), *Child Rights and International Discrimination Law* (Routledge, 2019).

'Childism' may also be seen through an intersectional lens.[52] Although research has been limited to the impact of discrimination on children belonging to a particular identity, highlighting the nature of 'childhood' as an identity itself does not take attention away from other forms of discrimination experienced by children. Intersectionality evidences the difficulty of capturing distinct forms of discrimination through one status-based characterisation of discrimination. It sheds light on the complex and multi-layered nature of disadvantages that may be experienced uniquely by different subjects, failing perfect capture by the ground-based discrimination framework. Disadvantage suffered by children belonging to other identity groups will therefore add to the potential disadvantage suffered on the ground of childhood. Intersectionality is best seen as a critique to a discrimination law framework, however, demonstrating the law's persistent incapacity to grasp the complexity of inequality as a social phenomenon rather than as a fix of the discrimination law framework.[53]

As mentioned above, however, non-discrimination as a legal term contains technical requirements that must be observed in any argumentation of disadvantage. Discrimination against children can therefore be seen through multiple lenses depending on what distinction resulting in disadvantage(s) is observed. A distinction between children and a distinction between children and adults will therefore result in differing descriptions within a framing of non-discrimination. The question as to which ground qualifies the discrimination endured by children is therefore dependent on the analysis of the comparator. In other words: children are treated differently, but compared to whom?

3.4 *The Comparator Problem*

The presence of cognate or identifiable groups lies, therefore, at the centre of discrimination law. As a comparative concept, discrimination defines the disadvantage endured by one particular group in relation to another. The advantaged group is defined as a comparator – an examination of the differential

52 On intersectionality in the children's rights context, *see* J. Dixon Weaver, 'Intersectionality and Children's Rights', In J. Todres and S.M. King (eds.), *The Oxford Handbook of Children's Rights Law* (Oxford University Press, 2020).

53 *See* K. Crenshaw, 'Demarginalizing the Intersection of Race and Sex: A Black Feminist Critique of Antidiscrimination Doctrine, Feminist Theory and Antiracist Politics' 1989 *University of Chicago Legal Forum* (1989); Although 'internal' perspectives have been proposed. For instance, Atrey argues that intersectionality captures better the complexities of relative disadvantage within the central case methodology in discrimination law. *See* Atrey, *supra* note 39.

treatment will therefore verify if and to what extent the different groups were treated differently (direct discrimination) or suffered the effects of a determinate action differently (indirect discrimination) without reasonable justification.[54] 'Childism' (sometimes also termed 'adultism') describes differential treatment suffered by children in comparison with adults. For Adami, "[c]hildism characterizes children as defined by their lack of adult abilities and, therefore, as inferior to adults. On this basis, children are assigned or denied certain perceived abilities, skills, or character traits".[55] This articulation describes, through a discrimination lens, existing debates from children's rights law on the paternalism and agency-denying approaches present in children's rights discourses.[56] As summarised above, picturing children as vulnerable subjects may fail to respect their agency and autonomy. From a non-discrimination perspective, such a distinction in treatment could be argued to result in disadvantage for children and, lacking justification, considered discriminatory.

In the children's rights context, however, non-discrimination has been widely focused on distinctions in treatment on the basis of children's membership to certain identity-groups. Meanwhile, discrimination on the grounds of childhood or childism has been widely ignored.[57] Article 2(1) prohibits "discrimination of any kind, irrespective of the child's or his or her parent's or legal guardian's race, colour, sex, language, religion, political or other opinion, national, ethnic or social origin, property, disability, birth or other status". Some have suggested that it is evident from the wording of the provision that the CRC is focused on distinctions between children, as opposed to disadvantages suffered by children in comparison to adults.[58] The clearest element in that regard is the omission of age as a prohibited ground. Given the instrument's focus on children, the status of 'childhood' is presupposed, outlining instead several grounds or statuses that might apply to children.[59] Archard concludes, therefore, that childism "is not the discrimination that Article 2 concerns".[60]

---

54 For a distinction in the children's rights context, *see* Daly et al., *supra* note 3.

55 Adami, *supra* note 29, p. 128.

56 *See* Peleg, *supra* note 4; M. Luttrell-Rowland, *Political Children: Violence, Labor, and Rights in Peru* (Stanford University Press, 2023).

57 *See* Adami, *supra* note 29; E. Webb, 'Discrimination against Children', 89 *Archives of Disease in Childhood* (2004) p. 804.

58 *See* Archard, *supra* note 50.

59 This could, for instance, also be said about the Refugee Convention, whose Article 3 states that its provisions shall apply "to all refugees without discrimination as to race, religion or country of origin".

60 Archard, *supra* note 50, p. 45.

What seems like exaggerated detail to wording is central through a non-discrimination lens, particularly given the importance of a comparator for assessing a distinction in treatment. As mentioned above, discrimination is characterised by an unjustified differential treatment in a comparable situation. Identifying a difference in treatment will therefore rely first on the identification of such comparable situation. The conclusion above establishes that for the CRC the comparator is assumed: *children* ought not to be discriminated against on particular grounds amongst each other.[61] Discrimination against children in comparison with adults may therefore fall outside the scope of the CRC. This conclusion is challenged, however, by the fact that the very existence of the Convention is built on the premise of according rights to children.[62] Childism may thus fall under other articles of the Convention. As Sutherland explains, childism may be inconsistent with provisions of the Convention such as the child's evolving capacity or the cluster of participation rights.[63] But the comparator issue is not delimited to the applicability of the Convention.

In a case concerning child tax credit, the Supreme Court of the United Kingdom found a "fundamental problem in the [appellants'] argument", seen as "[c]hild tax credit does not affect children and adults in comparable ways".[64] That the importance of identifying the comparator cannot be underestimated was also made evident in the case of *Bah* v. *The United Kingdom*, where the European Court of Human Rights (ECtHR) identified *ex officio* a better fitting comparator for the applicant's situation.[65] While the applicant had argued for discrimination on the grounds of nationality, supposing that a British national would have been treated differently in the according of special housing, the ECtHR decided that a better comparator would be another person without the same obstacles as to immigration status. This difference in framing can also have significantly different results. For example, in the case

61 It is important to note that, "[a]lthough the CRC is premised on the categorisation of children as a group distinct from adults and Article 2 frames age-based discrimination in terms of differences between children and adults, it must be remembered that children are not a homogenous group and that age-based distinctions may also arise as between children themselves". Breen, *supra* note 51, p. 64.

62 Archard, *supra* note 50, p. 45.

63 E.E. Sutherland, 'Article 2 of the United Nations Convention on the Rights of the Child: Non-discrimination and Children's Rights', In M. Skivenes and K. Søvig (eds.) *Child Rights and International Discrimination Law* (Routledge 2019) p. 28.

64 *R (on the application of SC, CB and 8 children) (Appellants)* v. *Secretary of State for Work and Pensions and others Respondents*) [2021] Supreme Court [2021] UKSC 26 [63].

65 *Bah* v. *the United Kingdom* [2011] ECtHR 56328/07 [42].

of *Bah* the ground of nationality would have received stricter scrutiny than the ground of immigration status.[66]

The selection of the comparator, along with the identification of the ground of discrimination in question, are important technicalities that may require attention in the framing of childism as discrimination. This is not to say, however, that the election of a comparator is the definitive element or even indispensable for a non-discrimination analysis. In fact, some cases of discrimination may even be argued to lack a proper comparator. For this among other reasons, approaches that place exaggerated importance to choosing the proper comparator have been criticised. Additionally, different approaches may place focus on the disadvantage itself as viewed, for instance, in the context of the victims' vulnerability. In this case, the concern will lie with the conceptualisation of children's vulnerability, a point that may be counterproductive for a more emancipatory argumentation.

Whatever the approach taken for assessing childism through a discrimination lens, the disadvantageous treatment must be analysed in terms of its justifiability. Since not all distinctions are discriminatory, the criteria for assessing their arbitrariness or justifiability must be addressed.

3.5 *How Justified Is Childism?*

As stated above, not all distinctions in treatment result in discrimination. The determination of the arbitrariness of the distinction depends on a test that assesses its justifiability. While childism may be presented as a disadvantage, arguments may still be put forward to the effect that distinctions in treatment between children and adults are justified.

As hinted at, the context of children's rights is faced with a difficult framing of the position of children as necessitating particular protection. Frameworks of vulnerability are therefore questioned in the risk of employing a paternalistic approach that silences children's voices, denying them agency. On the other hand, their particular position is recognised in concepts that prioritise their protection such as the BIC principle and other protection provisions such as the protection from violence (Article 19), protection from economic exploitation (Article 32), among others. In this connection, non-discrimination seems to encounter similar conundrums as it seeks to correct not only inequalities in treatment, but also its resulting disadvantages. Non-discrimination may thus be seen as a protective instrument, often picturing disadvantages as resulting

66 The CRC Committee, on the other hand, does not distinguish between grounds of differentiation. Even more, it lumps together administrative status and national origin, *see HM v. Spain* (CRC Committee) [11.5].

from certain vulnerabilities. The need for identifying a particular disadvantage may thus fall within the same risk of paternalism identified in children's rights law. A discrimination lens may therefore necessitate the identification of the position of a child as vulnerable and disadvantaged and in need of protection as compared to an adult (in the same situation). This will of course depend on the premise upon which a claim is substantiated.

A different outcome may result from framing a disadvantage through the very issue of the paternalism. In an instance in which agency is denied on the basis of childhood, for instance, an argument could be made that such distinction between a child and an adult is not justified. The challenge here still lies, however, in arguing for a disadvantage by highlighting its injustice. While such an argumentation could be made, it is unclear to what extent a framework of discrimination law is needed or useful in this regard. Challenging certain paradigms within children's rights law can perhaps be more easily done within that domain, without engaging with the additional challenges that underlie discrimination law. This is to say that, depending on how the narrative of discrimination grounds and comparators is developed, the assessment of the justifiability of a distinction in treatment may take different turns. Most importantly, it must be noted that the debates that surround children's rights, that is, the opposition between a 'liberationist' and a 'paternalist' approach, are likely to be mirrored in a debate on non-discrimination. This is likely to become evidenced during an analysis of justification. Is a policy that determines a certain age as the threshold for voting rights discriminatory, or is it justified according to how children's capacities are defined? While a discrimination lens may set the scene for such a debate, it unfortunately does not provide an immediate and concrete answer.

In sum, non-discrimination is a complex and incomplete concept, and despite its aspirations to equality and justice, it has been widely criticised as insufficient.[67] Additionally, challenges that define non-discrimination, particularly regarding structural forms of discrimination, are often obscured within its widely technical nature. For this reason, changes of paradigm such as the conceptualisation of 'childism' and the evolution of children's rights may encounter more problems than solutions, especially if argued for without attention to such technical difficulties within discrimination law. Nevertheless, the potential of non-discrimination cannot be ignored, and as argued above, an

67 C. O'Cinneide, 'New Directions Needed Exponential Inequalities and the Limits of Equality Law', In S. Atrey and S. Fredman (eds.), *Exponential Inequalities: Equality Law in Times of Crisis* (Oxford University Press, 2023).

argumentation that handles the technicalities of non-discrimination with care, may be able to achieve its desired objectives.

4 Best Interests of the Child *and* Discrimination on the Basis of Childhood: The Example of Voting Rights

The application of BIC or non-discrimination does not seem to immediately address the potential disadvantages captured by the concept of childism. Rather, issues arise that reinforce the difficulties expressed by childism itself. Namely, an opposition between a protection-focused perspective of children's rights and an agency-focused approach seems to underlie interpretations of BIC. A perspective of non-discrimination aimed at viewing childism as disadvantage between children and adults will inevitably call for an analysis of the 'justifiability' of the distinction between children and adults. Such analysis will involve a debate regarding the justification of a protective approach to children, facing therefore the opposition between a view of childism as a justified protection on the one hand and a disadvantage on the other.

This is not to say that engaging with these concepts in an argumentation that addresses childism is impossible. Care must be taken, however, in avoiding the pitfalls that surround these concepts, particularly when it comes to their legal technicalities. Additionally, if shortcomings are observed, critical perspectives in the evolution of the notions of substantive equality and intersectionality are welcome progress. So how can BIC and non-discrimination be engaged to challenge disadvantage on grounds of childhood?

As pointed out above, non-discrimination addresses disadvantages resulting from differential treatment between one group in relation to another. Childism, in this context, reflects the disadvantages suffered by children in relation to adults. An example such as political participation may aid in illustrating different facets of the argumentation. In this case, it could be argued that children are disadvantaged in relation to adults if their voice and participation is ignored in decisions that equally affect them. Considerable literature exists in the exploration of the justifiability of the exclusion of children from democratic processes. Weinstock argues that children are often excluded from voting rights under consequentialist rather than categorical arguments.[68] In other words, abstract worries about what could unfold if children were to be included in democratic processes end up informing what is essentially a cate-

68 D. Weinstock, 'What's So Funny about Voting Rights for Children?', 18 *The Georgetown Journal of Law & Public Policy* (2020).

gorical division between children and adults. For Todres, even the categorical arguments for the exclusion of children must be questioned.[69] Common definitions of the (lack of) competence of children could be considered arbitrary and stigmatising while failing to reach a convincing justification for defining and distinguishing 'children' as a single group.[70] For Runciman, questioning the connection of competence to voting rights is at the basis of the idea of universal suffrage.[71] Rather, voting rights stem from the fact of belonging to a democratic society and sharing in the consequences of its chosen directions,[72] an argument particularly developed in contexts of long-term effects which are likely to affect children and future generations. However, it is a distinct exercise to articulate this argumentation from a non-discrimination lens. From this perspective, the argument may start from the following consideration:

a) There is a distinction in treatment: adults are allowed to vote while children are not.

Two groups are identified in a comparison of treatment: the identifiable group 'children' is treated differently in relation to adults (the comparator), in that adults are allowed to vote while children are not. On which particular ground is that distinction based? Such distinction in treatment may be described as one of age. There are two problems with this ground. First, a distinction based on age may also apply to distinctions between children themselves.[73] In other words, it would not unequivocally address differential treatment between children and adults. Second, describing the distinction as one grounded merely on age may obscure the conceptions of childhood that inform the exclusion of children and that ought to be questioned.[74] Alternatively, and more fitting to the problematisation of 'childism', the distinction may be more clearly framed within the ground of 'childhood', establishing a comparison between children on the one hand and adults on the other. Conceptualising this distinction as one between children (a group identifiable as human beings in their childhood) and adults captures better the problematised pater-

69 J. Todres, 'Confronting Categorial Exclusions Based on Age: The Rights of Children and Youth', 36 *Harvard Human Rights Journal* (2023).

70 Ibid., p. 289.

71 D. Runciman, 'Votes for Children!', *Unleashing Children's Voices in New Democratic Primary Education* (Routledge, 2022) p. 180; *See also* Wall, *supra* note 28.

72 Runciman, *supra* note 71, p. 183.

73 Breen, *supra* note 51.

74 Compare G.L. Neuman and A.M Ibrahim, 'When Is Age Discrimination a Human Rights Violation?', 36 *Harvard Human Rights Journal* (2023) pp. 234–244 who problematises chronological age as a ground of discrimination through different lenses.

nalistic nature of the exclusion of children from political participation. A distinction based on childhood seems therefore to fulfil the technical requirement of an identifiable comparator more clearly for the situation of childism.

b) Not being able to vote is disadvantageous.

As mentioned above, not all distinctions in treatment are discriminatory. Certain distinctions may even be required according to factual inequalities. It must be demonstrated that the distinction is disadvantageous for a particular group in relation to the comparator. The instance of this distinction allows for an engagement with an argumentation that highlights agency as opposed to a lack of capacity. At this point, the engagement of BIC may be useful if argued in a less 'protection-oriented' and more 'agency-oriented' way,[75] although direct reliance on the cluster of participation rights in the CRC[76] may do a better job in this regard.[77] The disadvantage may be qualified as an exclusion from the decisions that directly influence shared consequences for children and adults alike.[78] The determination of such disadvantage, highlighting the exclusion from the democratic process but not from the distribution of its consequences will also inform the argumentation regarding the justifiability of the distinction.

c) The distinction is not justified.

Once a disadvantageous distinction in treatment has been identified as occurring between the identifiable groups (here children versus adults) and on a particular ground (childhood), its justifiability is examined. As not all distinctions in treatment are automatically considered discrimination, certain elements must be identified before this distinction may be considered wrongful. Although different courts and treaty-bodies engage in this exercise differently, certain commonalities appear. The analysis of the justifiability of a distinction is often termed a proportionality test (in the broad sense). Distinctions in treatment must be lawful (sanctioned by law), have a legitimate aim, be necessary (a needed action without less intrusive alternatives) and proportionate

75 It must be highlighted that this does not mean that the limitations of BIC are resolved within a non-discrimination lens.

76 F. Ang et al., 'Participation Rights in the UN Convention on the Rights of the Child', In F. Ang et al., (eds.), *Participation Rights of Children* (Intersentia, 2006).

77 C. Marshall et al., 'Face to Face: Children and Young People's Right to Participate in Public Decision-Making', In T. Gal and B. Duramy (eds.), *International Perspectives and Empirical Findings on Child Participation: From Social Exclusion to Child-Inclusive Policies* (Oxford University Press, 2015).

78 Runciman, *supra* note 71, p. 183.

(in the stricter sense; the action must be proportionate to the sought objective). Despite different approaches to the proportionality test and critiques to its adequacy in a non-discrimination analysis,[79] its technicalities cannot be ignored in a claim of discrimination, be it within a court case or in the development of policy.

As the analysis follows a step-by-step process, the finding of incompatibility in an initial step such as the unlawfulness of a measure will be enough to find a violation of non-discrimination. However, taking the argument that a distinction on the basis of childhood in the enjoyment of voting rights is discriminatory is likely to be concentrated on the proportionality (in the strict sense) of a particular measure. This is because, in terms of a) lawfulness and b) legitimacy of the aim, a) the age condition of voting rights is usually defined by law, often times by the constitution; and b) it is difficult to argue, even in questioning a protectionist approach, that the aim of distinguishing between children and adults in guaranteeing democratic processes is *illegitimate*. The purported aim may be twofold: to protect children against involvement in matters that they do not understand, and to safeguard the quality of the democratic processes (by keeping out those who do not fully understand it).[80] While it does not seem *prima facie* to be illegitimate (although one may disagree), it may still be disproportionate.

Assessing the proportionality (in the strict sense) of such measure would raise the balancing between two opposing interests, namely the protection of children against involvement in matters they do not understand (which would feature as the legitimate aim) on the one hand and the fulfilment of children's agency and participation in political life on the other hand. Within this proportionality assessment, it is likely that the BIC may serve to shift the debate from one approach to the other, provided that it is understood in the emancipatory, rights-based way in which the CRC Committee reads it. It may be argued, for instance, that it is in the best interests of the child in general to be able to actively participate in the democratic processes that directly affect them, rather than being silenced as a protective measure. Additionally, the necessity of such measure may also be questioned, arguably since alternatives may exist for protecting children which do not impede their participation in political life. It goes without saying that no guarantees exist for the success of such argumentation in a court or in a legislative process, especially since additional considerations must be made. For instance, a significant difficulty

79 A. Nilsson, 'Same, Same but Different: Proportionality Assessments and Equality Norms', 7 *Oslo Law Review* (2020) p. 126.

80 *See, similarly*, Todres *supra* note 69, p. 289.

arises in legally questioning one age-based distinction while arguing for another in lowering the voting age. Different proposals have been made for a better inclusion of children in democratic processes.[81] A legal argumentation would therefore benefit from a well-defined articulation of childhood as a category that stands to benefit from democratic participation. This is not only a matter of how children's rights or non-discrimination is conceptualised and interpreted, but also an issue of policy-making that will also see variation in the way different societies conceive of childhood.

5 Conclusion

In conclusion, BIC and non-discrimination are complex legal concepts that do not necessarily provide clear solutions in addressing childism, that is, disadvantageous treatment of children because they are children. Nevertheless, a careful engagement with their technicalities ('handle with care'), as well as the coordinated employment of both concepts may point to an avenue for a more coherent argumentation regarding the discriminatory nature of childism. The success of such argumentation depends on factual circumstances as well as judicial and democratic procedures. A conceptual engagement with these concepts, however, aids in a clearer visualisation of the potential and challenges with addressing childism through law.

An example such as political participation may aid in illustrating different facets of the argumentation. It could be argued that children are disadvantaged in relation to adults if their voice and participation is ignored in decisions that equally affect them. The argument that a distinction on the basis of childhood in the enjoyment of voting rights is discriminatory is likely to be concentrated on the proportionality (in the strict sense) of a particular measure. Assessing the proportionality (in the strict sense) of such measure would raise the balancing between two opposing interests, namely the protection of children against involvement in matters they do not understand (which may be invoked as the legitimate aim) on the one hand and the fulfilment of children's agency and participation in political life on the other hand. Within this proportionality assessment, it is likely that the BIC may serve to shift the debate from one approach to the other, provided that it is understood in the

81 *See, for instance*, M. O'Neill, 'Radical Democratic Inclusion: Why We Should Lower the Voting Age to 12', 91 *Royal Institute of Philosophy Supplements* (2022) p. 185; Runciman, *supra* note 71.

emancipatory, rights-based way in which the CRC Committee reads it. A significant difficulty arises however in legally questioning one age-based distinction while arguing for another in lowering the voting age. A legal argumentation would therefore benefit from a well-defined articulation of childhood as a category that stands to benefit from democratic participation.

CHAPTER 4

Confronting Age Discrimination: The Importance of Article 2 of the Convention on the Rights of the Child

Claire Breen

Abstract

Age discrimination is not widely recognised in international and regional human rights law. The inertia around recognising age discrimination stems from a general reliance on age-based distinctions; the Convention on the Rights of the Child being a key example. This inertia has profound implications for the implementation of children's rights, particularly as uninterrogated age-based distinctions can mask age discrimination. To counter this threat, the child's right to be free from discrimination must include discrimination based on age. This chapter illustrates the key role that Article 2 of the Convention on the Rights of the Child must play in that regard. Yet, age-based distinctions may have an important role in navigating the (sometimes contradictory) complexities that come with being a child. This chapter offers a nuanced understanding of age-based distinctions that seeks to ensure equality and avoid age discrimination so as to navigate such complexities in a more meaningful way.

1 Introduction

As the only global or regional treaty that relies on age to determine its personal scope, the Convention on the Rights of the Child[1] (CRC) is central to discussions around age discrimination. Age discrimination is taken here to mean detrimental treatment because of one's age. Accepting that Article 2 prohibits age discrimination is critical. It will give better effect to the spirit and purpose of the CRC. This is because it will ensure that children are not discriminated against on the basis of their age or on the basis of being a child.

1 UN Convention on the Rights of the Child (1989).

In that regard, this chapter starts with an exploration of age discrimination in UN and regional human rights frameworks. The focus of the chapter then moves to the CRC, which is arguably premised on recognising the differences between children and adults, and what that distinction means for the rights of the child and concomitant states' obligations. It outlines the extent to which the CRC reflects states' views on the legitimacy of age distinctions, and the subsequent slow evolution in considering age as a form of discrimination. The chapter continues with an examination of Article 2's prohibition of discrimination, and why it extends to the prohibition of age discrimination, whilst also noting the (slow) evolution of the recognition of age discrimination in other areas of international and regional human rights law.

In an attempt to understand the inertia around acceptance of age as a form of discrimination, and in keeping with the theme of this edited collection 'being treated like a child', the chapter will explore varying attitudes to age discrimination and what such attitudes may mean for the implementation of children's rights generally, and the child's right to non-discrimination in particular. Because it is still important to recognise that age-based distinctions do play an important part in ensuring equality and acknowledging difference, the chapter considers the need for a nuanced understanding of equality that can accommodate differences that are based on age, with a view to ensuring that such differences lead to positive outcomes for children.

In an effort to distinguish age-based distinctions which are justifiable from those which mask age discrimination, this chapter concludes with three core caveats around the use of such distinctions. *One*, age-based laws and policies (e.g. minimum ages) should not be a vehicle to permit on-going negative attitudes towards children, especially those that are grounded in historical, structural and hierarchical attitudes that regard children as 'less than' adults. *Two*, laws and policies that are regarded as necessary to secure positive outcomes for children (e.g. exclusion from certain types of work) must also be interrogated to ensure that the outcomes are, in fact, positive for children; such determinations must be informed by the CRC's Guiding Principles (the right to non-discrimination being one). *Three*, it is also necessary to look beyond the matter of 'age' in age discrimination, and properly consider the complexities of how 'childhood' is to be understood. Read together, these caveats call for a more meaningful approach that recognises the differences between children and adults that takes account of the (sometimes contradictory) complexities that come with being a child. Recognising that Article 2 of the CRC prohibits age discrimination is a key step in ensuring that being 'treated like a child' is no longer shorthand for age discrimination that undermines the implementation of children's rights.

2 Age Discrimination in Human Rights Law

The variability of attitudes towards age as a distinguishing characteristic can be seen in legal responses, at the global and regional level. Age discrimination is mentioned explicitly in only two of the core UN human rights treaties; only the Migrant Workers' Convention prohibits age discrimination,[2] whilst the preamble of the Convention on the Rights of Persons with Disabilities simply refers to difficult conditions faced by persons with disabilities who are subject to multiple or aggravated forms of discrimination including age-based discrimination.[3] Age is not enumerated in the prohibited grounds of discrimination in most regional human rights,[4] the exceptions being two European Union treaties and then only as regards employment matters.[5]

But the jurisprudence of the UN and regional human rights monitoring mechanisms show some changes in attitude. The Committee on the Elimination of Racial Discrimination has identified age as being a factor that can contribute to the circumstances of multiple or double discrimination against children or women of a specific group.[6] Age has been recognised as discrimination on grounds of "other status". In 1996, the Committee on Economic, Social and Cultural Rights (CESCR Committee) noted, in relation to the

2 International Convention on the Protection of the Rights of All Migrant Workers and Members of Their Families (1990) Art. 7.

3 Convention on the Rights of Persons with Disabilities (2007) Preamble, para. (p).

4 *See*, African Charter on Human and Peoples' Rights (1982) Art. 2; Arab Charter on Human Rights (2004) Art. 3; American Convention on Human Rights (1969) Art. 1; A-52 Additional Protocol to the American Convention on Human Rights in the Area of Economic, Social and Cultural Rights (1988) Art. 3; Protocol 12 to the European Convention on Human Rights and Fundamental Freedoms on the Prohibition of Discrimination (2000) Art. 1; European Social Charter (Revised) (1996) Art. E; European Convention for the Protection of Human Rights and Fundamental Freedoms (1950) Art. 15. European Union legislation currently is limited to protections in the employment context by Council directive 2000/78/EC of 27 November 2000 establishing a general framework for equal treatment in employment and occupation; Protocol to the African Charter on Human and Peoples' Rights on the Rights of Older Persons in Africa (2016) (not yet in force); African Youth Charter (2006); Ibero-American Convention on the Rights of Youth (2005).

5 Charter of Fundamental Rights of the European Union (2000) Art. 21; Consolidated Version of the Treaty on the Functioning of the European Union (2012) Art. 10 and 19; ASEAN Human Rights Declaration (2012) Art. 2; Inter-American Convention on Protecting the Human Rights of Older Persons (2013) Art. 3; Inter-American Convention Against All Forms of Discrimination and Intolerance (not yet in force) Art. 1(1).

6 CERD, *General Recommendation No. 31, Prevention of Racial Discrimination in the Administration and Functioning of the Criminal Justice System*, CERD/C/GC/31/Rev.4. (2005) Preamble.

rights of older people, that it was not possible to conclude that the International Covenant on Economic, Social and Cultural Rights 1966 (ICESCR)[7] comprehensively prohibited discrimination on the grounds of age. However, it did note that the range of matters in relation to which such discrimination could be accepted would be very limited.[8] By 2009, however, the CESCR Committee was able to affirm that "[a]ge is a prohibited ground of discrimination in several contexts".[9] The Human Rights Committee has recognised age as an "other status" category under Article 26, albeit in relation to two retirement cases.[10] It has recommended that age be included as a prohibited ground of discrimination.[11] The European Court of Human Rights has regarded age to be a prohibited ground of discrimination within the category of "other status".[12] But, in doing so, the court has observed that age discrimination should not be equated to discrimination on the grounds of ethnic origin, gender or sexual orientation, where the latter "would require particularly convincing and very weighty reasons" for it to be justifiable under the European Convention on Human Rights (ECHR).[13] The Court noted that, in general terms, the ECHR allows states to treat certain groups of people differently, where such treatment can be justified. Unless the measure is "manifestly without reasonable foundation", states are usually allowed a wide margin of appreciation as regards their general measures of economic or social strategy because national authorities are better placed to judge what is in the public interest on social and economic grounds.[14] In finding that a national court's determination that siblings under the age of 14 should not be awarded compensatory damages for the death of their sister because their age meant that they would not be as negatively affected by her death

7 International Covenant on Economic, Social and Cultural Rights (1966).

8 CESCR, *General Comment No. 6 on the Economic, Social and Cultural Rights of Older Persons*, E/1996/22 (1996) para. 12.

9 CESCR, *General Comment No. 20: Non-discrimination in Economic, Social and Cultural Rights*, E/C.12/GC/20 (2009) para. 29.

10 *Love* v. *Australia*, CCPR/C/77/D/983/2001 (25 March 2003) para. 8.3; *Canessa Albareda and Others.* v. *Uruguay*, CCPR/C/103/D/1637/2007 (24 October 2007) para. 9.3–9.4.

11 HRC, *Concluding Observations, Hong Kong, China*, CCPR/C/CHN-HKG/CO/4 (2022) para. 9.

12 *See Schwizgebel* v. *Switzerland*, App. No. 25762/07, Eur. Ct. H.R. (10 June 2010) para. 85; *Khamtokhu and Aksenchik* v. *Russia*, App. No. 60367/08 and 961/11, Eur. Ct. H.R. (24 January 2017) para. 62; *Dudgeon* v. *United Kingdom*, App. No. 7525/76, Eur. Ct. H.R., 117 (22 October 1981) para. 117.

13 *Šaltinytė* v. *Lithuania*, App. No. 32934/19, Eur. Ct. H.R. (26 October 26, 2021) para. 63.

14 Ibid., para. 64.

to be discriminatory, the Court found that there was no reasonable justification for such a determination.[15]

"Other status" may be the only option currently to push and expand the jurisprudence to recognise age discrimination. But there are risks and weaknesses with this approach. This implicit protection is in dispute, and practice is "far from consistent among human rights bodies".[16] "Other status" incorporates a wide range of variable characteristics, where such variability can impact on determinations of justifications for different treatment, and so the legitimacy of legal and policy goals. Being an unenumerated ground indicates a lack of consensus that the distinction is problematic and unjustifiable, which make it more challenging to establish discrimination.

3 The Centrality of Age to Children's Rights: Distinctions and Discrimination

3.1 *Age as a Defining Feature of Children's Rights*

In terms of international human rights law, the Declaration on the Rights of the Child 1924[17] was an initial step in differentiating between children and adults.[18] Other than in the title, the child is not extended any rights under the 1924 Declaration, which is framed quite strongly on the themes of protection and vulnerability and the obligations of adults (rather than states) towards children. The 1924 Declaration and the 1948 Universal Declaration on Human Rights[19] formed the basis of the 1959 UN Declaration on the Rights of the Child,[20] which recognised children as rights-holders. At the same time, the

15 *Deaconu* v. *Romania*, App. No. 66299/12 (26 January 2019) para. 38.

16 OHCHR, *Normative Standards in International Human Rights Law in Relation to Older Persons: Analytical Outcome Paper* (2012). *See also*, HRC, *Normative Standards and Obligations under International Law in relation to the Promotion and Protection of the Human Rights of Older Persons*, A/HRC/49/70 (2022).

17 Geneva Declaration of the Rights of the Child of 1924, *adopted* Sept. 26, 1924, League of Nations Official Journal Special Supplement 21, at 43.

18 D. Fotterell, 'One Step Forward or Two Steps Sideways: Assessing the First Decade of the United Nations Convention on the Rights of the Child', in D. Fotterell (ed.), *Revisiting Children's Rights: 10 Years of the UN Convention on the Rights of the Child* (Brill Martinus Nijhoff, Leiden, 2002) p. 2.

19 Universal Declaration of Human Rights, UNGA Res 217 A(III) (10 December 1948) Art. 25.

20 Declaration of the Rights of the Child, A/RES/1386(XIV) (1959). Z. Moody, 'The United Nations Declaration of the Rights of the Child (1959): Genesis, Transformation and Dissemination of a Treaty (Re) Constituting a Transnational Cause', 45(1) *Prospects*, pp. 15–29.

1959 Declaration proclaimed that by reason of their physical and mental immaturity, children needed special care and protection. Principle 1 proclaims that the child shall enjoy the rights set out in the Declaration without discrimination, on the grounds enumerated in that article. That children's rights are based on their status as a special group in need of care and protection continues through both the ICESCR 1966 and the International Covenant on Civil and Political Rights 1966.[21]

Article 1 of the CRC[22] continues international law's differentiation between children and adults, defining a child as a human being aged under 18 years (unless a state's legal age of majority makes earlier provision). The drafting process indicates that the major concern was setting the upper age at 18 years, as different states had different ages of majority, and different culturally informed views about the end of childhood.[23] In the context of multiple and intersecting discrimination, the issue of sex discrimination and different ages of majority was noted during the drafting of Article 1.[24]

That a legal distinction between children and adults was required was not debated, given states' stance that such distinctions were necessary because of children's physical and mental immaturity.[25] The preamble to the Convention also indicates that rights are extended to children because of the special protection and care that is warranted by their physical and mental immaturity.[26] Article 1 continues the practice of using chronological age to differentiate children from adults, and thus the rights held by children and those held by adults. Article 1 does not prevent states from setting their own legislative boundaries as to particular age limits; as the representative of New Zealand observed "it would be very difficult to declare an across-the-board age and that the end of childhood would be related to specific issues (right to leave home, vote, drive a motor vehicle, have sexual intercourse, etc.) which would be covered by spe-

---

21 ICESCR, *supra* note 7, Art. 10; International Covenant on Civil and Political Rights (1966) Art. 23 and 24.

22 CRC, *supra* note 1.

23 *See for example*, OHCHR, *Legislative History of the Convention on the Rights of the Child*, HR/ PUb/07/1 (2007) pp. 130, 256, 264, 305, 311. *See generally*, T. Abebe, 'Interdependent Rights and Agency', in K. Hanson and O. Nieuwenhuys (eds.), *Living Rights, Social Justice, Translations* (Cambridge University Press, Cambridge, 2012).

24 OHCHR, ibid., p. 307.

25 Ibid., p. 314.

26 CRC, *supra* note 1, Preamble, para. 9. *See also*, D. Archard and J. Tobin, 'Art. 1: The Definition of a Child', in J. Tobin (ed.), *The UN Convention on the Rights of the Child: A Commentary* (Oxford University Press, Oxford, 2019) p. 32.

cific legislation in each country.[27] The potential for such domestic distinctions to be discriminatory was not considered in the drafting of the CRC.

3.2 *Age Discrimination within Article 2 of the CRC*

Age discrimination did not feature in the 1959 Declaration, and it was not considered in the drafting history of Article 2 of the CRC (which did make passing mention of extensive state practice in enacting legislation that created levels of dependency and responsibility).[28] Age discrimination, therefore, is not amongst the prohibited grounds of discrimination set out in Article 2(1) which states that; a child – or their parent or legal guardian – must not be discriminated against on the basis of race, colour, sex, language, religion, political or other opinion, national, ethnic or social origin, property, disability, birth or other status. Article 2(2) requires States Parties to ensure that children are not discriminated against or punished because of the status, activities, expressed opinions, or beliefs of their parents, legal guardians, or family members. In sum, Article 2's right to discrimination means that the child is to be protected from discrimination based on their own status as a child, as well as that of their parents. The Convention ring-fences rights for children, and recognises the special status of children and childhood.

The CRC Committee has made some attempts to engage with age discrimination. Its stronger statements have been in conjunction with other UN human rights treaty monitoring bodies. The CRC Committee, in its joint General Comment with the Committee on the Elimination of All Forms of Discrimination against Women, noted that harmful practices are grounded in discrimination based on age, among other things.[29] The CRC Committee and the Committee on Migrant Workers have stated that migrant children are entitled to enjoy their rights under both Conventions, yet they experience substantive inequality and discrimination, and their age in a factor in that experience.[30] They have affirmed that the fundamental principle of non-

27 OHCHR, *supra* note 23, p. 303.

28 Ibid., p. 314.

29 CEDAW and CRC, *Joint General Recommendation No. 31 of the Committee on the Elimination of Discrimination against Women/General Comment No. 18 of the Committee on the Rights of the Child on Harmful Practices*, CEDAW/C/GC/31/Rev.1–CRC/C/GC18/Rev.1 (2014) para. 16(c).

30 CMW and CRC, *Joint General Comment No. 3 (2017) of the Committee on the Protection of the Rights of All Migrant Workers and Members of Their Families and No. 22 (2017) of the Committee on the Rights of the Child on the General Principles Regarding the Human Rights of Children in the Context of International Migration*, CMW/C/GC/3-CRC/C/GC/22 (2017) para. 3.

discrimination applies to all migrant children regardless of their age.[31] The Committees have distinguished between non-discrimination and the differential treatment of migrants where the latter must be lawful and proportionate; differential treatment is treatment that has a legitimate aim and is in line with the child's best interests and international human rights norms and standards.[32]

The CRC has observed that age limits may be used to curtail the rights of the child to have their voice heard. In that regard, the Committee has stated that Article 12 is not subject to any limit based on age, and it has discouraged the introduction of any age limits by States Parties which would restrict the child's right to be heard.[33] In relation to the child's best interests, the Committee has also emphasised that the term 'children' refers to all persons under the age of 18 years without discrimination of any kind, in line with Articles 1 and 2 of the Convention.[34] Somewhat indirectly, the CRC Committee has alluded to age discrimination with its acknowledgment that "[a]dolescence itself can be a source of discrimination."[35]

In its Concluding Observations, the CRC Committee has expressed concern that the effective realisation of the rights enshrined in the CRC may be compromised by the age of the child. The Committee has noted with concern that the New Zealand Bill of Rights Act 1990 and the Human Rights Act 1993 prohibit age discrimination from the age of 16 years only.[36] It recommended that Aotearoa New Zealand ensure that children under the age of 16 years are not unjustly discriminated against on the basis of age.[37] The Committee had previously expressed concern about the lack of consistent age limits across the domestic law of Aotearoa New Zealand[38] and called upon the state to ensure full protection against discrimination on any ground.[39] The Committee ex-

---

31 Ibid., para. 21.

32 Ibid., para. 22.

33 CRC, *General Comment No. 12: The Right of the Child to be Heard*, CRC/C/GC/12 (2009) para. 21.

34 CRC, *General Comment No. 14 on the Right of the Child to Have His or Her Best Interests Taken as a Primary Consideration*, CRC/C/GC/14 (2013) para. 21.

35 CRC, *General Comment No. 20 (2016) on the Implementation of the Rights of the Child during Adolescence*, CRC/C/GC/20 (2016) para. 21.

36 CRC, *Concluding Observations on the Sixth Periodic Report of New Zealand*, CRC/C/NZL/CO/6 (2023) para. 15.

37 Ibid., para. 16.

38 CRC, *Concluding Observations on the Fifth Periodic Report of New Zealand*, CRC/C/NZL/CO/5 (2016) para. 14.

39 CRC, *Concluding Observations on the Fifth Periodic Report of the United Kingdom of Great Britain and Northern Ireland*, CRC/C/GBR/CO/5 (2016) para. 15.

pressed concern at the insufficient progress in ensuring that British children under the age of 18 years were protected from age discrimination.[40] In addition to recommending that the United Kingdom take legislative and other measures to ensure protection against age discrimination, the Committee called upon the state to address discriminatory stereotypes against children and to promote a positive image of children as rights-holders.[41]

After expressions of concern about inconsistencies in age limits in Norway,[42] the Committee recommended that Norway carefully examine the possibility of expanding legislation to provide protection to children against discrimination on the grounds of their age.[43] The Committee subsequently welcomed the adoption of the 2018 Equality and Anti-discrimination Act, section 6 of which prohibits, inter alia, age discrimination.[44] The Committee has also welcomed the prohibition of age discrimination in Sweden's Discrimination Act 2008,[45] yet has expressed deep concern at the absence of data on discrimination against children disaggregated by age,[46] and has called upon Sweden to collect such data including for the purpose of identifying and analysing discrimination on the basis of age.[47] Similarly, although welcoming a variety of action plans adopted by Finland to counter discrimination, the Committee was deeply concerned about persistent discrimination against children and adolescents on the basis of, inter alia, age.[48]

That children are not a homogenous group has been recognised by the CRC Committee in relation to the right of the child to have their voice heard.[49] The CRC Committee's recognition of the specific needs of children in early child-

40 CRC, *Concluding Observations on the Combined Sixth and Seventh Periodic Reports of the United Kingdom of Great Britain and Northern Ireland*, CRC/C/GBR/CO/6-7 (2023) para. 19.

41 Ibid., para. 20(f). *See also*, CRC, *supra* note 39, paras. 21–22.

42 CRC, *Consideration of Reports Submitted by States parties under Article 44 of the Convention, Concluding Observations: Norway*, CRC/C/NOR/CO/4 (2010) para. 19.

43 Ibid., para. 20.

44 CRC, *Concluding Observations on the Combined Fifth and Sixth Periodic Reports of Norway*, CRC/C/NOR/CO/5-6 (2018) para. 3.

45 CRC, *Concluding Observations on the Fifth Periodic Report of Sweden*, CRC/C/SWE/CO/5 (2015) para. 3(c).

46 CRC, *Concluding Observations on the Combined Sixth and Seventh Periodic Reports of Sweden*, CRC/C/SWE/CO/6-7 (2023) para. 16(a).

47 Ibid., para. 17(a).

48 CRC, *Concluding Observations on the Combined Fifth and Sixth Periodic Reports of Finland*, CRC/C/FIN/CO/5-6 (2023) para. 15.

49 CRC, *supra* note 33, para. 21.

hood,[50] as well as its statement that adolescence can be a source of discrimination,[51] is further evidence that the CRC Committee recognises the particular needs of children at different stages of development and thus the basis for any potential discrimination amongst children.

Article 2's prohibition of discrimination of "any kind" and its inclusion of the phrase "or other status" can comfortably be interpreted to accommodate age discrimination. Yet, as indicated above, there are some drawbacks to the use of 'other status' as a means to introduce or expand age as a prohibited ground of discrimination. Age discrimination is not broadly recognised within the framework of international and regional human rights law; to the extent that it has been recognised (in the context of older people) the implication is that age-based distinctions, with their tendency not to enquire into negative stereotyping, may make it more difficult to challenge successfully the justifications for age distinctions or even introduce positive measures to eradicate age-based discrimination.[52] The lack of enquiry into negative stereotyping based on age certainly has implications for children's experiences of age discrimination, as outlined above.[53]

But, does the absence of explicit references to age discrimination mean that the CRC Committee is not concerned about the negative stereotyping of children within some states? Negative stereotyping may go beyond matters of simple chronology, and the CRC Committee has expressed concern about negative public attitudes towards young people leading to stereotyping, stigmatisation and social exclusion. Adolescents, for example, often bear the brunt of such negativity, being viewed as both "dangerous or hostile", and "incompetent and incapable".[54] Such concerns about discriminatory conduct appeared to be based on life stages, such as childhood,[55] which are bookended by chro-

50 CRC, *General Comment No. 7 (2005): Implementing Child Rights in Early Childhood*, CRC/C/GC/7/Rev 1 (2006) para. 2.

51 CRC, *supra* note 35, para. 21.

52 OHCHR, *supra* note 16; *See also*, A. Gosseries, 'What Makes Age Discrimination Special: A Philosophical Look at the ECJ Case Law', 43(1) *Netherlands Journal of Legal Philosophy* (2014) p. 70.

53 *Supra* note 36–48 and accompanying text.

54 CRC, *supra* note 35, para. 21.

55 A. Daly et al., 'UN Convention on the Rights of the Child, Article 2 and Discrimination on the Basis of Childhood: The CRC Paradox?' 91(3) *Nordic Journal of International Law* (2022) pp. 435–439. *See* chapter 1 in this anthology.

nological ages. Negative stereotyping of children and poor treatment on the basis of childhood is also evidenced in wider research.[56]

Given that wider research shows that children themselves are aware that they are being discriminated against because of their age,[57] it is time that the CRC Committee takes a more consistent and explicit approach to recognising age discrimination and its multiple and/or intersectional effect on children's right to non-discrimination, and children's rights more widely. The CRC Committee has made some effort in this regard with its observation that many of the multiple forms of discrimination that it has identified "have particular implications in adolescence and necessitate an intersectional analysis and targeted holistic measures"[58] and in relation to children with disabilities.[59] In addition to referring to the enumerated grounds of discrimination in Article 2, the CRC Committee also stated that attention should be given to any other forms of discrimination that might undermine children's health, and that the implications of multiple forms of discrimination should also be addressed.[60] The failure to identify age within the multiple and intersecting forms of discrimination experienced by children and street situations was a missed opportunity.[61]

The Committee has made important strides in targeting state behaviours towards children that are prohibited when it comes to adults with corporal

---

56 A. Daly et al., *Challenges to Children's Rights Today: What do Children Think? A Desktop Study on Children's Views and Priorities to Inform the Next Council of Europe Strategy for the Rights of the Child* (Council of Europe, Strasburg, 2016) pp. 29–30.

57 Ibid.

58 CRC, *supra* note 35, para. 21.

59 *See for example*, CRC, *Concluding Observations on the Fifth Periodic Report of Bangladesh*, CRC/C/BGD/CO/5 (2015) paras. 52(b) and 53(b); CRC, *Concluding Observations on the Combined Second and Third Periodic Reports of Brunei Darussalam*, CRC/C/BRN/CO/2-3 (2016) paras. 49(b) and 50(b); CRC, *Concluding Observations on the Combined Fourth and Fifth Periodic Reports of Ethiopia*, CRC/C/ETH/CO/4-5 (2015) para. 53; CRC, *Concluding Observations on the Combined Third to Fifth Periodic Reports of Nepal*, CRC/C/NPL/CO/3-5 (2016) para. 46(b); CRC, *Consideration of Reports Submitted by States Parties under Article 44 of the Convention, Concluding Observations: Algeria*, CRC/C/DZA/CO/3-4 (2012) para. 30(b); CRC, *Concluding Observations on the Combined Third and Fourth Periodic Reports of China*, CRC/C/CHN/CO/3-4 (2015) para. 58(b); CRC, *Concluding Observations on the Combined Third to Sixth Periodic Reports of North Macedonia*, CRC/C/MKD/CO/3-6 (2022) para. 30(f).

60 CRC, *General Comment No. 15: The Right of the Child to the Enjoyment of the Highest Attainable Standard of Health (art. 24)*, CRC/C/GC/15 (2013) para. 8.

61 CRC, *General Comment No. 21 on Children in Street Situations*, CRC/C/GC/21 (2017) para. 26.

punishment being a prime example.[62] But, the failure of the Committee to sufficiently emphasise that these types of practices are examples of children being discriminated against because of their age and because they are children somewhat obscures the potential for Article 2 to be a vehicle for the prohibition of age discrimination. It overlooks the cumulative nature of intersectional discrimination and it deprives children, and society more widely, from the benefits of taking an intersectional approach the combined effect of which will have greater power than an approach to discrimination that separates or omits age.

The CRC Committee's gradual move towards addressing age-based discrimination is a welcome development. Equally welcome, is the Committee's recognition that the discrimination experienced by children may be more deeply rooted in negative attitudes towards children. In this way, the Committee's comments are beginning to reflect the fact that the discrimination that is experienced by children is historical, structural and hierarchical. Its calls upon States Parties to address such discrimination reflect the view that Article 2(1) of the CRC should be read in light of Article 1; where the state is exercising its powers in a manner that results in unjustifiably detrimental impacts upon a certain group – the shared characteristic being that they are under the age of 18 years – then children are being discriminated against because they are children.[63]

4 Some Bases for Age Discrimination Inertia

As the previous paragraphs and sections indicate, there has been a degree of inertia in recognising age as a form of discrimination within the jurisprudence of the CRC Committee, and the human rights legal framework more generally. Part of the reason for this inertia, it is suggested, is the important legal function that age-based distinctions play within states, and which reflects often deeply embedded – and often negative – attitudes towards the young (and the old) because of their age; that the phrase 'being treated like a child' may have negative connotations is not without legal and social foundation. The implications for interpreting Article 2 of the CRC as including age discrimi-

62 Daly et al., *supra* note 55, pp. 439–440.

63 B. Abramson, *Article 2 the Right of Non-discrimination* (Martinus Nijhoff Publishers, Leiden, 2008).

nation go wider than the Convention, and provide a platform to challenge the ready acceptance that age-based distinctions are justifiable, and the associated denial that age can be the basis for unequal and discriminatory treatment.

Chronological age refers to the passage of time since an individual's birth.[64] As a proxy for decisions and judgements, chronological age is an attractive tool because its measurements can be easily verified and administrated.[65] It has been co-opted into law so that particular points in time in an individual's life are imbued with legal significance.

This apparent simplicity belies a conceptually complex issue, however, because age is also a social construct that has biological, psychological, and social dimensions.[66] Age may be expressed in numerical terms but the meaning and symbolism attached to age originates in, and is mediated by, wider social processes and cultural contexts.[67] The use of age as a proxy is a convenient basis for wider social judgements and decision-making, as "[i]n all societies, age is one of the bases for the ascription of status and one of the underlying dimensions by which social interaction is regulated".[68] Yet, despite the wide use of age-based distinctions, or indeed because of the wide use of age-based distinctions, there appears to be a reluctance to accept age as a form of discrimination, no matter how old or young. A range of arguments have been advanced for drawing a distinction between age discrimination and other forms of discrimination.[69] Some arguments are based on the view that discrimination can only stem from characteristics that an individual has no control over and/or cannot change to avoid discrimination, such as race, ethnicity, sex, and/or disability. Another argument is that because our age is constantly changing everyone will experience the advantages and disadvantages that may be associated with age. Even where age discrimination is rec-

64 R. A. Settersen and B. Godlewski, 'Concepts and Theories of Age and Aging', in V. L. Bengtson and R. A. Settersen (eds.), *Handbook of Theories of Aging* (Springer, New York, 2016).

65 B. L. Neugarten et al., 'Age Norms, Age Constraints, and Adult Socialization', 70(6) *American Journal of Sociology* (1965) p. 710.

66 Settersen and Godlewski, *supra* note 64.

67 J. MacNicol, *Age Discrimination: An Historical and Contemporary Analysis* (Cambridge University Press, Cambridge, 2006).

68 Neugarten et al., *supra* note 65, p. 710.

69 *But see*, B. D. Mezmur, 'Based Solely on Their Date of Birth? Rethinking Age Discrimination Against Children under the Convention on the Rights of the Child', 36(2) *Harvard Human Rights Journal* (2023) p. 264, citing M. Liebel, 'Adultism and Age-Based Discrimination against Children', in D. Kutsar and H. Warming (eds.), *Children and Non-discrimination: Interdisciplinary Textbook* (University Press of Estonia, Tartu, 2014).

ognised, it is often seen as a less harmful form of discrimination.[70] Some of the inertia also stems from the social and economic benefits of age-based distinctions (for example 'child benefit' being received by families for children under a certain age).

Arguments that reject the potential for age-based distinctions to be discriminatory stem from age's unique features of being simultaneously 'immutable' (unchangeable over time) and 'mutable' (changeable over time).[71] Age is regarded as an immutable characteristic because, like one's sex or race, it cannot be controlled or changed. But, at the same time, age is a mutable characteristic, it changes over the course of life in the same way that other identity traits or characteristics, such as religion, class, and disability may also change over time.

The mutability of age argument is similar to the argument that age-differential treatment can be compatible with equality of opportunity to a greater extent than other differential treatment. Both arguments view change as coming with age and any discrimination associated with age is different to other forms of discrimination because everyone will experience the advantages and disadvantages that come with different age groups over the course of their life.[72]

It is also argued that age-differential treatment is not as demeaning as other differential treatment. It is not aimed at protecting a group that "is socially reviled, penurious, or cut off from the mainstream of society and/or marked by the badge of social opprobrium".[73] A final argument is that age-differential treatment is also advanced as a rational means of promoting social and economic objectives, such as those around social and employment legislation including the retirement age[74] or various employment and/or educational policies aimed at young people that are intended at benefitting them and wider society.[75]

70 S. Fredman, 'The Age of Equality', in S. Fredman and S. Spencer (eds.), *Age as an Equality Issue: Legal and Policy Perspectives* (Hart, Oxford, 2003) p. 21.

71 A. A. Boni-Saenz, 'Age, Time, and Discrimination', 53(3) *Georgia Law Review* (2018) p. 850.

72 S. Goosey, 'Is Age Discrimination a Less Serious Form of Discrimination?' 39(3) *Legal Studies* (2019) pp. 534, 535.

73 Ibid., p. 537, citing S. Issacharoff and E. W. Harris, 'Is Age Discrimination Really Age Discrimination: The ADEA's Unnatural Solution', 72(4) *New York University Law Review* (1997) pp. 780–840.

74 Ibid., 535.

75 Ibid., citing A. Gosseries, 'What Makes Age Discrimination Special: A Philosophical Look at the ECJ Case Law', 43(1) *Netherlands Journal of Legal Philosophy* (2014) pp. 59–80.

If the core of these arguments are accepted, then discrimination only arises when a distinction (i) relates to an immutable characteristic or a fundamental choice; (ii) perpetuates exclusion; (iii) is demeaning; (iv) is attached to a historical legacy of relative disadvantage, or where the group in question is politically disenfranchised; and (v) can be excused because it serves an economic and social function.[76]

The call to recognise age discrimination offers an important opportunity to evaluate what we understand discrimination to be, and why the inertia around age discrimination must be overcome.

5 Arguments for Recognition of Age Discrimination

Arguments that the immutability of age makes it an unsuitable ground for discrimination simply reaffirm a view of discrimination where it is the characteristic that gives rise to the problem. These arguments also ignore the fact that it is the social constructs that surround that characteristic that are the problem, especially when these social constructs inform legal responses (or lack thereof). Denying that age is a form of discrimination because it is mutable (universal and transitory) is of limited value because the changes that accompany the ageing process are inevitable, whereas people can change religions or political opinions. The latter changes may come because of chance or choice;[77] they are not, and should not be, inevitable.[78] Similarly, an individual may be born with an immutable disability, or accident or illness may result in a disability at any stage in an individual's life. It also signals an acceptance of historical and structural inequalities and negates the harm caused by such inequalities. The mutability and equality of opportunity arguments overlook the fact that age will bring changes, but individuals may still be treated differently simply because of their age.

Like race and sex discrimination, age discrimination can stem from prejudice and negative stereotyping about the particular moral or social worth of members of particular groups.[79] Young people might be stereotyped as dangerous, untrustworthy and unreliable, whilst older people might be viewed as

76 E. Dewhurst, 'Is Age Exceptional? Challenging Existing Rationales and Exploring Realities', 36(2) *Harvard Human Rights Journal* (2023) p. 248.

77 Boni-Saenz *supra* note 71, p. 850.

78 J. Baars, 'Concepts of Time in Age and Aging', in G. Scarre (ed.), *The Palgrave Handbook of the Philosophy of Aging* (Palgrave, London, 2016) pp. 71–72.

79 Goosey, *supra* note 72, *p.* 541.

useless, senile and a burden to society.[80] Indeed, ageism was initially identified in relation to the systematic stereotyping of, and discrimination against, old people because they are old; negative stereotypes of old people "allowed younger generations to see older people as different from themselves; thus they subtly cease to identify with their elders as human beings".[81] The opposite can be true also, as older generations' focus on difference can prevent them from identifying young people as human beings. If ageist social and cultural beliefs are regarded as normal and acceptable, or merely less harmful, it can be more difficult to challenge age-based distinctions that are enshrined in law. Finally, assertions that age-based distinctions are unique because of their economic and social functions overlooks the fact that race or sex distinctions can also be justified on the grounds of advancing equality and assisting disadvantaged groups.[82]

Age-based distinctions may be socially, legally, and politically acceptable, and the lines of age discrimination law may not be sufficiently certain. This is not, however, a valid justification to refuse to engage with the possibility that age-based distinctions may be discriminatory. The unquestioning acceptance of age-based distinctions reinforces negative stereotypes and prejudices towards people of a certain age and obscures any associated harm. The normalising of such behaviours, socially and legally, can mean that the actual harm on members of such groups is never recorded or analysed. Such normalisation can also serve to minimise or even obscure serious human rights violations against individuals within certain age groups, such as children. In short, age-differential treatment is not different or special, nor necessarily less serious. It can still inflict the same types of harms as other discrimination and many of the justifications for positive differential treatment, on the basis of race or sex for example, can be extended to age discrimination.

Recognising age as a basis of discrimination has wider implications not only because it is a characteristic in its own right, but because it may be one of the additional characteristics that gives rise to multiple discrimination.[83] Multiple discrimination, or discrimination on more than one ground, has been described in three ways, ranging from a purely siloed approach to an intersec-

---

80 Ibid.

81 R. N. Butler and M. I. Lewis, *Aging & Mental Health: Positive Psychological Approaches* (The C.V. Mosby Company, St. Louis, 1973) p. 12.

82 Goosey, *supra* note 72, p. 542.

83 L. Roseberry, 'Multiple Discrimination', in M. Sargeant (ed.), *Age Discrimination and Diversity. Multiple Discrimination from an Age Perspective* (Cambridge University Press, Cambridge, 2011) pp. 16–40.

tional approach. First, sequential multiple discrimination arises when a person suffers discrimination on different grounds on separate occasions. For example, a woman with a disability may suffer discrimination on one occasion because of her gender, and on a different occasion may suffer discrimination because of her disability. This is the traditional 'single axis' approach to discrimination that looks at a single identity trait in insolation so that the disadvantages suffered by persons with more than one identity trait commonly targeted for discrimination are overlooked. Secondly, additive multiple discrimination occurs when a person suffers discrimination on more than one ground on the same occasion, such as a woman experiencing discrimination at a given point in time because she is a woman with a disability. Thirdly, intersectional discrimination arises when two or multiple grounds operate simultaneously and interact in an inseparable manner, producing a qualitatively different[84] form of discrimination, the impact of which is greater than the mere sum of the individual grounds of discrimination.[85] Efforts to tackle discrimination may be inadequate where there is a failure to acknowledge an identity trait, such as age, as a source of discrimination, which will impact on an assessment of how various identity characteristics interact with each other and the form of (intersectional) discrimination that eventuates. It is for these reasons that age discrimination is so significant to children and their rights. Children can for example suffer discrimination because they are young, female, have a disability, and because they are a member of an ethnic minority, and so on. It is important then that their age/youth is considered in terms of the disadvantageous treatment that it may involve.

6 Age Distinction or Age Discrimination?: The Impact on Children and Their Rights

The impact of the failure to take age discrimination as seriously as other forms of discrimination is heightened when it comes to children. Views about the (im)utability of age and whether age can be regarded as a basis of discrimination informs the tendency not to accept that children can experience discrim-

84 S. Fredman, *Intersectional Discrimination in EU Gender Equality and Non-discrimination Law* (European Commission: Directorate General for Justice and Consumers, Brussels, 2016) pp. 7, 27–28.

85 K. Crenshaw, 'Demarginalizing the Intersection of Race and Sex: A Black Feminist Critique of Antidiscrimination Doctrine', *University of Chicago Legal Forum* (1989) p. 140.

ination because of their age, where age is a defining characteristic of what it is to be a child, experience childhood, and be child-rights holder.

Like the wider discourse around race, sex, and age discrimination, the children's rights movement has been distinguished from efforts to recognise the rights of other traditionally oppressed groups, such as women, racial or ethnic minorities or persons with disabilities, because, it is argued, these groups cannot change the characteristics that give rise to the discrimination that they experience, unlike the maturation process of child to adult. Fredman's explanation for the distinctions is that "[w]e have all been young, and we will all, if we are fortunate, become old. Thus, the basic opposition between "self" and "other" – which marks much of racism and sexism – is not present in the same way."[86] Even if it is recognised that children do experience age discrimination, such discrimination is regarded as justifiable because it is temporary and it will cease once the child becomes an adult. For children, arguments that any inequalities will balance out over the course of the individual's life[87] means that any inequality and discrimination will be resolved by the fact that they will one day grow up. This view is problematic because it suggests that some discrimination, and its attendant negative impact upon a whole section of society for 18 years is permissible. It ignores too the fact that many children die for reasons that may be connected to discriminatory attitudes, law and policies.

In addition to the transitory nature of the subordination of children rendering it different to the subordination of other groups is the related justification that children need to be cared for; their dependency is temporary and those that look after children have no vested interest in prolonging that dependence, unlike other (genuine) oppressors.[88] This view reflects much of the academic discourse around age-based distinctions that revolves around the perceived (in)competency of children and young people and their inability to engage in rational decision-making, which traditionally served to deny the extension of rights to children.[89] Equally, however, age limits are advanced as a means to ensure that young people are afforded a healthy and gradual development. Age limits – particularly around education and employment – have been designed to allow young people to gradually ease

86 S. Fredman, *supra* note 70, p. 21.

87 Goosey, *supra* note 72, p. 540.

88 O. O'Neill, 'Children's Rights and Children's Lives', 98(3) *Ethics* (1988) p. 462.

89 *See, generally* C. Breen, 'The Ageing of Article 2(1): The Child's Right to be Free from Age-Based Discrimination', in M. Skivenes and K. H. Søvig (eds.), *Child Rights and International Discrimination Law* (Routledge, London, 2019) pp. 55–69.

into adult society.[90] This approach echoes arguments about the role that social and economic policies play in overcoming the disadvantage experienced by certain groups in society. In the context of children, many of law's age-based distinctions are premised on protecting children from themselves (e.g. protection of children from legal access to alcohol), but with the additional premise of the need to protect wider society from children (e.g. by preventing children from voting before they are ready to make 'sound' decisions on politics). These schemes are often characterised as benevolence and based on generalisations or stereotypes about reaching the specific chronological age. They are a continuation of longstanding debates around the capacity and competency of children to engage in behaviours and/or exercise their rights.[91]

Children do not always see themselves as vulnerable, and indeed their power as active agents in their lives and the lives of others must be recognised. At the same time, however, children can be far more at risk than adults because of their lack of experience and dependent status.[92] Matters of competency can be seen in relation to perceptions of children and young peoples' decision-making abilities as reflected in legislation governing driving, drinking alcohol, or firearms use. Many of the assumptions underpinning such schemes are, however, increasingly called into question by developmental psychology research. Such research shows that adolescent decision-making competency, for example, varies in relation to the decision that they are making. On the one hand, decision-making by adolescents around what are already risky activities, such as driving, drinking alcohol, and using firearms may be impacted by the fact that the social or emotional competence that regulates such decision-making develops later in adolescence.[93] Similar findings have been made in developmental neuroscience research, which shows that brain development governing cognitive processes is not uniform. On the

90 C. Breen, 'Voter Eligibility and Age Discrimination: The View From Aotearoa New Zealand', 36(2) *Harvard Human Rights Journal* (2023) p. 306.

91 C. Breen, *Age Discrimination and Children's Rights: Ensuring Equality and Acknowledging Difference* (Brill Martinus Nijhoff, Leiden, 2006) pp. 2–8; G. L. Neuman and A. M. Ibrahim, 'When Is Age Discrimination a Human Rights Violation? Special Edition on Age Discrimination', 36(2) *Harvard Human Rights Journal* (2023) pp. 223–246.

92 Daly et al., *supra* note 56, pp. 29–30.

93 M. E. Hay, 'Incremental Independence: Conforming the Law to the Process of Adolescence', 15(3) *William & Mary Journal of Women & Law* (2008) pp. 666, 679–80. *See generally*, G. Icenogle et al., 'Adolescents' Cognitive Capacity Reaches Adult Levels Prior to Their Psychosocial Maturity: Evidence for a 'Maturity Gap' in a Multinational, Cross-Sectional Sample.' 43(1) *Law and Human Behavior* (2019) pp. 69–85.

other hand, by the age of 16 years, adolescents' cognitive development is the same as adults when matters of determining who and what to vote for.[94] In essence, adolescents mature intellectually before they mature socially or emotionally, a difference that plays out in the cognitive process involved and the type of decision that they are making.[95] The findings of both research disciplines show that competence in young people is variable. Much like adults, different types of decisions make different sorts of demands on individuals' brains and abilities. Blanket assumptions of incompetency and inability to make rational decisions need to be interrogated.

Differential treatment based on negative stereotyping that leads to a denial of rights is a traditional marker of discrimination. Even if the temporary nature of age discrimination – whether such a view is based on the (im)mutability of age and/or the temporary subordination of children because of their transitory dependency – for the individual child was acceptable, it does not excuse the permanent nature of the discrimination experienced by children as a societal group. For children, individually and as members of the group, the failure to interrogate age-based differences, and, as necessary, to recognise and prohibit age discrimination serves to internalise the identity that adult society gives to children; the identity of being less than adults. It is to be expected then that many children can – and do – end up feeling that their own interests and concerns are not important simply because their interests and concerns are often different to adults' values and norms and are not 'mainstream'. Even where adults and children share the same values and concerns, which is often the case, children's views are not acknowledged or acted upon – or they are often actively dismissed – because the opinion-holder is a child. In this regard, and despite her denial of age as a form of discrimination in relation to children, there is merit in Fredman's wider observation that:

> [T]he problem is not the diversity of characteristics, but the detrimental treatment attached to it. Thus the aim should not be to eliminate difference, but to prohibit the detriment attached to such difference, prefera-

94 Breen, *supra* note 90, p. 307.

95 L. Steinberg, 'The Science of Adolescent Brain Development and its Implications for Adolescent Rights and Responsibilities', in J. Bhaba (ed.), *Human Rights and Adolescence* (University of Pennsylvania Press, Philadelphia, 2014) p. 66; V. E. Hamilton, 'Democratic Inclusion, Cognitive Development, and the Age of Electoral Majority', 77(4) *Brooklyn Law Review* (2012) pp. 1507–1510.

> bly by adjusting existing norms to accommodate difference so that equality can also stem from differential but legitimate treatment.[96]

Understandings of inequality and discrimination need to be informed by children and their experiences of exclusion on the basis of their age, particularly where such exclusion results in injustice, harm and oppression[97] and can point to the changes that are needed to those fundamental historical and societal structures that perpetuate inequality against children.

Ageist attitudes towards children may also reflect wider social biases, as "childhood cannot be totally separated from other variables: class, gender, ethnicity, disability, sexual orientation ..."[98] For example, media portrayals of children with disabilities often refer to disability benefit dependency.[99] A poor, female child with disabilities from an ethnic minority may experience discrimination deriving from all of her characteristics, whilst discrimination that targets teenage, single mothers may impact both mothers and their children.[100] With children, age is not merely an add-on to other types of discrimination, it is embedded in the subordination and inequality that children may experience, and age discrimination may exacerbate these disparities. And, as noted above, age can intersect with other identity characteristics to create and compound more pernicious, yet also subtle, forms of disadvantage that for children stem from an adult-centric approach to discrimination.[101] Efforts to tackle discrimination against children, such as those enumerated in Article 2 will always be compromised if one source – perhaps the central source – of oppression is not identified or recognised.[102] The benign nature of age distinctions may conceal, deliberately or otherwise, other forms of discrimination, or a focus on forms of discrimination may conceal discrimination based on

96 S. Fredman, *Discrimination Law* (Oxford University Press, Oxford, 2011) p. 13.

97 M. Moosa-Mitha, 'A Difference-Centred Alternative to Theorization of Children's Citizenship Rights', 9(4) *Citizenship Studies* (2005) pp. 369–388.

98 M. D. A Freeman, 'Introduction', in M. D. A. Freeman (ed.), *Law and Childhood Studies: Current Legal Issues* (Oxford University Press, Oxford, 2012) p. 5.

99 Daly et al., *supra* note 56, p. 31.

100 E. Sutherland, 'Article 2 of the United Nations Convention on the Rights of the Child: Non-discrimination and Children's Rights' in M. Skivenes and K. H. Søvig (eds.), *Child Rights and International Discrimination Law: Implementing Article 2 of the UN Convention on the Rights of the Child* (Routledge, London, 2019) p. 30.

101 *But see*, K. Konstantoni and A. Emejulu, 'When Intersectionality Met Childhood Studies: The Dilemmas of a Travelling Concept', 15(1) *Children's Geographies* (2017) pp. 6–22.

102 C. I. Ravnbøl, 'Intersectional Discrimination against Children: Discrimination against Romani Children and Anti-discrimination', *Innocenti Working Paper* No. IDP 2009–11 (UNICEF Innocenti Research Centre, Florence, 2009) pp. 14–18.

age.[103] Within that consideration are echoes of the diversity of views of who is a child and what constitutes childhood. In other words, if age is a social and cultural construct, then age should be used to interrogate those constructs and their manifestation in law and policy.

7 Equality, Non-discrimination, and Children's Rights

Debates about whether to recognise that children may be discriminated against because of their age has sat against wider debates around children's rights. These debates are important because, ultimately, they shape perceptions of children as rights-holders.

The 1970's Child Liberationists regarded the incapacity argument as a form of inequality and they sought to challenge it by calling for children and adults to be treated the same.[104] However, there are difficulties with their insistence on formal equality because of its potential to reinforce inequality. An insistence on formal equality that regards children as being the same as adults is problematic, where it is the adult that is the comparator, and adult characteristics are the measure to be achieved. Existing power relationships and hierarchies remain unchallenged when the adult is the measure of all things and children are assessed according to their resemblance with adults.[105] It is also an exercise that often ends up with the child being found to be deficient and 'less than'. Despite calls to reject equality as a basis to counter age discrimination,[106] there is a benefit to using a comparator analysis if it highlights just how reinforced our an adult-centric world is, with its associated social institutional practices and beliefs that inform law and policy.

A more nuanced approach to achieving equality requires a fundamental re-examination of the structures that perpetuate such inequality; substantive equality provides such a nuanced framework. Substantive equality calls for the removal of barriers to the advancement of vulnerable or disadvantaged groups (equality of opportunity), where it is those that are excluded that iden-

103 M. Liebel, 'Discriminated Against Being Children: A Blind Spot in the Human Rights Arena', in M. Liebel (ed.) *Children's Rights from Below: Cross-Cultural Perspectives* (Palgrave Macmillan, New York, 2012) p. 98.

104 R. Farson, *Birthrights* (Macmillan, Oxford, 1974); J. C. Holt, *Escape from Childhood* (EP Dutton, New York, 1974).

105 Compare: C. A. MacKinnon, *Feminism Unmodified: Discourses on Life and Law* (Harvard University Press, Cambridge, 1987) p. 34.

106 Boni-Saenz, *supra* note 71, p. 850.

tify the barriers.[107] But, the removal of barriers may not be enough; positive action to ensure that every individual has a genuinely equal chance of satisfying the criteria for access to a particular social good such as education, employment, healthcare, and political representation (equality of results) may also be needed. Ensuring that everyone has a genuinely equal chance of accessing these social goods may also require new ways of thinking about what those measures should be,[108] an exercise that may be more successful with the input of those who have previously been excluded, such as children. Equality would be measured without reference to adults, where (children's) difference is not a negative or a 'less-than'.[109]

Stepping away from difference as a negative would be a further way of removing barriers. Instead of the liberal definition of equality as the right of citizens to be equal and different, equality should be re-interpreted to mean that all citizens are 'differently equal'. By emphasising difference first, it is suggested that it is through difference that equality is defined, rather than difference being transcended through a claim to equality.[110] Difference-based theories offer alternative interpretations of oppression and equality. Difference-based theories regard difference as central to achieving equality, rather than difference being regarded as the source of oppression and exclusion. This approach means that difference is not viewed as a negative characteristic that must be changed for equality to be achieved. Taking a different view of equality, in this way, can change our understanding of what (in)equality actually is, which can then lead to changes how we measure if, and when, equality is achieved.

The right to non-discrimination can operate as a tool to achieve equality. Conduct that treats a child negatively because of a particular characteristic, such as ethnicity or gender, may be regarded as direct discrimination and a violation of the child's right to non-discrimination. Indirect discrimination also allows an individual to challenge unintentional discrimination or conduct that is not designed with the intention to produce a discriminatory effect but which, nonetheless, imposes a specific disadvantage on members of certain groups. Recognising that discrimination may also be indirect allows situations of structural bias, where the equal treatment of individuals results in

107 Fredman, *supra* note 96, pp. 14–17.
108 Ibid., pp. 18–19.
109 MacKinnon, *supra* note 105, p. 378.
110 N. Yuval-Davis, 'Ethnicity, Gender Relations and Multiculturalism', in R. D. Torres et al., (eds.), *Race, Identity and Citizenship: A Reader* (Blackwell, Oxford, 1999).

unequal outcomes, to be challenged.[111] The main advantage of this approach for the child's right to non-discrimination on the basis of age is that it can challenge situations of structural bias and conduct that were not designed to be discriminatory, or simply not assessed for their potential discrimination. Nonetheless, the contribution of this view of discrimination is contingent on children being regarded as a group who must not be discriminated against. Conduct that is aimed at treating an individual negatively because they are a child is often less clearly prohibited, as is evidenced by the sporadic evolution of age discrimination. The result is continuing structural and systematic discrimination against children where "conventional discrimination analysis mirrors the power relations that form hierarchies that define inequalities rather than challenging and equalizing them".[112]

8 Children, Rights and Age: Three Core Caveats

The use of age limits to organise society in itself promotes the view that treating younger people differently on the basis of their age is unproblematic, or at least not as problematic as treating someone differently on the grounds of ethnicity, gender, or disability, and any of the other prohibited grounds of discrimination enumerated in human rights treaties. This view is clearly open to challenge when such distinctions are discriminatory. Yet, acknowledging difference can be key to achieving equality. Where age-based distinctions are used, three core caveats are suggested.

One, age-based laws and policies should not discriminatory. They should not be a vehicle to permit on-going negative attitudes towards children, especially those that are grounded in historical, structural and hierarchical attitudes towards children that regard children as 'less than' adults. Laws and policies that are regarded as necessary to secure positive outcomes for children must also be interrogated to ensure that the outcomes are, in fact, positive for children, determinations that must also be informed by the Convention's Guiding Principles. The justifications for the differentiation must be advanced and interrogated; the procedural element for the determination plays a key role. In terms of human rights law, the right to non-discrimination can be regarded as a tool for achieving of equality. Law or policy that results in a child being treated negatively because of a particular

111 *See generally*, Fredman, *supra* note 96, pp. 177–190.

112 C. A. MacKinnon, 'Intersectionality as Method: A Note', 38(4) *Signs: Journal of Women in Culture and Society* (2013) p. 1023.

characteristic may be regarded as direct discrimination, and it should be prohibited unless such differentiation can be justified. The question of whether the differentiation is justifiable, and not discriminatory, needs to be examined against legitimacy, rationality and proportionality as informed by the Convention's Guiding Principles and their promotion of a child-centric perspective on the legitimacy of such distinctions.[113] But even where law and policy does not explicitly turn on age, the same mechanism for its justification must be applied to ensure that it does not lead to indirect discrimination.

The matter of justification leads to the second caveat. More is now known about the extent of children's capacity for decision-making and autonomy. There is an appeal to viewing age related laws and policies through the lens of psychological development or social conceptions of maturity, if decision-makers can calibrate the law against the relevant markers of maturity to ensure developmentally appropriate rights and responsibilities.[114] This calibration exercise should draw from "context-specific research across the social and developmental sciences, in addition to more traditional policy considerations".[115] Such calibration should also ensure that the 'right' science is matched to the 'right' question.[116] But research findings of this nature must not viewed in isolation from the wider context of childhood experiences and state action.[117] This combined approach should allow existing norms to be adjusted to accommodate difference so that equality can also stem from differential but legitimate treatment. In this way, age-based distinctions may come under closer scrutiny. But, viewed through the lens of the CRC, there is more to this calibration exercise. The question of whether age-based distinctions should continue as a means of organising society should take into account the Guiding Principles of the Convention.[118]

Three, it is also necessary to look beyond the matter of 'age' in age discrimination. Age-based distinctions are still only a proxy for wider social and cul-

113 C. Breen, *supra* note 91, pp. 42–43.

114 C. Ryan, 'The Law of Emerging Adults', 97 *Washington University Law Review* (2019) p. 1165.

115 V. E. Hamilton, 'Adulthood in Law and Culture' 91(1) *Tulane Law Review* (2016) p. 59.

116 Steinberg, *supra* note 95, p. 65; L. Steinberg, 'Should the Science of Adolescent Brain Development Inform Public Policy?', 64(8) *American Psychologist* (2009) p. 744.

117 K. Silbaugh, 'Developmental Justice and the Voting Age', 47(2) *Fordham Urban Law Journal* (2019) pp. 272–282.

118 CRC, *Treaty-Specific Guidelines Regarding the Form and Content of Periodic Reports to be Submitted by States Parties under Article 44, paragraph 1(b), of the Convention on the Rights of the Child*, CRC/C/58/Rev.3 (2015).

tural attitudes towards age, and, in the current context, children and childhood. Care needs to be taken to avoid the reductionism inherent in age as a justification of law and policy. Rather, age should be used to facilitate an expansive understanding – and accommodation – of the complexities of 'childhood' and what it means to be a child. In this way, discussions of age as a proxy should prompt discussion of whether children are being discriminated against simply because they are children.

Read together, these caveats call for an approach that recognises the differences between children and adults that takes account of the (sometimes contradictory) complexities that come with being a child, in a more meaningful way.

9 Conclusion

Age-based distinctions can serve a positive purpose as they denote the differences between children and adults. Given the extent to which chronological age regulates our lives and legal relationships, there is a dearth of age-based discrimination research and a failure to consistently examine if, and how, such distinctions may perpetuate inequality and discrimination within a particular group whose shared characteristic is their age. The extent of the recognition that children experience age discrimination is even more underexplored, even where the exercise of state power has unjustifiably detrimental impacts. Paternalistic attitudes around physical and mental immaturity prevail and serve to excuse negative wider social attitudes towards children that may then be reflected in law and policy based on an uninterrogated use of age-based distinctions. Denying the potential for age to be discriminatory makes it harder to establish a historical legacy of relative disadvantage and/or marginalisation, particularly where age operates to compound other forms of discrimination. As such, age discrimination raises some important questions, not only for the question for how age-discrimination should be understood, but for our understandings of discrimination more generally.

As the only global or regional treaty that relies on age to determine its personal scope, the CRC Convention is central to discussions around the role of age in ensuring equality and acknowledging difference. The Convention's centrality is heightened by its near universal ratification. Accepting that Article 2 prohibits age discrimination is critical in giving better effect to the spirit and purpose of the CRC in a number of ways. One, it would put states on notice that age-based laws and policies should no longer be a vehicle to permit on-going negative attitudes towards children, especially those that are grounded in historical, structural and hierarchical attitudes that regard children as 'less than' adults. Two, it would allow laws and policies that are regarded as necessary to secure positive outcomes for children to be more thoroughly interrogated to ensure that the outcomes are, in fact, positive for children; such determinations must be informed by the Convention's Guiding Principles (the right to non-discrimination being one). Three, it would facilitate the need to look beyond the matter of 'age' in age discrimination, so as to be able to examine the complexities of being a child, which are heightened by the complexities of how 'childhood' is to be understood.

CHAPTER 5

Adultism, Normative Power, and Voting Age Discrimination

John Wall

Abstract[1]

The argument made here is that age discrimination against children must be addressed as not only a legal but also a normative problem. It is an expression not only of children's denial of rights but also what can be called historically engrained systems of patriarchy or adultism. Consequently, age discrimination calls for an equally systemic critique of childism, in analogy to similar critiques of feminism, decolonialism, and anti-racism. This argument is illustrated by the issue of age discrimination in the right to vote across international and national law. The problem is shown to lie not just in law itself but also in underlying attitudes about normative power. Age discrimination is thereby shown to raise profound questions about what appears normal and settled in society and law in order to reimagine what is equal and just.

1 Introduction

Discrimination law across nations and internationally is much more concerned with matters of gender, race, ethnicity, nationality, sexuality, and disability than it is with matters of age. When age discrimination is mentioned, it predominantly refers to the elderly and not the young. Even the Convention on the Rights of the Child ('CRC'), which promulgates non-discrimination as one of children's core rights in Article 2, does so in terms of other factors such as those above, but not age itself (unless included under "other status").[2] Legal and scholarly discourse, likewise, understands children as objects of various forms of intersectional discrimination, but rarely in their status of being chil-

1 This article is a substantially modified version of J. Wall, 'Adultism and Voting Age Discrimination', 36 *Harvard Human Rights Journal* (2023) pp. 329–340. Reproduced with permission.

2 UN Convention on the Rights of the Child (1989).

DOI:10.1163/9789004708433_006

dren as such. Considering that persons under the age of eighteen (the UN's definition of children) constitute fully a third of the world's population, and considering that children often receive differential treatment as children under the law and in societies, it is clearly problematic that age discrimination against the young is not a matter of academic, social, and legal concern.

My argument in this chapter is that age discrimination against children can be properly understood when it is examined as not just occasional but normative. That is, it is an expression of what can be referred to as adultism: meaning, not just mistreatment or neglect of children, but a more profound and systemic historical bias that is just as fundamental as sexism, racism, classism, and other long recognized structures of power. To make this argument, I consider the case of children's worldwide lack of rights to vote. Children's placement outside the democratic franchise, I claim, constitutes classic age discrimination by denying a basic and prima facie universal human right to children as a group without justification that can stand up to reasonable scrutiny. Of course, there are many other instances that could be examined, and voting is merely a small part even of political empowerment. However, as for other marginalized groups, suffrage is one basic touchstone of equal societal inclusion. As a remedy to adultism in this and any instance, I propose an equally systemic critique from the perspective of childism, one that aims to be just as transformative as critiques from feminism, decolonialism, anti-racism, and the like. In the end, resolving age discrimination against children, in voting rights or elsewhere, is both a legal matter and one demanding underlying reconfigurations of normative power.

2 Adultism as Discrimination by Age

While researchers have developed powerful ways to understand and confront sexism, racism, colonialism, and many other forms of social marginalization, it is relatively less obvious what it might mean to develop a critical analysis of adultism, or the marginalization of children specifically as children. Even childhood studies scholars tend to borrow critical lenses from feminism, decolonialism, queer theory, and the like that were originally developed without children particularly in mind.[3] One of the reasons adultism is so difficult to unpack is that much of critical theory has sought to over-

3 J. Wall, 'Childism: Transforming Critical Theory in Response to Children', in S. Balagopalan et al. (eds.), *The Bloomsbury Handbook of Theories in Childhood Studies* (Bloomsbury, New York, 2023) pp. 208–222.

come adult groups, such as racial minorities, women, the colonized, indigenous people, and the poor, are oppressed by being constructed as childlike.[4] That is, anti-discrimination campaigns have often used the notion that certain members of society should not be treated as children. An indication of the invisibility of childhood is the widespread use of the term 'patriarchy' to refer only to the oppression of women, when in fact the 'pater' or father figure is also inherently oppressive of children. Adultism is then firmly established in contemporary normative assumptions and arguably even discrimination's most intractable root.

The concept of adultism, along with similar terms such as ageism and infantization, has taken on various meanings over time. The term 'adultism' itself first entered the English lexicon in a book by the popular education writer Patterson Dubois in 1903. Dubois uses the word in a non-systemic way to refer to "the undue interposition by the adult of ... his adult point of view", which he argues reflects an undue sense of "absolute possession, unlimited right, and infallible judgment".[5] This use of the term describes an immediate and direct imposition of adult privilege under certain circumstances. It retains this sense all the way up into the 1970s, when, for example, the influential developmental psychologist Jack Flasher uses it to describe caregivers' occasional "misuse of power" over children.[6] The feminist scholar Elise Boulding uses the term "ageism" to refer to the possibility for "segregation" against children's (and the elderly's) rights such as to family nurturance and political expression.[7] Even the well-known education theorist John Holt, who argues for many kinds of systemic children's empowerment, including the universal right to vote, refers to what he calls "ageism" in the limited sense of adults' frequent attempts to suppress children's self-expression.[8]

The idea of adultism began to take on what I would call more robustly normative meanings in the 1990s, largely in response to theoretical developments in deconstructionism, third-wave feminism, anti-racism, and decolonialism. Scholars started to unpack what is means not only for adults to dominate over children, but also for adulthood as a social category to occupy a systemically superior status that hinges on childhood's marginalization.

4 T. Rollo, 'The Color of Childhood: The Role of the Child/Human Binary in the Production of Anti-Black Racism', 49.4 *Journal of Black Studies* (2018) pp. 307–329.

5 P. Dubois, *Fireside Child-Study: The Art of Being Fair and Kind* (Dodd, Mead and Company, New York, 1903) pp. 8 and 35.

6 J. Flasher, 'Adultism', 13 *Adolescence* (1978) pp. 517–523.

7 E. Boulding, *Children's Rights and the Wheel of Life* (Transaction Books, 1979).

8 J. Holt, *Escape from Childhood* (Penguin, New York, 1974) pp. 1–4.

Adultism is understood as normative when it establishes adulthood as the normal or default understanding of human being, the central or primary experience of what it means to be a political person. It is not just that adults sometimes mistreat children, but that societies are historically structured around a binary opposition of empowered adulthood and disempowered childhood.

There are three ways the concept of adultism can be understood normatively, each more complex than the last. Initially, scholars like John Bell and Barry Checkoway in the 1990s describe the adultistic way in which broadly accepted attitudes construct childhood as in some way inferior. Bell argues that contemporary societies give permission to adults (and children) to assume an attitude of "disrespect of the young".[9] Adults are able to subject children to physical punishment, ban them from public spaces, and deny them real voices in schools, for example, because of a deeper and unquestioned cultural acceptance of adult superiority. Similarly, Checkoway explains that, in the political sphere, "adultism refers to all the behaviors and attitudes that flow from the assumption that adults are better than young people, and are entitled to act upon young people in many ways without their agreement".[10] Adultism is understood here as the expression of the deep-seated historical belief that adulthood is a privileged status.

In the early 2000s, scholars and practitioners develop a second way of thinking about adultism as normative by describing it as a legally enforced structure of "discrimination". More than just a broad-based assumption of adult entitlement, adultism can refer to established systems of anti-child bias built into social relations, institutions, and law. The psychologists Jocelyn Gregoire and Christin Jungers argue, for example, that children's therapists need to be aware of the "systematic discrimination against young people" that undermines children's well-being and self-esteem across families, schools, and social systems.[11] The psychoanalyst Elisabeth Young-Bruehl similarly explores the ways that "discrimination against children" pervades social relations across families and social institutions (though she somewhat confusingly uses the word "childism" in place of "adultism").[12] In the same way, the

9 J. Bell, 'Understanding Adultism: A Major Obstacle to Developing Positive Youth-Adult Relationships', *YouthBuild USA* (1995) p. 1.

10 B. Checkoway, 'Adults as Allies', 38 *Partnerships/Community* (1996) p. 14.

11 J. Gregoire and C. Jungers, *The Counsellor's Companion: What Every Beginning Counselor Needs to Know* (Routledge, New York, 2007) p. 65.

12 E. Young-Bruehl, *Childism: Confronting Prejudice against Children* (Yale University Press, New Haven, CT, 2011).

sociologists Lucien Lombardo and Karen A. Polonko argue that, "similar to sexism, racism and classism, adultism refers to a system of structured inequality or oppression that permeates relationships between children and adults".[13] Describing adultism in terms of discrimination makes it possible to see how the prioritization of adult points of view has real structural impacts on children's opportunities and lives.

But there is a third and to my lights more complex and critical concept of adultism that likewise arises in the early 2000s, this time not out of psychology but out of childhood studies. Here, adultism refers to a normative structure of power. It establishes adulthood as the assumed subject of social and political power and therefore childhood as rightly disempowered. The field of childhood studies insists that children be understood, not in terms of their development into adults, but rather in terms of their own agency, diversity, and lived experience.[14] It then becomes possible to understand adultism as the normative prioritization of adulthood over childhood perspectives. As the feminist theorist Mehmoona Moosa-Mitha describes it, adultism is the reduction of children and youth to a status of "difference" from the "norm", to their being "not-yet-citizens" who remain "invisible" to adult-dominated social imaginations.[15] Or, as I have put it in my own work, adultism constitutes "the social and political foundations on which children's lives and experiences are already imagined and pre-constructed".[16] Adultism in this sense refers to the unwritten normative assumptions that justify the empowerment of adults by means of the disempowerment of children.

Adultism is best tackled if it is critically understood. It certainly involves the mistreatment of children and the institutionalization of anti-child practices, attitudes, and systems. But underlying these visible phenomena is a less easily

13 L. Lombardo and K.A. Polonko, 'Interdisciplinary Contributions to the Prevention of Child Maltreatment', 4 *Int'l J. Interdisc. Soc. Sci.: Annual Review* (2010), pp. 89 and 94; *see also* A. Fletcher, *Facing Adultism* (CreateSpace Independent Publishing, 2015), pp. 3–4.

14 A. James and A. Prout, *Constructing and Reconstructing Childhood*, 2nd Edition (RoutledgeFalmer, New York, 1997); S. Spyrou et al. *Reimagining Childhood Studies* (Bloomsbury, New York, 2018); S. Balagopalan et al. *The Bloomsbury Handbook of Theories in Childhood Studies* (Bloomsbury, New York, 2013).

15 M. Moosa-Mitha, 'A Difference-Centered Alternative to Theorization of Children's Citizenship Rights', 9.4 *Citizenship Studies* (2005), pp. 369–388.

16 J. Wall, 'From Childhood Studies to Childism: Reconstructing the Scholarly and Social Imaginations', 20.3 *Children's Geographies* (2022) pp. 257–270; J. Wall, *Ethics in Light of Childhood* (Georgetown University Press, Washington DC, 2010); J. Wall, 'Adultism', in M. Tesar (ed.), *The Bloomsbury Encyclopedia of Social Justice in Education* (Bloomsbury, New York, forthcoming 2025).

recognizable structure of largely invisible normative assumptions pervading the histories, languages, and cultures that are the social air we all breath. Just as with sexism, racism, and other social conditions, adultism creates a double bind. It not only excludes children from social systems but also undermines their power to fight for inclusion in the first place. Children are then discriminated against in the profound sense of being normatively disempowered. They lack the right to be seen and heard as legitimate social agents in their own right. They are understood to be second-class human beings: less rational, less developed, less competent, and less valued as citizens. From this point of view, age discrimination is not just occasional or even necessarily visible, but an expression rather of historically engrained constructs of adulthood as the normative center of power.

3 The Right to Non-discriminatory Voting

One of the central battlefields of historical anti-discrimination campaigns has been the right to vote. Over time and across the world, the poor, women, racial and ethnic minorities, and others have fought and sometimes died for inclusion in this most fundamental of human rights. They have done so because, in democratic societies, suffrage is a key groundwork for political dignity and empowerment. Voting is far from the only way to exercise political power, nor is it often the most powerful. Indeed, historical suffrage movements themselves had to rely on other powers such as free speech, organization, assembly, and public argument. Nevertheless, few adults who have the right to vote would willingly give it up, as it is one of the most basic mechanisms for trying to influence political life.

This battle for voting rights has always faced deep-seated normative biases. In the United States, for example, where "all men are created equal", voting rights initially belonged at its founding in 1776 by some estimates to only six percent of the population: namely, those who qualified as landowning white men.[17] Somehow "all men" was assumed to mean only a tiny minority. Even in 1919, when the United States granted suffrage to women twenty-one and over, voting rights were expanded thereby only to fifty-seven percent of

17 J. Lepore, 'Rock, Paper, Scissors: How We Used to Vote', *The New Yorker*, Oct. 13, 2008, <www.newyorker.com/magazine/2008/10/13/rock-paper-scissors> [https://perma.cc/WPR7-3KYE]; D. Ratcliffe, 'The Right to Vote and the Rise of Democracy, 1987–1828', 33 *Journal of the Early Republic* (2013); and C. Williamson, *American Suffrage from Property to Democracy, 1760–1860* (Princeton University Press, Princeton, NJ, 1960) pp. 20–39.

the people. And this does not even count the Jim Crow laws of the time that effectively barred suffrage to racial minorities.[18] Similar stories can be told of the emergence of voting rights across countries. The fight for suffrage has not involved a simple extension of one idea of suffrage to more and more people. It has involved overcoming profound historical biases against entire classes of people, biases that construct those classes as unfit for political power by nature.

There is now a world-wide, if largely unknown, suffrage movement for the third of humanity who are children under eighteen years of age.[19] Most policy debate considers 'universal' suffrage already to have been achieved with voting rights for adult men and women. But, of course, people under eighteen are just as profoundly impacted by democratic choices. And they can be just as active participants in political life. They have contributed time and time again to democratic causes such as women's suffrage, anti-war campaigns, labor movements, climate strikes, Black Lives Matter marches, anti-gun crusades, child and youth parliaments, non-binary gender rights, and a great deal much else.[20] Children have even succeeded in gaining rights to vote in the twenty or so countries (starting with Nicaragua in 1984) and countless cities (including several in the United States) that have lowered the voting age to sixteen – even if, as I and others have argued, merely lowering voting ages to sixteen retains an adultist logic that you have to be at least adult-like to vote.[21]

---

18 United States Census Bureau, *National Intercensal Tables: 1900–1990*, <www.census.gov/data/tables/time-series/demo/popest/pre-1980-national.html> [https://perma.cc/SU5S-KQSA].

19 UNICEF Data, 'How Many Children are there in the World?', UNICEF, <data.unicef.org/how-many/how-many-children-are-in-the-world/> [https://perma.cc/Y26C-7E8C]. In the United States, the population under 18 is 22%. Kids Count Data Center, 'Total Population by Child and Adult Populations in United States', The Annie E. Casey Foundation, <datacenter.kidscount.org/data/tables/99-total-population-by-child-and-adult-populations#detailed/1/any/false/2048,574,1729,37,871,870,573,869,36,868/39,40,41/416,417> [https://perma.cc/37C9-JT5H].

20 M. Cummings, *Children's Voices in Politics* (Peter Lang, New York, 2020), pp. 4–6; J. Josefsson and J. Wall, 'Empowered Inclusion: Theorizing Global Justice for Children and Youth', 17.6 *Globalizations* (2020), pp. 1043–1060; *see also* M. Cummings, 'Silence is Poison: Explaining and Curing Adult "Apathy"', in J. Wall (ed.), *Exploring Children's Suffrage: Interdisciplinary Perspectives on Ageless Voting* (Palgrave Macmillan, New York, 2022), pp. 27–46.

21 J. Wall, *Give Children the Vote: On Democratizing Democracy* (Bloomsbury, New York, 2022).

The movement to end adultist voting discrimination has been led by both children and adults. This movement has been forced to take on barely visible normative prejudices that confine children to the political margins. Discrimination in this case comes down, not just to unequal opportunities to access political institutions, but to widely held presuppositions that construct children's voting as out of the question. The very idea lies beyond the general political imagination. It remains largely unthinkable, both in society and in the academy, that adults should not exercise their long-held right to political domination over children.

Nevertheless, as early as the 1970s, social reformers like John Holt and Richard Farson began to argue for "the right to vote for people of any age": in their case, on the grounds that being subject to laws in which one has no say "is the most serious injustice".[22] Sixteen-year-old Vita Wallace argued in 1991 in the popular U.S. magazine *The Nation* that it is "discriminatory" and hence "unconstitutional" to ban children from voting because "children of all ages must be given the same power to elect their representatives that adults have, or they will continue to be unfairly treated".[23] The German child-led organization KinderRÄchTsZÄnker (KRÄTZÄ) filed lawsuits in the German courts against children's voting discrimination in 1995–96 and again in 1998, resulting in their suit being dismissed on the grounds that children lack the legal standing to sue in the first place.[24] Another German child-led group, We Want the Vote, tried and failed again in 2014.[25] In the United States, the ten-year-old Kid Governor of Oklahoma, Charlotte Anderson, gave a speech to the Edmond Democratic Women arguing for the elimination of all voting age discrimination.[26] The National Youth Rights Association (NYRA) in the US held a conference on "Age of Youth" in which children, youth, and adults explored strategies for achieving ageless voting rights as an urgent anti-

---

22 J. Holt, *Escape from Childhood* (Penguin, New York, 1974), pp. 99–110; R. Farson, *Birthrights: A Bill of Rights for Children* (Macmillan Publishing, New York, 1974).

23 V. Wallace, 'Give Children the Vote', *The Nation*, Oct. 14, 1991, p. 439.

24 KinderRÄchTsZÄnker (KRÄTZÄ), *Constitutional Appeal Against the Voting Age* (July 1997), <http://en.kraetzae.de/vote/faq/> [https://perma.cc/K3T8-9TLX]; *see also* a publication by one of KRÄTZÄ's founders, M. Weiman, *Wahlrecht für Kinder: Eine Streitschrift* [*Suffrage for Children: A Polemic*] (2002). *See also* similar arguments made by another German youth organization, founded in 1997 and still working today, Foundation for the Rights of Future Generations, <www.intergenerationaljustice.org> (last visited May 2022) [https://perma.cc/78R8-MDWU].

25 *We Want the Vote*, <www.intergenerationaljustice.org/activities/projects/we-want-to-vote/> (last visited May 2022) [https://perma.cc/246N-MEZJ].

26 Charlotte Anderson, 'Let. Kids. Vote.' Speech to the Edmond Democratic Women (2021), <www.youtube.com/watch?v=G5fC-IDa5u8>.

discrimination concern.[27] These are just a few of many examples of what has gradually grown into a wide-ranging, if largely under the public radar, children's suffrage movement.

Children have increasingly been joined, especially since the 2000s, by adult-led organizations, which have both adopted the issue into existing work or been formed specifically to advance the cause. These groups include international organizations such as Plan International, Demos, Children's Rights International Network (CRIN), and the Children's Voting Colloquium (co-founded in 2019 by myself and activist Robin Chen). And they include national groups like Freechild Institute (US), Association for Children's Suffrage (US), Kids Can't Vote (US), Children's Voice Association (Finland), and Amnesty International UK (United Kingdom).[28] The issue has also been advanced in recent years in numerous op-eds in publications like *The New York Times*, *Washington Post*, *The Guardian*, *New Republic*, and *Vox.com*; on radio shows such as on PBS and BBC4; and in white papers, Ted Talks, and blogs.[29] While not yet recognized in larger political discourse, the issue of ageless voting has been taken up across diverse segments of child and adult activism.

4 Voting Competence

There are two main arguments about adultism or age discrimination at the heart of the above movements. These are advanced by both activists and a growing chorus of academic researchers. Both arguments are about rights to non-discrimination in not just a legal and institutional sense but also a normative and systemic one. That is, both claim that what is called for is to make democracies more fully democratic by deconstructing adultistic biases that marginalize children from their just right to power.

The first argument has to do with competence. Advocates of ageless suffrage claim that the prevailing notion that voters need a supposedly "adult" competence excludes children on illegitimate grounds. The reality is that, even on the present system, no age restriction properly distinguishes capable from non-capable voters. Contra widespread assumptions, often voiced by

27 National Youth Rights Association (NYRA), 'Age of Youth Conference' (Oct. 24, 2020), <www.youtube.com/watch?v=8Li4OooD-FM>.

28 J. Wall, 'Introduction', in J. Wall (ed.), *Exploring Children's Suffrage: Interdisciplinary Perspectives on Ageless Voting* (Palgrave Macmillan, New York, 2022), pp. 1–24.

29 Ibid.

political theorists,[30] many young children do in fact understand politics, engage in democratic deliberation, and bring to the table their own political ideas and experiences. And many adults – from the politically incurious and naive to those with cognitive disabilities and dementia – arguably do not, or at least not in a way that is only present in adults. Competence has long been ruled out as a legitimate bar to suffrage, as it is impossible to measure accurately and, just as importantly, easily stands in as a proxy for biases of class, race, gender, and much else. As the political philosopher Nicholas Munn puts it, "the accepted standard for capacity for political participation is minimal, and many of those excluded [from voting] in virtue of their age could in fact satisfy the standard if they were subject to the same restrictions as adults".[31]

In a democracy, the capacity to vote should be defined broadly rather than narrowly, as an inclusive right rather than an exclusive privilege. The purpose of democracy is not to have the supposedly competent decide for everyone else. Rather, it is to pool the population's diversity of competencies and experiences in order to arrive at the most widely possible informed policies. According to the political scientist Claudio López-Guerra, the "franchise capacity" is present in most children if it is correctly understood in democratic terms: that is, as "the ability to experience the benefits of enfranchisement and the harms of disenfranchisement".[32] Competence really means the capacity to claim a stake in political outcomes. Or, as I have argued myself, anyone who wants to vote has already, by wanting it, demonstrated the requisite capacity to do so. The desire itself to vote proves that one understands what voting is for and why it is important to exercise.[33] Certainly there can be no

30 D. Archard, *Children, Family and the State* (Ashgate, Burlington, VT, 2003); P. Cowley and D. Denver, 'Votes at 16? The case against', 41 *Representation* (2004), pp. 57–62.

31 N. Munn, 'Against the Political Exclusion of the Incapable', 35 *Journal of Applied Philosophy* (2018), pp. 601–614; N. Munn, 'How Low Can You Go? The Capacity to Vote Among Young Citizens', in J. Wall (ed.), *Exploring Children's Suffrage: Interdisciplinary Perspectives on Ageless Voting* (Palgrave Macmillan, New York, 2022), pp. 47–66; S. Lecce, 'Should Democracy Grow Up? Children and Voting Rights', 9.4 *Intergenerational Justice Review* (2019) pp. 133–139; B. Kiesewetter, 'Dürfen wir Kindern das Wahlrecht vorenthalten?' ['Should we deny children the right to vote?'] 95 *Archiv für Rechts und Sozialphilosophie* (2009).

32 C. López-Guerra, *Democracy and Disenfranchisement: The Morality of Electoral Exclusions* (Oxford University Press, New York, 2014), p. 6.

33 J. Wall, *Give Children the Vote: On Democratizing Democracy* (Bloomsbury, New York, 2022); J. Wall, 'Why Children and Youth Should Have the Right to Vote: An Argument for Proxy-Claim Suffrage', 24.1 *Children, Youth & Environments* (2014), pp. 108–123; J. Wall, 'The Case for Children's Voting', in J. Wall (ed.), *Exploring Children's Suffrage: Interdisciplinary Perspectives on Ageless Voting* (Palgrave Macmillan, New York, 2022), pp. 67–88.

literacy tests, bans for lack of knowledge, or rulings against incivility or cognitive incapacity.[34]

Drawing age distinctions around voting competence can arguably be described as discriminatory in a legal sense. Wouter Vandenhole shows that UN rights treaty bodies have used two main definitions of legal discrimination. One, found in the UN's conventions against racial and gender discrimination (the International Convention on the Elimination of all Forms of Racial Discrimination ['ICERD'] and the Convention on the Elimination of All Forms of Discrimination against Women ['CEDAW']) defines discrimination as "any distinction, exclusion or preference on prohibited grounds, with the purpose or effect of impairing the equal enjoyment of rights".[35] On this definition, barring children from the vote could be argued to both directly harm children by robbing them of democratic equality and dignity, and indirectly cause harm by giving their interests less weight in policy. However, this view requires demonstrating that a voting ban is not, in fact, as widely assumed, in children's best interests, on the presupposition that children do not know what would be in their political best interests in the first place. The other definition of discrimination, used by the European Court of Human Rights, is "the differential treatment in comparable situations without an objective and reasonable justification".[36] Here again, one could argue that no clear justification has been given, or could be given, for denying children equal treatment when it comes to suffrage. However, it is also the case, as with the first definition, that general public opinion would find that there is indeed an "objective and reasonable justification", namely children's lack of adult competence.

Resolving these legal questions would require tackling the underlying issues of largely invisible normative discrimination. Whether children are being denied "equal enjoyment of their rights" without "objective and reasonable justification" can only be settled by examining fundamental historical assumptions about the natures of voting and childhood. Similar arguments had to made in the past about why suffrage was being denied to women, minorities, the poor, and so on. For children, the case is not especially complicated, however controversial it may be. Based on the considerations above, it is that voting discrimination takes place whenever the right to vote is denied

---

34 E. Wiland, 'Should Children Have the Right to Vote?', in D. Boonin (ed.), *The Palgrave Handbook of Philosophy and Public Policy* (Palgrave Macmillan, New York, 2018).

35 W. Vandenhole, *Non-Discrimination and Equality in the View of the UN Human Rights Treaties Bodies* (Intersentia, 2005) p. 83.

36 Ibid.

to a member of a polity desiring it. There is no reasonable justification for barring suffrage on the basis of age. There may be rights that are legitimately limited by age – such as marriage, driving, and making life-threatening medical decisions – since these can be shown to cause obvious direct or indirect harm. But the right to vote carries no such risk apart, perhaps, from a paper cut. The right to vote cannot legitimately be abridged on any competence grounds at all, however socially accepted those grounds may be.

The deeper problem of discrimination in this case is then the unsupported normative presumption of childhood incompetence. Voting ought not be a social entitlement but a fundamental freedom, one that can legitimately be abridged only for exceptional and well-grounded reasons. Children already have freedom rights such as to expression, conscience, assembly (to a point), and protest; voting is the same kind of freedom right extended into politics. As the pediatric scholar Neena Modi argues, children's voting rights could be understood on the same basis as their medical decision rights: as freedoms a child can exercise for themselves in developing ways over time with the support of caregivers.[37] Or as the legal scholar Joanne Lau puts it, if there really is a substantive competence ground for voting, then "we ought either to disenfranchise the elderly, if we do not enfranchise children, or enfranchise children of an age group that has the same proportion of capacity as the elderly".[38] Children are discriminated against when it comes to voting rights for no other reason than that they are children.

5 Voting Consequences

The other main argument made about voting age discrimination concerns, not competencies, but consequences. Here the claim is made that denying children suffrage places their concerns and perspectives at a systematic societal disadvantage. Representatives are less beholden to the interests of constit-

37 N. Modi, 'A Radical Proposal: To Promote Children's Wellbeing Give Them the Vote', *BMJ* 361 (2018); N. Modi, 'A View from Paediatric Medicine: Competence, Best Interests, and Operational Pragmatism', in J. Wall (ed.), *Exploring Children's Suffrage: Interdisciplinary Perspectives on Ageless Voting* (Palgrave Macmillan, New York, 2022) pp. 197–214.

38 J. Lau, 'Two Arguments for Child Enfranchisement', 60 *Political Studies* (2012); P. Cook, 'Against a Minimum Voting Age', 16 *Critical Rev. Int'l Soc. & Pol. Phil.* (2013); J. Tremmel and J. Wilhelm, 'Democracy or Epistocracy? Age as a Criterion of Voter Eligibility', in J. Tremmel (ed.), *Youth Quotas and Other Efficient Forms of Youth Participation in Ageing Socieites* (Springer, New York, 2015), pp. 125–47; L.M. Umbers, 'Enfranchising the Youth', 23 *Critical Rev. Int'l Soc. & Pol. Phil.* (2018).

uents who cannot vote them out of office, resulting in policies that systematically favor people eighteen and older over people under eighteen, and across all political, economic, health, social, and even educational and family spheres. The political philosopher Stefan Olsson argues that children's suffrage would constitute "a way to guarantee that the people who really are deciding on the laws, the elected officials, do not forget to consider all interests equally".[39] Likewise, the economist Luigi Campiglio demonstrates that children's lack of voting rights places them at a disadvantage when it comes to long-term, inter-generational economics.[40] Or, as I have put it, children's enfranchisement would "make politicians accountable to the real complexities of children's lives".[41] When hard choices have to be made about resources, rights, and priorities, an adultist voting system presses children's already disadvantaged position even further into the margins of political decision-making.

The usual assumption is that children's voting would harm both children and adults by inflicting uninformed ideas on societies.[42] It is asserted that voting would "adultify" children, robbing them of their childhoods both in politics and in other spheres like criminal justice and sexual protection.[43] And it is claimed that children's suffrage would undermine the responsibilities of parents and teachers toward children's care.[44] But these arguments ignore the existing and more profound disadvantages arising from children's disenfranchisement itself. By lacking a part in choosing their political representatives, children are reduced to second-class citizens without equal dignity in their own right or influence over the systems on which they rely. They cannot pressure governments to address, for example, their being the poorest social group, their lack of health and education resources, their denial of justice protections, or their need for urgent climate action. The rea-

39 S. Olsson, 'Children's Suffrage: A Critique of the Importance of Voters' Knowledge for the Well-Being of Democracy', 16 *International Journal of Children's Rights* (2008) pp. 55–76.

40 L. Campiglio, *Prima le Donne e i Bambini* [*Women and Children First*] (Il Mulino, Bologna, 2005); L. Campiglio and L.A. Lorenzetti, 'Generational Economics', in J. Wall (ed.), *Exploring Children's Suffrage: Interdisciplinary Perspectives on Ageless Voting* (Palgrave Macmillan, New York, 2022), pp. 155–176.

41 J. Wall, *Give Children the Vote: On Democratizing Democracy* (Bloomsbury, New York, 2022).

42 G. Scarre, 'Children and Paternalism', 55 *Philosophy* (1980).

43 K. Silbaugh, 'Developmental Justice and the Voting Age', 47 *Fordham Urb. L.J.* (2020).

44 M. Guggenheim, *What's Wrong with Children's Rights* (Harvard University Press, Cambridge, MA, 2005).

son voting rights advantage people's lives is that democracies generally work, since they force elected leaders to take voters' concerns into account.

What is more, overcoming voting adultism would systematically benefit adults, social institutions, and democracies. As with other groups in history, adding voices to the democratic discourse pressures politicians to make more broadly and complexly informed policy choices. In the case of children's suffrage, it would most likely result, for example, in better funding and support for child-related professionals such as teachers, paediatricians, and social workers; longer-term economic policy, public health, and climate action; and a fresh wave of new insights into solving social issues such as gender rights, justice reform, and migration.[45] Overcoming adultism in voting rights adds a third more pixels to the policy-making screen. Indeed, as the political theorist Michael Cummings argues, it would strengthen democracy itself by improving democratic engagement and building in greater resistance to authoritarianism: "The civic disengagement and loss of social capital plaguing democracies today is rooted in the systemic silencing of people's political voice during their early years."[46]

An adultist voting system is thus normatively discriminatory when it comes to consequences as well. It is built on unexamined historical assumptions about the likely political impacts of children's voting empowerment. In reality, children are not uninformed, easily influenced, and incompetent political beings whose suffrage would harm themselves and others, but instead a diverse class of full human beings and citizens whose ideas and perspectives are very much needed in making informed political policies. The adultism of denying children their equal rights is not just that some adults treat some children badly, but that adults as a class are implicitly assumed to be superior to children as such. It constructs a binary opposition in which adulthood is empowered at the expense of the empowerment of childhood. But this deep-rooted societal norm distorts democracy and harms us all.

---

45 B. Franklin, 'Children's Political Rights', in B. Franklin (ed.), *The Rights of Children* (Basil Blackwell, New York, 1986), pp. 24–53; L. Campiglio, 'Political Participation, Voting, and Economic Policy: Three Problems of Modern Democracies', in A. Breton (ed.), *Understanding Democracy: Economic and Political Perspectives* (Cambridge University Press, New York, 1997); L. Campiglio, 'Children's Right to Vote: The Missing Link in Modern Democracies', 12 *Soc. Stud. Child. & Youth* (2009); P. van Parijs, 'The Disenfranchisement of the Elderly, and Other Attempts to Secure Intergenerational Justice', 27 *Phil. & Publ Aff.* (1999); K. Hinrichs, 'Do the Old Exploit the Young? Is Enfranchising Children a Good Idea?', 43 *Arch Europ Sociol* (2002).

46 M. Cummings, *Children's Voices in Politics* (Peter Lang, New York, 2020), p. 288.

6 Addressing Adultism in International Voting Rights Law

Responding to children's voting rights discrimination involves in part reinterpreting international law. Legal scholars have taken steps in recent years to rethink international human rights conventions as well as the CRC in more child-responsive ways. Partly international law itself suggests more inclusive ways forward, and partly it has to be reinterpreted or even reframed from a broader normative perspective. In any case, it is possible to begin with international law to start rethinking voting rights as no longer discriminatorily adultist and hence as more truly universal.

International law is particularly interesting in this respect, as it reveals in stark terms the gap between legal rights and adultist biases. The 1948 Universal Declaration of Human Rights ('UDHR'), for example, states in Article 21.3 that "the will of the people shall be the basis of the authority of government; this will shall be expressed in periodic and genuine elections which shall be by universal and equal suffrage".[47] This language is echoed also in the 1966 International Covenant on Civil and Political Rights ('ICCPR'), which asserts in Article 25 that "Every citizen shall have the right and the opportunity ... [t]o vote and to be elected at genuine periodic elections which shall be by universal and equal suffrage".[48] All countries in the world are bound through international customary law to the UDHR, and most, including the United States, have ratified the ICCPR, the landmark international law on political rights.

But, of course, the world's apparently inclusive affirmation of "universal and equal suffrage" is nowhere understood to extend to citizens under the age of eighteen (or in a few countries sixteen). This is not because international law provides an explicit rationale for children's exclusion. Nor is it because human rights committees have explored the question and validated national age restrictions on objective or reasonable grounds. Rather, children's non-enfranchisement is simply taken for granted. It is an assumed dimension of voting rights that is not thought to require justification. But such is the very essence of normative discrimination: in principle guaranteeing a universal human right while in practice withholding it from entire social groups, in this case a third of humanity, without argument. The only explanation for this clear self-contradiction is the presence of systemic and widespread historical adultism.

---

47 *Universal Declaration of Human Rights*, GA Res 217A, UNGAOR, UN Doc A/810 (Dec. 9, 1948).

48 International Covenant on Civil and Political Rights (1966).

A related problem is found in the CRC, the key international framework on children's rights and history's most widely ratified treaty. There have been broad critiques of the CRC as a discriminatory document in and of itself, in that it separates children's rights from larger human rights frameworks, thereby giving free reign to children's differential treatment (as indeed just illustrated with the UDHR and ICCPR).[49] The CRC may be adultist by its very act of separating 'children's' rights from 'human' rights. In addition, the CRC famously excludes any reference to political rights, defining even its freedom rights, as Aoife Nolan demonstrates, in almost entirely apolitical terms.[50]

But the actual language of the CRC contains a similar paradox as in larger human rights law in that it could be argued to simultaneously deny and require children's universal rights to vote. Most of the discussion in the scholarship here has focused on Article 12, which asserts in part children's "right to express [their] views freely in all matters affecting the child".[51] On one hand, Article 12 limits free expression in ways that would be unacceptable for adults: only "to the child who is capable of forming his or her own views" (not to all children), in "all matters affecting the child" (not other matters too), and in accordance with "age and maturity." Childhood is framed in terms of 'capacity' instead of inherent human dignity.[52] On the other hand, Article 12's demand for free expression in "all matters affecting the child" would seem to include politics broadly and electing representatives in particular. General political matters do indeed very much affect children. The Amnesty International lawyer Katherine Walton argues in this vein that since Article 12 affirms freedom of expression in all matters impacting children's lives, it necessarily affirms the freedom to vote.[53] Similarly, the legal scholar Aoife Daly argues that Article 12 in effect calls out states' voting age "discrimination" because "we fail to permit children the right to political influence, and we fail ourselves by imposing a

49 A.T.-D. Imoh and S. Okyere, 'Towards a More Holistic Understanding of Children's Participation: Foregrounding the Experiences of Children in Ghana and Nigeria', 112 *Child. & Youth Serv.'s Rev.* (2020); A. Quennerstedt, 'Children, But Not Really Humans? Critical Reflections on the Hampering Effect of the "3 p's"', 18 *International Journal of Children's Rights* (2010).

50 A. Nolan, 'The Child as Democratic Citizen: Challenging the Participation Gap', *Public Law* (2010) pp. 126–141.

51 UN Convention on the Rights of the Child (1989).

52 R. Sandland, 'A Clash of Conventions? Participation, Power and the Rights of Disable Children', 5.3 *Social Inclusion* (2017), pp. 93–103.

53 K. Walton, 'Votes for Children: The Case for Universal Suffrage', *Amnesty International UK*, Oct. 6, 2019, <www.amnesty.org.uk/blogs/childrens-human-rights-network-blog/votes-children-case-universal-suffrage> [https://perma.cc/4Y4S-K232].

lack of diversity on the civil processes in which we engage".[54] Although CRC Article 12 does not explicitly mention voting, then, it can be read to demand it implicitly once adultistic assumptions are removed.

In my view, an even stronger case can be made from CRC Article 13.[55] Article 13 states that "[t]he child shall have the right to freedom of expression; this right shall include freedom to seek, receive and impart information and ideas of all kinds". It further insists that there can be "restrictions" on this freedom "only" in the following instances: "(a) For respect of the rights or reputations of others; or (b) For the protection of national security or of public order (ordre public), or of public health or morals."[56] As in Article 12, the freedom to impart "ideas of all kinds", while appearing not to impinge on politics, in fact patently includes it. Political "information" is information a child may wish to "impart", including via the choice of representatives. In addition, Article 13 is closely related to Article's 15's guarantee of the right to "freedom of association", which is another way to interpret the act of voting. But most importantly, Article 13 explicitly forbids restrictions on the right to freedom of expression outside of strictly limited cases. These restrictions echo standard language throughout international law (such as in ICCPR articles on freedoms of expression, movement, thought, conscience, religion, assembly, and association). They prevent freedom of expression from violating the rights of others as well as national security, public order, health, and morals. Clearly, children's voting no more falls under any such restriction than adults' voting. On the contrary, it would be easier to argue that it is adult-only voting that fails in "respect of the rights or reputations of others" by denying equal treatment and dignity to children. CRC Article 13 thus makes an even clearer argument than Article 12 that children are owed the right to vote as a matter of freedom of expression without any unreasonable restriction.

Finally, one could point to CRC Article 41, which requires states not to exclude children from any larger human rights. As it says, "nothing in the present Convention shall affect any provisions which are more conducive to the realization of the rights of the child" in national and international law. Since the right to vote would in fact be "more conducive" to realizing children's rights,

54 A. Daly, 'Free and Fair Elections for Some? The Potential for Voting Rights for Under-18s', in D. Keane and Y. McDermott (eds.), *The Challenge of Human Rights: Past, Present, and Future* (Edward Elgar, Cheltenham, UK, 2012).

55 J. Wall, *Give Children the Vote: On Democratizing Democracy* (Bloomsbury, New York, 2022), pp. 33–34.

56 UN Convention on the Rights of the Child (1989).

and since it is explicitly required in the UDHR and ICCPR to be universal and equal, CRC Article 41 can be read to override any remaining ambiguity in the matter. If the CRC does construct children's rights in a discriminatory manner by separating them from larger human rights law, then Article 41 effectively reverses this situation by holding states to their larger human rights commitments when it comes to children. This is especially the case when it comes to children's suffrage, as little could be imagined to promote the realization of children's rights more – at least, once unreasonable normative biases against children are recognized – than their right to have an impact on the formation of their rights.

7 Addressing Adultism in National Voting Rights Law

In terms of national law, there have, as noted, been increasing attempts to sue for children's voting non-discrimination, and these have been joined by a growing body of legal scholarship. These have for some time gone beyond the more broadly acceptable campaigns for votes at sixteen[57] and parental proxy votes for children up to eighteen.[58] Such arguments retain strongly adultistic biases toward the adult as the voting rights standard. These national legal efforts to end all voting age discrimination face similar paradoxes in

57 D. Hart and R. Atkins, 'American Sixteen- and Seventeen-Year-Olds Are Ready to Vote', 633 *The Annals of the American Academy of Political and Social Science* (2010), pp. 201–222; V.E. Hamilton, 'Democratic Inclusion, Cognitive Development, and the Age of Electoral Majority', *Faculty Publications*, The College of William & Mary Law School Scholarship Repository (2012) pp. 1447–1513.

58 A. Toulemon, *Le Suffrage familial ou suffriage universel integral* [Family suffrage or integral universal suffrage] (1933); J.-Y. Le Naour and C. Valenti, *La famille doit voter: Le suffrage familial contre le vote individual* [The family must vote: Family suffrage versus individual voting] (2005); J. Gesley, 'Family Voting as a Solution to Low Fertility? Experiences from France and Germany', *Glob. L. Guest Post*, Apr. 19, 2018, <blogs.loc.gov/law/2018/04/family-voting-as-a-solution-to-low-fertility-experiences-from-france-and-germany/> [https://perma.cc/P2ML-WSHK]; H. De Quetteville, 'Germany Plans to Give Vote to Babies', *Daily Telegraph*, July 9, 2008, <www.telegraph.co.uk/news/worldnews/europe/germany/2275407/Germany-plans-to-give-vote-to-babies.html> [https://perma.cc/8KNR-XRM2]; Deutscher Bundestag, *Fragen zum Wahlrecht von Geburt an*, WD 3 - 3000 - 157/17, 8–10 (Sept. 7, 2017), <www.bundestag.de/resource/blob/531942/6669f3e29651882065938fc6a14fd779/wd-3-157-17-pdf-data.pdf> [https://perma.cc/F9J9-5EQF]; J. Rutherford, 'One Child, One Vote: Proxies for Parents', 82 *Minn. Law Rev.* (1998); R W. Bennett, 'Should Parents Be Given Extra Votes on Account of Their Children: Toward a Conversational Understanding of American Democracy', 94 *Nw. U. L. Rev.* (2000).

national law as found above internationally. That is, national law can be argued to demand ageless suffrage even as it is used in reality to oppose it.

The most developed discussions here are in Australia, Canada, and the United States. The Australian legal expert Robert Ludbrook argues, for instance, that because laws in every Australian state prohibit "age discrimination" in general, these implicitly apply to age discrimination in voting, since voting rights are fundamental rights. As he puts it, Australian democracy needs children's suffrage "if [its] political leadership and [its] political and social policies are to truly reflect the views of all sections of [the Australian] community".[59] Also in Australia, Robert Goodin and Joanne Lau suggest that children's voting rights are justified by the concept of legal "suretyship", a mechanism of combined competencies that ensures that "all the voters are 'co-signatories' with regard to electoral outcome".[60] In Canada, Cheryl Milne explains why a legal case can be made to use anti-discrimination law to amend Section 3 of the *Canadian Charter of Rights and Freedoms* "to strike down the age restriction [on voting rights]" on the grounds of political non-discrimination being fundamental to Canadian citizenship.[61]

In the United States, the anti-discrimination argument for ageless voting has revolved chiefly around the US Constitution's Fourteenth Amendment Equal Protection Clause, which guarantees that "no state shall ... deny to any person within its jurisdiction the equal protection of the laws".[62] The Constitution offers no legal precedent for barring children's voting, only for protecting voting for adults. As the legal scholar Samantha Godwin argues in detail, children's suffrage is demanded by a rigorous application of established equal protection jurisprudence. According to Godwin, "a persuasive case can be made that children represent a suspect class for equal protection purposes [similar to suspect classes around race, religion, and national origin], and that children's fundamental rights are implicated in many of the restrictions against them".[63] Voting is a constitutionally established fundamental right that is denied to children without a compelling state interest or legitimate state encroachment.

---

59 R. Ludbrook, 'Should Children Have the Right to Vote?', *Nat'l. Child. & Youth L. Ctr.* (1995).

60 R.E. Goodin and J.C. Lau, 'Enfranchising Incompetents: Suretyship and the Joint Authorship of Laws', 24 *Ratio* (2011).

61 C. Milne, 'Legality of Age Restrictions on Voting: A Canadian Perspective', in J. Wall (ed.), *Exploring Children's Suffrage: Interdisciplinary Perspectives on Ageless Voting* (Palgrave Macmillan, New York, 2022), pp. 177–196.

62 U.S. CONST. amend. XIV, § 1.

63 S. Godwin, 'Children's Oppression, Rights, and Liberation', 4 *Nw. Interdisc. L. Rev.* (2011).

Along with co-authors Sonja Grover and Robin Chen, I have argued along similar lines that childhood is a legitimate "suspect class" when it comes to voting rights protection, and furthermore that, according to *Dunn* v *Blumstein* (1972), voting is a "fundamental interest" whose "derogation must be subject to strict scrutiny by the Courts".[64] So far, US courts have refused to consider childhood a suspect class on the peculiar reasoning that "[h]olding that 'posterity' or even just minor children are a suspect class would hamstring governmental decision-making", subordinating non-discrimination interests to political and economic expediency.[65] However, since voting is indeed a fundamental interest for all citizens, providing them with political dignity and the ability to influence matters that affect them, no such government interest can in fact justifiably outweigh it.

Although no international or national laws therefore establish ageless suffrage, it is also arguably the case that they require it on fundamental anti-discrimination grounds. The democratic right to vote is a universal and equal freedom that can legitimately be denied only for exceptional reasons. As we have seen, however, not only would children's voting rights present no more risk than adults', but, on the whole, they would result in widespread and systemic advantages for children, societies, and democracies. What is more, children deserve to be treated as a suspect class for discrimination purposes when one considers the long history of adultism around the world. A fundamental human right like voting is evidently denied for such a large class of human beings only because of uncritical adultist assumptions about political competencies and consequences. In the realm of voting rights, absent significantly more compelling evidence against them, children are discriminated against simply because of their age.

8 From Adultism to Childism

Because adultism is normative, it calls for not only the application of existing law but also the more fundamental critique of underlying systems and assumptions. As in the case of voting rights, it is one thing to note discrepancies in law, another to rewrite law from the point of view of those it marginalizes.

---

64 S. Grover et al., 'The Legal Case for Children's Right to Vote in the United States', 31 *The International Journal of Children's Rights* (2023) p. 803.

65 *Juliana v. United States*, 339 F. Supp. 3d 1062 (D. Or. 2018) Decided Oct 15, 2018 (Case No. 6:15-cv-01517-aa, United States District Court for the District of Oregon, Eugene Division Juliana v. United States 947 F.3d 1159 (9th Cir. 2020), p. 34.

This task is especially clear when it comes to voting rights, as it is voters who elect the representatives who write law and policy in the first place. Suffrage movements over history have always had to do more than demand equal protection under the law. They have also had to mount deeper challenges against who is considered a rightful political being and policy-making citizen in the first place. Such is especially the case for children, since being like a child has often functioned as the ultimate trope of second-class citizenship. Responding to adultism cuts at the root of political disempowerment not only for children but for us all.

The effort to rethink social and legal norms in light of childhood can be termed 'childism'.[66] As I and others have defined this concept, childism is analogous to feminism, decolonialism, anti-racism, queer theory, disabilities studies, transhumanism, and other critical theories. Specifically, "[c]hildism offers the needed critical lens for deconstructing adultism across research and societies and reconstructing more age-inclusive scholarly and social imaginations", a lens that aims therefore at "empowering children's experiences of difference to transform larger social norms and systems".[67] If adultism is engrained within law and society's often hidden historical norms, then childism responds by challenging the very languages, cultures, and power structures on

---

66 J. Wall, 'Childhood Studies, Hermeneutics, and Theological Ethics', 86.4 *Journal of Religion* (2006) pp. 523–548; J. Wall 'Human Rights in Light of Childhood', 16.4 *International Journal of Children's Rights* (2008) pp. 523–543; J. Wall, *Ethics in Light of Childhood* (Georgetown University Press, Lanham, MA, 2010); S. Wadsworth 'The Year of the Child: Children's Literature, Childhood Studies, and the Turn to Childism', 27.2 *American Literary History* (2015) pp. 331–341; J. Sundhall, 'A Political Space for Children? The Age Order and Children's Right to Participation', 5.3 *Social Inclusion* (2017) pp. 164–171; J. Wall, 'From Childhood Studies to Childism: Reconstructing the Scholarly and Social Imaginations', 17.6 *Children's Geographies* (2019) pp. 257–270; H. Warming, 'Childism', in D. Cook (ed.), *The SAGE Encyclopedia of Children and Childhood Studies* (SAGE, Thousand Oaks, CA, 2020); T. Biswas and N. Mattheis, 'Strikingly Educational: A Childist Perspective on Children's Civil Disobedience for Climate Justice', 54.2 *Educational Philosophy and Theory* (2021), pp. 145–157; T. Abebe and T. Biswas, 'Rights in Education: Outlines for a Decolonial, Childist Reimagination of the Future', 199 *Fennia – International Journal of Geography* (2021); Childism Institute, <www.childism.org/> [https://perma.cc/YQH6-6LKC]; J. Wall, 'From Childhood Studies to Childism: Reconstructing the Scholarly and Social Imaginations', 20.3 *Children's Geographies* (2022) pp. 257–270; T. Biswas and J. Wall, 'Childist Theory in the Humanities and Social Sciences', 37.4 *Children & Society*, Special Issue on "Childism," ed. T. Biswas and J. Wall, (2023); T. Biswas, 'Becoming good ancestors: A decolonial, childist approach to global intergenerational sustainability', 37.4 *Children & Society* (2023).

67 J. Wall, 'From Childhood Studies to Childism: Reconstructing the Scholarly and Social Imaginations', 17.6 *Children's Geographies* (2019), pp. 257 and 268.

which such norms are built. Third-wave feminists like Judith Butler, Luce Irigaray, and Leslie Heywood called not just for women's equality to men but also for rethinking gender as a social category.[68] Likewise, childism calls for not only children's equality to adults but also for rethinking age in social understandings of equality and politics.

A particularly relevant childist concept when it comes to voting law is the ontological idea that social relations are "deeply interdependent".[69] The traditional adultist assumption is that there is a binary opposition between independent adults and dependent children. This independence-dependence binary has often been used to justify divisions between adults too: landowners over the poor, free men over slaves, men over women, the abled over the disabled, and so on. To construct a group as "dependent" or "child-like" is to justify their second-class citizenship. It is to suggest that they are unfit for the full range of social and political rights and power. However, as children's lived experiences teach especially clearly, no person of any age is simply dependent or independent. Human beings are social creatures who survive and thrive only because they are thoroughly interdependent: socially, culturally, economically, linguistically, familially, historically, biologically, and of course also politically. It is an adultist myth that anyone lives independently of others, even relatively so. Rather, from birth to death, human (and nonhuman) lives gain their possibilities and meanings only through a vast range of close and distant networks of social interdependence.

This point about human interdependence has already been made by feminists such as those above. What childism could be said to add is that social interdependence is 'deep' in the sense of involving both horizontal relationships and vertical inter-reliances.[70] That is, human interdependence means that people are at once both subjects and objects of power: both exercisers

---

68 J. Butler, *Gender Trouble: Feminism and the Subversion of Identity* (Routledge, New York, 1990); L. Irigaray, *An Ethics of Sexual Difference*, trans. C. Burke and G.C. Gill (Cornell University Press, Ithaca, NY, 1993); L. Heywood, *Third Wave Agenda: Being Feminist, Doing Feminism* (University of Minnesota Press, Minneapolis, MN, 1997).

69 J. Josefsson and J. Wall, 'Empowered Inclusion: Theorizing Global Justice for Children and Youth', 17.6 *Globalizations* (2020) pp. 1043–1060.

70 T. Biswas, 'Becoming good ancestors: A decolonial, childist approach to global intergenerational sustainability', 37.4 *Children & Society* (2023); F. Borg and K. Sporre, 'Children's Empowered Inclusion in Early Childhood Education for Sustainability', in S.L. DeZutter (ed.), *International perspectives on educating for democracy in early childhood: recognizing young children as citizens* (Routledge, New York, 2023), pp. 260–278; J. Wall, 'Childism: Transforming Critical Theory in Response to Children', in S. Balagopalan et al. (eds.), *Bloomsbury Handbook of Theories in Childhood Studies* (Bloomsbury, New York, 2023), pp. 208–222.

of power alongside others and reliant on power systems for support. Citizens are 'subjects' in both senses of the term: subjects of polities and subject to them. Children rely on others and societies for care, economic support, learning, and so on. But equally, adults rely on others and societies for work, protections, being heard, and much else. People depend on each other in many different ways, but no one is simply 'dependent' overall. Rather, childism suggests that the binary opposition of independence and dependence is not a social reality but a form of prejudice used to maintain adultist structures of power.

Take again the case of rights to vote. For various historical reasons, voting is currently assumed to express voters' competent, free, and individual independence.[71] Before the onset of the adult franchise about a century ago, with the inclusion of women, voting was understood quite differently. When voting was restricted to wealthy landowning men at the dawn of modern democracies, voters were assumed to represent not only themselves as individuals but also their dependent families and tenants. Even when all men starting in the 19th century started gaining suffrage, they were understood to vote on behalf of their wives and children as well. It is now clear that such an arrangement is unjust and undemocratic, since it assumes that one segment of the population can speak politically on behalf of another. Such an arrangement clearly marginalizes social differences. The solution to this problem was to grant the franchise to women, which transformed the very notion of voting from an act performed in part on behalf of families to an act performed independently.

However, as we have seen, this normative construction of democracy has justified the continued and unfortunate disenfranchisement of children. It enshrines the assumption that only adults can vote with fully responsible independence. Childism makes it possible to see that voting is neither a representation of dependent persons by independent ones, as in the past, nor a representation of independent persons simply, as in the present. Rather, it needs to be reconstructed as a representation of deep interdependence, that is, of both difference and interconnectedness. Voting is properly understood as an act undertaken both on one's own behalf and on behalf of others. The right to vote is a right to be included as both an object and a subject in an inter-reliant political network.

---

71 D. Runciman, 'The Paradox of Political Representation', 15.1 *Journal of Political Philosophy* (2007), pp. 93–114; C. López-Guerra, *Democracy and Disenfranchisement: The Morality of Electoral Exclusions* (Oxford University Press, New York, 2014); J. Wall, 'Democratizing Democracy: The Road from Women's to Children's Suffrage', 18.6 *International Journal of Human Rights*, Special Issue, ed. S. Grover (2014), pp. 646–659.

9 Childist Voting Rights in Practice

Concretely speaking, there would be many ways of practicing voting rights along such childist lines. My own proposal is that age-inclusive suffrage could be achieved by means of a new imagination of voting rights for all as a 'proxy-claim' right to vote.[72] Currently, voting rights are not claimed by the electorate but granted by governments, usually at age eighteen. A proxy-claim right to vote, in contrast, would belong to everyone from birth to death. Every citizen would have a 'proxy' right to vote that is exercised on their behalf by their legal guardian, which, however, every citizen would have the right to 'claim' to exercise on their own behalf whenever they so desire. The proxy side of such a voting right ensures that anyone dependent on others for political representation is not thereby denied democratic power. Most likely this would include infants, young children, adults with severe cognitive disabilities, persons with incapacitating health conditions, older adults with dementia, and other groups. In many countries this would mean a proxy vote for roughly 20 per cent of the population, 10 per cent children and 10 per cent adults. The claim side of such a voting right ensures that anyone with the minimum needed ability could, if they liked, exercise their voting right on their own behalf. The right to claim your vote would not rest on achieving some predetermined age. Rather, it would rest, as argued above, on the simple desire to vote.

Such a proxy-claim system of voting would overcome the problem of systemic adultist discrimination in contemporary voting law. It does not simply extend existing adultist constructions of voting rights to children, as if an independence-only voting practice could include children adequately. Merely extending individual voting rights to children would leave the youngest of children, as well as adults who cannot vote independently, even more politically marginalized than they are now. The more fundamental restructuring proposed here reflects the social reality of every citizen's deep interdependence. The proxy side recognizes that citizenship involves reliance on one another; and the claim side recognizes that it nevertheless involves the representation of differences. Most countries already have proxy voting for incapacitated and elderly adults (as well in some cases for adults traveling abroad or in the military); there is no reason it should not be extended also to younger children. Older children would be able to claim their right to vote on their

---

72 J. Wall, *Give Children the Vote: On Democratizing Democracy* (Bloomsbury, New York, 2022).

own behalf whenever they, and not their guardians or governments, wished to do so.

This new understanding of the right to vote brings to bear a deepened normative perspective that can overcome the contradictions found above in international suffrage law. In terms of the UHDR and ICCPR, it would resolve the ambiguity of explicitly demanding "universal and equal" suffrage while implicitly tolerating only adult suffrage. The proxy side of a proxy-claim vote would make universal and equal suffrage a reality for the large number of both children and adults who for one reason or another are unable to vote on their own behalf. In terms of the CRC, a new interpretation of voting would redress its discriminatory potential for denying children's human rights in the name of affirming them. Proxy-claim voting would ensure that the freedoms of expression guaranteed in Articles 12 and 13 really do apply to "all matters affecting the child" and that they truly recognize the right to "impart information and ideas of all kinds" without undue restriction. Mere dependency on others in specific economic and emotional respects is not a reason for being denied political representation. On the contrary, as CRC Article 2 could be understood to suggest, no limitation of rights should discriminate against children simply because they are children. If voting rights should not discriminate by gender, ethnicity, race, class, or other factors, for the same reasons neither should they discriminate by age.

However structured in practice, an age-inclusive right to vote illustrates the point that age discrimination is socially normative and so ultimately calls for transforming the underlying systems in which it is rooted. Existing voting rights are not only enshrined in law but also representative of a deeper adultistic logic. The age discrimination involved demands a childist response that can not only change law but also build new normative imaginations. Proxy-claim voting sounds necessarily peculiar because voting systems have not been imagined to include children fully as children. The same profound shift, however, also sounded strange when other discriminated against groups like women, minorities, and the poor gained suffrage as well. The work of overcoming normative discrimination involves a difficult struggle with entrenched power systems.

10 Conclusion

The problem of age discrimination against children is consequently profound. It concerns more than just children's occasional denial of respect or rights. Rather, age discrimination is the expression of a normatively systemic adultism. It is written into the fabric of historical and contemporary societies, politics, and laws. As the case of children's voting rights makes especially clear, age discrimination against children rests on a largely invisible groundwork of unquestioned assumptions. The continued denial of suffrage to children, even after it has been extended to every other major group, reflects adultistic/paternalistic prejudices against children as a class. By recognizing the problem as one of normative age discrimination, it is possible to see that children are being denied a fundamental human right without reasonable grounds. Above all, addressing age discrimination against children calls upon both children and adults to question what appears normal and settled in society and even law in order to imagine what is truly equal and just.

CHAPTER 6

Decolonizing Age Discrimination against Children in Intergenerational Relationships: Alternative Generationing and Generativities

Lucia Rabello de Castro

Abstract

The aim of this chapter is to discuss how discrimination against children in the CRC is couched in terms of an age episteme which naturalizes and essentializes age power differentials between adults and children. Such a normalization of social positions based on age ensues the superiority of adults over children legitimating intergenerational relations of domination and discrimination against children. A critique of the age episteme is forwarded in order to deconstruct the underpinnings of age classifications which imply a specific teleology of human subjectivity geared to the attainment of instrumental rationality as a universal way to be human. The age episteme plays an important role in developmental paradigms which have grounded claims to civilize and subordinate, not only children, but also nations. This paper argues for other possible ways to generate the child and the adult in intergenerational relationships. Based on empirical data it is argued how the irrevocable interconnectedness and interdependence among generations can generate alternative ways of intergenerational solidarity that eschew the prejudiced and exclusionary relationships among children and adults based on age.

1 Introduction

Intergenerational relationships foreground the impasses of how modern societies deal with social change and permanence. Modern generations of children and youth have been regarded as potentially cultural and moral reservoirs of society's progress,[1] embodiments of an open, indeterminate and better future to be eventually achieved[2] as well as the promising continuation of

1 K. Mannheim, *The Problem of Generations. Essays in the Sociology of Knowledge* (Routledge and Kegan Paul, London, 1952 [1928]).

2 E. Erikson (ed.), *The Challenge of Youth* (Anchor Books, New York, 1965).

novel revolutionary ideals.[3] In this vein, children and youth have often embodied change as a promise, and an indicator, of cultural and social evolution. However, at stake also lies the concern that the openness and the indeterminacy of the future should be pursued in alignment with the values that older generations cherish and deem important. Both the modern educational institutions as well as the legal-juridical apparatus of modern societies are supposed to ensure that such indeterminacy of the future can be regulated. Thus, children and youth stand as the targets which summon up the special endeavours of educational and legal-juridical institutions, the former responsible to transmit and preserve a society's cultural legacy, and the latter to control the incommensurate ways whereby novelties can deviate from what is positivized as right.

The Convention of the Rights of the Child (CRC) of 1989, approved by the General Assembly of the United Nations and its worldwide signatories, addresses States Parties in their obligations towards what is considered the rights of children. It consists of both a movement towards ensuring dignity for the less powerful, but also of normatizing the scope and the nature of adults' actions towards children. However, it is to be noted that across the entire document of the CRC the term 'adult(s)' is mentioned only twice – articles 37 and 42 – whilst the term 'parent(s)' appears in numerous articles. This fact conveys the conception that *the child* should be straightforwardly regarded as part of a kin structure – the modern family – but with limited social, political and juridical status herself as a social category. Children are then signified as the others of parents, rather than of adults in CRC. Thus, despite being referred to as children, they are familialized[4] as sons or daughters which is the positionality that is recurrently evoked in the legal text to the formulation and assignment of rights. In this sense, the particular position of the child in the CRC is articulated with the ways that adult-child intergenerational relationships are conceptualized as foremost familial ones. This aspect somewhat contradicts Hafen's[5] claim and concern that the CRC embraces the notion of

3 X. Xu, 'Chairman Mao's Child: Sparkling Red Star and the Construction of Children in Chinese Cultural Revolution', 36:4 *Children's Literature Association Quarterly* (2011) pp. 381–409.

4 For the concept of 'familialization' *see*, J. Qvortrup, 'Nine Theses about 'Childhood as a Social Phenomenon'', in J. Qvortrup (ed.), *Childhood as a Social Phenomenon: Lessons from an International Project* (The European Centre for Social Welfare Policy and Research, Vienna, 1993).

5 B. Hafen and J. Hafen, 'Abandoning children to their autonomy: The United Nations Convention on the Rights of the Child', 37:2 *Harvard International Law Journal* (1996) pp. 449–491.

the autonomy of the child to the point of abandoning children to themselves. Rather, the issue points to the limitations present in the CRC concerning how the conceptual autonomy of the child subject – her singular personality – is foregrounded mostly in child-parent terms, and not in terms of child-adult relationships at large.

In modern societies, intergenerational solidarity is guaranteed by prescribed norms of behaviour, a set of obligations to be undertaken by States and their adult citizens. The Convention of the Rights of the Child states obligations of the older generation so that the adequate provision care and protection of the young are ensured. Furthermore, in Article 2, protection should aim to ban all forms of discrimination, such as race, gender, disability, colour, sex, language, religion, political or other opinion, national, ethnic or social origin, property and status. However, such a legalistic encoding of the older generation's appropriate attitudes and duties toward the younger overlooked the adult bias concealed in the intergenerational power relations of the new solidarity pact announced by CRC. As Daly, Thorburn Stern and Leviner[6] have shown, over and above the multifarious discriminations against children, they face discriminations *qua* children, on account of being children. Contradictorily enough, and despite advances in the construction of legal frameworks for children's rights, being a child constitutes itself a condition that is evocative of discredit, if not, exclusion, rejection and discrimination. In this sense, one can wonder how solidarity and reciprocity bonds between generations fare in societies where children do not have the respect of adults, even if their legal rhetoric implies intergenerational care and provision. Or still, when adults do not support children as equals, what are the effects of generational non-reciprocity on the construction and the development of the goods of a society towards its conservation and renewal?

In this chapter I will examine age discrimination against children as it is effected in intergenerational relationships of modern societies equipped with legal instruments, such as the CRC and the national codes that were elaborated as a consequence of it, which should supposedly ban all forms of discrimination against children. It does not seem a coincidence that Article 2 of CRC has not listed age as one form of discrimination, and one can wonder how, for adults, even those acting on behalf of children, it is difficult to ascertain the 'blind spots' that veil relationships of prejudice, hostility, exclusion

6 A. Daly et al., 'UN Convention on the Rights of the Child, Article 2 and Discrimination on the basis of Childhood: the CRC paradox?', 91:3 *Nordic Journal of International Law* (2022) pp. 419–452.

and discrimination towards children. Thus, ageism[7] has been referred to as a form of ill-treatment of children based on prerogatives of a given superiority of adults, irrespective of context, situation, time and history. Adultism[8] can be conceived as a form of ageism, once age becomes the basis of discrimination – a normative systemic discrimination – which structures societies around the opposition of empowered adults on one side and disempowered children on the other. Moreover, the familial conception of the autonomy of the child embraced by the CRC favours a vision of the child as a privatized subject whose limited scope of action in the domestic sphere is viewed mainly in relation with her parents. I will argue that a critique of age and the epistemology that underpins this concept becomes a necessary step not only to enhance the advances of legal rights to children, but also, to move towards more fair and convivial intergenerational relationships between children and adults at large. Both the CRC and national codes on children's rights, like the Brazilian *Estatuto da Criança e do Adolescente* (Child and Adolescent Statute), are underpinned by criteria of age to establish both what is a child and what he/she is entitled to. However, as I argue here, age criteria were elaborated and established in the scope of the modern episteme of science, development and colonization/civilization that allowed the hierarchization of peoples, nations and cultures. It established and naturalized the hierarchical position of dominance and superiority of adults over children.[9] Therefore, a critique of age becomes imperative to deconstruct a legal order based on this notion which, despite its apparently neutral objectivity, veils a specific teleology of human life that posits the attainment of a specific rationality normalized as universal and human specific.[10] Modern intergenerational relationships have been

---

7 J. C. Westman, 'Juvenile ageism: Unrecognized prejudice and discrimination against the young', 21 *Child Psych Hum Dev* (1991) pp. 237–256. <https://doi.org/10.1007/BF00705929>; K. King, 'Exploring age-based oppression: ageism, adultism and their potential interactions', 22(1) *Taboo* (2024) pp. 71–85.

8 *See* J. Wall, in this volume.

9 A. Nandy, 'Reconstructing childhood: a critique of the ideology of adulthood', In A. Singh and S. Mohapatra (eds.), *Indian Political Thought* (Routledge, New York, 2010) pp. 203–214.

10 Different critiques with regards to modern scientific rationality can be found in feminist scholarship (*see*, for instance, D. Haraway, *Simians, Cyborgs and Women. The Reinvention of Nature*, Routledge, New York, 1990), anti-colonial scholarship (*see*, for instance, S. Wynter, 'Unsettling the Coloniality of Being/Power/Truth/Freedom: Towards the Human, After Man, Its Overrepresentation – An Argument', 3.3 *CR: The New Centennial Review*, 2003, pp. 257–337), and postcolonial scholarship (*see*, for instance, A. Bilgrami, 'Gandhi, Newton and the Enlightenment,' In A. Singhand and S. Mohapatra (eds.), *Indian Political Thought*, Routledge, London, 2010, pp. 163–174).

structured around the unproblematized power relationships and the superior knowledge of adults/parents in relation to children based on age differences which reinforce systemic intergenerational inequalities.

So, if we are going to move forward from intergenerational relations based on the index of age – which has established a 'biological truth' that underpins and legitimates age power differentials, we must inquire what sort of intergenerational relationships are otherwise possible. Based on two empirical case studies with Brazilian children and adolescents, I will discuss the agonistic construction of alternative intergenerational grammars and new generativities[11] when adults and children/adolescents struggle against established intergenerational practices which doom children to silencing and social and political invisibility. One case study discusses the political movement of school occupations by secondary students in Brazil which shows how students dispute with elders their ascribed position of inferiority that is constantly fixed on them and are able to act politically informed by their own situated perspectives. On the other hand, students are also able to establish alliances with some groups of adults, based on shared political and ethical values. The other case study discusses the collective movements of children in their demands for playtime at school. Notwithstanding their doubts about their capacities, children were able to construct their singular points of view on the need for playtime at school, materializing their claims for fairness and reciprocity in expressive and artistic ways rather than deploying well thought rational arguments. Children were thus able to establish dialogue with incredulous adults and sensitize them about the fairness of their demands. These two empirical case studies instigate us to think about other possible ethical and political arrangements between generations, and most specifically between children and other adults outside the family. These examples urge us to decolonize the cornerstones of the hierarchically positioned age superiority of adults/parents, leading to age discrimination, and envisage new generativities between the young and the old based on values such as the search for justice, equality and solidarity between generations.[12]

---

11 H. Wydra, 'Generations of Memory: Elements of a Conceptual Framework', 60(1) *Comparative Studies in Society and History* (2018) pp. 5–34.

12 E.B. Weiss, 'In fairness to our children: international law and intergenerational equity', 2 Childhood (1994) pp. 22–27.

2 Age as a Foundational Epistemology of the Superiority of Adults over Children

It is important to observe that in the CRC the term 'age' appears in the very first article of the convention to define what a child is. Thus, age becomes the sole and paramount criterion to distinguish a child in its difference from its others (parents). Furthermore, in article 12, the notion of age is signified as maturity in a clear reference to the assumption of children's 'lack of maturity'. In many different articles (31, 32, 37, 38 and 40) references to age in the CRC point to the same understanding of the child's lack of capacity or maturity.

The question that must be asked is how the notion of age came to be enshrined as a universal parameter of individual's capacities in our present societies so that its use in legal texts seems incontrovertible. Age has been deployed as a seemingly self-evident index of divisions and characterizations to classify cognitive, emotional and moral capacities. It has been deployed to define the child in scholarship,[13] professional practice,[14] legal texts and ordinary child-adult relationships. In daily life, adults use age as a rule of thumb to understand and decide about what children should and should not do, to forbid and authorize them, and to reproach or celebrate their actions and behaviours, a quantifiable and universal index of children's level of understanding and overall capacity. The label of 'childish' attached to a child's behaviour is often pejoratively invoked whenever children deceptively show attitudes and behaviours below what is perceived to be their chronological age. The legal system of modern societies, as noted above, reverberates conventional wisdom recurring to age to define individual's autonomy, rights and duties. In present modern societies parameters of moral agency and legal responsibility are couched in age cutting points. For instance, age comes to define thresholds of criminal responsibility, of civic participation in elections and of individual autonomy and choice to wander about without anyone's consent, even if such fixed age thresholds have been subject to scholar interrogation.[15] The criterion

13 B. Thorne, 'Theorizing age and other differences', 11:4 *Childhood* (2004) pp. 403–408; B. Thorne, 'What's in an age name?', 15:4 *Childhood* (2008) pp. 435–439.

14 G. Mantle et al., 'Establishing Children's Wishes and Feelings for Family Court Reports. The significance attached to the age of the child', 13:4 *Childhood* (2006) pp. 499–518.

15 For instance, *see*, K. Hanson, 'Editorial – Children's Participation and Agency when they don't 'do the right thing'', 23:4 *Childhood* (2016) pp. 471–475; S.E. Merry, 'Relating to the Subject of Human Rights: The Culture of Agency in Human Rights Discourse', in M. Freeman and D. Napier (eds.), *Law and Anthropology* (Oxford University Press, Oxford, 2009) pp. 385–407.

of age has become what authorizes the entrance of adolescents into the brave new world of paid work, licensed drugs and unaccountable sex. Age has thus established an entrenched episteme that essentializes what children are, or can be, in the sense of defining their limited abilities in relation to adults which leads to differential positions of capacity and power.[16]

The age episteme calls for problematization, once its supposedly universality veils its historical conditions of production – European modernity. The notion of age emerges in the historical context of an 'enlightened' vision of the human subject whose instrumental rationality was to prevail over her own passions and the 'more-than-human-world'.[17] Such rational competence was to be acquired through the process of education along a progressive and scalar temporality[18] when the future is seen as indeterminate,[19] thus demanding early modelling of individual assets and capacities. This very process of ascertaining and evaluating progressive abilities posited what these should be, legitimating thus a view of human-ness as the uni-dimensional development and attainment of instrumental rational capacities and autonomy.[20] In this vein, the episteme of age has also forwarded a politics of age whereby asymmetries in the distribution of cognitive, moral, social and political competences came to be connected with social power according to an age hierarchization. Adults' abilities and competences, defined by what Wynter called the Man Structure[21] – embodied by the white, European, bourgeois adult male – provided the end state towards which human-ness should tend to.

At the backdrop of such an age epistemology lies modern societies' perspective of progress which, as Koselleck[22] and others have pointed out, has, since the 18th century, provided a conceptual framework for changes both

16 L. R. de Castro, 'Age epistemology and the politics of age', In C. Baraldi and L. R. de Castro (eds.) *Global Childhoods in International Perspective: Universality, Diversity and Inequalities*, Sage Studies in International Sociology (Sage, London, 2020), pp. 33–50.

17 M.P. Bellacasa, *Matters of Care: Speculative ethics in more than human worlds.* (University of Minnesota Press, Minneapolis, 2017).

18 J. Piaget, *Seis Estudos de Psicologia,* (Forense, Rio de Janeiro, 1971).

19 A. Rénaut, *La libération des enfants* (Hachette, Paris, 2002).

20 J. Broughton, 'Piaget's Structural Developmental Psychology. Knowledge without a Self and without History', 24 *Hum. Dev.* (1981) pp. 320–346; J. Henriques et al., *Changing the Subject. Psychology, Social Regulation and Subjectivity* (Routledge, London, 1984); J. Morss, *Growing Critical. Alternatives to Developmental Psychology* (Routledge, London, 1996).

21 S. Wynter, 'Unsettling the Coloniality of Being/Power/Truth/Freedom: Towards the Human, after Man, its Over-representation. An Argument', 3:3 *CR – The New Centennial Review,* (2003) pp. 257–337.

22 R. Koselleck, *Historias de conceptos* (Ed. Trotta, Madrid, 2012).

epochal and biographical. Accordingly, there is a direction in human history towards evolution and improvement which is continuous and steady even if minor throwbacks can take place. The focus on ontogenetic changes conduced inevitably to an interest in the child – as the baseline of human ontogenetic development. Ontogeny performed the progressive nature of human development investigated by early psychologists, like A. Gesell[23] and C. Buhler[24], and later by Jean Piaget, captivated by the neatness of the model to explain human change as regular patterns of increasing complexity along biographical time. At the cornerstone of such a model lay a linearly sequential and cumulative conception of temporality which organized the transformative processes of individuals, species and societies as improved patterns of ability and performance as time goes by. On one side, the concept of chronological age, constructed as an individual scale starting at point zero (birth), organized the timing of human changes teleologically ordered towards its apex, adult rationality; on the other, the great epochal historical stages depicted the progressive development of western civilisation, from barbarism to the Enlightenment. Peters summarizes: "I take it as axiomatic that, in talking about development, there must be *a prior conception of the end-product* and that the processes which contribute to it must be sequential".[25] Following Jean Piaget, he sees the end-product as the acquisition of rationality and autonomy – inherited as human specific – to be adequately accomplished, it is admitted, with correct environmental stimuli.

Children, as those beings whose capacities are not still what they ought to be, became depicted as subjects of *evolving capacities,* a conception embodied in Article 5 of the CRC. Lansdown notes that children do not acquire competencies merely as a consequence of age, although he acknowledges that "age is widely assumed as a proxy for competence", and that "...it is impossible to discount the concept of phases altogether ... there is clear evidence of biologically based universality in children's physical development".[26]

Age differentiation in western modernity has underscored adults' peculiarities as a complete and final state of socialization and humanness in detriment of children's attributed imperfect and transient competencies as part of a the-

23 A. Gesell, *Infancy and Human Growth* (MacMillan, New York, 1928).

24 C. Buhler, *From Birth to Maturity* (Routledge and Kegan Paul, London, 1935[1951]).

25 R. Peters, 'The development of reason', In S. Modgil and C. Modgil (eds.), *Toward a Theory of Psychological Development* (NFER Publ., Windsor, 1980), pp. 40–67.

26 G. Lansdown, *The Evolving Capacities of the Child* (UNICEF/Save the Children, Florence, 2005).

ory of progress whereby an adult ideology came to be enforced.[27] Positive laws, and also the CRC, are constructed on the basis of this model of human differentiation assuming the age scale as a non-problematical indicator of social, moral and cognitive competence. Thus, the universalized use of age scales has led to an in-built prejudiced view of the child, as well as of the adult, leading to fixed ways of inter-relationality between adults and children that is also present in legal texts.

CRC and other legal texts have assumed age as an unproblematic concept in the definition of what is maturity and competence. Underpinning the notion of subjectivity thus endorsed lie concepts such as individual autonomy, agency, cognitive and moral independence which have been critiqued as they stand as substantive evolving attributes of *individuals* not allowing for relational perspectives of human subjectivity. Butler[28] has insisted on the notions of human precarity, vulnerability and suffering to indicate a new social ontology of the human subject in which human subjectivities can be conceived as a *set of active interrelationships, assemblages.* Such a way to understand the human presence in the world entails an 'ethics of co-inhabitation' and interdependence. This and other theories of human subjectivity which foreground interdependence as one of its constitutive aspects, should challenge the conception of the human subject present in CRC which puts on opposite sides, the developing immature child and the cognizant superior adult.

3 A Critique of Age and Its Far-Reaching Multi-scale Program of Domination

Development and progress have been widely critiqued as the basis of an explanatory model both of historical[29] and biographical changes[30] where the concept of age has played such a formidable role in the latter. If we assume that children differ from adults – which is a rather uncontroversial point – the crucial point lies in determining by what criteria they differ, and how these differences come to be differentially valued. So far, the rationale has been to

27 Nandy, *supra* note 9.

28 J. Butler (ed.), *Vulnerability in Resistance* (Duke University Press, Durham, 2016); J. Butler, *Precarious Life: The Powers of Mourning and Justice* (Verso, London, 2020).

29 A. Escobar, *Encountering Development* (Princeton University Press, Princeton, 1995).

30 J. Morss, *Growing Critical. Alternatives to Developmental Psychology* (Routledge, London, 1996).

account for, and legitimate, children's less economic, social and political power in terms of age, and concomitantly, their lesser abilities.

The view that the beginning of human life is emptied and devoid of any substantive or relevant disposition has raised quite different appraisals both from philosophical and empirical sides. H. Bergson[31] has long ago noted that it is in childhood that lies a whole range of human possibilities that are acted out as if one could play different personalities at the same time. As one grows old, choices have to be made that constrict, and impoverish, human life: one is gradually reduced to being one sole subject, owner of one sole life, as Bergson puts it. In the same vein, following H. Michaux, Charbonnier[32] notes that children disclose an enormous privilege vis à vis other life phases: being strangers in the world nothing is given or evident for them, what constitutes in itself a most potent ethical horizon for human action. Similarly, arguing from the perspective of empirical studies with babies, the long-standing work of D. Stern[33] has shown the intense, rich and complex forms of vitality that make up the lives of infants from the very start, a picture quite at odds with the view that presents it as asocial and emptied. Some of these initial capabilities, many of them quite unknown by an adult-centred society, show that infants and small children dispose of different and complex ways of subject-object relationship and that this primary intersubjectivity is impregnated by a unique and dense body-affect-sensory experience[34] that is lost in adulthood.

The notion of a univocal sequential temporality underpinning the human differentiation process seals children's destiny towards one form of being a human adult in westernized societies. Furthermore, the linear temporality of the age scale has conformed a rigid separation of beings, so that if one is a child, one cannot be an adult. Intermingling states and ambiguity of beings become a logical aberration, thus the difficulty to think of the adult as not the child yet, as pointed out by Charbonnier, or that children and adults are not opposite states or beings[35] and that they have more in common than they differ.

It must be underscored that what is at stake here is *one specific model of the human adult subject* characterized by the individual's instrumental rationality

---

31 H. Bergson, *Oeuvres* (PUF, Paris, 1959).

32 S. Charbonnier, 'La conquête de l'enfance: uchronie de l'émancipation', In A. Kerlan and L. Loeffel (eds.), *Repenser l'enfance?* (Hermann, Paris, 2012) pp. 219–230.

33 D. Stern, *The Interpersonal World of the Infant* (Basic Books, New York, 2000); D. Stern, *Forms of Vitality* (Oxford University Press, Oxford, 2010).

34 T. Ogden, *The Primitive Edge of Experience* (Jason Aronson, Northvale, 1989).

35 P. Alderson, *Childhoods Real and Imagined,* vol. 1, (Routledge, London, 2013).

and her individual autonomy to choose which foregrounds a vision of human completeness based on a fiction of adulthood that is both derogative of the differential humanness of children and, in fact, in disaccord with real adults' demonstrated capacities to choose what is rational and morally good. Age markers and the episteme they presuppose, biased by an adultist ideology,[36] have for long been used to constrict the view about human-ness, and its infinite forms to materialize its universality,[37] into a progressive scale towards instrumental rationality and autonomous self-sufficiency. This has led to the maintenance of social, economic and political inequities between generations based on the differential social power attached to the adult and the child social positions. The internationally-validated legal framework of children's rights, the CRC, is based on essentialized differences between the adult and the child imbued by humanitarian advocacy and motivation to protect children. In this way, international provisions to forbid child labour and employment (art. 32), child participation in armed conflicts (art. 38) and 'inadequate' recreational activities (art. 31) are made considering that children, by themselves, are incapable to decide about these matters. However, as Hanson and Nieuwenhuys[38] point out international legislation of children's rights is locally translated by children and their social networks who must make sense of very abstract and often not locally sensitive norms in order to assimilate them into their already established values and moral economies. Frequently, what children see as what is right and fair to them does not comply with the top-down rules of international legislation conceived in distant metropolitan centres.

Recently, a critique of the development/progress paradigm – which substantiates the construction of age as an unequivocal index of human capacity – has been provided by decolonial scholarship[39] which has pointed out the relationship between the supremacist and martial perspective of the 'enlightened' vision of the human subject and its desire to dominate, conquer and

---

36 J. Wall, 'Childism: Transforming Critical Theory in Response to Children', in S. Balagopalan et al. (eds.), *The Bloomsbury Handbook of Theories in Childhood Studies* (Bloomsbury, London, 2024) pp. 208–222.

37 A. Sekyi-Otu, *Left Universalism, Africacentric Essays* (Routledge, New York, 2019).

38 K. Hanson and O. Nieuwenhuys, 'Living Rights, Social Justice, Translations', in K. Hanson and O. Nieuwenhuys (eds.), *Reconceptualizing Children's Rights in International Development: Living Rights, Social Justice, Translations* (Cambridge University Press, Cambridge, 2016) pp. 3–25.

39 W. Mignolo, 'The decolonial option', In C. Walsh and W. Mignolo (eds.), *On Decoloniality: concepts, analytics, praxis* (Duke Univ. Press, Durham, 2018) pp. 103–226; A. Dirlik, 'Developmentalism: A Critique', 16:1 *Interventions: International Journal of Postcolonial Studies* (2014) pp. 1–20.

colonize. The 'rational ego' who knows over and above, and from a supposedly 'universal vantage point',[40] equals the 'conqueror ego' who knows what is best for his inferior others – children for example, colonized peoples, Blacks, women and so on. Decolonial theorists have underscored how such an idealized vision of the subjectivity has favoured extractivist imperial relationships among nations from the 16th century onwards whereby colonized people, mainly of the Southern regions of the world, were seen as those *others* to be civilized, protected and developed. This process of colonization bore the downgrading of the others' cultures, languages and modes of existence, together with the inculcation of the belief of universal (and better) modes of knowledge and being.[41] In this sense decolonial theory has highlighted how colonization stands as the 'darker side of European Modernity'[42] since, in the name of civilization, Christianization and progress, many and different forms of oppression, inferiorization and cruel treatment have been legitimated. Thus, the notions of development/progress and civilization have served as legitimating narratives for the construction of the modern world system from a European vantage point, where colonial peoples, first of America, and later of Asia and Africa, came to signify their own selves and cultures, as *different and inferior*. Thus, development narratives have curbed both nations' future trajectories and children's alternative self-projects providing an overarching multi-scale binding program of domination, both of countries as well as of the younger generations.

In many indigenous social groups in Brazil[43] children's social position is vital to how these societies can secure their collective existence. For instance, among the Guarani and Kayapó's groups, who believe that children's beings are still ambiguously placed in-between this world and the world of spirits, children are those who, by virtue of being somewhat *other*, are most capable of mediating social contacts with the non-indigenous, the gods, or even, the enemies.[44] Thus, in these groups, it is through children's capacities, *not ages that demarcate their incapacities*, that the group's sociability with others is socially regulated and cosmologies of world transformation are played out.

40 S. Castro-Gómez, 'Ciencias sociales, violencia epistémica y el problema de la 'invención del otro'', In E. Lander (ed.), *La Colonialidad del saber: eurocentrismo y ciencias sociales* (Ciccus/Clacso, Buenos Aires, 2011) pp. 163–180.

41 V.Y. Mudimbe, *The invention of Africa* (Indiana University Press, Bloomington, 1988).

42 W. Mignolo, *Local Histories/Global Designs. Coloniality, Subaltern Knowledges and Border Thinking* (Princeton Univ. Press, Princeton, 2000).

43 A.L. Silva et al. (eds.), *Crianças Indígenas. Ensaios Antropológicos* (Fapesp/Global, São Paulo, 2002).

44 A. Tassinari. 'Concepções indígenas de infância no Brasil', 7:13 *Tellus* (2007) pp. 11–25.

Colonization, and its long-lasting structures of domination and hierarchization of peoples and cultures, named as coloniality,[45] have ensured the maintenance of economic and political inequalities among nations, much in the same way that age, through its long-lasting ideology – ageism, or adultism – has ensured that adults take themselves as superior beings relative to children. In this vein, it is also time to question the legal frameworks of our modern liberal societies, based on this over-represented ideal of the human subjectivity – the sovereign, rational, autonomous individual – with regards to its straightforward alignment with a logic of human hierarchization and domination.

4 Alternative Generational Ethics and Politics in the Contemporary World

Ageism/adultism consists of practices of discrimination against children sealing a kind of intergenerational bond pregnant with prejudice and domination. The field of Childhood Studies[46] consolidated since the 80's performed a major role towards de- and reconstructing the conceptualization of childhood and children and their role in society establishing a new paradigm for the social sciences in this area of studies. During these almost fifty years of social science scholarship on childhood it is now undoubtedly a truism to affirm that the child is a social actor that contributes effectively to the configuration of our society, to its destiny and its transformations. However, not so obvious are developments in the field that discuss and posit that children have a share in the economic division of labour of modern societies which is performed through school work;[47] or that, children's suffrage can contribute to improve

45 A. Quijano, 'Colonialidad del poder, eurocentrismo y América Latina', in E. Lander (ed.), *La colonialidad del saber* (Ciccus/Clacso, Buenos Aires, 2011) pp. 219–264.

46 There are too many important and seminal works that forwarded the main conceptual and theoretical framework of the field, but to quote a few of them: A. James and A. Prout (eds.), *Constructing and Reconstructing Childhood* (The Falmer Press, London, 1990); A. James et al. (eds.), *Theorizing Childhood* (Polity, Cambridge, 2004); C. Jenks, *Childhood* (Routledge, London, 2005); W. Corsaro, *The Sociology of Childhood* (Pine Forge Press, Thousand Oaks, 1997); J. Qvortrup (ed.), *Childhood as a Social Phenomenon: lessons from an International Project* (European Centre for Social Welfare Policy and Research, Vienna, 1993); J. Qvortrup et al. (eds.), *The Palgrave Handbook of Childhood Studies* (Palgrave Macmillan, London, 2009).

47 J. Qvortrup (ed.), *Childhood Matters. Social Theory, Practice and Politics* (Avesbury, Aldershot, 1994); H. Wintersberger, 'Costs and Benefits – The Economics of Childhood', in J. Qvortrup (ed.) *Childhood Matters* (Avesbury, Aldershot, 1994) pp. 213–247.

our present perishing democracies and refresh the ethical basis of social conviviality;[48] or that, the transformative potential of education and its institutions depends on acknowledging and undertaking the co-partnership and collaboration of children themselves[49] to quote just a few examples. In this sense, despite advances in social theorizing about childhood, social practices, including those inspired by legal texts, such as the CRC, still cling to outdated repertoires of thinking, feeling and relating to children that are resilient to change.

Children and youth, on their part, have often taken a prominent role in changing their own conditions of existence that are deemed unfair and harmful standing up to struggle and claim for a different society in many parts of the world. The conventional image of the docile student who learns and acquiesces to adult authority has been superseded by the multifarious children's activisms in the social, cultural and political arenas that have foregrounded children's engagements to change the status quo. Twum-Danso Imoh[50] relates the major role that children took in the Soweto uprising, South Africa, long ago as 1976, where many of them were killed; Cordero-Arce, Liebel and Kattan[51] discuss the struggles of Latin American children organized in labour movements demanding their rights to work with dignity which is essential to their own and their family survival; the extensive work of Alderson[52] in

48 J. Wall (ed.), *Exploring children's suffrage: interdisciplinary perspectives on ageless voting.* (Palgrave Macmillan, New York, 2022); J. Wall et al., 'The health and well-being case for children's suffrage', 8 *Lancet Child Adolesceent Health* (2024) <https://doi.org/10.1016/S2352-4642(24)00020-8>; A.G. Ferreira Jr, *Ferenczi e Winnicott. Uma leitura psicanalítica e descolonial sobre a confusão e a invenção de línguas entre adultos e crianças* (Appris, Curitiba, 2022).

49 T. Abebe, 'Refusals for liberating childhood from the trap of schooling?', 30:2 *Childhood* (2023) pp. 109–115; T. Abebe and T. Biswas, 'Rights *in* education: outlines for a decolonial, childist reimagination of the future- commentary to Ansell and colleagues', 199:1 *Fennia. International Journal of Geography* (2021); L. R. de Castro et al., *Falatório: Participação e democracia na escola* (Contracapa/Faperj, Rio de Janeiro, 2010); J. Nair (ed.), *Uncommon Schooling* (Orient Blackswan, Telangana, 2022).

50 A. Twum-Danso Imoh, 'Adults in Charge: The Limits of Formal Child Participatory Processes for Societal Transformation', in B. Sandin et al. (eds.), *The Politics of Children's Rights and Representation* (Palgrave Macmillan, London, 2023) pp. 59–80.

51 M. Cordero-Arce, 'Who is (to be) the Subject of Children's Rights?', In S. Spyrou et al. (eds.), *Re-imagining Child Studies* (Bloomsbury Academic, London, 2019) pp. 169–197; M. Liebel, 'Protecting the rights of working children instead of banning child labour', 23 *International Journal of Children's Rights* (2015) pp. 529–547; N.S. Kattan, 'Contribuciones desde los movimentos de niños, niñas y adolescentes trabajadores a la discusión em torno al trabajo infantil', 31 *DESIDADES – Revista Científica da Infancia, Adolescencia e Juventude* (2021).

52 P. Alderson, 'Human rights and democracy in schools. Do they mean more than 'picking up litter and not killing whales'?', 7 *International Journal of Children's Rights* (1999)

English schools show how children's claims of injustice and ill-treatment at school have led to institutional changes to make schools more democratic and more effective in their aims. A myriad of experiences of children's participation[53] has shown the scope and diversity of children's actions which, unfortunately, many a times are not recognized as truly self-represented actions, or are regarded as merely adjunct to adults' initiatives. Such a reading unveils the prejudice that still targets children's capacities to act as political and social actors, an eloquent indication that, albeit ample evidence of children's capacities, the definition of who can be counted as a citizen, and who is an able political subject, still lies in the hands of powerful adults.

A certain intergenerational politics is established when children are excluded from contributing with the destinies of our societies. Most importantly is the impoverishment in the way social problems and impasses are understood and dealt with since adults' perspectives cannot be challenged, othered and thus altered. On this point Wyness[54] argues that unless we look at certain social and political issues through a lens of intergenerational connectedness – children's and adults' lives being inextricably *interrelated* – creative solutions to social impasses will not be found. A case in point is children's and youth's claims for climate security[55] which have foregrounded the self-centred/selfish ethical position of the adult generation concerning its obligations towards the preservation and care of the world for those others to come. This has opened wide a case of *intergenerational injustice* since an unlimited emphasis on growth, consumption and development in the present seems at odds with the preservation of a hospitable world for all – the elders, the young and those still to be born. Adults' greed and voracity under present capitalist economies, albeit hard to be constrained, should evoke public reproval and restraint. From the vantage point of the youth, their long-term life perspective must be taken into account as a legitimate basis for changes in how natural and human resources should be deployed otherwise grounding claims for intergenerational justice.

---

pp. 185–205; P. Alderson, 'School students' views on schools councils and their daily lives at school', 14:2 *Children and Society* (2000) pp. 121–134.

53 B. Percy-Smith and N. Thomas (eds.), *A Handbook of Children and Young People's Participation* (Routledge, New York, 2012).

54 M. Wyness, 'Children's participation and intergenerational dialogue: Bringing adults back in the analysis', 20:4 *Childhood* (2012) pp. 429–442.

55 A. Daly, 'Climate competence: youth climate activism and its impact on international human rights law', 22:2 *Human Rights Law Review* (2022).

In some parts of the world experimentations of interconnected solidarity and reciprocity between generations are on the way, like for instance in the Landless Workers' Movement of Brazil (*Movimento dos Trabalhadores Rurais Sem Terra,* MST) and the Zapatista Movement in Mexico (*Ejército Zapatista de Liberación Nacional,* EZLN).[56] Both these movements contest, and struggle against, the present capitalist economic order which continues to produce unfair geopolitical as well as intergenerational relationships. Against seemingly evident patterns of intergenerational relationships worldwide, in MST and EZLN movements, other ethical and political perspectives embed their intergenerational conviviality so that practices of knowledge transmission are entwined with those of political participation. As a politically invested condition, childhood takes part in the collective and transformative engagements of adults towards a new world order in the context of alarming and deadly symptoms of our present decayed world.

Paradoxically enough, the 'conceptual autonomy of the child',[57] a notion which is necessary to forward advances in legal and social practices of age discrimination against children, must come to grips with the empirical relational embeddedness of children's (also adults') lives. Although it is clear that children must be seen in their own terms, as a distinct social category, the legal framework that is constructed to positivize their prerogatives and rights must be conceptualized taking into consideration those very important social networks and relationships where they belong and participate in. Interconnected solidarity of children and adults in many social groups, like those of the Zapatista and the MST, for instance, should caution one not to overrepresent children's rights against those of the elders. Thus, fundamental as it may be to think children as conceptually autonomous, the legal encoding of rights must allow for circumstances where *social relationalities* take precedence over *individualities* so that children's rights should also resonate the rights of their significant adult others, and vice-versa. To give conceptual autonomy to the child implies the painstaking conceptual maneuver to also theorize the child as part and result of a generative partnership with the adult in which both partners can enjoy freedom and pleasure whilst being able to carry out their reciprocal obligations.

---

56 L. R. de Castro. 'Children, Childhood and Decolonial Theory', In S. Balagopalan et al. (eds.), *The Bloomsbury Handbook of Theories in Childhood Studies* (Bloomsbury, London, 2024) pp. 125–142.

57 K. Hanson, 'Editorial. International Legal Procedures and Children's Conceptual Autonomy', 22:4 *Childhood* (2015) pp. 427–431.

In what follows I discuss empirical examples of how novel ways of generationing[58] between adults and children can ensue when age discrimination against children is overcome, in open relationalities between generations which attempt to eschew the dogmatic essentialism of age as a marker of fixed social intergenerational identities.

5 In Quest of Fairness and Reciprocity in Intergenerational Relationships

5.1 *Intergenerational Alliance Based on Shared Political and Ethical Values*

In this section I discuss the results of an empirical research project which investigated the secondary students' school occupations in Brazil,[59] a political movement that spread all over the country during 2015 and 2016. The occupations of schools by adolescents attested the condition of utter abandonment and negligence to which state schools were left in Brazil, or, in other words, how older generations have committed themselves to youngsters' welfare with regards to the provision of educational opportunities. Although, since the proclamation of the Brazilian Republic in 1889, Brazil has upheld republican values of universal dignity and equality, to this day it has not succeeded in providing universal high quality public education to all youth. It has been a major political fact that secondary students came out in the public scene to question the quality of the education they were receiving, making this issue a locus of inter and intragenerational dispute and a field of political antagonism.[60] As such, the politicisation of the issue of educational transmission brings into question assumptions about how not-so-modern societies, like

58 Throughout this chapter the notion of generation has been used to mean an important dimension of how modern societies are structured. According to L. Alanen, "the notion of generational structuring – or 'generationing' for short – refers to the complexity of social processes through which people become (are constructed as) 'children' while other people become (are constructed as) 'adults'". *See* L. Alanen, 'Childhood as a generational condition: children's daily lives in a central Finland town', In L. Alanen and B. Mayall (eds.), *Conceptualizing Child-Adult Relationships* (Routledge/Falmer, London, 2001) pp. 129–143.

59 L. R. de Castro and R. Tavares, 'Direitos geracionais e ação política: os secundaristas ocupam as escolas', 46 *Education Pesq SP* (2020); L. R. de Castro, 'Righting Adults' Wrongs: 'Generationing' on the battlefield. A decolonial approach', 29:3 *Childhood* (2022) pp. 355–370.

60 C. Mouffe, *The Return of the Political* (Verso, London, 1993).

Brazil, have fared in establishing structures and practices of generationing,[61] in view of the many impasses that have foreclosed the fulfilment of the country's egalitarian ideals of educational provision to all children and adolescents. The present conditions of the public educational system evidence the generational, but also the racial and social class[62] discriminations against children and youth, since those who go to the public system are the badly-off Black children, who live in *favelas* or peripheric zones of the city who cannot afford paying for their education. This ampler generational, also racial and class, discrimination is zoomed in and it is possible to see how at the level of daily school practices adults play out such determining conditions of intergenerational interdependence. This major political event of the secondary school students' occupations consisted of a most opportune investigation scenery to analyse the *different* ways whereby intergenerational connectedness was constructed.

Secondary students faced fierce opposition from the state governments where schools were located. Thus, adults in the position of educational officers, government representatives and many politicians outlawed students' movements, moreover, took whatever measures to discredit the students. They were referred to as delinquents, yobs, good-for-nothing youth who did not value education, and were doing harm to their peers and society. Many head teachers, who were liable to be fired out if they supported the students' movement, also aligned with top-scale educational officers, though quite a few opted for a compromising solution making a semblant adherence to the official position, but at the back giving some support to the students' occupation. For students, head teachers figured as icons of the appalling condition of schools; icons of conformity to authority; of a repressive and regressive educational system; of ingrained indifference toward the less powerful, thus becoming the emblematic focus of the students' revolt. On the other hand, politicians were criticized for serving the economic elite that ignores

61 L. Alanen, 'Explorations in generational analysis', In L. Alanen and B. Mayall (eds.), *Conceptualizing Child-Adult Relationships* (Routledge/Falmer, London, 2001) pp. 11–22.

62 The fundamental education in the Brazilian educational system consists of nine years of schooling, and then children go to the second cycle of education of three more years of schooling. Only in the 1988 Citizen Constitution education became a universal right to children, an irrevocable duty of the State. Before that, during Brazilian Republic, this duty oscillated between the family and the State, or the latter was not charged explicitly with this obligation. As a country that maintained over two hundred years of African slavery, and has not yet fully faced the ingrained consequences of such a tragedy, the educational services destined to the population of Afrodescendant children still bear the long-standing traces of racial, class and generational discrimination.

republican ideals and disregards intergenerational solidarity. The preoccupation of politicians with capital accumulation, the students feel, makes politicians turn their backs to all claims of subaltern groups. For the students, political struggle should be the only way to oppose those who hold so much power and remain impervious to claims for justice.

The opposition to these elders is underpinned by students' rejection of an attributed position of incompetence, or of passivity, contentedly accepting whatever is handed out to them as educational provision. What has come to the fore in students' narratives is the unfairness of the relationality between adults and children which fuelled and legitimated antagonism and political struggle. The adversarial stance assumed by these adults (head teachers, politicians and education officers) with regard to the students' demands for decent education yielded a politicized relationship that denounced their withdrawal from the intergenerational pact of solidarity denying students' generational rights to education.[63] Thus, the intergenerational connectedness was one of conflict and fierce opposition between children and those adults who were exercising positions of power to maintain a system that was unfair to a great majority of youngsters.

On a diametrically opposite side, stood a majority of teachers who backed up the students' movement inspired by ideals of more equality and fairness between generations[64] taking actively part in the occupations, in assemblies and in carrying out learning and cultural activities that happened during this period. In many states teachers had gone on strike just before the students' occupations[65] which, for the students, became almost an incentive for them to occupy the schools. Thus, for students, school teachers were clearly their allies, once a perceived convergence of interests existed between themselves

---

63 L. R. de Castro and R. Tavares, 'Participation Rights in Brazilian Schools: towards the politicization of adult-child relationships?', In A.Vergara et al. (eds.), *South American Childhoods since the 1990s: Neoliberalisation and the Exercise of Children's Rights* (Springer Nature, London, 2022).

64 C. Catini and G. Mello, 'Escolas de luta, educação política', 37:137 *Educação and Sociedade Campinas* (2016); L.P. Barbosa, *Educación, Resistencia y Movimentos Sociales: la praxis educativo-politica de los Sin Tierra y de los Zapatistas* (Universidade Nacional Autónoma de México, México, D.F. 2015); T. Cockburn, 'Partners in power: A radically pluralistic form of participative democracy for children and young people', 21 *Children and Society* (2007) pp. 446–457 <https://doi.org/10.1111/j.1099-0860.2006.00078.x>.

65 After the presidential coup that deposed the elected president Dilma Rouseff, a significant shift towards neoliberal 'adjustment' measures took place in Brazil, with enormous and deleterious consequences to the public education system: privatization, downsizing of schools, curriculum reforms, worsening of work conditions, the freezing of teachers' salaries and so on.

and their teachers. Furthermore, teachers were considered intellectual mentors of the occupation movement, as their struggle for better working conditions implied the refusal to countenance the deterioration of state education or its privatization. Thus, the goal of improving the conditions of state education positioned teachers and students on an equal footing within the unequal structure of educational opportunities. Students and teachers realized that they shared the very same fate within the structure of distribution of economic resources and educational opportunities, finding that they were equally positioned as outsiders, partaking jointly of the ill-effects of a precarious state educational system and of political choices handed down by hegemonic political groups. The shared experience of toiling, either as a student or as a teacher under deteriorated conditions of the educational system, aligned students shoulder to shoulder with teachers, over and above generational differences and positionalities defined by the pedagogic bond. As teachers and students – adults and adolescents – they became engaged in this mutually relevant struggle constructing an altogether different generational configuration, as co-actors, co-partners and co-generators of a wished-for educational situation which could be fairer to both children and adults. Honig[66] postulates that generation can be regarded as an epistemological concept within a theory of 'the generativity of the social', thereby eschewing a conceptualization that distinguishes opposing groups, or lineal descent, in order to highlight the emergence of novel and unexpected social practices. It seems that here, both teachers' and students' subjectivities are affected by the indifference of the elites who defy ideals of an egalitarian society. For students and teachers, education is considered a value and a common[67] relating to ideals of citizenship, inclusion and equality, as well as a political vision of the future. Such an experience of co-generativity between teachers and students, as a novel form of intergenerational interdependence, is oriented by the sharing of moral and political values and points at alternative configurations that interdependence between generations can assume.

It is to be noted that teachers' and students' alignments were discursively framed as a conjoined search for fairness and justice. Students explicitly

66 M-S. Honig, 'How is the child constituted in Childhood Studies?', In J. Qvortrup et al. (eds.), *The Palgrave Handbook of Childhood Studies* (Palgrave Macmillan, New York, 2011) pp. 62–77.

67 For a discussion of the notion 'common', *see* G. Esteva, 'Commoning in the New Society', 49:1 (issue suppl_1) *Community Development Journal* (2014) pp. i144–i159; G. Caffentzis and S. Federici, 'Commons against and beyond capitalism', 49:1 (issue suppl_1) *Community Development Journal* (2014) pp. i92–i105; J. Gilbert, *Common Ground: Democracy and Collectivity in an Age of Individualism* (Pluto, London, 2014).

claimed that their *rights* to a good education were being violated (though they did not refer to CRC or our national statute of children's and adolescents' rights, the ECA). The students' alignment with their adult-teachers became a reality on account of their teachers' explicit actions of solidarity when the students occupied the schools which demonstrated the teachers' embodied and practical commitment with the students' struggle and their interdependence with them.

5.2 *Reciprocity Claims and Children's Demands for Playtime: An Experimentation towards Alternative Intergenerational Bonds*

It may seem startling the fact that in many state schools in Rio de Janeiro, Brazil, at present, there is no playtime scheduled along children's school day. Although the right to play is enshrined in Article 31 of the CRC, and the Committee on the Rights of the Child highlights it as a key right of children, in the Brazilian educational legislation, *Lei de Diretrizes e Bases* (Bill of Directives and Bases of National Education) there is no provision for playtime at school. As I, and a team of research assistants, were working on the theme of school councils, the insistence of students' claims about their lack of playtime instigated us to look at this issue a bit further.[68] Since 2018 to this day I, and my collaborators, have been researching the nature, context and effects of this claim on children's and teachers' school experiences.[69] In the following I discuss some of the results, foregrounding how such a generational demand is listened to by the elders – researchers, teachers and educational staff – and what sort of legitimacy children provide to their claims as they address it to adults. As children could be listened to in their demands about playtime, they were able to position themselves as legitimate interlocutors in the process of making sense of school experience. This constituted an opportunity for adults to embark upon experimentations of intergenerational connectedness brought about by children's process of claim-making and addressing.

Even for myself and my research assistants, listening to children's claims about playtime was difficult to decode and ascertain initially. Being in school

68 L. R. de Castro, "Precisamos falar do recreio!' A construção do comum pelas crianças na escola', 14:29 *Childhood and Philosophy*, Rio de Janeiro (2018) pp. 129–148.

69 From 2018 to this day our methodological approach encompassed a variety of forms: initially ethnography and participant observation, then discussion groups with children and teachers, drama, video and collage workshops and interviews. These different approaches sought to understand how material and spatial elements took part in, and produced childrens' action systems in view of collectively making sense of their experience and establishing 'commons'. Playtime has been conceptualized as a students' common.

we could overhear the veiled complaint about not having proper playtime couched in different ways: in rather incisive terms such as "with no breaktime school is like a prison", or "adults have forgotten that they were children once and liked to play", or in subtler terms as "the thing I most love to do in school is to talk to my friends". But also, by intense affective moods, like grumbles, insignificant gestures, playfulness and anger. As we talked about this issue with school staff, we were quite astonished to hear how they thoroughly dismissed the importance of playtime based on a wide gamut of reasons: schools did not have enough space, or enough staff to look after them in playtime; children did not 'merit' to have playtime as they often behaved badly; they would hurt one another; they were too ruthless and could damage school property and others.

The international legislation, CRC, in its art. 31, states children's right to "rest and leisure, … and to engage in play". This is the only reference to play in the whole document. In the same vein, in the Brazilian Statute of Adolescents' and Children's Rights, ECA,[70] the term 'play' is mentioned just once in article 16 which deals with the right to freedom. In the Brazilian National Educational Bill (*Lei de Diretrizes e Bases da Educação Nacional*)[71] which sets the normative framework for education in the whole country, there is no provision for playtime at school, and the term 'play' is nowhere mentioned.

Children's claims for playtime led the research process to navigate a gradual epistemic reconstruction which encompassed their erratic complaints about their lack of playtime. As we fared in this direction, we were able to get closer to their grievances and their cherished ways to imagine that another school is possible. It is noteworthy that, as Ferguson[72] analyses children's play in present capitalist societies, she notes how play, as a sensuous, imaginative and autotelic activity counteracts capitalist designs for subjectivities who must channel their energies and motivations to instrumentalized labor that is required to produce value for capital. Then it is not a coincidence that it is precisely those children of the disadvantaged social classes that attend public schools in Rio de Janeiro that are left with no playtime, though vehemently reclaiming it back.

---

70 Brasil, *Estatuto da Criança e do Adolescente, Law 8069 of 13_07_1990*, (Brasília: Sec. Nac. dos Direitos da Criança e do Adolescente, 2022).

71 Brasil, *Lei de Diretrizes e Bases da Educação Nacional, Law 9394 of 20_12_1996*, (Brasília: Senado Federal, 2005).

72 S. Ferguson, 'Children, Childhood and Capitalism: a social reproduction perspective', in T. Bhattacharya (ed.), *Social Reproduction Theory. Remapping class, recentering oppression* (Pluto, London, 2017) pp. 112–130.

Although children discredited themselves about their competence to demand and their right to claim about playtime, as they were given opportunity to be listened to, they produced singular justifications for its existence. From less sophisticated arguments, such as *'we are children then we need and/or like to play'*, to the understanding that what they do at school is work, and like teachers, or any working man or woman, pauses to rest are important. With more sagacity than any scholar, they could enumerate a long list of benefits – social, cultural, communicational, psychological – of playtime to their own wellbeing as well as to social conviviality at school. Most importantly, the fairness of their playtime claims was foregrounded, rather than elocution, as an ethically based communication with adults[73] whose compassion and identification was demanded and reciprocity expected. After all, "weren't adults once children and, as such, couldn't they remember their need to play?", or, "why can't adults understand that after two or three hours listening to them in the classroom we need to refresh our minds?".

For some limitation of space here, I will not be able to bring the full picture of the vicissitudes of children's relationships with adults, specially school staff, as we, researchers, proceeded to investigate this subject. Despite the scientifically celebrated importance of play in childhood,[74] the banning of playtime from the daily students' schedule of the school day seemed to, at first, raise no worry or uneasiness, except for the kids. It is not that teachers did not see *the reasons why* (*and children's right*) to have playtime but, on account of diverse practical reasons that made their lives less burdensome, they'd rather not to attend to the claims about the right to play. The rights' framework was surely in the minds of adults, but these expectations seemed thwarted by many daily demands and emergences as well as, contradictorily enough, children's right to be protected. There was a frequent claim by teachers that if children were left to themselves in the courtyard they would hurt one another, be violent and unruly, so better to avoid trouble for teachers and pain for children. Thus, the rights' idiom was used in many different ways by teachers to justify their ambivalence: even if they agreed in principle with children's claims of playtime, they argued that it could not be a reality in school. However, some

73 S. Critchley, *Infinitely Demanding. Ethics of commitment, politics of resistance* (Verso, London, 2007).

74 J. Huizinga, *Homo Ludens: o jogo como elemento da cultura* (Perspectiva, São Paulo, 2008); S. Lester and M. Maudsley, *Play, Naturally* (NCB, London, 2007); H. Maturana and G. Verden-Zöller, *Amar e Brincar* (Pala Athena, São Paulo, 2004); B. Evans et al. (eds.), *Play and Recreation, Health and Well-being* (Springer Nature, London, 2016).

changes could be seen in teachers' initial suspicious incredulity and condescending distrust of children's claims.

First of all, in some schools teachers agreed to take part in conversation groups about playtime.[75] This was a significant movement away from the often rigid refusal to not having anything else to say or do about the matter. These groups propitiated teachers reflecting more deeply about their own positions and having to elaborate them further in view of children's demands. In one school staff agreed to be interviewed by the students on the subject as a demand made by children themselves. In another school the teacher of Music agreed to collaborate with researchers to help students write the verses of their rap on 'stories about playtime'. By and large, teachers' incredulity, suspicion and derision gave way to a timid self-interrogation about their own opinions. In two schools teachers told researchers that they were giving playtime to children on a more frequent basis and they evaluated this positively as it had improved students' relationships with them. Even if many teachers remained indifferent we could note that there was a significant change in teachers' ethical sensitiveness making them more conscious about a respectful attitude towards children's opinions. Maybe these changes will not be residual and long-standing, it is hard to know as the research project is still on the way in these schools. However, these partial results do indicate that through this 'experimentation' brought about by the fact that a research process was taking place in these schools many teachers could make changes in their ways of listening to children's demands and try out new gestures towards alternative generativities based on intergenerational solidarity and interconnectedness, and a more equal regard towards their students.

6 Concluding Considerations

Modern societies face the enormous challenges of overcoming age discrimination, an ailing social and political condition that denies children a status of citizen. Although the CRC has ensured children's rights against diverse discriminations, to this day children are often looked down and disrespected *for the fact of being a child.* In the present chapter I have provided a critique of age and ageism as the epistemological ground on which the moral and

75 In this part of our ethnography which took place from the end of 2022 to the end of 2023 five schools participated in the research process. It has been a long and intensive involvement of the researchers, children and school staff and so far only part of the results have been fully analysed.

psychological superiority of adults is based, a product of the 'enlightened' view of the human subject and history geared to actualize the supremacist and martial ideals of progress of European modernity. I have argued that the age episteme has provided an in-built discrimination against children that is present in legal texts, such as the CRC. Thus, on the one side, children's positive rights can enhance non-discrimination practices against them, though, on the other, as inscribed in CRC, rights must be also problematized as the result of ethical 'blind-spots', one of them being how 'low age' stands as a synonym for immaturity and incapacity.[76] Not only do children suffer from age discrimination, but it also curtails the enormous possibilities of human creativity and expansion leading to an impoverishment of social generativities in adult-child relationships. In both empirical examples discussed above, co-generational relationships between adults and children could enhance conviviality, learning and pleasure on both sides. In some groups in Latin America, like the Zapatista,[77] young and older generations must act in concert and solidarity to secure their own survival and autonomy.

To face the irrevocable interconnectedness and interdependence among generations I have discussed alternative ways of intergenerational solidarity that eschew the prejudiced and exclusionary relationships among children and adults based on age. The legal codes of modern societies, like the CRC, have had the aim to establish new regulations about intergenerational relationships banning discriminations against children. These can be turned quite ineffective if, concurrently, a change of mentalities and sensitivities does not also take place establishing, thus, reinvigorated forms of social respect, equality and dignity between adults and children.

---

76 *See also* Alderson, this volume.

77 *See* de Castro, *supra* note 56.

CHAPTER 7

Nondiscrimination/Equality and Children's Rights in the Climate Crisis

Aoife Daly

Abstract

There are a number of groups who will disproportionately suffer due to the climate crisis. One of these groups are those who are under 18 years. Children are active agents who are leading efforts to combat climate change, but they are generally not permitted to vote, and cannot influence climate policy (though it will affect them the longest). There are a number of difficulties with positioning children/youth in the nondiscrimination/equality framework, including the fact that under-18s are frequently excluded from frameworks prohibiting unfair discrimination. The CRC has generally not resulted in explicit consideration of age discrimination against children (i.e. detrimental treatment for being young/under 18) in the same way that has happened for other groups like women and ethnic minorities. Yet there is potential for doing so, primarily through CRC Article 2. Child/youth climate petitions (e.g. the *Duarte Agostinho* – 'Portuguese youth' – petition to the European Court of Human Rights) are increasingly invoking the principle of non-discrimination/equality. It is argued in this article that although such climate litigation is not always legally successful, the reliance on the principle of non-discrimination/equality is a significant transformation in the legal status of children.

1 Introduction

The principle of nondiscrimination/equality (taken here to mean the same thing) is enshrined in every international and regional international human rights instrument. Article 2 of the United Nations Convention on the Rights of the Child ('CRC') specifies that states will ensure that children enjoy their CRC rights "without discrimination of any kind". There is still, however, limited recognition in law and practice that children face discrimination because

© AOIFE DALY, 2025 | DOI:10.1163/9789004708433_008

they are children, that is, 'on the basis of childhood'.[1] Attention has almost solely been provided in law, practice and academia to discrimination against children on the basis that they belong to particular minority groups such as racial or ethnic minorities; those with disabilities; or due to gender or legal status.[2] As Liebel describes it, "i.e. in comparison to other children, however not in relation to adults".[3]

Yet there are ample grounds for identifying that discrimination against children and young people[4] is in fact an important issue in children's rights. Daly, Thorburn Stern, and Leviner point to examples including disadvantageous legal protections (e.g. protection from assault) to status offences (noncriminal act that is considered a legal violation only because of a youth's status as a minor, such as curfew violations targeted solely at under 18s).[5] Liebel also provides examples of discrimination based on age, such as the restriction on children accessing particular rights and services, often with little or no justification.[6] In many countries for example, age-based discrimination in wages is sanctioned and regulated, such as in the Netherlands where there is no minimum wage for workers below the age of 15; and a 15-year-old is entitled to only a third of the full adult minimum wage.[7]

One emerging issue is that children are arguably affected more detrimentally by climate change than those of us who are older. There has never been a more pressing challenge than the current climate crisis to consider new legal avenues for progressing children's rights. There are increasingly dire warnings about severe ecological harms from amongst other environmental threats, climate change.[8] It has been projected that, without adequate miti-

1 M. Liebel, 'Adultism and age-based discrimination against children', in D. Kutsar and H. Warming (eds.) *Children and non-discrimination* (CREAN, 2014) p. 123; A. Daly et al., 'UN Convention on the Rights of the Child, Article 2 and Discrimination on the basis of Childhood: The CRC Paradox?' 91:2 *Nordic Journal of International Law* (2022) pp. 419–452.

2 *See e.g.* M. Skivenes and K. H. Søvig (eds.), *Child rights and international discrimination law. Implementing article 2 of the United Nations Convention on the Rights of the Child* (Routledge, New York, 2019).

3 Liebel, *supra* note 1, p.123.

4 Children (under 18s) and youth (15–22 years) intersect greatly, however the focus in this chapter will be on those who are under 18 years. The term 'children and young people' will be used to refer to those under 18 years.

5 Daly et al., *supra* note 1.

6 Liebel, *supra* note 1, p. 123.

7 Liebel, *supra* note 1, p. 122.

8 Intergovernmental Panel on Climate Change (IPCC), *Climate Change 2022: Impact, Adaptation, Vulnerability, 'Summary for Policymakers'* (IPCC, 2022) <www.ipcc.ch/report/sixth-assessment-report-working-group-ii/> accessed 1 April 2022.

gation policies, global heating will accelerate towards 3.2°C by the close of the century.[9] It has been made clear by medical and other experts that, globally, children will be amongst those most seriously affected by the climate crisis.[10] As far back as 2015 the UN International Children's Emergency Fund (UNICEF) stated that "[t]here may be no greater, growing threat facing the world's children – and their children – than climate change".[11]

The phrase 'intergenerational justice' has therefore been essential to the climate justice movement.[12] De Spiegeleir and Brucher distinguish between two forms of intergenerational justice: (i) fairness between current generations and generations yet to be born and (ii) fairness between older and younger generations currently alive today.[13] This chapter is concerned with the latter as this is where children's rights become relevant – they are, of course, part of the younger generations currently alive today (the other part comprising of young adults). It can be difficult however to distinguish between i and ii however, particularly as both children's rights and the rights of future generations are being invoked together in litigation. Also, thousands of children are born every minute, and they therefore transfer from being amongst those yet to be born, to being a part of the 'child' category.[14] The popularity, and also the vagueness, of the term 'intergenerational justice' has likely impacted how the rights/interests of children and young people are addressed in climate cases, as is outlined in Section 4.3.

Children and young people have been at the forefront of climate action. As outlined in this article, they will disproportionately suffer from the conse-

9 UNEP, *Emissions Gap Report 2020* (9 December 2020) <www.unep.org/emissions-gap-report-2020> Accessed 1 April 2022.

10 N. Watts et al., 'The 2019 Report of The Lancet: Countdown on health and climate change: ensuring that the health of a child born today is not defined by a changing climate', 10211 *The Lancet* (2019) p. 1836.

11 UNICEF, 'Unless We Act Now: The Impact of Climate Change on Children' (2015) <www.unicef.org/reports/unless-we-act-now-impact-climate-change-children> Accessed 8 March 2022.

12 A. Daly, 'Intergenerational rights are children's rights: Upholding the right to a healthy environment through the UNCRC', 41:3 *Netherlands Quarterly of Human Rights* (2023) pp. 132–154.

13 A. de Spiegeleir and A. Brucher, 'Climate Docket and the Future in the Case Law of the European Court of Human Rights', *Colombia Law Blog*, 20 March 2023 <https://blogs.law.columbia.edu/climatechange/2023/03/20/climate-docket-and-the-future-in-the-case-law-of-the-european-court-of-human-rights/>.

14 *See further* Daly, *supra* note 12.

quences of the climate crisis. Of course certain categories of children and young people – those who are economically disadvantaged for example – are disproportionally vulnerable to harm caused by climate change. Can age-based nondiscrimination/equality arguments be mobilised to mitigate the climate crisis in the interests of children and young people? It has been argued that in regard to environmental issues, the wellbeing of each individual can be better protected when their status as collectivities is taken into account through the principle of nondiscrimination/equality.[15] This point, Kaya opines, is already evident through litigation, whereby the particular vulnerabilities of groups are being argued, sometimes successfully. She points to groups such as "younger generations, the elderly and indigenous people"[16] – I would add, people with disabilities.[17] A key argument put forward in many of these cases is that the response by governments to the climate crisis is inadequate or slow, and that this violates the equality rights of children/youth and of future generations.[18]

This article examines how the principle of nondiscrimination/equality applies to children's rights and interests in the climate crisis. Section 1 outlines how the principle of nondiscrimination/equality can apply to the detrimental treatment of children as opposed to adults. In Section 2, children's rights in the climate crisis are considered. In Section 3, the relevance of the principle (nondiscrimination/equality) to the climate crisis in general is examined. Section 4 considers the emerging trend of the reliance on the principle of non-discrimination in children/youth-related climate cases. Finally, the potential for further relying on the principle of nondiscrimination/equality is considered. It is argued that it is important to use the principle to progress the rights of children/young people as a group in the climate crisis, so that their specific needs are better recognised.

15 R. Kaya. 'European court of human rights on addressing environmental discrimination against collectivities', 9:4 *The Lawyer Quarterly* (2020).

16 Ibid.

17 *See e.g.* ECtHR, *Verein KlimaSeniorinnen Schweiz* and *Others* v. *Switzerland, no. 53600/20*, judgment (Grand Chamber) of 9 April 2024. The Court stated in *KlimaSeniorinnen* that "populations at 'highest risk' of temperature-related morbidity and mortality include older adults, children, women, those with chronic diseases, and people taking certain medications" (para. 510).

18 N. J. Chalifour et al., 'Coming of Age in a Warming World: The Charter's Section 15 (1) Equality Guarantee and Youth-Led Climate Litigation', 17 Journal of Law and Equality (2021) p. 1.

2 How the Principle of Nondiscrimination/Equality Is Relevant to Children in the Climate Crisis

Article 2 of the CRC provides that "States Parties shall respect and ensure the rights set forth in the present Convention to each child within their jurisdiction" and that "States Parties shall take all appropriate measures to ensure that the child is protected against all forms of discrimination". Although the ground of age is not explicitly included, the argument can be made that it falls under the heading of "other status."[19] The implementing body for the CRC, the Committee on the Rights of the Child, has not yet had the opportunity to clarify this. The principle is commonly accepted in other international/regional courts however. The European Court of Human Rights has previously held for example that 'age' is included among 'other status' under Article 14 (*Schwizgebel v. Switzerland* [No. 25762/07], 10 June 2010).

The Committee on the Rights of the Child rarely frames child-specific discriminatory practices – corporal punishment, for example – explicitly as age discrimination. The Committee generally considers only the rights of traditionally disadvantaged groups of children such as girls and ethnic minorities under Article 2.[20] There are a handful of exceptions to this, for example the Committee's 2016 general comment on adolescents makes reference to discriminatory attitudes against adolescents. The Committee plainly states: "Adolescence itself can be a source of discrimination".[21] The Committee has also recommended abolishing provisions on status offences "in order to establish an equal treatment under the law for children and adults".[22] So the trend appears to be that the Committee does not often refer to age discrimination against children, but the Committee has not completely ignored it, nor has it ruled it out as a principle for children's rights. This gives cause for optimism about the use of CRC Article 2 to counter age discrimination against children. Breen has argued that recent developments in the jurisprudence of the CRC

19 *See e.g.* W. Vandenhole et al., *Children's Rights: A Commentary on the Convention on the Rights of the Child and its Protocols* (Edward Elgar Publishing, Cheltenham, 2019) para. 2.14.

20 Daly et al., *supra* note 1.

21 UN Committee on the Rights of the Child (CRC), *General comment No. 20 (2016) on the implementation of the rights of the child during adolescence*, CRC/C/GC/20, 6 December 2016, para. 21.

22 Vandenhole et al., *supra* note 19.

Committee indicates "an evolving recognition that children may be subject to age-based discrimination".[23]

The limited acknowledgment by the Committee (and others more broadly) of age and/or childhood as grounds for discrimination against children is surprising in light of the numerous examples where children are treated detrimentally in state policy and practice as compared with adults. There is however a growing body of literature which aims to position children as at risk of discrimination in the same way that other distinct groups can be. Wall points to the concept of adultism, explored through literature, which is "the idea that societies need to be examined for the ways they discriminate against children as children".[24] Though there has been a lack of attention to the question as to whether CRC Article 2 protects against age discrimination, at least some commentators understand that it does. Breen argued in *Age Discrimination and Children's Rights*, a 2006 monograph, that children should be considered in the context of the equality and non-discrimination, because every differential treatment of children should be proportionate and justifiable.[25] She opines that a failure to do so makes it difficult for those using the law to "access, explore and embrace the differences between children and adults"[26] and to avoid the assumption that children are "less than adults".[27] Vandenhole likewise argues that "the approach to age discrimination in children's rights law should be aligned as much as possible with the approach taken to (age) discrimination more generally in human rights law".[28] Liebel has been writing from a discrimination perspective for some time, particularly in relation to working children.[29]

As for what non-discrimination means in the CRC context exactly, the word "'discrimination' is not explicitly defined in the text. Vandenhole points out however that the jurisprudence of the Committee on the Rights of the Child indicates that discrimination constitutes "differential treatment in similar

23 C. Breen, *Age Discrimination and Children's Rights* (Martinus Nijhoff Publishers, 2006) p. 64.

24 J. Wall, 'Children's Rights and Voting Age Discrimination', 36 *Harvard Human Rights Journal* (2023) p. 327.

25 Breen, *supra* note 23.

26 Breen, *supra* note 23, p. 67.

27 Ibid.

28 W. Vandenhole, 'Age discrimination exceptionalism?', *Harvard Human Rights Journal online* (2022).

29 M. Liebel, 'Economic and Labour Rights: A Blind Spot in the Discourse on Children's Rights', 39 *Nordic Journal of Human Rights* (2021).

cases without an objective and reasonable justification".[30] The Committee, in its Concluding Comments on the report of Belgium for example outlines that: "the general principle of non-discrimination in the Convention prohibits differences in treatment on grounds that are arbitrary and objectively unjustifiable".[31]

Indirect discrimination can also occur, however. This is when a policy or rule applies to everyone, but has an unintended, detrimental impact on a particular group of people. Seemingly neutral policies can detrimentally affect children, as their unique needs can be ignored, leading to disadvantage for them. This is accepted under international and regional human rights instruments. Article 14 of the ECHR is violated for example when a State Party, without objective and reasonable justification, fails to treat differently persons whose situations are significantly different (*Thlimmenos v. Greece* [2001] 31 EHRR 15). Laws and practices that exclude groups can violate article 14, as can those which ignore the unique needs of a specific group. It has been held by the court for example that the Netherlands gave insufficient consideration to women's rights in the context of pension policies (*Hoogendijk v The Netherlands* [2005] App. no. 58641/00).

It can be argued that in failing to adequately mitigate the climate crisis states are, without objective and reasonable justification, failing to treat children differently to adults, when their situations are significantly different. Their situations are different for a number of reasons, including their exclusion from voting and the fact that they will on average live much longer than adults. Governments are failing to sufficiently curb carbon emissions. The Paris Agreement is a legally binding international treaty which seeks to keep the rise below 1.5 degrees Celsius. The Executive Secretary of UN Climate Change said in 2022 "we are still nowhere near the scale and pace of emission reductions required to put us on track toward a 1.5 degrees Celsius world".[32] In 2023 a UN Climate Change report found that national climate action plans

30 W. Vandenhole (ed.), *Non-discrimination and equality in the view of the UN human rights treaty bodies* (Intersentia, Antwerpen, 2005).

31 UN Committee on the Rights of the Child (CRC), *Consideration of reports submitted by states parties under article 44 of the Convention. Concluding observations of the Committee on the Rights of the Child: Belgium*, (2002) CRC/C/15/Add.178, 13 June 2002, para. 6.

32 UN Climate Press Release, 'Climate Plans Remain Insufficient: More Ambitious Action Needed Now', *United Nations Climate Change* (26 October 2022) <https://unfccc.int/news/climate-plans-remain-insufficient-more-ambitious-action-needed-now>.

remained insufficient to limit global temperature rise to 1.5 degrees.[33] In failing to stop climate change, governments give insufficient consideration to the needs of children in the climate crisis.

The effects of this crisis is not distributed equally. There are a number of groups disproportionately affected by the climate crisis, such as those living in the Global South – colonisation and limited resources have resulted in a lack of mechanisms to cope with the devastating effects of climate change such as drought and rising sea levels.[34] These countries are least responsible for causing the crisis, yet face its most severe consequences and have the least capacity to cope.[35] Of all the groups, however, it can be argued that those who are young are (on average) worst affected, particularly those in the Global South, because of a number of factors which will be outlined in the next section.

3 Children's Rights and the Climate Crisis

In General Comment (No 26) of the UN Committee on the Rights of the Child on children's rights and the environment with a special focus on climate change[36] the Committee makes the point that the climate and environmental crisis is "an urgent and systemic threat to children's rights globally" and that States are under an obligation to immediately take action to protect children's rights in what it refers to as a 'triple planetary crisis' involving the climate crisis, biodiversity loss and pollution (paras 63–64). The climate crisis is having catastrophic effects on the rights and interests of children. UNICEF points out for example that millions of children globally have been driven from their homes by weather-related events in the past six years (to 2023), amounting to 20,000 child displacements per day.[37]

---

33 UN Climate Change, *Nationally determined contributions under the Paris Agreement. Synthesis report by the secretariat*, 14 November 2023 <https://unfccc.int/documents/632334>.

34 Ibid.

35 E. Gibbons, 'Climate change, children's rights, and the pursuit of intergenerational climate justice', 16 *Health and Human Rights Journal* (2014).

36 *See* Committee on the Rights of the Child, *General Comment No. 26: Children's Rights and the Environment with a Special Focus on Climate Change* (2023), CRC/C/GC/26, 22 August 2023.

37 UNICEF, 'Children displaced in a changing climate Preparing for a future that's already underway' (2023) <https://www.unicef.org/reports/children-displaced-changing-climate> Accessed 29 May 2024.

This harm is due to increase rapidly in the future. Over one billion people under the age of 18 live in countries at extremely high risk in the climate crisis.[38] Their survival is therefore severely threatened. There are numerous reasons why children are disproportionately affected in the climate crisis. They are economically disempowered as compared with adults. They have physical vulnerabilities compared with the average adult, in that because they are rapidly developing to adulthood, their growth can be irreparably harmed by pollution. Compared with those who are older, children have a (generally) longer life span.[39] Children born in 2020 will experience an enormous increase in extreme weather events – up to seven times greater than people born in the 1960s.[40] They will be exposed to at least one climate/environmental hazard (i.e. harm from heatwaves, water shortages, cyclones, or flooding) in their lifetime.[41] Yet action by governments to mitigate the climate crisis is seriously lacking.[42] There is therefore a disproportionate, and therefore an objectively unjustifiable, impact of the climate crisis on children. It can be argued then that failing to mitigate the climate crisis violates CRC Article 2 as per the Committee definition of discrimination. It also appears to violate non-discrimination/equality provisions of other human rights instruments.

There is ample evidence that governments have given seriously inadequate consideration to the rights and interests of children as a group in climate policies. Every country in the world (save one – the US) has ratified the CRC and therefore committed to upholding the principle of the best interests of the child. This principle requires that in all relevant decisions by governments and others, the interests of children must be given due consideration. It has been argued however that states have consistently failed in the context of the climate crisis to adequately consider the best interests of children as a group, and

38 UNICEF, 'The climate crisis is a child rights crisis: Introducing the Children's Climate Risk Index' (2021) <https://www.unicef.org/reports/climate-crisis-child-rights-crisis> Accessed 18 June 2022.

39 R. Kaya, 'On Challenging the Disparate Impacts of Climate Change through European Discrimination Law by Refia Kaya. What do we mean by "disparate impacts of climate change"?', *blogdroiteuropeen* (22 January 2020) <https://blogdroiteuropeen.com/2020/01/22/on-challenging-the-disparate-impacts-of-climate-change-through-european-discrimination-law-by-refia-kaya/>. Accessed 18 June 2022.

40 W. Thiery et al., 'Intergenerational Inequities in Exposure to Climate Extremes', 374 *Science* (2021) p. 158.

41 Ibid.

42 Paris Agreement (opened for signature 16 February 2016, entered into force 4 November 2016), UK Treaty Series No 4 (2017).

that this is an international human rights law issue which should be invoked in climate cases and elsewhere.[43]

The CRC places extensive obligations on States to ensure that the best interests of children are adequately considered in all matters concerning them – including matters relating to environment and climate. In General Comment No. 14, the Committee outlines that states must conduct children's rights impact assessments, which involves "predicting the impact of any proposed law, policy or budgetary allocation which affects children and the enjoyment of their rights". Child impact evaluations must also be conducted, to evaluate the actual impact of implementation on children's rights.[44] These assessments that must be underpinned by the CRC general principles, and be based on input from children and other stakeholders.[45] They also require that states collect and disaggregate data on the children's rights impact of the climate crisis.[46]

It has been found however that in climate policy-making most States do not explicitly give primary consideration to children's rights and interests. Research conducted in 2020 by UNICEF found that in only 34 per cent of countries examined could their climate plans (Nationally Determined Contributions – a requirement under the Paris Agreement) be described as 'child sensitive'.[47] There are many States then which are falling well short of their CRC obligations to explicitly consider children's rights in environmental/climate policies. It has also been pointed out that children and young people are largely ignored in environmental policymaking environments, which causes many of them great frustration.[48] This failure to consider children's interests

43 Daly, *supra* note 12.

44 Committee on the Rights of the Child, *General Comment No. 5* (2003), CRC/GC/2003/5, 27 November 2003. In the context of the environment in particular, *see* UNHRC, *Children's Rights and the Environment: Report of the Special Rapporteur* on the issue of human rights obligations relating to the enjoyment of a safe, clean, healthy and sustainable environment, A/HRC/37/58, 26 February–23 March 2018.

45 Committee on the Rights of the Child, *General Comment No. 14* (2013) *on the right of the child to have his or her best interests taken as a primary consideration*, CRC/C/GC/14, 29 May 2013, para. 99.

46 E. D. Gibbons, 'Climate change, children's rights, and the pursuit of intergenerational climate justice' 16 *Health and Human Rights Journal* (2014) p. 27.

47 UNICEF, *Climate & Environment Discussion Paper* (November 2021).

48 *See* A. Lio and I. Literat, ''We Need You to Listen to Us': Youth Activist Perspectives on Intergenerational Dynamics and Adult Solidarity in Youth Movements', 14 *International Journal of Communication* (2020).

in climate plans, considering the disproportionate impact, can clearly be argued to constitute detrimental treatment of children which is objectively unjustifiable.

4 Nondiscrimination/Equality in the Climate Crisis

Can the principle of nondiscrimination/equality assist children in the climate crisis? Ganty[49] points out (albeit in the context of socio-economic status) that the prohibition of discrimination is an empowering legal tool in the protection of disadvantaged people. It can assist in scrutiny of disadvantage; it can have a role in combating stereotypes and stigma, and can have "an important cross-cutting function in cases of multiple discrimination". Children are a particularly disadvantaged group, they are frequently overlooked in policy-making, and it is ironic that they are generally excluded from national equality frameworks.[50]

A number of groups of people suffer disproportionate harm in the climate crisis as noted above, including Indigenous people, the elderly and those with disabilities.[51] The Inter-American Court of Human Rights has recognised that environmental damage is experienced to a greater degree amongst groups that are already in a vulnerable situation; and so states are legally obliged, under international human rights law, to deal with this in accordance with "the principle of equality and non-discrimination".[52] There are structural inequalities at play in the climate crisis – those on low income are least able to deal with the effects of climate change for example – and authorities are unwilling to correct such inequalities.

The climate crisis is at present upfolding because of the failure of governments all over the world to take adequate action. They are failing for example to take action against fossil fuel companies, to curb deforestation, and otherwise tackle the main causes of climate change. One attraction for using the nondiscrimination/equality approach is that it facilitates the framing of differ-

49 S. Ganty, 'Poverty as Misrecognition: What Role for Antidiscrimination Law in Europe?', 21:4 *Human Rights Law Review* (2021) pp. 962–1007.

50 Daly et al., *supra* note 1.

51 R. Kaya, 'The Recommendation to Recognize Environmental Discrimination' *Leuven Blog for Public Law*, 2022 <https://www.academia.edu/92688810/The_Recommendation_to_Recognize_Environmental_Discrimination> Accessed 29 May 2024.

52 Inter-American Court of Human Rights, *Advisory Opinion (OC-23/17) of November 15, 2017, requested by the Republic of Colombia: the Environment and Human Rights*, 15 November 2017, para. 27.

ential treatments as problems of inaction by authorities. Kaya points out that most cases relating to indirect discrimination "rely on the fact that no action was taken to correct an injustice that resulted from a general rule that was the same for everyone".[53] In discrimination cases relating to the environment/ climate, then, it can be argued that in its inaction the state is disregarding the needs and rights of socially vulnerable individuals, including children and youth.

So where is the relevance here for children's rights in the climate crisis? Historically, adults (and adult perspectives) have human societies, cultures and narratives in the systems in which we live around the world.[54] Children and young people operate in "social, legal, political and economic structures that marginalise their interests and voices".[55] In spite of this, discourse in relation to age discrimination and the law most frequently focus on the rights of the elderly.[56] The focus on the elderly is predictable – these individuals are of course part of the adult group (and can face significant discrimination in society). The elderly also have the right to vote so are of interest to those seeking election.

The disenfranchisement of under 18s (they are generally excluded from the right to vote) creates a democratic deficit when it comes to the formation of climate policy. This leaves a democratic gap which means that states arguably have significant obligations when it comes to ensuring the best interests of children. It has been argued that, since children are disenfranchised, this increases the duties of courts when children's rights are being litigated. This has been recognised by courts in other jurisdictions and has influenced court decision-making accordingly. Columbian case SU-225/98 for example concerned the right to health of children. The Constitutional Court decision related to the failure of the Ministry of Health and District Secretary of Health of the Santa Fé of Bogotá to ensure the provision of free meningitis vaccines to children of mothers participating who were without access to healthcare (due to partici-

53 R. Kaya, 'Challenging Environmental Exposures Through Discrimination Law in Europe', 20:1 *Ankara Avrupa Çalışmaları Dergisi* (2021) pp. 195–219.

54 J. Wall, 'From childhood studies to childism: reconstructing the scholarly and social imaginations', 20:3 *Children's Geographies* (2019) pp. 257–270.

55 L. Parker et al., 'When the Kids Put Climate Change on Trial: Youth-Focused Rights-Based Climate Litigation around the World', 13:1 *Journal of Human Rights and Environment* (2021) pp. 64–89.

56 R. Kaya, 'Environmental vulnerability, age and the promises of anti-age discrimination law', 28:2 *Review of European, Comparative and International Environment Law* (2019) pp. 162–174.

pation in the informal sector of the economy).[57] The Colombian Constitutional Court stated in its decision that in relation to a social state which is right based, preferential treatment is owned by the political community to people and circumstances of disadvantage and exclusion from participation from public policy-making. The court emphasised that although responsible for decisions relating to budgets and tax policies, the case of the rights of children is different because this group lacks participation in the political processes and therefore decisions which affects this group. This essentially recognises that children, who are without the right to vote, have limited if any opportunities to influence the elected branches of government. Judicial intervention therefore is more justifiable, and in fact more necessary when it comes to children's rights being enforced.

It should also be considered that children's 'vulnerability' is another argument in favour of recognition of children's rights to nondiscrimination andequality. For those who emphasise children's agency, children's vulnerability is overemphasised. However it is not to suggest that children are weak when we use the terms 'victim' or 'vulnerable'.[58] Instead, here 'vulnerability' denotes the universal potential of human suffering, in the way described by Martha Fineman for example.[59] It is important to note that vulnerability has proven in the European Court of Human Rights to be a useful concept for applicants for some groups. Under the ECHR for example, a 'vulnerability criterion' under article 14 allows the courts to favour the applicants by highlighting the applicants' group affiliation.[60] In *DH and others v Czech Republic*, the court adopted a vulnerability criterion, an approach demanding that a respondent state provide 'special protection' to vulnerable groups.[61] The 2019 landmark decision *JD and A v UK* is also relevant. The ECtHR ruled the U.K.'s bedroom tax to violate article 14 of the European Convention on human rights. The applicant in this

57 Constitutional Court decision regarding the failure of the Ministry of Health and District Secretary of Health of the Santa Fé of Bogotá to provide free meningitis vaccines to children of mothers participating in the informal sector of the economy and therefore without access to healthcare, Judgement SU-225/98, 20 May 1998 <https://www.escr-net.org/caselaw/2020/judgment-su-22598> Accessed 29 May 2024.

58 A. Hefti, 'Intersectional victims as agents of Change in International Human Rights-based climate litigation', *Transnational Environmental Law* (2024) pp.1–26.

59 M. A. Fineman, 'The vulnerable subject: anchoring equality in the human condition', 20:1 *Yale Journal of Law and Feminism* (2008), *Emory Public Law Research Paper* no. 8–40.

60 S. Y. Kim, 'Les Vulnerables: evaluating the vulnerability criterion in article 14 cases by the European Court of human rights', 41:4 *Legal Studies* (2021) pp. 617–632.

61 European Court of Human Rights, Case of *D.H. and others* v. *the Czech Republic*, Application no 57325/00, merits and just satisfaction, 13 November 2007, p. 182.

case was in a social protection scheme relating to severe domestic violence and her 'panic room' was levied as a spare room, reducing her housing benefit by 14 per cent. The key point in the case according to the court about the fact that she had a vulnerable status as a victim of domestic violence. When an applicant is particularly vulnerable, this reduces the margin of appreciation of the respondent state, and requires the state to give weighty reasons for the differential treatment.[62] The applicant needed a spare room, and the UK failed to reasonably justify applying the bedroom tax to the room. The UK had violated article 14 therefore, by applying the bedroom tax to this vulnerable applicant who the court described as falling within a 'small and easily identifiable group'.[63]

Children and youth can fit in at least two of the groups of vulnerability identified by the court. Heri categorises the types of vulnerability recognised by the Court:

> The first category is dependency-based vulnerability, which concerns minors, the elderly, and those with psychosocial and cognitive disabilities. A related category, which accounts for the bulk of the Court's references to vulnerability under Article 3, concerns vulnerability due to state control. In addition, applicants may be considered vulnerable due to experiences of victimisation or a feeling of vulnerability, because of a context of migration, discrimination or marginalisation, or due to pregnancy or situations of precarious reproductive health, unpopular views, or the intersection of various sources of vulnerability.[64]

Children are of course very dependent on adults for the exercise of their rights, and children and youth both can be considered as marginalised from political processes and power. The Court has long referred to this its jurisprudence under Article 8 ECHR that there is an obligation on states to provide effective deterrence against the sexual abuse of children and other vulnerable individuals, see for example *Stuart v UK*.[65]

---

62 European Court of Human Rights, Case of *JD and A* v. *UK*, Case no. 32949/17 ND 34614/17, 24 October, 2019, p. 89.

63 Ibid, p. 105.

64 C. Heri, *Responsive Human Rights: Vulnerability, Ill-treatment and the ECtHR* (Hart Publishing 2021).

65 European Court of Human Rights. *Stuart* v. *UK,* App no 41903/98, Decision of 6 July 1999, para 1, citing *Stubbings and others* v. *United Kingdom*, 22083/93, 22095/93, 6 July 1996, para. 64.

There are a number of arguments therefore that can be employed to emphasise that children and young people require special protection in the climate crisis, and that failures by states to act may breach the principle of non-discrimination and equality.

5 Recent Cases/Applications Invoking Nondiscrimination/Equality for Children and Youth

There has been an explosion in climate cases in recent years, many of them involving child and youth litigants. These cases have different legal arguments and bases. Some of these cases are based on domestic constitutional law; some on international human rights law (and its domestic implementation); and some, like the *Sharma* case[66] in Australia, on principles of tort law (a civil wrong that causes a claimant loss or harm).

One can track the use of the themes, or explicit arguments, of nondiscrimination/equality as the climate applications/cases have emerged at both national and international level. Donger notes that by 2021, 30 per cent of child/youth climate cases invoked the principle of nondiscrimination/equality on the basis of age[67] – a significant amount, considering the absence of nondiscrimination/equality cases relating to children and youth up until this time. In fact, the number of children's rights arguments invoked in child/youth-related climate cases has been very narrow. Donger points out that it has consisting mainly of two principles: arguments for children's rights to have their best interests considered as a primary matter (Donger found that by 2021, it was invoked in seven cases); and age-based discrimination (by 2021, invoked in nine cases).[68] This is a stunning turn of events for children's rights – a principle which was almost never associated with children as a group (non-discrimination and equality) appears to be now one of the two primary rights principles invoked in climate cases concerning children and young people.

It is clear, however, that the principle, although invoked, is not necessarily successfully invoked. In the majority of the cases examined by Donger (six), the principle was ultimately not addressed. In a handful (two), the violation was expressly rejected, and another case, the judicial decision was pending. More recent research focusing on 'youth' climate cases (i.e. where the appli-

66 Federal Court of Australia, *Minister for the Environment* v. *Sharma* (2022) FCAFC 35.

67 E. Donger, 'Children and youth in strategic climate litigation: Advancing rights through legal argument and legal mobilization', 11 *Transnational Environmental Law* (2022).

68 Ibid, p. 227.

cants are from eight to 25 years old) finds the vast majority of cases unsuccessful or pending.[69] Nevertheless, the fact that the principle is being invoked can be argued to be a sea change; a transformational moment in itself. There are different iterations and approaches in the arguments used which will now be considered.

5.1 *Reliance on Equality/Nondiscrimination Arguments*

Greater levels of reliance on arguments relating to nondiscrimination/equality for children are evident in climate cases in the past few years. It seems that the earliest was the Juliana case, the flagship of the US climate case efforts led by NGO Our Children's Trust.[70] In *Juliana, et al. v. United States of America, et al.*[71] the application states that:

> The affirmative aggregate acts of Defendants in the areas of fossil fuel production and consumption irreversibly discriminate against Plaintiffs' exercise of their fundamental rights to life, liberty, and property, and abridge central precepts of equality. The affirmative aggregate acts of Defendants in the areas of fossil fuel production and consumption have caused and are causing irreversible climate change. As a result, *the harm caused by Defendants has denied Plaintiffs the same protection of fundamental rights afforded to prior and present generations of adult citizens.* (Emphasis added)

This constitutes a distinct use of argument comparing children and adults, in terms of the effects of the climate crisis. The Juliana case remains ongoing, most recently (as of June 2024) the applicants are appealing the 2024 decision of the court to dismiss.[72]

In the unsuccessful petition of *Armonda Ferrao Carvalho and Others v. The European Parliament and Council of the European Union*, the point was raised that Article 21 of the Charter prohibits any discrimination based on age. The applicants argued that consequently:

---

69 Climatalk, *Global Trends in Youth Climate Litigation* (2024) <https://climatalk.org/2024/04/16/global-trends-in-youth-climate-litigation-booklet/ > Accessed 29 May 2024.

70 Our Children Trust website <www.ourchildrenstrust.org/> Accessed 29 May 2024.

71 United States District Court for the District of Oregon Eugene Division, Case no: 6:15-cv-01517 (D.Or. 2018) p. 292.

72 Sabin Centre for Climate Change Law, *Juliana* v. *United States* <https://climatecasechart.com/case/juliana-v-united-states/> Accessed 29 May 2024.

> This principle of equal treatment should clearly be applicable in respect of equality between children and young people, and older people, and requires broader intergenerational justice … [U]nless drastic action is taken now, today's children will face environmental conditions in their future lives that are far worse than those enjoyed by present day adults.[73]

Although unsuccessful, there is again explicit emphasis on children, a group that is explicitly referenced in the petition.

At national level, there appears to be countries whose laws are particularly well disposed to equality arguments, and this has been harnessed in climate cases with child litigants. In the 2023 application of *Children of Austria v. Austria*, 12 children filed a complaint with the Austrian Constitutional Court claiming that the Federal Climate Protection Act (adopted in 2011 to implement emission reduction obligations under European law) violates 1) the rights of children under the Austrian constitution as well as 2) the fundamental right to equality before the law.[74] The applicants claimed that the principle of fair burden sharing is not being observed, and that this involves unequal treatment of children as compared with adults, as the future freedoms of children become more and more restricted, whilst Austria's carbon budget becomes more rapidly exhausted. The application was found inadmissible, on the basis that repealing the law would amount to an act of legislation by the court.

Canada has been another key jurisdiction in this regard. Section 15 of the *Canadian Charter of Rights and Freedoms* states that everyone is equal before and under the law without discrimination based on age. This context is one of the very, very few in which to date legal arguments have been made relating to age discrimination and children in cases that do not relate to the climate crisis. The equality provision in the Charter has for example been used (albeit unsuccessfully) to argue that those under 18 years should have the right to vote. The most recent attempt is the petition of *Penney-Crocker et al. v Can-*

---

73 Order of the General Court (Secod Chamber). T-330/18, *Armonda Ferrao Carvalho and Others* v. *The European Parliament and Council of the European Union*, ECLI:EU:T:2019:324, Application at <https://peoplesclimatecase.caneurope.org/wp-content/uploads/2018/08/application-delivered-to-european-general-court.pdf> Accessed 29 May 2024, *see* p 27.

74 Sabin Centre for Climate Change Law, *Children of Austria* v. *Austria*. Filing date 2023 <http://climatecasechart.com/non-us-case/children-of-austria-v-austria/> Accessed 12 March 2023.

ada.[75] It makes sense therefore that in the youth led climate cases which have arisen there, youth are arguing that the Canadian government is violating their rights under the Charter by perpetuating climate change.

In *Mathur v Ontario*, 2020 ONSC 6918 (CanLII) and *Mathur v His Majesty the King in Right of Ontario*, 2023 ONSC 2316 (CanLII), the applicants relied on section 15 (as well as section 7, the right to security of the person) to argue that Ontario's greenhouse gas emissions reduction violated in the Charter. The application was unsuccessful at trial on the basis of a failure to show deprivation of the applicants' rights under section 7; and because any disproportionate impact experienced by youth would be caused by climate change itself and not by Ontario's greenhouse gas reduction target (at paras 177–183). An appeal was heard in 2024 and judgment was reserved. In the ongoing Canadian *La Rose*[76] case 15 youth likewise argue that the Canadian government is violating their rights under the Charter by perpetuating climate change. The application very explicitly relies on the argument that government conduct related to climate change constitutes unjustifiable age-based discrimination. The petition by children/youth aged 10 to 19 (seven are from Indigenous communities), involves the invocation of a right to equality, as enshrined in section 15(1) of the Canadian Charter of Rights and Freedoms. The Motions Judge did not accept the argument relating to section 15 of the Charter on the basis that the appellants did not point to a "law" that was the source of the alleged discrimination – a necessity, according to the Motions Judge. It has been argued however that this is a clear error of law, in that section 15 does not require a law to be the source of the discriminatory conduct.[77]

5.2 *Challenges of Nondiscrimination/Equality Arguments*

There are a number of challenges for success and cohesion of nondiscrimination/equality arguments in climate applications/cases concerning children. One challenge is that references to nondiscrimination/equality can appear tokenistic. We see in some applications, reference being made to nondiscrimination/equality, but without elaboration. The *Sacchi* application is one such

75 *Justice for Children and Youth, Penney-Crocket et al.* v. *Canada* [Voting Age Challenge] <https://jfcy.org/en/cases-decisions/vac/> Accessed 29 May 2024.

76 *La Rose* v. *Canada*, 2020 FC 1008, at para 27.

77 Federal Court of Appeal, *La Rose* v. *Her Majesty the Queen*, November 24 2020 <https://climatecasechart.com/wp-content/uploads/non-us-case-documents/2020/20201124_T-1750-19_appeal.pdf> Accessed 29 May 2024; Find other documents at Sabin Centre for Climate Change Law, La Rose v Her Majesty the Queen <http://climatecasechart.com/non-us-case/la-rose-v-her-majesty-the-queen/> Accessed 29 May 2024.

instance. The *Sacchi* application involved 16 children petitioning the UN Committee on the Rights of the Child.[78] Although it did not proceed to a full hearing, the Committee's resulting pronouncement constituted the first time that a UN body found that a state can, in certain circumstances, be held responsible for the impacts of its carbon emissions on the rights of children inside *and* outside of its territory.[79]

This is a case involving an explicit argument by (all) *child* applicants that the failure of governments to take action to increase climate mitigation denies them equality with *adults*. By its nature, this is a nondiscrimination argument, even if it not described explicitly as such. The *Sacchi* petition of course by its nature, being taken in relation to CRC rights, involved arguments about children versus adults. In the application it is stated that:

> Two foundational principles of the Convention are at stake in the climate crisis: non-discrimination and the prioritization of the best interests of the child. Both principles are undermined by delaying climate-change mitigation, because delay shifts the burden onto children and future generations, with irreversible human rights consequences.
>
> Saachi petition, para 192

This is a welcome, if vague reference to discrimination. There is no further explanation of the point, nor is there explicit reference to Article 2, which is not amongst the articles of the CRC explicitly invoked, namely the best interest principle (Article 3); the right to life (Article 6); the right to health (Article 24), and the right of Indigenous children to their own culture (Article 30).[80] Of course, the application is just one part of the trajectory of a particular legal or quasi-legal action. Further steps in an application (a later hearing perhaps) may include an elaboration on the point, as was the case in *Duarte Agostino.*

In the 2020 *Duarte Agostinho* petition the six youth applicants alleged breaches of the European Convention on Human Rights. They invoked

78 *Sacchi and others* v. *Argentina and others*, Petition Submitted under Article 5 of the Third Optional Protocol to the United Nations Convention on the Rights of the Child (23 September 2019). Hereinafter *Sacchi.*

79 A. Daly, 'Climate crisis: how states may be held responsible for impact on children', *The Conversation*, (20 October 2021) <https://theconversation.com/climate-crisis-how-states-may-be-held-responsible-for-impact-on-children-170130> Accessed 29 May 2024.

80 The Committee declined to examine the petition on its merits, due to a failure to exhaust domestic remedies, though it established important precedent in recognising State responsibility for transboundary harm. *See further* Daly, *supra* note 79.

Articles 2 (the right to life), 8 (family life) and 14 (freedom from discrimination). In the application, the argument was made that climate policies of states are placing most of the economic and environmental burden on the younger generation.[81] The child and youth litigants together argued that insufficient attention was being given to burden-sharing of the consequences of carbon emissions. Inadequate reduction of carbon emissions in the present, they argued, will disproportionately affect the younger generation. Ultimately the petition was unsuccessful on the basis that it did not exhaust domestic remedies.[82] Back in 2020, the reference to nondiscrimination provision of the ECHR- Article 14 (para 28) was incredibly ground breaking, considering the serious lack before this lack of nondiscrimination legal arguments in relation to children and youth. It is notable however that the reference appears just once across the 20 pages, and there is no elaboration.[83] In later submissions however, there was further argumentation made in relation to the relevance of the point, it just is not publicly available.[84]

Another challenge for success and cohesion of the nondiscrimination/equality argument in applications/cases is that, as noted above, many of these cases involve both under and over 18s as litigants; and/or arguments that the interests of 'younger people' are harmed by climate change. This could be taken to mean those under 18 years but also young adults. The focus of 'youth' arguments are not particularly on under 18s (i.e. children), and so are unlikely to provide detailed arguments about nondiscrimination/equality for children. The focus is more likely on nondiscrimination and young people.

In the Dutch *Urgenda* case for example – the first case in which citizens established that their government has a legal duty to prevent climate change[85]

---

81 *See* petition at Global Legal Action Network website <https://youth4climatejustice.org/case-documents/>, Accessed 3 June 2021.

82 *See further* C. Heri, 'On the Duarte Agostinho Decisio', *Verfassungsblog*, 15 April 2024, <https://verfassungsblog.de/on-the-duarte-agostinho-decision/> Accessed 29 may 2024.

83 Sabin Centre for Climate Change Law, Duarte Agostinho and Others v. Portugal and 32 Other States <https://climatecasechart.com/non-us-case/youth-for-climate-justice-v-austria-et-al/>

84 *See* a recording of the hearing, available at https://vodmanager.coe.int/cedh/webcast/cedh/2023-09-27-1/en

85 Supreme Court of the Netherlands, *The State of the Netherlands* v. *Urgenda Foundation*, (20 December 2019), case 19/00135 (English translation) <https://www.urgenda.nl/wp-content/uploads/ENG-Dutch-Supreme-Court-Urgenda-v-Netherlands-20-12-2019.pdf> (Supreme Court decision).

– the Hague Court of Appeal recognized that young generations are disadvantaged by government policies, stating that:

> It is without a doubt plausible that the current generation of Dutch nationals, in particular but *not limited to the younger individuals in this group*, will have to deal with the adverse effects of climate change in their lifetime if global emissions of greenhouse gases are not adequately reduced.[86] (Emphasis added)

The applicants did not explicitly invoke the non-discrimination principle. Kaya points out however that nevertheless the unequal, and therefore discriminatory, effects of climate change on 'younger people' has through *Urgenda* been legally documented in a European climate change case.[87] Whilst not squarely a children's rights argument, it is a significant development that this momentous case acknowledged that the court accepted the disproportionate effects of the climate crisis on children and youth.

5.3 *'Intergenerational Justice/Equity' and Future Generations in Climate Cases*

As noted above, the principle of 'intergenerational justice/equity' has been drawn upon to argue that the current generations owe duties to future ones. In any case, the "present bias" of public climate policies means that carbon budgets have been depleted greatly across many states for the twenty-first century.[88] There is irrefutable scientific evidence that children/youth and future generations will therefore bear a disproportionate burden in relation to the action which will need to be taken in the future, as well as the harm that will result from present government inaction.[89] The principle of intergenerational equity has a long history across numerous cultures, but in the context of international law it was elaborated by Brown Weiss in 1989. She outlines that the basic premise of the principle is that:

---

86 The Hague Court of Appeal. *The State of the Netherlands* v. *Urgenda Foundation* (9 October 2018), case 19/00135 (English translation) Para 37, <https://www.urgenda.nl/wp-content/uploads/ECLI_NL_GHDHA_2018_2610.pdf>

87 Kaya, *supra* note 39.

88 *See* N. Chalifour et al., 'Coming of age in a warming world: The Charter's Section 15 (1) equality guarantee and youth-led climate litigation', 17 *Journal of Law and Equality* (2021).

89 Ibid.

> [A]ll generations are partners caring for and using the Earth. Every generation needs to pass the Earth and our natural and cultural resources on in at least as good condition as we received them.[90]

Another important principle arising in climate cases is that of the rights of future generations. Defining it is clearly not straightforward, as the term 'future generations' is frequently left undefined where it is included in national Constitutions.[91] The *Maastricht Principles on The Human Rights of Future Generations* provides the definition that future generations are "those generations that do not yet exist but will exist and who will inherit the Earth"[92] – this is quite a vague definition. In the *Neubauer* case (2021) the German Supreme Constitutional Court suggested the more specific definition that 'future generations' were those who are alive ten years from the year the case was decided.[93] Yet there is a lack of clarity and consensus on the matter, particularly on whether children are to be included in the definition. A number of academic commentators consider the definition of future generations to encompass children,[94] but others do not.

The principle of the rights of future generations has proven useful in climate cases as it is enshrined in the laws of numerous countries. German Basic Law for example states: "Mindful also of its responsibility toward future generations, the state shall protect the natural foundations of life and animals by

---

90 E. Brown Weiss, 'Climate Change, Intergenerational Equity, and International Law', 9:3 *Vermont Journal of Environmental Law* (2008) p. 615.

91 A. Nolan, 'Children's Rights and Future Generations' Rights – Ensuring Mutual Support', paper presented at *Children/Youth and the Right to a Healthy Environment* (11 November 2022); Centre for Children's Rights and Family Law, University College Cork <https://www.ucc.ie/en/law/research/ccrfl/> Accessed 30 March 2023.

92 Maastricht Principles on The Human Rights of Future Generations, Article 1, adopted on 3 February 2023; On definitions of future generations *see also* A. Nolan, 'The Children are the Future – Or Not? Exploring The Complexities of the Relationship between the Rights of Children and Future Generations", *EJIL Talk!*, 26 May 2022, <https://www.ejiltalk.org/the-children-are-the-future-or-not-exploring-the-complexities-of-the-relationship-between-the-rights-of-children-and-future-generations/> Accessed 27 May 2022.

93 Sabin Centre for Climate Change Law, *Neubauer et al.* v. *Germany BvR 2656/18/1 BvR 78/20/1 BvR 96/20/1 BvR 288/20*. *See* http://climatecasechart.com/non-us-case/neubauer-et-al-v-germany/ Accessed 9 January 2023.

94 S. Skogly, 'The Right to the Continuous Improvement of Living Conditions and Human Rights of Future Generations – A Circle Impossible to Square?', in J. Hohman and B. Goldblatt (eds.), *The Right to the Continuous Improvement of Living Conditions Responding to Complex Global Challenges* (Hart Publishing, 2021).

legislation and, in accordance with law and justice, by executive and judicial action, all within the framework of the constitutional order."[95]

A number of climate cases appear to have a mix of children's legal entitlements, and a focus on different generations. In *Sacchi*, the applicants referred in their arguments to the notion that "states are stewards of public commons held in trust for the good of future generations"; and emphasised that it has been recognized by human rights treaty bodies.[96] The applicants also highlight that the idea that states must act now to safeguard posterity is incorporated into domestic law around the world. For example, the German Constitution recognizes "responsibility toward future generations".[97] In the *Duarte Agostinho* application[98] to the ECtHR, also, the applicants make reference to 'the concept of intergenerational equity' alongside 'the requirement (under Article 3(1) of the UN Convention on the Rights of the Child) that the 'best interests of the child' must be 'a primary consideration.'[99]

There has been a similar trend in youth climate cases at domestic level, whereby a mix of children's legal entitlements, and a focus on different generations is evident in arguments. In Australia, children and youth made attempts to prevent coal mining in the case of *Sharma*.[100] In this (ultimately unsuccessful)[101] tort law-based application, the applicants argued that the relevant legislation should be interpreted as involving the need to "ensur[e] a healthy environment for the benefit of future generations".[102] The argument was also made in the 2023 filing *Children of Austria* v. *Austria* that the danger posed to present and future generations (posed by the failure to mitigate climate change) related to the state's obligations to take adequate measures to

---

95 The German Basic Law of the German Federal Republic Article 20a (added 1994). English translation at: <www.gesetze-im-internet.de/englisch_gg/englisch_gg.html> Accessed 6 May 2024.

96 *Sacchi, supra* note 78, para 167.

97 Ibid.

98 *See* application to the Court at Global Legal Action Network website <https://youth4climatejustice.org/> Accessed 3 June 2021.

99 The applicants cite *Neulinger* v. *Switzerland* App No 41615/07, (ECtHR GC 6 July 2010), para. 132, in relation to the best interests principle.

100 *Minister for the Environment* v. *Sharma* [2022] FCAFC 35.

101 An initial success was overturned on appeal by the Full Court of the Federal Court of Australia.

102 *Sharma and others* v. *Minister for the Environment* [2021] FCA 560, 274.

protect child well-being.[103] In *La Rose*[104] it is argued that that the young litigants have public interest standing to represent their rights and the "rights of all children and youth in Canada, present and future".[105]

The *Juliana* case likewise appears to have a mix of children's legal entitlements, and a focus on different generations. These foci are then taken together with an equality argument by litigants. *Juliana, et al.* v. *United States of America, et al.* No: 6:15-cv-01517 (D.Or. 2018), proceeding § 292 states that:

> The affirmative aggregate acts of Defendants in the areas of fossil fuel production and consumption irreversibly discriminate against Plaintiffs' exercise of their fundamental rights to life, liberty, and property, and abridge central precepts of equality. The affirmative aggregate acts of Defendants in the areas of fossil fuel production and consumption have caused and are causing irreversible climate change. As a result, the harm caused by Defendants has denied Plaintiffs the same protection of fundamental rights afforded to prior and present generations of adult citizens.

It has been argued elsewhere that it is possible that arguments relating to both 'intergenerational equity' and 'the rights of future generations' could possibly be distracting those taking cases from the realisation of the potential usefulness of CRC rights,[106] which have after all been committed to by almost all countries in the world. There is a clear preference for future generation arguments evident from analysis of the case law. Donger examined the 33 child/youth-focused climate applications filed before 2021 which reference rights,[107] and established that 90 per cent of the arguments advanced in these applications refer to intergenerational equity. Less than 10 per cent were found to refer to the best interests principle.[108] A larger percentage of cases refer to nondiscrimination/equality for children as noted above. However it is still far less than cases referring to 'intergenerational equity' and 'the rights of fu-

103 *Children of Austria v. Austria* Filing Date: 2023. *See* Sabin Center for Climate Change Law, *Global Climate Change Litigation database* <http://climatecasechart.com/non-us-case/children-of-austria-v-austria/> Accessed 12 March 2023.

104 *La Rose* v. *Canada*, 2020 FC 1008, *see* Plaintiffs' Statement of Claim, at para 27.

105 *See further* N. J. Chalifour et al. 'Coming of Age in a Warming World: The Charter's Section 15(1) Equality Guarantee and Youth-Led Climate Litigation', 17 *Journal of Law & Equality* (2021).

106 Daly, *supra* note 12.

107 Donger, *supra* note 67, p. 270.

108 Ibid, p. 277.

ture generations'. This tendency to focus on the rights of future generations could well be detracting from a focus on the rights of children, who are here now. This seems like a missed opportunity when there is an issue being widely litigated – the climate crisis – on which there appears to be some acceptance that children are affected disproportionately.

6 Conclusion

The climate and environmental crises are arguably the most serious threat to children's rights globally. States are under an obligation to immediately take action to protect human rights, and yet national climate action plans remained insufficient to limit global temperature rise to 1.5 degrees.[109] In climate policy-making most States do not explicitly give primary consideration to children's rights and interests.[110]

Indirect discrimination occurs when a seemingly neutral policy or rule has an unintended, detrimental impact on a particular group of people. It can be argued that in failing to adequately mitigate the climate crisis states are, without objective and reasonable justification, failing to treat children differently, whose situations are significantly different. Their situations are different for a number of reasons, including their exclusion from voting and the fact that they will on average live much longer than adults.

There is a growing body of literature which aims to position children as at risk of discrimination in the same way that other distinct groups can be. The Committee on the Rights of the Child does not often refer to age discrimination against children, but it has referred to it occasionally, and has not ruled it out as a principle for children's rights. This gives cause for optimism about the use of CRC Article 2 to counter age discrimination against children. The phrase "intergenerational justice" has been essential to the climate justice movement,[111] and as well as examining the dichotomy of old versus young in the climate crisis, it presents adults versus children as a frame for legal analysis.

In climate litigation, children/youth are one of a handful of groups who are arguing that their particular vulnerabilities is an issue of equality/nondis-

109 UN Climate Change, *Nationally determined contributions under the Paris Agreement. Synthesis report by the secretariat*, 14 November 2023 <https://unfccc.int/documents/632334 > Accessed 29 May 2024.

110 UNICEF, *Climate & Environment Discussion Paper* (UNICEF, November 2021).

111 Daly, *supra* note 12.

crimination where governments fail to mitigate the climate crisis.[112] Two significant factors exist. Children are generally excluded from the right to vote, and so arguably judicial intervention therefore is more justifiable (this was recognised in Columbian case SU-225/98 in the Constitutional Court). Furthermore, when an applicant is particularly vulnerable, states arguably are required to give weighty reasons for the differential treatment. Children have dependency-based vulnerability as well as vulnerability due to state control.[113] Their vulnerability has been recognised extensively by for example the ECtHR.[114]

The equality/discrimination argument has, before climate cases, been almost completely avoided when children's interests arise in court. Yet explicit arguments relating to nondiscrimination/equality have been engaged in climate applications/cases at both national and international level.[115] This is a very notable transformation for children's rights, despite the fact that the principle is not necessarily successfully invoked.

Greater levels of reliance on arguments relating to nondiscrimination/equality for children are evident in climate cases in the past few years. It seems that the earliest was the *Juliana* case, This constitutes a distinct use of argument comparing children and adults, in terms of the effects of the climate crisis. At national level, there appears to be countries whose laws are particularly well disposed to equality arguments, and this has been harnessed in climate cases with children litigants, such as in the 2023 application of *Children of Austria v. Austria*. Canada has been another key jurisdiction in this regard, due to Section 15 of the *Canadian Charter of Rights and Freedoms* which states that everyone is equal before and under the law without discrimination based on age. In the (unsuccessful) *Mathur v Ontario*, 2020 ONSC 6918 (CanLII) and *Mathur v His Majesty the King in Right of Ontario*, 2023 ONSC 2316 (CanLII), as well as the ongoing Canadian *La Rose*[116] case children and youth have argued that the Canadian government is violating their rights under the Charter by perpetuating climate change. These applications very explicitly rely on the argument that government conduct related to climate change constitutes unjustifiable age-based discrimination.

112 Kaya, *supra* note 39.

113 Heri, *supra* note 64.

114 *Stuart* v. *UK* App no 41903/98, Decision of 6 July 1999, para 1, citing *Stubbings and Others* para. 64.

115 Donger, *supra* note 67.

116 *La Rose* v. *Canada*, 2020 FC 1008, online: <https://decisions.fct-cf.gc.ca/fc-cf/decisions/en/item/487686/index.do> plaintiffs' statement of claim, at para 27.

There are some notable trends in the invocation of the principle of nondiscrimination/equality for children in these cases. One point is that references to nondiscrimination/equality can appear tokenistic. In the *Sacchi* application for example,[117] reference is made to nondiscrimination/equality, but without elaboration. It is a welcome, if vague reference to discrimination. Another point is that it is the interests of 'younger people' that are referenced – this means that the focus is on 'youth' arguments rather than on those relating to under 18s (i.e. children), as in the Dutch *Urgenda* case for example. These cases are therefore unlikely to provide detailed arguments about nondiscrimination/equality for children. The focus is more likely on nondiscrimination and young people.

Another crucial point is that the principle of the rights of future generations has proven useful in climate cases as it is enshrined in the laws of numerous countries.[118] A number of climate cases appear to have a mix of children's legal entitlements, and a focus on different generations – the *Juliana* case, for example.[119] These arguments relating to both 'intergenerational equity' and 'the rights of future generations' are attractive for litigators as they are grounded in national law provisions, but they could possibly be distracting from the need to fully elaborate children's right to equality/nondiscrimination.

Although arguments relating to nondiscrimination/equality for children are not necessarily *successfully* invoked in climate cases, arguably the consequences of raising these arguments is quite profound. First, it has explicitly proclaimed children as the equals of adults, as they access adult spaces and make rights claims in a way that they have never done before. It is somewhat tragic that it is in the context of an existential threat to humanity that they, as a group, will be left to deal with longer than those of us who are older.

The second point is that these cases in which nondiscrimination/equality arguments are being used, sometimes *do* have profound legal consequences. The *Sacchi* application,[120] although it did not proceed to a full hearing, involved the Committee recognising that a state can, in certain circumstances, be held responsible for the impacts of its carbon emissions on the rights of

117 *Sacchi, supra* note 78.

118 The German Basic Law of the German Federal Republic Article 20a (added 1994). English translation at: <https://www.gesetze-im-internet.de/englisch_gg/englisch_gg.html> accessed 6 May 2024.

119 *See, Juliana, et al.* v. *United States of America, et al.* No: 6:15-cv-01517 (D.Or. 2018), proceeding § 292.

120 Sacchi, *supra* note 78,

children inside *and* outside of its territory.[121] Through the *Urgenda* case, the discriminatory, effects of climate change on 'younger people' has been legally documented in a European climate change case.[122]

Irrespective of the success of these cases, it is crucial to invoke the principle to progress the rights of children/young people as a group in the climate crisis, so that their specific needs are better recognised. Age-related environmental vulnerabilities[123] of children must be addressed meaningfully. The use of the principle fills a gap in international human rights law. It encourages focus on children as a group which the principle of the best interest of the child has not managed to do, considering most States do not explicitly give primary consideration to children's rights and interests.[124] The principle has the effect of drawing explicit attention to discrimination against children in the climate crisis, and making it clear that it is unacceptable. Child-involved climate cases will likely continue to proliferate and litigators and their representatives will learn how to better achieve legal victories. Legal success with the principle of nondiscrimination/equality for children will obligate law makers and others to explicitly outline how they are ensuring that children's needs are adequately considered in the climate crisis.

---

121 Daly, *supra* note 79.

122 Kaya, *supra* note 39.

123 Kaya, *supra* note 56.

124 UNICEF, *Climate & Environment Discussion Paper* (UNICEF, November 2021).

CHAPTER 8

Working Children: Children without Childhood or Opponents against Age-Based Discrimination?

Manfred Liebel

Abstract[1]

Working children are not only discriminated against because they are still children, but also because they live in a way that is not foreseen in the prevailing pattern of childhood from the Global North: they work. Their discrimination is expressed, among other things, by the fact that their work is not recognised and that they are more economically exploited than adults, as well as by the fact that they are denied labour rights and participation in all matters that affect them as working children. To counteract their discrimination, the author argues for rethinking childhoods as well as work. In this context, he refers to the concept of adultism as a fundamental feature of a society in which adults determine how young people should live and in which children are prevented from participating in a meaningful way. The author explores the forms of adultism and discrimination against working children and describes the specific ways in which they experience and resist it.

1 Introduction

Working children are among the most discriminated young people. They are not only discriminated against because they are still children, but also because they live in a way that is not provided for in the prevailing Western-European pattern of childhood: they work. This pattern, which has spread throughout the world over the last 250 years, provides special educational reservations for children in which they are separated from the 'seriousness of life' and the 'adult world'. It is understood as an *incomplete* or *immature* preparatory stage for what is imagined to be perfect adulthood. It goes hand in hand

1 The chapter is based on an intensive exchange with Philip Meade and collaboration with activists in the ProNATs association, which campaigns for the rights of working children (*see* https://pronats.org/en/). I would like to thank the anonymous reviewers and Monique Voltarelli for comments on the manuscript.

with children being subordinate to adults and excluded from activities that are considered essential for social production and reproduction. This attribution is sometimes criticised as the 'infantilisation' or 'colonisation of childhood' and is considered characteristic of an 'adult-centred' society.[2] In this context, discrimination against working children is expressed, among other things, in the fact that their work is not recognised and they are economically exploited to a particularly high degree compared to adults, as well as in the fact that they are denied labour rights and participation in all matters that affect them as working children.

To counteract their discrimination, I consider it necessary to rethink childhood as well as labour/work. Instead of understanding childhood as a state in which children are excluded from any kind of work, children (can) also work without jeopardizing their lives and well-being and restricting their life prospects. However, this requires a society to change in such a way that work can become a life-affirming activity that enhances the lives of people of all ages and makes them more satisfying.

In this chapter, I examine the specific ways in which and the specific reasons why working children are discriminated against in societies with capitalist modes of production – which today affects the largest part of the world. I pay particular attention to those aspects and reasons that go hand in hand with the low age and minority status of children. I describe a society in which the young age of children becomes a major reason for discrimination as *adultist*. This is a society in which adults generally determine – either directly through their authoritarian stance, or indirectly by framing norms and expectations or denying resources – how young people should live and in which children are prevented from participating in a meaningful way in the matters that affect their lives.[3] In the case of working children, adultism takes on special forms.

---

2 *See e.g.* A. Prout, *The Future of Childhood* (Routledge-Falmer, London and New York, 2005); G. S. Cannella and R. Viruru, *Childhood and Postcolonization: Power Education, and Contemporary Practice* (Routledge-Falmer, New York and London, 2004); M. Liebel, *Decolonizing Childhoods: From Exclusion to Dignity* (Policy Press, Bristol and Chicago, 2020); X. Bañales, 'Decolonization: 'A Framework to Understand and Transgress Adultism", 22:1 *Taboo: The Journal of Culture and Education,* Special issue: Adultism (2024), pp. 7–27.

3 *See* 22:1 *Taboo: The Journal of Culture and Education,* Special issue: Adultism (2024); P. Alderson, 'Adultism', in D. T. Cook (ed.), *The SAGE Encyclopedia of Children and Childhood Studies* (Sage, Thousand Oaks, 2020), pp 538–542; A. Fletcher, *Facing Adultism* (Common Action Books, Olympia, WA, 2015); B. A. LeFrançois, 'Adultism', in T. Teo (ed.), *Encyclopedia of Critical Psychology* (Springer, New York, 2014), pp 47–49.

First, I will outline what I mean by working children, discrimination and adultism. I will then discuss the specific ways in which working children are affected by discrimination in societies with a capitalist mode of production, paying particular attention to labour and participation rights. Finally, I will use the example of the movements of working children to show how children defend themselves against the superiority of adults and the discrimination that goes hand in hand with this, and what can be learnt from this for an open and adultism-critical understanding of childhood.

2 Who Are Working Children and What Is Age-Based Discrimination?

Contrary to the dominant notion enshrined in many laws, that the role of children is to be prepared in school for their role as future workers, millions of children around the world continue to engage in activities that directly contribute to the reproduction of life.[4] Many of these children, especially in the regions of the Global South[5], do so to contribute to the livelihoods of their families, who need the economic cooperation of their children. Other children, especially in the regions of the Global North, engage in activities to have their own income, to participate in the lives of adults and to be more independent from their parents. When I refer to these activities as work, I do not only have in mind activities that are paid, but all activities that are essential to life or – in the words of Karl Marx – that produce 'use values' or contribute to the reproduction of life.[6] This includes, for example, looking after younger siblings or taking on tasks in the household of one's own family or of other people in the neighbourhood and wherever else.

The vast majority of working children live in regions of the Global South, i.e. areas whose people were colonised by European powers and are still suffering the consequences (even if some of these sufferings are meanwhile home-

4 *See e.g.* M. Liebel, *A Will of Their Own: Cross-Cultural Perspectives on Working Children* (Zed Books, London and New York, 2004); M. Bourdillon et al., *Rights and Wrongs of Children's Work* (Rutgers University Press, New Brunswick and London, 2011); V. Morrow and J. Boyden, *Responding to children's work: Evidence from the Young Lives study in Ethiopia, India, Peru and Vietnam. Summative Report* (Young Lives, Oxford, 2018).

5 I use the terms Global South and Global North not in a geographical but in a geopolitical sense.

6 *See e.g.* T. Bhattacharya (ed.), *Social Reproduction Theory* (Pluto Press, London, 2017); R. Rosen, 'Childhood in and through Social Reproduction Theory' in S. Balagopalan et al. (eds.), *The Bloomsbury Handbook of Theories in Childhood Studies* (Bloomsbury Academic, London, 2023), pp. 690–725.

made).[7] The statistics and reports of the International Labour Organisation (ILO)[8] are focussed on these regions, but they only cover a small part of the children working there, because they only understand as work what contributes to the 'economic value added', i.e. work for third parties that is remunerated somehow – in money or in kind. They also provide only very limited information about how the conditions vary under which children work. And – perhaps even more important – they provide no information at all about what the work means to the children and what they themselves think about it.

In the reports and statistics, working children do not appear as subjects, but are reified as a 'social problem' under the label of *child labour*. In the concept of the 'worst forms of child labour' (ILO Convention 182)[9], the understanding of labour is even extended to processes such as child trafficking, recruitment of children for use in armed conflict or the use of children for prostitution and pornography, whereby it is only a question of what children are used for. Something seems happening to them that can supposedly only be remedied by measures taken by the state or other authorities. Working children are treated as if they were something to be banned or 'abolished', for example by striving for 'child labour-free zones' or decreeing blanket bans on work up to a certain age. All of this may be well-intentioned, but it does nothing to protect them; in fact, it usually increases their vulnerability.[10] Moreover,

7 This also applies to many children of migrants from these countries who live, for example, in Southern Europe. *See* L. Gaitán et al. (eds.), *Children's Lives in Southern Europe: Contemporary Challenges and Risks* (Edward Elgar Publishing, Cheltenham UK and Northampton, MA, 2020); or in the USA: J. T. Mortimer, *Working and Growing Up in America*. (Harvard University Press, Cambridge, MA and London, 2003); E. Estrada, *Kids at Work: Latinx Families Selling Food at the Streets of Los Angeles* (New York University Press, New York, 2019).

8 *See e.g.* International Labour Organisation and UNICEF, *Child Labour: Global Estimates 2020, Trends and the Road Forward* (ILO and UNICEF, New York, 2021).

9 C182 – Worst Forms of Child Labour Convention, 1999 (No. 182), <https://normlex.ilo.org/dyn/normlex/en/f?p=NORMLEXPUB:12100:0::NO::P12100_ilo_CODE:C182>.

10 *See e.g.* B. Hungerland et al. (eds.), *Working to be someone: Child focused research and practice with working children* (Jessica Kingsley Publishers, London and Philadelphia, 2007): Bourdillon et al., *supra* note 4; E. V. Edmonds and S. Maheshwor, 'The Impact of Minimum Age of Employment Regulation on Child Labor and Schooling: Evidence from UNICEF MICS Countries', 1:14 *IZA Journal of Labor Policy* (2012), pp. 1–14; P. Bharadwaj et al., 'Perverse Consequences of Well-Intentioned Regulation: Evidence from India's Child Labor Ban', *NBER Working Paper No. 19602* (October) (National Bureau of Economic Research, Cambridge, MA, 2013); D. I. Putnick and M. H. Bornstein, 'Is Child Labor a Barrier to School Enrolment in Low- and Middle-Income Countries?', 41 *International Journal of Educational Development* (2015), pp. 112–120.

these practices make working children invisible as people who feel, think, speak, and (want to) act. This already brings us to a form of discrimination that could be called 'epistemic injustice'[11] or even 'epistemic violence'.[12] In contrast, some regional branches of NGOs, such as *Save the Children, Defence for Children International, terre des hommes, Enda Tiers-Monde* or *Concerned for Working Children* take a more differentiated position. For the reasons mentioned, they reject a blanket ban on child labour and advocate a policy that recognises the subjectivity and views of working children.[13]

When I speak of working children here, I am using a term chosen by working children of the Global South themselves. It is the result of a decades-long learning process, handed down from generation to generation, in which children constitute themselves as social subjects who do something vital and which they understand as an integral part of their identity.[14] These processes take place predominantly in age-appropriate groups of children, sometimes taking the form of child-led social movements and organisations.[15] By describing themselves as working children, children oppose a discriminatory way of

11 M. Fricker, *Epistemic Injustice: Power and the Ethics of Knowing* (Oxford University Press, Oxford, 2007).

12 G. C. Spivak, 'Can the Subaltern Speak?' in C. Nelson and L. Grossberg (eds.), *Marxism and the Interpretation of Culture* (University of Illinois Press, Urbana, IL, 1988), pp. 66–111.

13 Some examples: *Save the Children's Position on Child Labour*, February 2019, available at <https://resourcecentre.savethechildren.net/pdf/child_labour_position_feb_2018.pdf/>; Defence for Children International, 'DCI's Position on Child Labour: A Contribution to Debate and Practice', February 2002; available at <https://www.dci-is.org/Static/childldesk/DCIs-position-on-CL-menu-5-sousmenu-1.html>; 'Terre des Hommes calls for participation of working children in identifying sustainable solutions', June 2021; available at <https://reliefweb.int/report/world/terre-des-hommes-calls-participation-working-children-identifying-sustainable-solutions>. In Africa, the NGO Enda Tiers-Monde accompanies the African Movement of Working Children and Youth. *See e.g.* <https://endatiersmonde.org/aiovg_videos/how-to-join-the-movement-of-working-children-and-youth-in-africa/>. In India, the NGO Concerned for Working Children is committed to the self-organisation of working children. *See* <https://www.concernedforworkingchildren.org/empowering-children/childrens-unions/> (all retrieved 22 July 2024).

14 Since for most children in the Global North work is not existentially necessary and comprises only a small temporal share of their lifetime, they rarely see themselves explicitly as working children.

15 On the origin and significance of working children's movements, *see* M. Liebel et al. (eds.), *Working Children's Protagonism: Social Movements and Empowerment in Latin America, Africa and India* (IKO, Frankfurt/M. and London, 2001); Liebel, *supra* note 4; O. Nieuwenhuys, 'From Child Labour to Working Children's Movements' in J. Qvortrup et al. (eds.), *The Palgrave Handbook of Childhood Studies* (Palgrave Macmillan, Basingstoke, 2009), pp. 289–300; J. K. Taft, *The Kids are in Charge: Activism and Power in Peru's Working Children Movement* (New York University Press, New York, 2019); E. van Daalen,

speaking that sees children's vital activities not as work that deserves recognition, but at best as 'help' for close adults. This reproduces a pattern of childhood according to which it is incompatible with a 'proper childhood' to take responsibility for one's life through work and other activities. From my point of view, working children are not 'children without childhood',[16] but they embody other childhoods that have yet to be deciphered and which I understand in this chapter as an alternative design to the uniform Eurocentric pattern of childhood. In this way, I wish to contribute to a better understanding of the discrimination against working children and to counteract it.

Age-related discrimination is receiving increasing attention in research and policy. However, the focus has so far been primarily on older people, usually called *ageism*. Age-based discrimination of young people, also referred to as *adultism* or *adult-centrism*, on the other hand, is still largely a research desideratum and is only gradually being considered as a policy challenge.[17] In the following, when I refer to age-based discrimination against young people as a structural feature of societies, I will speak of adultism or adult-centred societies.

The UN Convention on the Rights of the Child (CRC)[18] does not explicitly mention (young) age as a possible ground for discrimination. Article 2 calls on the States Parties to respect and ensure the children's rights "without discrimination of any kind, irrespective of the child's or his or her parents or legal guardian's race, colour, sex, language, religion, political or other opinion, national, ethnic or social origin, property, disability, birth or other status". The UN Committee on the Rights of the Child is increasingly addressing the issue of age, but it still plays a minor role in the General Observations of the State

---

Decolonising the Global Child Labour Regime: The ILO, Trade Unions and Organised Working Children (PhD Thesis, University of Geneva, Faculty of Law, 2020).

16 *See e.g.* M. Winn, *Children without Childhood: Growing Up to Fast in the World of Sex and Drugs* (Penguin Books, New York, 1984); UNICEF, *Zur Situation der Kinder in der Welt. Kinder ohne Kindheit* (S. Fischer, Frankfurt/M., 2006); M. Winkel, 'Children Without Childhood: Robbed Innocence and Its Implications for Violence', 1 *Voices in Bioethics* (2014), pp. 1–5.

17 *See* M. Liebel, 'Adultism and age-based discrimination against children', in D. Kutsar and H. Warming (eds.), *Children and non-discrimination. Interdisciplinary textbook* (Children's Rights Erasmus Academic Network – CREAN and University of Estonia Press, 2014), pp. 119–143. M. Liebel and P. Meade, *Adultism: A Critical Introduction to Discrimination Against Children* (Policy Press, Bristol, 2026).

18 UN Convention on the Rights of the Child (1989).

Reports and the General Comments.[19] Moreover, working children are hardly considered in these contexts.

Discrimination is always rooted in unequal power, in the case of age-based discrimination on the greater power that adults usually have over children. It is a form of exercising power by older people over younger people, which has negative consequences for the younger people.[20] It can manifest itself in verbal and symbolic forms, such as how adults speak about and to children, or how children are portrayed figuratively. It can manifest itself in physical and material ways, such as violence, paternalism, violation of physical and psychic integrity, or denial of rights and vital resources. Or it can happen seemingly 'by itself' whereby norms are set according to which children are judged as inadequate, insufficient or incompetent. In the broadest sense, it negates children as social subjects, making them invisible as persons with specific characteristics, up to and including the threat of extermination.

In the case of working children, who are the focus of this chapter, an *intersectional* perspective and a broad understanding of discrimination are particularly important.[21] Working children are never discriminated against solely because they are children, but also because as working children they live in ways that are not envisaged in the prevailing pattern of childhood or are seen as backward and harmful to the development of society. Age-based discrimination or the adultist treatment of working children manifests itself primarily in

- that children's work is equated with economic exploitation and condemned as harmful in a blanket manner, mainly with reference to their young age,
- that protection from the negative consequences of work is achieved solely through prohibitions on work and that working children are denied any labour rights,

19 *See* A. Daly et al., 'UN Convention on the Rights of the Child, and Article 2 discrimination on the basis of childhood: The CRC Paradox?', 91:3 *Nordic Journal of International Law* (2022), pp. 419–452.

20 *See e.g.* Liebel, *supra* note 17; Fletcher, *supra* note 3; M. Liebel and P. Meade, 'Adultism, children's political participation and voting rights' in M. Liebel (in collaboration with R. Budde, U. Markowska-Manista and P. Meade), *Childhoods of the Global South: Children's Rights and Resistance* (Policy Press, Bristol, 2023), pp. 98–115.

21 *See* M. Liebel and P. Meade, 'Intersectional tensions in theorizing adultism', 22:1 *Taboo: The Journal of Culture and Education,* Special issue: Adultism (2024), pp. 96–123. In the case of working children, adultism is particularly intertwined with the discriminatory dimensions of classism, sexism and racism.

– that working children are denied the right to participate in policy decisions and actions that affect their work and their lives.

3 Discrimination by Equating Children's Work with Economic Exploitation

Today it is common to equate the work of children up to a certain age with economic exploitation. 'Exploitation' is a kind of metaphor meant to signal that the mere fact that a child is working is reprehensible and to be rejected. While a distinction is occasionally made between exploited work (*child labour*) and non-exploited work (*child work*), the dominant idea is that work is unsuitable for children and robs children of their childhood.

In the prevailing view of children's work, wage labour becomes the measure of all things. By attributing a 'value' only to this, all other forms of work, especially those described as 'reproductive', are devalued. From such a perspective, most of the labour practised by children today can neither be adequately analysed nor valued. This applies to the Global South as well as to the Global North.

If we really want to get to the fundaments of child exploitation in its social contexts, it is necessary to understand it as an unequal social relationship between persons or social groups (classes) in which one side, due to greater power and possibly by force, gains economic advantages at the expense of the other side. Its essence is that one side becomes the object of the other.

It is obvious that exploitation in the sense outlined here is common in contemporary capitalist societies. While the manifestations and trajectories of exploitation have changed throughout history, and in some respects violence and arbitrariness in working conditions have been reduced or regulated by protectory legal norms, exploitation remains a common reality as economic and political power continues to be unequally distributed. As deregulation and informalisation of labour relations and labour markets continue to increase worldwide, exploitation is taking on more blatant forms and dimensions again. New forms of exploitation are emerging as classic wage labour or *dependent* work is being replaced by forms of *fictitious self-employment* in growing parts of the economy.[22]

22 *See e.g.* S. Edgell, *The Sociology of Work: Continuity and Change in Paid and Unpaid Work*. Second Edition (Sage, London, 2010); U. Bröckling, *The Entrepeneurial Self: Fabricating a New Type of Subject* (Sage, London, 2016).

A large part of children's work takes place under these conditions. On the one hand because they have no legal possibility to enter formal employment relationships due to the ban on child labour and only have access to informal work, and on the other hand because they are considered particularly flexible and are easy prey for those who have power over them due to their marginal and subordinate social position. It is also important to remember that economic exploitation is not limited to traditional labour relations. Today, it also increasingly takes place in the run-up to work, in the field of digital media and on the commodity market. Young people are being instrumentalised with their creativity to increase the design and marketing of products as 'trendsetters'. For young people, work and non-work can no longer be strictly separated in terms of space, time and concepts.

One way of understanding the nature of exploitation and the associated discrimination against children is to ask why their labour is valued less and exploited more than that of adults. This is expressed, for example, in the fact that they are generally paid less than the comparable work of adults, or that there is no payment at all, with the indication that it is not 'real' work, but a form of 'help', 'initiation' or 'training'. Or that the wages are not paid to the children but to the parents and the work of the children is treated as a seemingly self-evident part of the family labour force. Or that children are not 'rewarded' with money, but (if at all) with goods in kind. But discrimination is also expressed in the fact that it is not considered necessary to grant working children the same labour rights that apply to adults (see section 4).

Like the economic exploitation of adults, the exploitation of children is a structural phenomenon of capitalist societies. But the reference to the structures and functioning of capitalist economies is not sufficient to explain the risks of exploitation and discrimination of working children. Nor can it be used to understand the different levels of risk and the specific and quite different forms and degrees of exploitation to which children are exposed in the South on the one hand and in the North on the other.

The subordinate social position of children in the age hierarchy can be considered a risk factor for the exploitation of children that cannot be directly derived from the functional laws of the capitalist economy. To describe this, as is usually done, as 'weakness' is problematic insofar as it suggests that it is a primarily biological phenomenon. In fact, however, the weakness of children, which makes them more susceptible for external interests and purposes, is largely the result of a social construction, i.e. it results from social power relations, and it is therefore also changeable. Children's weakness manifests itself in two directions: as disregard for their subjectivity and as exclusion from social responsibility.

The subjectivity of children is despised above all in authoritarian and strongly hierarchically structured societies in which postulates of equality and individual as well as collective rights do not play a significant role. This is often the case in societies of the Global South, where communal forms of life and work based on reciprocity are dissolving under the pressure of 'modernisation', globalisation and individualisation, without new rules and institutions of coexistence and social responsibility being able to develop.[23] In the 'advanced' societies of the North, a higher value is placed on the subjectivity and protection of children, but in the same breath children are excluded from the 'society of adults' and 'infantilised'.[24] Here, it is above all the bourgeois ideology of childhood that places children in a status of dependency and makes them disadvantaged.

In her now classic theoretical study on 'The Differentiation of Children's Labour in the Capitalist Labour Market', economist Diane Elson[25] attributes the 'dominant' forms of work that disadvantage children to three 'authority sources' which, according to her, mark the 'seniority system' of contemporary capitalist societies: 1. the authority of the adults in the family; 2. the requirements of the educational system, which is also governed by adults; 3. the 'needs' of capitalism for the easy and profitable utilisation of labour power.

> The seniority system obviously encompasses a range of gradations, not simply the division between children and adults, but children are at the bottom of it. And this means it is extremely difficult for them to secure full recognition in monetary terms for the skills they possess and for the contribution they make to family income. Only when they have passed over to adult status can they be recognised as 'skilled' or 'breadwinners' – or rather, only when the boys have passed over to adult status, for the girls the problem remains.[26]

The low status of children has the result that a) the children's abilities are poorly regarded; b) children are primarily given tasks that are considered eco-

---

23 C. Katz, *Growing Up Global: Economic Restructuring and Children's Everyday Lives* (University of Minnesota Press, Minneapolis, 2004); M. Liebel, 'Children without Childhood? Against the Postcolonial Capture of Childhoods in the Global South', in A. Invernizzi, et al. (eds.), *'Children Out of Place' and Human Rights* (Springer, Cham, 2017), pp. 79–98.

24 Cannella and Viruru, *supra* note 2; Prout, *supra* note 2, pp. 7–34; K. Wells, *Childhood Studies* (Polity Press, Cambridge, 2018), pp. 147–157; Liebel, *supra* note 2, pp. 9–32.

25 D. Elson, 'The Differentiation of Children's Labour in the Capitalist Labour Market', 13 *Development and Change* (1982), pp. 479–497.

26 Ibid., p. 493.

nomically less valuable, especially so-called 'reproductive' jobs; c) despite the large quantity of work that they do, children are not recognised as workers with their own rights.[27]

Elson brings the educational system into the picture, because the 'pupil role' that it assigns to children makes their out-of-school work appear a marginal activity compared with their school obligations. This activity deserves no recognition and may even be devalued and discriminated against as a possible source of interference with what is important school performance. In the societies of the Global South, work is the main activity for most children, and they often struggle to reconcile their work with their educational interests and, in some circumstances, with school attendance. Quite a few children would not be able to attend school at all without their earnings from work. However, from the point of view of those who want to promote 'development' towards more 'modernity', children's work is seen exclusively and even as the main obstacle to regular and successful school attendance. The enforcement of compulsory education is seen as an alleged magic cure to eradicate child labour. This pushes children into a marginal social position that limits rather than expands their opportunities to achieve better living and working conditions.

Elson describes the seniority system as a socially constructed age hierarchy 'in which those in junior positions are unable to achieve full social status. They are not full members of the society.'[28] According to her, their subordination does not mean that they lack the personal capacity for autonomous behaviour; indeed, many children have more ability than many adults. What, on the other hand, it brings with it is the 'lack of public means for recognition of the right to autonomy; and the lack of public means to sustain and extend autonomy'.[29] In the seniority system, the lack of readiness of adults to question their own power over children manifests itself. 'The desire of adults to preserve adult power over children, through constructing certain forms of family, for instance, and certain forms of education, has given children an unenviable choice between exploitation at work and subservience in home and school.'[30] By contrast, children should

27 Ibid., p. 491; *see also* O. Nieuwenhuys, 'The Household Economy and the Commercial Exploitation of Children's Work: The case of Kerala' in B. Schlemmer (ed.), *The Exploited Child* (Zed Books, London and New York, 2000), pp. 278–291, with special reference to the Global South.

28 Elson, *supra* note 25, p. 491.

29 Ibid., p. 492.

30 Ibid., p. 494.

be granted an appropriate income of their own as their right, as well as the connection between education and income-generating activities. The exclusion of children from the sphere of work, even if it is the capitalist labour market, 'simply changes the way in which children are subordinated, rather than ending that subordination'.[31]

4 Discrimination by Denying Labour Rights

Working children are also discriminated against by being denied labour rights. These are defined in international law as the rights set out in the conventions of the International Labour Organisation (ILO).[32] The most important of these conventions are summarised in the ILO Declaration on Fundamental Principles and Rights at Work. This declaration highlights the following 'fundamental principles' or 'core labour standards':

- Freedom of association and the effective recognition of the right to collective bargaining
- The elimination of all forms of forced or compulsory labour
- The effective abolition of child labour
- The elimination of discrimination in respect of employment and occupation
- A safe and healthy working environment.[33]

Looking at the labour rights enshrined in international law, it is easy to see the contradictory statements on children. The ILO's Fundamental Principles do not include age provisions on 'freedom of association' and the 'elimination of discrimination in respect of employment and occupation', so they should apply to all workers regardless of their age. Yet the ILO principles contain a provision that is incompatible with this logic. When the ILO Principles refer to

31 Ibid., p. 495.

32 Labour rights are to be distinguished from economic rights, which are codified in the International Covenant on Economic, Social and Cultural Rights (ICESCR, 1966). They are a continuation of the rights first formulated in the Universal Declaration of Human Rights of 1948. Economic rights and labour rights differ in the sense that economic rights are intended for all people, while labour rights apply only to those who are in an employment relationship. For details *see* M. Liebel, 'Economic and labour rights – a blind spot in the discourse on children's rights', 39:2 *Nordic Journal of Human Rights* (2021), pp. 163–179. In the following, I will only deal with labour rights.

33 *The International Labour Organization's Fundamental Conventions.* Second impression (International Labour Office, Geneva, 2003), amended in 2022, available at https://www.ilo.org/ilo-declaration-fundamental-principles-and-rights-work (retrieved 28 September 2024).

the 'effective abolition of child labour' as a fundamental right, this can logically only be understood as a right of adults, since children are affected by it but are not seen as a separate subject of this right. As the Principles are based on ILO Conventions, they are governed by Convention No. 138, which sets minimum age requirements for employment.[34] While these provisions are intended to meet the special needs of children and to protect them, they constitute a serious restriction of their rights. They raise the question of whether they are an age-specific form of discrimination by implicitly nullifying the claimed function of child protection. For example, it is not possible for working children under the minimum age to claim rights in their workplace.

The same logical contradiction is reproduced in the CRC. Article 32 of this Convention, the only one directly related to children's work, reads as follows:

> 1. States Parties recognize the right of the child to be protected from economic exploitation and from performing any work that is likely to be hazardous or to interfere with the child's education, or to be harmful to the child's health or physical, mental, spiritual, moral or social development.
> 2. States Parties shall take legislative, administrative, social and educational measures to ensure the implementation of the present article. To this end, and having regard to the relevant provisions of other international instruments, States Parties shall in particular:
> (a) Provide for a minimum age or minimum ages for admission to employment,
> (b) Provide for appropriate regulation of the hours and conditions of employment,
> (c) Provide for appropriate penalties or other sanctions to ensure the effective enforcement of the present article.

Although the CRC does not use the term child labour as do the relevant ILO conventions, the requirement to set a minimum age or ages for admission to employment also contradicts the stated right of all children to be protected from economic exploitation or hazardous work. If protection for children is to be achieved only through exclusion from work, it is insufficient and may even entail additional risks for children. To avoid this, children who start or con-

34 ILO Convention No. 138, concerning Minimum Age for Admission to Employment (1973).

tinue working for whatever reason must be entitled to rights at work and to protection measures.[35]

Regarding the rights of working children, legal scholars Karl Hanson and Arne Vandaele speak of a 'difference dilemma'.[36] This means that working children can be considered both as workers and as children. As workers, they are entitled to the same labour rights as adults. On the other hand, as children they also need special rights because of their specific developmental needs, their relative powerlessness and their greater vulnerability. The latter is the purpose of the CRC, which contains both rights that correspond to the rights of adults and specific rights that differ from the rights of adults. The difference dilemma arises when children are deprived of rights that adults possess by reference to their situation, or when children's rights are accompanied by the restriction of universal human rights. Such restrictions can also increase children's vulnerability and discrimination.

Regarding labour rights, the question arises whether, in addition to the right to protection from exploitation and hazardous work, children are also granted other rights that are considered essential for adults. This applies to the following rights, which can be found in various formulations both in the ICESCR[37] and in some ILO conventions and their Fundamental Principles (here summarised):

- the right to work and to free choice of employment
- the right to just and favourable conditions of work
- the right to protection against unemployment
- the right to equal pay for equal work, without any discrimination
- the right to form and to join trade unions for the protection of his or her interests, including the right to collective bargaining
- the right to rest and leisure, including reasonable limitation of working hours and periodic holidays with pay.

35 The UN Committee on the Rights of the Child has not yet drafted a General Comment on Article 32. It recommends that States Parties ratify the ILO conventions on child labour but, unlike the ILO, emphasises the indivisibility of the CRC rights and in particular respecting the views and associations of (working) children. *See* UNICEF, *Implementation Handbook for the Convention on the Rights of the Child*. Fully revised third edition (UNICEF Regional Office for Europe, Geneva, 2007), pp. 479–501.

36 K. Hanson and A. Vandaele, 'Working Children and International Labour Law: A Critical Analysis', 11:1 *International Journal of Children's Rights* (2003), pp. 73–146; K. Hanson and A. Vandaele, 'Translating working children's rights into international labour law', in K. Hanson and O. Nieuwenhuys (eds.), *Reconceptualizing Children's Rights in International Development: Living rights, Social Justice, Translations* (Cambridge University Press, New York and Cambridge, 2013), pp. 250–274.

37 ICESCR, *supra* note 32.

The fact that work continues to belong to the lives of many children, and that it is part of their childhood, makes it seem appropriate to grant all adult economic and labour rights to children as well. I shall illustrate, why, unlike labour prohibitions, this would help protect working children from exploitation, preserve their human dignity, and improve their working and living conditions. This would also contribute to making social rights enshrined in the CRC real, such as the rights to health (Art. 24), social security (Art. 26), adequate standard of living (Art. 27), education (Art. 28 and 29), and rest and leisure (Art. 31).

It should also be borne in mind that the right to form independent associations and to promote common interests in an organised manner, is also, as a general matter, established in the CRC. Article 15 states as follows:

> (1) States Parties recognize the rights of the child to freedom of association and to freedom of peaceful assembly.
> (2) No restrictions may be placed on the exercise of these rights other than those imposed in conformity with the law and which are necessary in a democratic society in the interests of national security or public safety, public order (ordre public), the protection of public health or morals or the protection of the rights and freedoms of others.

Although these rights are not formulated as economic or labour rights, they have this meaning for children who work or want to work. Working children in many regions of the Global South have long used these rights by forming their own social movements and organisations. They usually do not call themselves trade unions but social movements, but they (also) fulfil trade union tasks. The main reason why they are not part of the trade union movement so far is that adult trade unions refuse to accept working children as equal members. That forces working children to form their own organisations as a response to the discrimination they experience because of their age.

The refusal to grant children labour rights is particularly stubbornly advocated by most trade unions and the ILO. After the Second World War, the ILO initially tried to align its long-term goal of abolishing child labour with the need to protect working children. However, this 'two-plank approach',[38] which included the goal of regulating and 'humanising' child labour, was re-

38 E. van Daalen and K. Hanson, 'The ILO's Shifts in Child Labour Policy: Regulation and Abolition', 11 *International Development Policy* (2019), pp. 133–150.

placed in the 1990s by the single goal of the complete eradication of child labour, starting with its 'worst forms'.[39]

One of the conventions that the ILO considers to be a particularly important part of its framework is ILO Convention No. 138, which sets minimum ages for employment.[40] It does not refer to human rights in general or children's rights in particular but defines measures to prevent children from working below the specified age limits. Although working conditions for children vary greatly, the Convention assumes that age alone is decisive in determining that work is harmful to children and should therefore be prevented by all legal means. Here, as in the numerous previous conventions against child labour,[41] it becomes obvious that their main purpose is to ward off wage competition feared by children. While humanitarian motives are cited, it has not yet been proven that this Convention has contributed significantly to improving the situation of working children. On the contrary, various studies have shown that excluding children from work simply because of their young age has had counterproductive effects and has actually worsened the situation of many working children, including their families.[42] Moreover, they provide evidence that other rights of children are also violated by child labour elimination policies and that they can unduly undermine survival strategies and livelihoods, as well as access to education and other social rights. For the same reasons, some child rights practitioners have long advocated for the 'unwritten right' of children to work under fair conditions and for fair wages.[43]

Although the difficulties in this area have been documented in research for years, neither the ILO nor governments have yet undertaken a holistic assessment of the supposed protection of children through measures and programmes to eliminate child labour.[44] Although the ILO Global Reports published since 2002 speak of a decline in child labour worldwide – at least up to

39 ILO Convention No. 182 concerning the Prohibition and Immediate Action for the Elimination of the Worst Forms of Child Labour (1999).

40 ILO Convention No. 138, *supra* note 34.

41 M. Dahlén, *The Negotiable Child: The ILO Child Labour Campaign 1919–1973* (Uppsala Universitet, 2007).

42 On references, *see* footnote 10.

43 J. Ennew, 'Outside Childhood: Street Children's Rights', in B Franklin (ed.), *The New Handbook of Children's Rights: Comparative Policy and Practice* (Routledge, London, 2002), pp. 388–403; *see also* M. Liebel et al., 'Working Children as Subjects of Rights: Explaining Children's Rights to Work', in M. D. Ruck et al. (eds.), *Handbook of Children's Rights: Global and Multidisciplinary Perspectives* (Routledge, London, 2017), pp. 417–453.

44 M. Bourdillon and W. Myers, *Child Protection in Development.* (Routledge and INTRAC, London, 2013); M. Bourdillon and R. Carothers, 'Policy on Children's Work and Labour', 33:4 *Children & Society* (2019), pp. 387–395.

the Covid-19 pandemic –, they also note that the conditions under which children work have deteriorated in many areas. Report after report emphasises that the planned complete elimination of child labour by 2025 can only be achieved if the pace accelerates significantly.[45] In this context, the participation of organisations of working children is not only a right enshrined in the CRC. It would also be an appropriate and obvious way for children to present their problems and name violations, and for policymakers to obtain information on the actual results of current policies and practices.

5 Discrimination by Denying Participation

At least since the adoption of the CRC, it has been repeatedly emphasised that children must have the opportunity to participate in decisions that affect them. In its General Comment No. 12,[46] the UN Committee on the Rights of the Child explicitly emphasises that this also applies to working children: They 'should be included in the search for a solution, which respects the economic and socio-structural constraints as well as the cultural context under which these children work' (para. 116). And: 'Children and, if existing, representatives of working children's associations should also be heard when labour laws are drafted or when the enforcement of laws is considered and evaluated' (para. 117). Nevertheless, working children are still denied the opportunity to exercise their participation rights.

45 ILO, *A Future without Child Labour. Global Report on Child Labour* (International Labour Office, Geneva, 2002); ILO, *The End of Child Labour: Within Reach: Global Report on Child Labour under the Follow-up to the ILO Declaration on Fundamental Principles and Rights at Work* (International Labour Office, Geneva, 2006); ILO, *Accelerating Action against Child Labour: Global Report on Child Labour under the Follow-up to the ILO Declaration on Fundamental Principles and Rights at Work* (International Labour Office, Geneva, 2010); ILO, *Making Progress against Child Labour: Global Estimates and Trends 2000–2012* (International Labour Office, Geneva, 2013). ILO, *Global Estimates of Child Labour: Results and Trends 2012–2016* (International Labour Office, Geneva, 2017).
ILO and UNICEF, *Child Labour: Global Estimates 2020, Trends and the Road Forward* (United Nations Children's Fund, New York; International Labour Office, Geneva, 2021).
ILO and UNICEF, *Child Labour: Global estimates 2024, Trends and the Road Forward* (International Labour Office, Geneva; United Nations Children's Fund, New York, 2025).

46 UN Committee on the Rights of the Child, General Comment No. 12: The right of the child to be heard, CRC/C/GC/12 (2009).

With the sole exception of the Children and Adolescents Code of Bolivia in 2014[47] that I am aware of, working children have never been included in the drafting of other laws and conventions affecting them. In the ILO, which has played a central role in international law on children's work since its founding in 1919, working children are not represented in the relevant bodies. While there have been occasional attempts to give children a voice at child labour conferences, this has always been limited to symbolic gestures by mostly former or non-workers.

In December 1996, the first intercontinental meeting of working children's movements took place in Kundapur, South India. At this meeting, which was attended by delegates from children's movements from 33 countries in Latin America, Africa and Asia, a declaration was adopted ('The 10 Points of Kundapur'), which demanded, among other things:

> We demand to be involved in the decision-making processes that affect us, whether it is at a local, national or international level. [...] Concerning the conferences that are being organised we demand participation on an equal footing (*e.g.* if there are twenty ministers, there should be twenty working children). We are prepared to discuss with ministers, but they do not represent us.[48]

For the first time, representatives of working children's movements were invited to an International Child Labour Conference, which was organised by the Dutch government together with the ILO in Amsterdam in February 1997. Eight children from Africa, Asia and Latin America participated. In the following years, informal meetings with representatives of the ILO took place from time to time at the request of the movements of working children, but participation in official ILO events was constantly refused.

---

47 This participation only came about after massive pressure from the Union of Working Children of Bolivia (UNATSBO). *See* M. Liebel, 'Protecting the Rights of Working Children instead of Banning Child Labour: Bolivia Tries a New Legislative Approach', 23:3 *International Journal of Children's Rights* (2015), pp. 491–509. The parts of the law that the children fought for, and which affected them have since been withdrawn by international pressure, particularly by the ILO and the US government. *See* M. Liebel, 'Children's Rights: Bolivia bows to International Pressure', *D+C – Development and Cooperation* (May 2019), pp. 14–15.

48 The full text of the declaration and the following discussions on the international level are documented in M. Liebel and A. Invernizzi, 'The Movements of Working Children and the International Labour Organization: A Lesson on Enforced Silence', 33:2 *Children & Society* (2018), pp. 142–153.

At none of the Global Child Labour Conferences held between 1997 and 2022 were representatives of the movements of working children allowed to participate. At the II Global Child Labour Conference, which took place in The Hague in 2010, the 'participation' of children was limited to a five-minute decorative performance by a Dutch children's dance group at the opening event and the apparently coordinated acceptance speech by a 14-year-old 'former child worker' from India at the end of the conference. The fact that working children were once again excluded from the III Global Child Labour Conference, which took place in Brasilia in 2013, led some NGOs to attempt at least for the IV Global Child Labour Conference, which was held in Buenos Aires in November 2017, to make the voices of working children heard. They organised a wide-ranging consultation in which more than 1800 working children from 36 countries participated.[49] However, even the representatives of these children were not allowed to present the results of the consultation at this conference. In coordination with the Argentinian government at the time, all persons under the age of 18 were even banned from attending the conference 'for security reasons.'[50] This blatant violation of the participation rights enshrined in the CRC prompted the Latin American Movement of Working Children (MOLACNATS) to file a complaint with the UN Committee on the Rights of the Child. In response to the protests since then by working children and some children's rights organisations, a 'Children's Forum' was held at the V Global Child Labour Conference in Durban (South Africa) in May 2022, but this forum was again limited to the ritual staging of the voices of a few children, sent by NGOS, who supported the ILO's position.[51]

Although the ILO occasionally calls on children to participate in discussions and sets up online platforms before its Child Labour Conferences (to which working children often have no access due to their precarious living conditions), it sets the questions and the framework and only allows opinions

49 *See* https://www.dialogue-works.com/wp-content/uploads/2018/05/T2T_Report_EN.pdf (retrieved 23 November 2024).

50 *See* E. van Daalen and N. Mabillard, 'A tale of two conferences: exploring the politics of global child labour policies' (2017), available at: https://www.opendemocracy.net/beyondslavery/edward-van-daalen-nicolas-mabillard/tale-of-two-conferences-exploring-politics-of-glob> (retrieved 26 July 2024).

51 *See* the film of the forum, which the ILO itself published on its website: <https://www.5thchildlabourconf.org/en/session/thematic-panel-12-children-forum>; *see also* the 'joint declaration' of working children's movements: <https://www.concernedforworkingchildren.org/news/2022/05/joint-declaration-of-the-movements-of-children-and-adolescent-workers-in-light-of-the-ilos-5th-global-conference-on-child-labour/> (both retrieved 26 July 2024).

to be expressed that are subordinate to the ILO's goal of banning all forms of child labour. Child rights advocates Antonella Invernizzi and Brian Milne pointed out more than 20 years ago that under these conditions the participation of working children even 'becomes discriminatory':

> On the one hand, there will be some children who will be allowed and encouraged to use their participatory rights *as long as they conform* to the controls that are now subtly being imposed on them. On the other hand, those children who are attempting to claim their rights through the channel of social action that conforms to the pertinent articles of the CRC will be chastised for so doing since they are speaking out for children *who work illegally*.[52]

In all attempts to give children a voice, it is noticeable that while there is some willingness to listen to them – especially by street and social workers who have direct contact with the children –, this is explicitly refused when they present themselves as *working* children and want to participate in decision-making.

6 How Working Children Resist Age-Based Discrimination

Working children, at least when they explicitly position and organise themselves as working children, come into contradiction with the prevailing pattern of childhood. By claiming to be recognised as working children, they express that they embody a different childhood or childhoods. This claim is perhaps most clearly expressed in their claiming the right to work *as children* and their understanding of children's *protagonism*.[53] Studies over various decades show that working children practise a kind of 'situated agency' in their daily confrontation with their living and working conditions and the

52 A. Invernizzi and B. Milne, 'Are Children Entitled to Contribute to International Policy Making? A Critical View of Children's Participation in the International Campaign for the Elimination of Child Labour', 10:4 *International Journal of Children's Rights* (2002), pp. 403–431, 404, emphasis in original.

53 On protagonism, *see* M. Liebel, 'Paternalism, Participation and Children's Protagonism', 17:3 *Children, Youth and Environments* (2007), pp. 56–73; M. Liebel, *Childhoods of the Global South: Children's Rights and Resistance* (Policy Press, Bristol, 2023), pp. 165–179; J. K. Taft, 'Protagonismo and Power: Building Political Theory with Young Activists', in S. Balagopalan et al. (eds.), *The Bloomsbury Handbook of Theories in Childhood Studies* (Bloomsbury Academic, London, 2023), pp. 180–193.

search for 'better forms of work', ranging from small improvements in their daily lives to more far-reaching demands for a socially and generationally just society.[54]

Unlike the right to protection from economic exploitation – codified in CRC Article 32 – the right to work, which organisations of working children have been demanding for decades,[55] is a claim that children themselves assert. The demand is the result of the experience of working children that existing laws and policies to protect them from exploitation have rarely, if ever, helped to improve their situation, but have increased their discrimination and vulnerability.

The discriminatory effects are a result of laws and policies that, while intended to protect children from exploitation, are based on the blanket assumption that all work necessarily harms children. Therefore, they do not consider the reasons that motivate children to take up or pursue work. The underlying belief is that work is unsuitable for children and therefore there is no need to consider their views. As a result, working children are seen as victims and objects in need of help, rather than as individuals who reflect on their situation and identity – and how they can solve their problems.

The claim for the right to work responds to the demand of working children for a higher social valuation of their work and their contributions not only to their own and their families' lives, but also to the production and reproduction of society in general. The children who demand the right to work have experience of work and exploitation, and of the inadequacy of many measures to protect them. These children demand solutions that consider their living conditions and experiences. They want to be respected as persons who have a stake in and can contribute to the solution of their problems. In this sense, they see the right to work as an instrument of self-determination, where they take control of their own situation.

As children do not yet have full access to political rights, they are often excluded from the most important opportunities for political participation.

---

54 *See e.g.* A. Invernizzi, *La vie quotidienne des enfants travailleurs. Stratégies de survie et socialisation dans les rues de Lima* (L'Harmattan, Paris, 2001); B. Leyra Fatou, *La niñas trabajadoras. El caso de México* (Los Libros de la Catarata, Madrid, 2012); L. Frasco Zuker et al., 'Agencia infantil situada. Un análisis desde las experiencias de niñas y niños que trabajan en contextos de desigualdad social en Argentina', 27:60 *Horizontes Antropológicos* (2021), pp. 163–190.

55 *See* M. Liebel, 'Do children have a right to work? Working children's movements in the struggle for social justice' in K. Hanson and O. Nieuwenhuys (eds.), *Reconceptualizing Children's Rights in International Development: Living Rights, Social Justice, Translations* (Cambridge University Press, New York and Cambridge, 2013), pp. 225–249.

They can neither contribute to legislation as citizens entitled to vote (or be voted for) nor can they interpret and make use of laws.[56] Children's perspectives and demands, which are collectively formulated and voiced by their social movements and organisations, are of particular importance. Children demand that adults, who are in a privileged situation compared to children, be more inclusive in terms of their needs and perspectives.

The consideration of how the right to work might come into play for children is not necessarily linked to the codification of the right. Like all human rights, the right to work can claim validity – before any formal codification in national laws or international conventions. It gains legitimacy through being articulated and practised by children themselves. For example, the 'twelve rights' formulated in the founding document of the *African Movement of Working Children and Youth* (MAEJT/AMWCY) in 1994[57] correspond in part to some articles of the CRC but are not included in any 'official' legal document. In contrast to governmental and intergovernmental legal documents, the 'twelve rights' are characterised by the fact that they relate specifically to the lives and interests of the working children who formulated them or to the children represented by this movement. In all countries where the movement is present, young members regularly assess the extent to which their 'twelve rights' are being put into practice and discuss the role of responsible adults and governments in supporting their goals.[58]

The right to work would also have significance for the implementation of other rights of children. The fundamental new beginning that the CRC promises by granting children the right to dignity and a self-determined social identity will not unfold its full potential as long as children remain dependent on and reliant on the goodwill of adults. If children can legally engage in economic activity and have their own income, they are more likely to expect to gain the independence and social significance necessary to assert their own rights in society.

---

56 J. Wall, *Give Children the Vote: On Democratizing Democracy* (Bloomsbury Academic, London and New York, 2021); Liebel and Meade, *supra* note 20.

57 *Voice of African Children: Work, Strength and Organisation of Working Children and Youth*. Occasional Papers no. 217 (Enda Tiers-Monde, Dakar, 2001), pp. 21–87.

58 *See* M Liebel, 'Children's Work, Education, and Agency: The African Movement of Working Children and Youth (AMWCY)', in G. Spittler and M. Bourdillon (eds.), *African Children at Work: Working and Learning in Growing Up for Life* (LIT, Zurich and Berlin, 2012), pp. 303–332; S. Fuchs, 'Towards the democratization of the future: The struggle for social recognition and economic success of a West African association of working children and youth', 26:2 *Childhood* (2019), pp. 139 –152.

In declarations and statements of the movements of working children,[59] the right to work does not refer to *any kind* of work, but children repeatedly emphasise that it should be 'work with dignity', 'light' or 'not too heavy work' and 'work appropriate to the child's abilities'. At first glance, this could be understood as children claiming only a limited right to 'child-specific' work. However, the context suggests that age is not the main criterion for them, but respect for human dignity. The understanding of the right to work for children aims at doing the 'best' work possible and actively counteracting any kind of exploitation and degradation at work. It thus contains a utopian surplus that points beyond the wage labour that prevails in capitalist society. Moreover, the children themselves want to decide whether the future work corresponds to their specific criteria or not.

A common characteristic of working children is that they are not simply different from adults and are often not strictly separated from their lives. They take on – often out of necessity, but also of their own free will – tasks that are attributed to adults according to the prevailing childhood pattern ('adult roles'). But this does not necessarily mean that they are to be regarded as little adults, as the stereotypes of 'adultification'[60] or 'children without childhood' suggest, but as people who shape their lives – often in exchange with close adults – more independently and responsibly than seems possible and desirable according to the Eurocentric concept of childhood. Through their existence and practices, they question the developmental time scheme underlying this childhood pattern, according to which childhood is always understood as a 'not yet' or a preliminary stage to adulthood.[61] This raises the question of

59 *See* https://pronats.org/en/materials/declarations (retrieved 26 July 2024).

60 The term is used to explain and brand the racially motivated repression of Black children and youth in the USA. For a critique of the term based on a problematic understanding of childhood as a 'time of innocence', *see* A. A. Gilmore and P. J. Bettis, 'Antiblackness and the Adultification of Black Children in a U.S. Prison Nation', in *Oxford Research Encyclopedia of Education* (2021), pp. 1–32; S. Patton, 'The Children of Children: Why the Adultification Thesis is a Misguided Trap for Black Children and Families', in C. J. Bergman (ed.), *Trust Kids! Stories on Youth Autonomy and Confronting Adult Supremacy* (AT Press, Chico, CA and Edinburgh, 2022), pp. 167–175. In a sense like the thesis of adultification, a study on Palestinian children in the territories occupied by Israel speaks of 'unchilding' the children: N. Shalhoub-Kevorkian, *Incarcerated Childhood and the Politics of Unchilding* (Cambridge University Press, Cambridge, 2019).

61 L. Rabello de Castro, 'Age epistemology and the politics of age', in C. Baraldi and L. Rabello de Castro (eds.), *Global Childhoods in International Perspective: Universality, Diversity and Inequalities* (Sage, Los Angeles, 2020), pp. 33–50; K. Hunfeld, 'The coloniality of time in the global justice debate: de-centring Western linear temporality', 18:1 *Journal of Global Ethics* (2022), pp. 100–117; C. da Rosa Ribeiro et al., 'Childhoods and

whether alternative ideas and patterns of childhood(s) are embodied in working children's mode of existence and self-understanding, which could contribute to rethinking the Eurocentric concept childhood.

7 Conclusion and Outlook

In this chapter, I did not perceive childhood as a social construction in a value-neutral sense, but as a contested site of political change. In this sense, I see children and childhood as normative re-constructions in which various interests and unequal power structures are manifested. From a normative point of view, childhoods are not mere statuses, but active expressions of corresponding interests and values. To call oneself or others a child or infant is to performatively participate in an ongoing public discourse.[62] Similar to philosopher Jacques Rancière[63] and ethicist John Wall,[64] I understand children and childhoods not as fixed structures, but as negotiations of power relations. Childhood is a sign of deviation from an assumed norm that can oppress or empower. According to Wall, being a child in the Western-European sense may entail structural advantages such as parental investment, educational resources, protection from exploitation or openness to growth. But it also always includes structural disadvantages such as being defined as 'not-yet-adult', being labelled according to developmental stage and age, being assumed to be dependent, overprotected or having a notion of innocence. These normative reconstructions intersect with equally powerful dynamics of the social systems of gender, ethnicity, class, and so on. Therefore, one cannot speak of the 'privileges of childhood', as is often done, since the supposed advantages of not yet being an adult are bought at the price of their 'infantilisation'.

Time: A Collective Exploration', 48:1 *Journal of Childhood Studies*, 2023, pp. 134–148; S. Balagopalan, 'Editorial: On racialized linear time and temporal "othering"', 0:0 *Childhood* (online), 2024, pp. 1–9. DOI: 10.1177/09075682241240839; P. N. Shabel, 'Intergenerational Present: Unexpected Proximity in the Adultist Temporality', 22:1 *Taboo: The Journal of Culture and Education,* Special issue: Adultism (2024), pp. 214–226.

62 *See* J. Butler, *Notes toward a Performative Theory of Assembly* (Harvard University Press, Cambridge, MA, 2018).

63 J. Rancière, *The Politics of Aesthetics* (Bloomsbury Academic, London and New York, 2013).

64 J. Wall, *Ethics in light of childhood* (Georgetown University Press, Washington, DC, 2010); J. Wall, 'Childhoods as Normative Reconstructions', in M. Tesar et al. (eds.), 54:3 *Infantographies: Education Philosophy and Theory* (Routledge, London, 2021), pp. 5–6.

This is especially true of the temporal construction of childhood as a stage prior to adulthood, in which the (chronologically measured) age of life is fetishised and turned into an unequal power structure. Such a power structure has so far manifested itself both in thinking and discourse about children and corresponding patterns of childhood, and in policies towards children and childhood. As sociologist Lucia Rabello de Castro[65] describes, age is often used as a universal index of children's level of understanding and capacity. According to her, it is necessary to analyse in depth the strong and often repeated discourse on age (in legal texts, common language and scientific explanations), which tends to consider age as an objective measure, for example, of the presence or absence of certain capacities. The author sees an example of this in the way age permeates different knowledge systems. She describes it as 'the notion of human life as the acquisition of rational competences according to progressive temporality, the perspective of the future as indeterminate and demanding early preparation, and the view of human capacities as individualized assets.'[66]

When childhood is categorised as a stage of life that is considered inferior, immature or incapable, what is sometimes referred to today as adultism or adult-centrism arises. In this sense, sociologist Santiago Morales and lawyer Gabriela Magistris[67] refer to adult-centrism as the analytical point of view from which the biological fact of being born, growing up and developing is seen in a straight line (chronological time) and in ascending order. This hierarchises the development of the subject not only in terms of age, but also in terms of the characteristics and values assigned to growth. From there, they see the emergence of hegemonic notions of childhood and adulthood that 'reaffirm a natural and desirable way of being a child; as a social representation assimilated as natural for children, it is the annulment and pathologization of all other ways of being a child, adolescent and young person. As such, children and young people from popular classes and/or non-Western cultures, who do not fit into this model of the child, are the targets of a set of policies deployed by states aimed at their control and normalization'.[68] This cultural practice of assigning age as a universal and natural fact is also a practice of

---

65 Rabello de Castro, *supra* note 61.

66 Ibid., p. 34.

67 S. Morales and G. Magistris (eds.), *Niñez en movimiento. Del adultocentrismo a la emancipación* (El Colectivo, Buenos Aires, 2018).

68 Ibid., p. 27, translated from Spanish. See also S. Morales and M. Martínez Muñoz, Adultocentrismo. ¿Qué piensan chicas y chicos? (Octaedro, Barcelona, 2024).

temporal power, which philosopher Elizabeth Freeman[69] calls 'chrononormativity'. In it, the body is linked to a socially meaningful embodiment through the management of time. According to her, the individual body thus simultaneously becomes a collective body to which certain properties are attributed.

This attribution of supposedly natural characteristics to being a child is questioned and challenged by the movements and struggles of working children. It is about the defence and recognition of human dignity, the search for humane living conditions and social relations, new forms of independence and coexistence, and thus liberation from paternalism and adultism. Children appear as actors with new individual and collective forms of agency, as children on the move who intervene and change the conditions of their lives. In doing so, they draw on new discourses and rights without considering them sufficient.

The childhoods that emerge in this way remain contradictory in themselves and must always be seen in relation to other childhoods. They can be seen as *liberating* and *emancipating* childhoods in the sense of a *utopia of possibility* in which prospects for future struggles and developments become visible. They do not produce 'new children' (in the sense of 'new men'), nor 'little adults', but rather redefine the generational order: young people understood as equals in the framework of social relations of equality and social justice, as well as recognition of diversity. The perspective is to overcome divisions and oppositions between adults and children in the sense of mutual respect and recognition of their specific needs and forms of communication.

---

69 E. Freeman, *Time Binds. Queer Temporalities, Queer Histories* (Duke University Press, Durham, 2010).

CHAPTER 9

The Devil Is in the Details(?): Age-Based Discrimination of Children in the Context of Migration

Rebecca Thorburn Stern

Abstract[1]

Recognition that discrimination can occur explicitly due to age/childhood – that children are discriminated against simply for being children – remains limited. Yet, numerous examples exist of children being treated less favorably than adults solely on the basis of age. This is also the case in migration law, despite various measures aimed at preventing the 'double vulnerability' of migrant children from placing them at a disadvantage compared to adults.

This chapter aims to examine discrimination based on age/childhood in the context of migration law by drawing on examples related to the child's right to be heard, the assessment of asylum claims, and access to family reunification. It explores the potential of the principle of non-discrimination, as expressed in Article 2 of the Convention on the Rights of the Child, to address adverse differential treatment of children relative to adults in migration contexts. The argument is made that systematically invoking Article 2 of the CRC to identify unequal treatment based on age has the potential to strengthen the rights of children in particularly vulnerable situations, such as migration, and to challenge prevailing assumptions about the legitimacy of, in practice, according children fewer or more limited rights than adults solely on the basis of age.

1 Introduction

Equality and non-discrimination are fundamental moral principles and parts of the foundation of the rule of law. The principle of non-discrimination is

1 The author is grateful to Anna Lundberg, the co-editors, other authors in this volume and participants in workshops held at the Centre for Children's Rights and Family Law, School of Law, University College Cork, and the MOBILE Centre, Faculty of Law, University of Copenhagen, for their valuable feedback on earlier drafts of this paper.

enshrined in every major human rights treaty, including the UN Convention on the Rights of the Child (CRC).[2] CRC Article 2.1 establishes that all of the rights set forth in the Convention pertain to every child within the State party's jurisdiction without exception and without discrimination of any kind "irrespective of the child's or her or his parent's or legal guardian's race, colour, sex, language, religion, political or other opinion, national, ethnic or social origin, property, disability, birth or other status". Besson and Kleber, in their commentary on Article 2, point to how the inclusion of a non-discrimination clause in the children's rights treaty reflects the role that the struggle against child discrimination has played in the development of children's rights. They describe Article 2 as "the culmination of the progressive emergence of children's rights".[3] Besson and Kleber refer to three kinds of child discrimination: between children and children, between children and adolescents, and between children and adults.[4]

Discrimination between children is the most common kind of child discrimination addressed: children being treated less favourably than other children due to gender, ethnicity, disabilities, or immigration status, or a combination of two or more characteristics.[5] However, recognition that discrimination can occur explicitly due to childhood – that children are discriminated for being children – remains limited. Yet, there are numerous examples of children being treated less favourably than adults solely on the basis of childhood.[6] In a growing body of literature recognizing this as an important issue in children's rights, unequal treatment due to childhood is analysed, arguing that such treatment under certain circumstances could constitute discrimination.[7]

---

2 United Nations Convention on the Rights of the Child (1989).

3 S. Besson and E. Kleber, 'Article 2: The Right to Non-Discrimination', in J. Tobin (ed.), *The UN Convention on the Rights of the Child. A Commentary* (Oxford University Press, Oxford, 2019) pp. 42, 70.

4 Besson and Kleber, *supra* note 3, at 42.

5 A. Daly et al., 'The UN Convention on the Rights of the Child, Article 2 and Discrimination on the Basis of Childhood', 91:3 *Nordic Journal of International Law* (2022) pp. 419–452.

6 *See examples in, e.g.,* M. Liebel, 'Adultism and age-based discrimination against children', in D. Kutsar and H. Warming (eds.) *Children and non-discrimination* (CREAN, 2014); Daly et al., *supra* note 5.

7 *See, e.g.*, S. Besson, 'The Principle of Non-Discrimination in the Convention on the Rights of the Child', 13:4 *The International Journal of Children's Rights* (2005) pp. 433–461; C. Breen, *Age Discrimination and Children's Rights: Ensuring Equality and Acknowledging Difference* (Martinus Nijhoff, Leiden, 2006); Liebel, *supra* note 6; D. Archard, 'Respecting Age: Discrimination against the Young and the Old', in M. Skivenes and K. H. Sovig (eds.) *Child rights and international discrimination law. Implementing Article 2 of the Convention on the Rights of the Child* (Routledge, New York, 2019); Besson and Kleber, *supra* note 3; C. Breen, 'The Ageing of

The idea is in essence, as phrased by Breen, that whereas "age-based distinctions are not uncommon and may often serve a practical purpose [...] when such distinctions directly or indirectly nullify or impair a right, age-based distinctions become age-based discrimination, unless such limitations are justified".[8] It is thus not held that children and adults can never be treated differently on the basis of age. Treating these two societal groups differently might in some cases even be necessary in order to secure equality and non-discrimination.[9] What is argued is that the principle of non-discrimination applies to unjustified unequal treatment based on childhood and there are no strong reasons for age discrimination exceptionalism, that is, for treating age discrimination of children in relation to adults differently than discrimination on other grounds.[10]

This position is the starting point of this chapter. The aim is to discuss discrimination on the basis of childhood in the context of migration law, exploring the potential of the principle of non-discrimination in addressing adverse differential treatment of children relative to adults within migration contexts. The choice of topic might require some explanation, as migration law at first glance might come across as a field where children in general are often treated differently, but usually more favourably, than adults.[11] Although

---

Article 2(1): The child's right to be free from age-based discrimination', in M. Skivenes and K. H. Søvig (eds.), *Child Rights and International Discrimination Law: Implementing Article 2 of the United Nations Convention on the Rights of the Child* (Routledge, New York, 2019) p. 63; Daly et al., *supra* note 5; J. Todres, 'Age Discrimination and the Personhood of Children and Youth', *Harvard Human Rights Online* (Dec. 2022) <https://harvardhrj.com/2022/12/age-discrimination-and-the-personhood-of-children-and-youth/>, visited on 27 May 2024; G.L. Neuman and A.M. Ibrahim, 'When is age discrimination a human rights violation?', 36:2 *Harvard Human Rights Journal* (2023) pp. 223–246; B. D. Mezmur, 'Based Solely on Their Date of Birth? Rethinking Age Discrimination Against Children under the Convention on the Rights of the Child', 36:2 *Harvard Human Rights Journal* (2023) pp. 261–281. On why age should not be treated any different than other discrimination grounds, *see* e.g. W. Vandenhole, 'Age discrimination exceptionalism?', *Harvard Human Rights Journal online* (2022). <https://journals.law.harvard.edu/hrj/2022/12/age-discrimination-exceptionalism/>, visited 19 May 2024 and E. Dewhurst, 'Is age exceptional? Challenging existing rationales and exploring realities', 36:2 *Harvard Human Rights Journal* (2023) pp. 247–260.

8 Breen (2019) *supra* note 7, p. 55, *see also* Breen (2006) *supra* note 7.

9 Breen (2006) *supra* note 7, p. 43.

10 See W. Vandenhole *supra* note 7.

11 Brittle and Desmet identify the principle of non-discrimination as a topic that should be accorded more attention in research on the rights of children in the context of migration. R. Brittle and E. Desmet, 'Thirty Years of Research on Children's Rights in the Context of Migration: Towards Increased Visibility and Recognition of Some Children, But Not All?', 28:1 *The International Journal of Children's Rights* (2020) pp. 36–65, 53. On discrimination

migration law in many ways is age-neutral – age is, for example, not a factor that independently motivates a residence permit being either granted or denied – being a child in the eyes of the law can have significant impact on decisions on legal status as well as for a person's rights during the migration process.[12] Being a child (that is, below the age of 18 years)[13] in the legal sense means that legal and policy measures adopted at the international, regional, and national levels aimed at protecting children's rights apply. Often, these measures provide for additional rights or less restrictive conditions than for adults in the same situation, with examples including access to family reunification, applicability of humanitarian grounds for residence permits, stricter time limits for detention, and more extensive rights to healthcare and education. Such acknowledgments in law and policy of the particular circumstances of children in a migratory context reflect the view that migrant children should first and foremost be seen and treated as children, not migrants, and that their particularly vulnerable situation should be taken into account, as should the principle of the best interests of the child.[14] It could thus be argued that in the migration context, being a child is in many ways an advantage, ensuring more safeguards and more generous rules.

However, being a child may also be a disadvantage in the migration context. The Committee on the Rights of the Child (CRC Committee) states that "in the context of international migration, children may be in a situation of double vulnerability, as children and also as children affected by migration who are (a) migrants themselves, either alone or with their families, (b) were born to migrant families in countries of destination or (c) remain in their country of origin while one or both parents have migrated to another coun-

---

in the migration context generally, see e.g. S. Atrey, C. Briddick and M. Foster, Guest Editor Introduction: Contesting and Undoing Discriminatory Borders' 22:3 *International Journal of Discrimination and the Law* (2022) pp. 210–223 and V. Stoyanova, S. Atalay and A. Loza, The Borders Within: When the right to non-discrimination confronts migration law' 25:2 *International Journal of Discrimination and the Law*, (2025) pp. 100–111.

12 What is of interest here is, in general, a person's chronological age; that is, the passage of time since an individual's birth. R.A. Settersen and B. Godlewski, 'Concepts and Theories of Age and Aging', in V. L. Bengtson and R. A. Settersen (eds.) *Handbook of Theories of Aging*, 3rd ed. (Springer, New York, 2016). On migrant children and legal status, see e.g. J. Lelliott, 'Unaccompanied Children in Limbo: The Causes and Consequences of Uncertain Legal Status' 34:1 *International Journal of Refugee Law* (2022) pp. 1–30.

13 *Cf.* CRC Article 1.

14 On 'child first, migrant second', *see e.g.*, H. Crawley, *Child First, Migrant Second: Ensuring that Every Child Matters*, ILPA Policy Paper (ILPA 2006) and C. McLaughlin, 'They Don't Look Like Children: Child Asylum-seekers, the Dubs Amendment and the Politics of Childhood', 44:11 *Journal of Ethnic and Migration Studies* (2018) pp. 1757–1773.

try".[15] CRC State parties are moreover obliged to "ensure that the best interests of the child are taken fully into consideration in immigration law, planning, implementation and assessment of migration policies and decision-making on individual cases".[16] Nevertheless, it has repeatedly been pointed out in scholarship that although great effort has gone into creating laws and policies aimed at taking the particular vulnerabilities of migrant children and the best interests principle into account, such measures are too often poorly implemented, misinterpreted or simply overlooked.[17] As a result, migrant children are not only at risk of being treated less favourably than citizen children (discrimination between children), but also less favourably than adult migrants in terms of available rights and agency in the process (discrimination between children and adults), to mention just two examples.

That individual children in migration contexts are directly or indirectly treated differently based on age, with children being differentiated from adults, is a fact. Nor is it contested that this is sometimes necessary; for instance, different rules apply to immigration detention for adults and chil-

15 Committee on the Rights of the Child, General Comment No. 6 (2005): Treatment of Unaccompanied and Separated Children Outside their Country of Origin, CRC/GC/2005/6, para. 1 and Joint General Comment No. 3 (2017) of the Committee on the Protection of the Rights of All Migrant Workers and Members of Their Families and No. 22 (2017) of the Committee on the Rights of the Child on the general principles regarding the human rights of children in the context of international migration, CMW/C/GC/3-CRC/C/GC/22, para. 3. *Cf. also* J. Ryngaert and W. Vandenhole, 'Undocumented Migration: Integrating the Children's Rights Concept of Nuanced Vulnerability in Human Rights Law', in E. Brems et al. (eds.) *Children's Rights Law in the Global Human Rights Landscape. Isolation, Inspiration, Integration?* (Routledge, Abingdon, 2017) pp. 210–230.

16 CMW/C/GC/3-CRC/C/GC/22, *supra* note 15, para. 29.

17 *See, e.g.*, J. Bhabha, 'Arendt's children: do today's migrant children have the right to have rights?', 31 *Human Rights Quarterly* (2009) pp. 410–451; J. Bhabha, 'Moving Children: Lacunae in Contemporary Human Rights Protections for Migrant Children and Adolescents', 30:3 *Revue Européenne des migrations internationals* (2014) pp. 35–57; B. Gornik, 'At the crossroads of power relations. The Convention on the Rights of the Child and unaccompanied minor migrants', in M. Sedmak et al., (eds.) *Unaccompanied Children in European Migration and Asylum Practices. In Whose Best Interests?* (Routledge, London, 2017); A. Lundberg, 'Management of "the unaccompanied." In search of a rights-based approach in the context of Swedish "crisis politics"', in J. Bhabha et al., (eds.) *Research Handbook on Child Migration* (Edward Elgar Publishing, Cheltenham, 2018) pp. 260–278; R. C. Smyth, 'The Human Rights Approach to 'Persecution' and Its Child Rights Discontents', 33:2 *International Journal of Refugee Law* (2021) pp. 238–276; R. Thorburn Stern, 'Great Expectations?: Some Thoughts on the Impact of Incorporation of the UN Convention on the Rights of the Child for Asylum-seeking Children in the Nordic Countries', 91:1 *Nordic Journal of International Law* (2022) pp. 17–43.

dren.[18] What this chapter posits is that there are situations where children and adults in the context of migration are treated differently on the basis of age, with negative effects for children, in ways that are difficult to justify. Drawing on literature on discrimination on the basis of childhood and selected examples from migration law where children, directly or indirectly, are treated less favourably than adults, this chapter argues that framing such treatment as discrimination as understood in human rights law, CRC Article 2 in particular, could be useful for shedding light on such unequal treatment and, ultimately, finding ways of counteracting it.

The outline of the chapter is as follows. Section 2 briefly presents how the principle of non-discrimination could apply to differential treatment of adults and children on the basis of age, with a particular focus on the non-discrimination clause in Article 2 of the CRC. Section 3 describes three examples of when migrant children are either directly or indirectly treated differently than adult migrants. The situations are the right to be heard in the migration process, conditions for family reunification in the context of European Union (EU) law, and assessment of asylum claims. The examples cover two kinds of situations: the first when a legal rule directly prescribes that children should be treated differently than adults – with negative consequences for the children – the second when indirect differential treatment as a result of seemingly neutral legal norms in practice has the effect of disproportionate disadvantages for children compared with adults. Section 4 considers the potential of using the principle of non-discrimination as a lens to highlight and challenge differential treatment of migrant children on the basis of age.

2 Age-Based Discrimination of Children in Human Rights Law

As mentioned above, the core human rights treaties, and numerous other legal instruments at the global and regional levels, include non-discrimination clauses. These can either be independent, protecting from discrimination in all fields (as Article 26 of the International Covenant on Civil and Political Rights[19] (ICCPR) and Protocol 12 of the European Convention for the Protection of Human Rights and Fundamental Freedoms[20] (ECHR)), or be possible to invoke only in combination with substantive rights in the treaty concerned

18 ECtHR, *Mubilanzila Mayeka and Kaniki Mitunga* v. *Belgium*, Appl. No. 13178/03, judgment of 12 October 2006.

19 International Covenant on Civil and Political Rights (1966).

20 Council of Europe, ETS No. 5.

(ICCPR Article 2.1, International Covenant on Economic, Social and Cultural Rights[21] (ICESCR) Article 2.2, ECHR Article 14, CRC Article 2.1). The provisions are open-ended in the sense that they are not limited to the grounds enumerated but also include a reference to 'other status'. The non-discrimination clauses impose both positive and negative obligations on states, with the aim to ensure equal enjoyment of rights.[22]

Although there is no single, established definition of 'discrimination', a definition often referred to in human rights law is that provided by the Human Rights Committee (HRC) in its General Comment on non-discrimination. The HRC holds discrimination to imply "any distinction, exclusion, restriction or preference which is based on any ground such as race, colour, sex, language, religion, political or other opinion, national or social origin, property, birth or other status, and which has the purpose or effect of nullifying or impairing the recognition, enjoyment or exercise by all persons, on an equal footing, of all rights and freedoms".[23] The HRC emphasises that "the enjoyment of rights and freedoms on an equal footing, however, does not mean identical treatment in every instance"[24] and that "not every differentiation of treatment will constitute discrimination, if the criteria for such differentiation are reasonable and objective and if the aim is to achieve a purpose which is legitimate under the Covenant",[25] thus indicating a need to distinguish between unequal treatment in general and unequal treatment constituting discrimination in a legal sense. At the regional level, the European Court of Human Rights (ECtHR) has held that discrimination refers to a difference in the treatment of persons in analogous, or relevantly similar, situations based on an identifiable characteristic, or 'status', which has "no objective and reasonable justification, that is, if it does not pursue a legitimate aim or if there is not a reasonable relationship of proportionality between the means employed and the aim sought to be achieved".[26] The Inter-American Court of Human Rights (IACtHR) adopts a similar understanding, describing 'discrimination' as "any exclusion, restric-

---

21 International Covenant on Economic, Social and Cultural Rights (1966).

22 Many pages have been produced on state obligations on this matter. For a brief overview, *see, e.g.*, O. de Schutter, *International Human Rights Law. Cases, Materials, Commentary*, 3rd ed. (Cambridge University Press, Cambridge, 2019) Chapter 7.

23 UN Human Rights Committee, *CCPR General Comment No. 18 Non-discrimination*, 10 November 1989, para. 7.

24 Ibid., para. 8.

25 Ibid., para. 13.

26 ECtHR, *Biao* v. *Denmark*, Appl. No. 38590/10, judgment (Grand Chamber) of 24 May 2016, paras. 89–90.

tion or privilege that is not objective and reasonable, and which adversely affects human rights",[27] though also emphasising that not all differential treatment is in itself offensive to human dignity and that discrimination only occurs when the distinction made is not reasonable, proportionate and objective.[28]

Human rights law recognises various forms of discrimination. *Direct* discrimination means that a person/group is treated unfairly compared with another person/group in a similar situation as a result of special attributes of that person/group, such as age. *Indirect discrimination* is when seemingly neutral and generally applicable laws, regulations, policies and social norms in practice result in disproportionate disadvantages for one category of individuals or groups compared with others. This is particularly important for children, as seemingly neutral policies can affect them detrimentally.[29] Discrimination can also be *structural*, which is when rules, norms, routines, patterns of attitudes and behaviour in institutions and other societal structures have the effect of creating obstacles for individuals or groups to achieve the same rights and opportunities available to the majority, or *intersectional*, which is when several discrimination grounds interact, leading to specific forms of discrimination.[30]

Very briefly, the principle of non-discrimination is understood as the prohibition of treating similar situations differently without objective justification.[31] The definition is, in Besson's words, made up of four components: "the differentiation of similar situations, the absence of legitimate ends, the lack of proportionality of means to ends and the use of suspect classifications".[32] There are different understandings and interpretations of 'proportionality'. Besson sums this up as follows: "[T]he means must be apt to attain the aim sought, be necessary means to do so and be the least restrictive means to reach that aim."[33]

27 IACtHR, Advisory Opinion OC-18/03 of September 17, 2003, requested by the United Mexican States, Juridical Condition and Rights of Undocumented Migrants, para. 84.

28 Ibid., paras. 89 and 84.

29 On direct and indirect discrimination, *see, e.g.*, de Schutter, *supra* note 22, Chapter 7.3.

30 On intersectional discrimination, *see, e.g.*, the discussion in S. Fredman, *Discrimination Law*, 3rd ed. (Oxford University Press, Oxford, 2022) Chapter 1.

31 Besson and Kleber, *supra* note 3, pp. 60–61.

32 Besson, *supra* note 7, p. 435. *Cf. also* T. Khaitan, *A Theory of Discrimination Law* (Oxford University Press, Oxford, 2015); Fredman, *supra* note 30, Chapter 1.

33 Besson, *supra* note 7, p. 436. *See also* M. G. Marcondes Smith and Wouter Vandenhole, 'Handle with Care': Addressing Disadvantage based on Childhood through a Non-

Distinguishing between what is considered discriminatory on the basis of age in lay terms and in legal terms can pose a challenge. Age has increasingly become recognised as a 'suspect classification', or, differently phrased, a non-legitimate ground for differential treatment. Classifications help identify the particular characteristics on which an individual's disadvantage is based. Two of the most recent core human rights treaties, the Convention on the Protection of Migrant Workers and their Families[34] and the Convention on the Rights of Persons with Disabilities[35] stand out, as they explicitly refer to (chronological) age as a protected characteristic in their non-discrimination clauses (two other core treaties, the ICCPR and the ICESCR do not, but instead refer to 'other status'). In the European context, the non-discrimination clause of the ECHR, Article 14, and the general prohibition of discrimination in Protocol 12 to the ECHR both mention only 'other status'. In contrast, the European Union Charter on Fundamental Rights[36] Article 21.1 specifically includes age as a discrimination ground.

Nevertheless, age, including young age, is increasingly recognised as a discrimination ground in the jurisprudence of UN human rights treaty monitoring bodies, including the CRC Committee, as part of what is covered by the reference to 'other status'.[37] The ECtHR has recognised that age may fall within the scope of 'other status' for the purposes of Article 14, but is yet to discuss it in the context of age-based unequal treatment of children compared with adults.[38] As a result of age discrimination in EU legislation having primarily focused on the employment context, case law from the Court of Justice of the European Union (CJEU) on age discrimination has generally taken aim at unequal treatment of older persons.[39] Age is furthermore a

---

discrimination Frame', in this volume and A. Nilsson, 'Same, Same but Different: Proportionality Assessments and Equality Norms', 7:3 *Oslo Law Review* (2020) pp. 126–144.

34 International Convention on the Protection of the Rights of All Migrant Workers and Members of their Families (1990).

35 Convention on the Rights of Persons with Disabilities (2006).

36 Charter of Fundamental Rights of the European Union, (2012) p. 391–407.

37 See e.g. UN Committee on Economic, Social and Cultural Rights, General Comment No. 20, Non-discrimination in economic, social and cultural rights, 2 July 2009, para. 29, W. Vandenhole et al., *Children's Rights: A Commentary on the Convention on the Rights of the Child and its Protocols* (Edward Elgar Publishing, Cheltenham, 2019) p. 56; Breen (2019), *supra* note 7, p. 63; Besson and Kleber, *supra* note 7, p. 42; Daly et al., *supra* note 5; Neuman and Ibrahim, *supra* note 7; Mezmur, *supra* note 7. *Cf also* A. Bruce, *Which Entitlements and for Whom? The Convention on the Rights of Persons with Disabilities and its Ideological Antecedents* (Lund University, Lund, 2014) p. 332, n. 837.

38 ECtHR, *Schwizgebel* v. *Switzerland*, Appl. No. 25762/07, judgment of 10 June 2010.

39 *See e.g.* H. Hejny, 'Justifying age discrimination in Europe: A case law analysis', 13:2 *The Journal of Aging and Social Change* (2023) pp. 15–28.

protected characteristic in a number of national jurisdictions.[40] However, explicit references to childhood in this context are limited, as is the case law on the topic.[41]

The applicability of CRC Article 2 on discrimination of children in relation to adults has been subject to debate.[42] Archard asserts that although children as a group may indeed be discriminated against in relation to adults, this does not fall within the scope of Article 2, as the provision only concerns "the discriminatory treatment of some children by comparison to other children".[43] Other scholars hold that CRC Article 2 is indeed relevant for discrimination of children compared with adults. Breen argues that "Article 2 frames age-based discrimination in terms of differences between children and adults" and that "the CRC is premised on the categorisation of children as a group distinct from adults".[44] Daly et al. hold that "the CRC Article 2 reference to 'other status' renders it possible to read into the right of children to be free from discrimination on the basis of childhood".[45] Mezmur recognises that although it is not obvious either from the text of Article 2 itself or the discussions during the drafting process how the CRC Committee is to address age-based discrimination against children, there is nevertheless a need for the Committee to do so.[46]

The 'similar situation' or comparability criteria (as in 'can adults and children be considered to be in a similar situation') poses a challenge. The comparator test in Atrey's words "helps establish this connection between discriminatory impact and its basis in grounds [...] the claimant has to show that a real or hypothetical individual or group, which does not share the claimant's personal characteristic, but is otherwise similarly situated, is better off".[47] Besson and Kleber note in their commentary on CRC Article 2 that the comparison between children and adults is probably "the most difficult assessment to

40 One example is Section 1 of the Swedish Discrimination Act (SFS 2008:567).

41 *See, e.g.*, S. Flacks, 'Is Childhood a Disability: Exploring the Exclusion of Children from Age Discrimination Provisions in the Equality Act 2010', 26:4 *Child and Family Law Quarterly* (2014) pp. 421–438; Mezmur, *supra* note 7, p. 268.

42 Breen (2006), *supra* note 7; Breen (2019), *supra* note 7; Besson and Kleber, *supra* note 3, pp. 47–48 and 61–63; Archard, *supra* note 7.

43 Archard, *supra* note 7, p. 45.

44 Breen (2006), *supra* note 7.

45 Daly et. al., *supra* note 5, p. 452.

46 Mezmur, *supra* note 7, p. 265.

47 S. Atrey, 'Comparison in intersectional discrimination', 38:3 *Legal Studies* (2018) pp. 379–395 (379–380).

perform"[48] due to the specificity of the situation of the child. On the one hand, they point out, there is a human rights treaty (the CRC) dedicated to the rights of this particular group of human beings, thus emphasising the difference between children and adults and the need to treat children differently.[49] On the other hand, Besson and Kleber argue, the very fact that there is a treaty on the rights of the child is a recognition that children are indeed rights holders and should be treated as such, just like adults.[50] They also hold that the CRC "does not endorse the view that children are always in a different position just because they are children and cannot be treated as adults".[51]

On the issue of justification of differential treatment, it should be stressed that it is only when such treatment lacks reasonable and objective justification that it may be deemed discrimination in the legal sense. As noted by the IACtHR, treating children and adults differently is not discriminatory *per se*.[52] The CRC Committee in its General Comment on the best interests-principle emphasises that the right to non-discrimination in CRC Article 2 "requires appropriate proactive measures taken by the State to ensure effective equal opportunities for all children to enjoy the rights under the Convention. This may require positive measures aimed at redressing a situation of real inequality"[53] – that is, treating children differently compared with, for example, adults. Limitations of children's rights may sometimes be required in order to protect them from harm (age limits on driving, drinking alcohol and sexual intercourse being some examples). The crux of the matter is what is considered legitimate, proportionate and hence justified – and why this is the case. There may be several, often intersecting, arguments for considering it justified to treat children and adults differently even if it results in negative outcomes for children as a group or individual children. These arguments may draw on the evolving capacities of the child, meaning that treating children and adults alike would be unfair as well as potentially detrimental to children, as children are in a state of psychological, mental, physical and social development.[54] In this perspective, the adult is the norm and the

48 Besson and Kleber, *supra* note 3, p. 60.

49 Ibid.

50 Ibid.

51 Ibid.

52 IACtHR, *supra* note 27, para. 115.

53 Committee on the Rights of the Child, General Comment No. 14 (2013) on the right of the child to have his or her best interests taken as a primary consideration (art. 3, para. 1), CRC/C/GC/14, para. 41.

54 *See e.g.* IACtHR, supra note 27, paras. 48–55; Archard, *supra* note 7, Breen (2019), *supra* note 7, p. 63.

child is the other, lesser. Differential treatment of adults and children may also draw on prevailing unequal power relations between adults and children, which help perpetuate the view that it is only 'natural' for adults to have more, or more broadly interpreted rights, and more influence over their own lives and the society in which they live than children.[55] Mezmur has recently noted that the sentiment of children being somehow less entitled to rights, or rather to less rights, while having subsided, still persists.[56] It might be that, as Sandland puts it, age-based discrimination is still seen as "inherent in the very idea that, by reason of age alone, children should be afforded less and lesser legal rights than adults".[57] It may also be justified by defining children based on their lack of abilities and therefore as inferior to adults *per se*. This approach, based on prejudice against children, which may lead to oppression and structural discrimination of children, is sometimes referred to as *childism*.[58] Given the complexity of the grounds of justification presented above, it is important to emphasise that whether the arguments could be considered objective justification for negative differential treatment based on childhood should, as stressed by Vandenhole, be assessed as much as possible in accordance with the same standards used in human rights law on discrimination generally.[59]

In a migratory context, negative attitudes and prejudice against children as a group – or just a lack of understanding of the challenges that being in a migratory situation can pose for a child – can have particularly detrimental consequences, given the child's vulnerable situation as both a minor and a

55 *See, e.g.*, Liebel, *supra* note 6, p. 123; E. Sevón, 'Who's Got the Power?: Young Children's Power and Agency in the Child-Parent Relationship', 6:4–1,*International Journal of Child, Youth and Family Studies* (2015) pp. 622–645; R. Thorburn Stern, *Implementing Article 12 of the UN Convention on the Rights of the Child: Participation, Power and Attitudes* (Brill/Nijhoff, Leiden, 2017); R. Sandland, 'Lessons for children's rights from disability rights?', in E. Brems et al. (eds), *Children's Rights Law in the Global Human Rights Landscape. Isolation, Inspiration, Integration?* (Routledge, Abingdon, 2017) p. 124; Gornik, *supra* note 17.

56 Mezmur, *supra* note 7, p. 261.

57 Sandland, *supra* note 55, p. 124.

58 On childism understood as prejudice, *see e.g.* E. Young-Bruehl, *Childism: Confronting Prejudice against Children* (Yale University Press, New Haven, 2012) and R. Adami, 'Childism – on Adult Resistance to Children's Rights', in R. Adami et al. (eds.), *The Rights of the Child. Legal, Political and Ethical Challenges* (Brill, Stockholm, 2023). On childism as a means of empowerment, *see e.g.* J. Wall, 'From Childhood Studies to Childism: Reconstructing the Scholarly and Social Imaginations', 20:83 *Children's Geographies* (2022) pp. 257–270 and T. Biswas and J. Wall, 'Childist theory in the humanities and social sciences', 37:4 *Child & Society* (2023) pp. 1001–1004.

59 Vandenhole, *supra* note 7.

person affected by migration. The combined statuses of 'child' and 'migrant' may work together to enhance the person's disadvantaged position. The next section offers examples of how unequal treatment of migrant children compared with migrant adults, with negative outcomes for children, may manifest.

3 Direct or Indirect Age-Based Discrimination of Migrant Children: Three Examples

3.1 *The Right to Be Heard in Migration Proceedings*

The right to be heard and to have one's views taken into account, as stated in CRC Article 12, is one of the CRC's four general principles and a prerequisite for the best interests principle to be applied correctly.[60] The CRC Committee emphasises that due to the particularly vulnerable situation of a migrant child, "it is urgent to fully implement their right to express their views on all aspects of the immigration and asylum proceedings".[61] Although the weight to be accorded to the views expressed by the child according to Article 12 is indeed to be related to the age and maturity of the child, gender, administrative matters, language issues or other factors cannot be invoked as an excuse for not allowing the child to be heard in matters affecting him or her. Yet, in several jurisdictions, the child's right to be heard in migration proceedings remains restricted compared with that of adults in the same situation. The Swedish Aliens Act Chapter 1, Section 11 prescribes that "in assessing questions of permits under this Act when a child will be affected by a decision in the case, the child must be heard, *unless this is inappropriate*" (author's italics). Account must be taken of what the child has said, to the extent warranted by the age and maturity of the child. The CRC Committee has criticised the exception of inappropriateness on the basis that it does not comply with Article 12, urging Sweden to abolish it.[62] In the preparatory works to the Aliens Act, it is explained that 'inappropriate' refers to situations concerning young children or children with mental health issues, but no reflection on the compatibility of the limitation with CRC Article 12 is offered.[63] The Finnish Aliens Act, Sec-

60 CRC/C/GC/14, *supra* note 53, para. 43. On Article 12 generally, see e.g. A. Parkes, *Children and International Human Rights Law. The Right of the Child to be Heard* (Routledge, London, 2013) and Thorburn Stern, *supra* note 55.

61 Committee on the Rights of the Child, General Comment No. 12 (2009) The right of the child to be heard, CRC/C/GC/12, para. 123.

62 Committee on the Rights of the Child, Concluding observations on the fifth periodic report of Sweden, 6 March 2015, CRC/C/SWE/CO/5, para. 20.

63 Government Bill (Prop.) 1996/97:25 Svensk migrationspolitik i globalt perspektiv, p. 298.

tion 6, contains a similar provision, stating that before a decision is made in a matter concerning a child over the age of 12 years, the child is to be heard *unless* it is "clearly unnecessary".[64] Younger children may be heard *if* they are sufficiently mature for their views to be taken into account. The preparatory works to the Finnish Aliens Act emphasise the importance of taking the child's views into account, but also states that hearing a minor is 'clearly unnecessary' in certain cases where the child's guardian has submitted an application on behalf of both themselves and their child, and where the child's best interests are not considered to be in conflict with those of the guardian.[65] The compatibility with CRC Article 12 is not commented upon, though the absence of an age limit in Article 12 is mentioned.[66] A third example is Switzerland, which on several occasions has been criticised by the CRC Committee for not allowing young children to be heard, for treating the child's right to be heard as a mere formality and for not considering the asylum-seeking child an individual rights holder.[67] Switzerland defended its approach by arguing that it is the Swiss State Secretariat for Migration's policy of hearing only children aged 14 years or over, as it is at this age children are generally presumed to have sufficient discernment, and also that the interests of children in general coincide with those of the parents.[68]

In all three cases, children's rights to be heard are made conditional upon an (adult) assessor determining whether they should be heard or not, an assessment that has no equivalent in the case of adult applicants, where it would be regarded as a restriction of the fundamental right to present one's case. In the case of children, however, not being heard may be presented as being in the child's best interests and for their protection.[69] Also contrary to what would be the case with an adult, it is presumed that the interests of one indi-

---

64 Utlänningslag 30.4.2004/301.

65 FvUB 4/2004 rd – RP 28/2003 rd RP 151/2003 rd, pp. 122–123. Asylum applications are a special case however, where children under the age of 15 "should also be heard, taking into account their age and level of maturity".

66 RP 28/2003 rd, pp. 122–123.

67 Committee on the Rights of the Child, *K.S. and M.S.* v. *Switzerland*, CRC/C/89/D/74/2019, 16 March 2022 and Committee on the Rights of the Child, *M.K.A.H.* v. *Switzerland*, CRC/C/88/D/95/2019, 3 November 2021.

68 CRC/C/89/D/74/2019, *supra* note 67, paras. 4.7 and 7.8.

69 However, research shows that children as young as 4 years of age can be interviewed for the purpose of criminal proceedings as long as the proper technique is used. A.C. Cederborg and M.E. Lamb, 'The need for systematic and intensive training of forensic interviewers', in T. I. Richardson and M. V. Williams (eds.), *Child abuse and violence* (Nova Science Publishers, 2008).

vidual applicant in general do not diverge from those of other applicants in the family. The child is not treated as an individual rights holder, but more as an accessory to the 'main applicants'.

3.2 *The EU Family Reunification Directive Integration Condition*

In the EU, the Family Reunification Directive (FRD)[70] is the key instrument regulating family reunification for third-country nationals residing lawfully in the territory of the Member States (Article 1). Family reunification is, according to FRD Recital 4, a way of making family life possible, recognising its role in promoting integration and creating sociocultural stability. The FRD applies to sponsors (third-country nationals residing in a destination state whom family members residing outside of the EU want to join, Article 2 c) with residence permits valid for one year or more, who have "reasonable prospects of obtaining the right of permanent residence" and whose family members are third-country nationals (Article 3.1).[71] If the conditions set out by the FRD are met, the Member States have a positive obligation to allow family reunification.[72] The conditions, as will briefly be outlined below, vary depending on several different factors, including whether the sponsor has been granted refugee status or not, the age of the sponsor or applicant, and the time spent legally by the sponsor in the Member State.

The family members for whom the Member State is obliged to grant family reunification under the FRD are spouses and minor children (Article 4.1).[73] However, the Directive allows for the Member State to, under certain conditions, impose an integration condition on the family reunification of minor children aged over 12 years who arrive independently from the rest of their family. Article 4.1 stipulates that the Member State is allowed to "verify whether [the child] meets a condition for integration provided for by its existing legislation on the date of implementation of this Directive". These conditions are to be met before the Member State authorises entry and residence

---

70 Council Directive 2003/86/EC of 22 September 2003 on the right to family reunification.

71 The Directive does not apply when the sponsor is an asylum seeker, holds a temporary protection status or an alternative protection status (Article 3.2), or is a family member of a Union citizen (Article 3.3). See CJEU, C-380/17, *K and B* v. *Staatssecretaris van Veiligheid en Justitie*, 7 November 2018, ECLI:EU:C:2018: 87.

72 CJEU, C-540/03, *European Parliament* v. *Council of the European Union*, 27 June 2006, ECLI:EU:C:2006:429, para. 60.

73 Member States may also allow for family reunification for additional categories of family members (Articles 4.2 and 4.3).

for the child.[74] There is no corresponding rule for spouses. Member States may indeed require certain conditions to be met by the sponsor before permission for entry and residence is granted to family members (Article 7.1) and may also require third-country nationals to comply with integration measures based on national law once present in the Member State (Article 7.2), but the 'stand-still clause' of Article 4.1 applies only to the aforementioned category of children. According to Recital 12 of the FRD, the possibility of limiting the right to family reunification in Article 4.1 "is intended to reflect the children's capacity for integration at early ages and shall ensure that they acquire the necessary education and language skills in school". The EU Commission, in its Communication on the application of the FRD, emphasises that Member States may not deny family members reunification only on the basis of not meeting an integration condition.[75]

In its 2006 ruling in *European Parliament* v. *Council of the European Union* the CJEU, when asked whether imposing an integration condition on children arriving independently, but not on adults, was discriminatory, held with reference to Recital 12 that the integration condition and the age limits set out in Article 4.1 are both legitimate as the aim is to facilitate integration, something that is more difficult for children over 12 years of age than for younger children.[76] The CJEU also held that the integration condition is not discriminatory as spouses cannot be compared with children due to the different objectives of family reunification: the objective of marriage is spending life together, whereas teenagers will not necessarily remain with their parents for a long time.[77] The Court, as Smyth points out, produces no scientific evidence in support of the 12-year limit, but seems merely to take it as a given, generally applicable to all children, regardless of their individual circumstances.[78] The CJEU also seems to find family life more important for adults than for teenagers, once again without providing any substantive support for its position. The justifications here are similar to those in the case of limitations to the

74 Communication from the Commission to the European Parliament and the Council on guidance for application of Directive 2003/86/EC on the right to family reunification /*COM/2014/0210 final*/, paras. 15–16.

75 Ibid., para. 16.

76 CJEU, C-540/03, *supra* note 72, paras. 67–68, 74.

77 CJEU, C-540/03, *supra* note 72, para. 75. Bottero criticises the integration condition in Article 4.1 in M. Bottero, 'Integration (of Immigrants) in the European Union: A Controversial Concept', 24:4 *European Journal of Migration and Law* (2022) pp. 516–544.

78 Smyth, *supra* note 17, p. 271, se also Bottero, *supra* note 77, (pp. 530–531).

child's right to be heard: it is in their best interests, and their status as rights holders is not accorded the same weight as would be the case with an adult.

3.3 *Assessment of Asylum Claims*

Being a child is not in itself enough to be granted refugee or alternative protection status. The best interests principle is not an independent ground for a residence permit or protection status, nor is age recognised as a protection ground.[79] A child claiming asylum must, like an adult applicant, make probable that she is eligible either for refugee status (that is that she, owing to a well-founded fear of being persecuted for reasons of race, religion, nationality, membership of a particular social group or political opinion, is outside the country of her nationality and is unable or unwilling to avail herself of the protection of that country)[80] or for alternative protection status.[81] Many asylum law instruments, guidelines and policy documents at the international, regional and national levels, including the 2009 United Nations High Commissioner for Refugees (UNHCR) Guidelines on International Protection on child asylum claims, explicitly state the need for the assessment of asylum claims to be carried out in a 'child-sensitive manner'82 and underline that a best interests assessment is an essential part of the asylum procedure.[83] Moreover, children may under certain circumstances be recognised as falling within the scope of the aforementioned protection ground 'particular social group', defined by the UNHCR as "a group of per-

---

79 For a discussion, *see, e.g.*, J. McAdam, *Complementary protection in international refugee law* (Oxford University Press, Oxford, 2007) and J. Pobjoy, *The Child in International Refugee Law* (Cambridge University Press, Cambridge, 2017).

80 Article 1A(2) of the Refugee Convention, which serves as a model for refugee definitions in other international legal instruments as well as on the national level.

81 *See, e.g.*, Directive 2011/95/EU of the European Parliament and of the Council of 13 December 2011 on standards for the qualification of third-country nationals or stateless persons as beneficiaries of international protection, for a uniform status for refugees or for persons eligible for subsidiary protection, and for the content of the protection granted (recast) (the EU Qualification Directive), Article 2 f) and Article 15, UNHCR, Guidelines on International Protection No. 8: Child Asylum Claims under Articles 1A(2) and 1F of the 1951 Convention and/or 1967 Protocol relating to the Status of Refugees, 22 December 2009, HCR/GIP/09/08, para. 4.

82 UNHCR, *supra* note 81, paras. 15–19, *see also* UNHCR, Executive Committee Conclusion No. 107 on Children at Risk, adopted in October 2007.

83 IARMJ/EASO, *Judicial analysis: Vulnerability in the context of applications for international protection* (Luxembourg: Publications Office of the European Union 2021); UNHCR, *2021 UNHCR Best Interests Procedure (BIP) Guidelines: Assessing and Determining the Best Interests of the Child* (UNHCR, Geneva, 2021) and CRC/C/GC/14, *supra* note 53, paras. 43 and 52–54.

sons who share a common characteristic other than their risk of being persecuted, or who are perceived as a group by society".[84] The characteristic will often be one which is innate, unchangeable or otherwise fundamental to identity, conscience or the exercise of one's human rights. That age may be such a defining common characteristic is recognised by the UNHCR[85] and, increasingly, also in case law.[86]

Drawing on the above, it would be fair to assume that being a child when seeking asylum would have substantial impact on the assessment of asylum claims. In recent years, adjudicators have increasingly recognised the particular vulnerabilities and needs of children, as well as the importance of applying a child-sensitive lens and taking the best interests principle into account.[87] However, as numerous scholars have pointed out, the adult-based norm for who is eligible for international protection remains strong, resulting in children's unique needs being disregarded and their protection needs assessed using an adult standard, something which may lead to children being denied asylum when such protection should have been granted.[88]

One example concerns the interpretation of the aforementioned well-founded fear criterion in the refugee definition. Crock and Yule opine that the fear requirement can be more problematic for children than for adults, for several reasons. Children may find it difficult to understand or articulate the future harm they are at risk of being subjected to. They may be not be able

---

84 UNHCR, Guidelines on International Protection No. 2: 'Membership of a Particular Social Group' within the context of Article 1A(2) of the 1951 Convention and/or its 1967 Protocol Relating to the Status of Refugees, HCR/GIP/02/02, 7 May 2002, para. 11.

85 UNHCR, *supra* note 81, paras. 49–50.

86 Pobjoy, *supra* note 79, section 5.2.3.2.

87 J. Pobjoy, 'Refugee Children', in C. Costello, M. Foster, J. McAdam (eds.), *The Oxford Handbook of International Refugee Law* (Oxford University Press, Oxford, 2021) p. 745. *See also* Smyth, *supra* note 17.

88 *See, e.g.*, J. Bhabha, 'Demography and Rights: Women, Children and Access to Asylum', 16:2 *International Journal of Refugee Law* (2004) pp. 227–243; UNHCR, *supra* note 81; L. Frydman and B. Bookey, 'Applying the refugee definition to child-specific forms of persecution', in J. Bhabha et al. (eds.), *Research Handbook on Child Migration* (Edward Elgar Publishing, Cheltenham, 2018) p. 203; S. Human, 'The importance of Article 2 of the Convention on the Rights of the Child for refugee children', in M. Skivenes and K. H. Søvig (eds.), *Child rights and international discrimination law. Implementing Article 2 of the Convention on the Rights of the Child* (Routledge, London, 2019) pp. 181–182; S. J. Diaz, 'Failing the refugee child: Gaps in the Refugee Convention relating to children', 20:3 *The Georgetown Journal of Gender and the Law* (2019) pp. 605–630; Pobjoy, *supra* note 87, pp. 745–749.

to connect the fear they experience to a relevant risk.[89] The latter might in particular be the case for children seeking asylum together with their families, where the decision to leave has usually been made by a parent or other adult and the children are not informed of the details of the perceived threat.

A second example is when the experiences and actions of children and adults are not accorded the same weight is assessing asylum claims. Crock and Yule note that children are often falsely assumed to be apolitical, unable to express political opinions or engage in political activities.[90] Krawiecki, commenting on US asylum case law, opines that adjudicators continue to struggle to recognise that "children's active civic engagement or assertion of their rights may lead to persecution".[91] Such misconceptions, and lack of recognition of children's agency, may result in 'political opinion' being overlooked as a protection ground for children, though the same or similar engagement in an adult might be considered sufficient grounds for asylum.

A shared characteristic for the situations regarding asylum claims outlined above is that though the intention may not be to treat children unfavourably compared with adults, the adult norms according to which child asylum claims continue to be assessed can result in their specific circumstances and vulnerabilities not being sufficiently taken into account. This puts them at risk of being treated unfavourably compared with adult asylum seekers. As Crock notes, "refugee jurisprudence, like asylum processes around the world, has developed with the adult asylum seeker as the norm".[92] The same situation may occur when children are judged based on traditional notions of their limited capabilities. In other words, the seemingly neutral norm of who is a refugee is in practice an adult-centred norm that, when applied to children, may result in disproportionate disadvantages for children as a group and in individual cases, and thus have a discriminatory effect.

---

89 M. Crock and P. Yule, 'Children and the Convention Relating to the Status of Refugees', in M. Crock and L.B. Benson (eds.), *Protecting Migrant Children. In Search of Best Practice* (Edward Elgar Publishing, Cheltenham, 2018) p. 102. *See also* UNHCR, *supra* note 81, para. 111.

90 Crock and Yule, *supra* note 89, p. 102.

91 S. Krawiecki (2022) 'Children Are Actors Too: In Search for Child Refugees' Agency', 43:1 *Children's Legal Rights Journal* (2022) pp. 1–16 (1). *See also* K.E. Smeda, 'Truth or Dare: A Framework for Analyzing Credibility in Children Seeking Asylum', 50:2 *Cornell International Law Journal* (2017) pp. 307–331.

92 M. Crock, 'Re-thinking the paradigms of protection: Children as Convention refugees in Australia', in J. McAdam (ed.), *Forced Migration, Human Rights and Security* (Bloomsbury Publishing, London, 2008) p. 157.

3.4 On Common Denominators

Some common denominators can be identified for the three examples of unequal treatment of migrant children compared with adult migrants outlined above. One is the traditional view of the child as an object of protection, rather than as an agent with the ability to act and influence outcomes. This approach is clearly visible in the case of limitations on the right to be heard in migration proceedings. Here, children's fundamental right to express their views and have them taken into account is subject to limitations based on adult appreciations of what is in the child's best interests and under which circumstances being heard is 'inappropriate' or 'unnecessary'. This appears to disregard the fact that the general principle of the right to be heard and to have one's views taken into account, as expressed in CRC Article 12, does not allow for such limitations.[93] The view of the child as an object rather than as a subject exercising agency is also visible in the context of assessment of asylum claims in that adjudicators and case workers seem to struggle to embrace the idea of children expressing political opinions or engaging in political activities, thus disregarding, or perhaps not identifying, grounds for international protection.

A second common denominator is the impact of adult-centred norms. Eligibility for refugee status or alternative protection status is in many cases interpreted in light of adult experiences, perhaps most visibly when asylum claims draw on 'adult-coded' activities such as political activism, but this could also be the case with for example LGBTQI-based claims or religious conversion.[94] Adult-centred norms also seem to guide the understanding of the weight to be accorded to the right to be heard in decision-making processes affecting one's life (such as the migration process), as well as the importance of family life for certain categories. An example is the EU FRD, in which family reunification appears to be more valuable for spouses than for teenagers due to the presumed duration of future family life. It has also been argued to impact the assessment of the well-founded fear criteria in relation to children (however, it should here be recognised that the weight to be accorded to the subjective criteria of 'fear' is debated).[95]

---

93 CRC/C/GC/12, *supra* note 61.

94 D. Hedlund and T. Wimark, 'Unaccompanied Children Claiming Asylum on the Basis of Sexual Orientation and Gender Identity', 32:2 *Journal of Refugee Studies* (2019) pp. 257–277.

95 *Cf.* A. Zimmermann and F. Herrmann, 'Article 1 A, para 2', in A. Zimmermann and T. Einarsen (eds.), *The 1951 Convention Relating to the Status of Refugees and its 1967 Protocol. A Commentary* (2 ed.) (Oxford University Press, Oxford, 2024) paras. 175–198.

A third common denominator is that children's interests and rights are not accorded the same weight as those of adults. Their right to be heard in asylum processes may be circumscribed if it is deemed unnecessary or if an adult has presented claims on their behalf. A child's right to family reunification can be made subject to integration conditions which do not apply to adults. Asylum claims presented by children may, as Smyth argues, be subject to doubts and suspicion and deemed not sufficiently substantive because children are not considered rights bearers at an equal level as adults.[96]

In summary, the examples presented in this section depict situations where the rights and experiences of migrant children are often considered less important than those of adult migrants. Directly or indirectly, whether intentionally or unintentionally, the adult (typically male) sets a standard against which children's capabilities, rights and experiences are assessed. The effect is that children, in certain cases, are treated worse than adults, despite the protection they should enjoy under the best interests-principle and the range of measures taken to account for children's dual vulnerability in a migration context.

4 Addressing Unequal Treatment of Children in the Context of Migration as Age-Based Discrimination : Some Reflections

As with age-based discrimination of children compared with adults in general, the criteria briefly outlined in Section 2 of this chapter must be fulfilled in order for unequal treatment to qualify as discrimination. This section addresses some of the key issues in relation to these criteria.

First, the identifiable characteristic due to which adult and child migrants are treated differently (when that is the case) is age/childhood, as described in the examples in the previous section. Second, on the comparator issue, one could argue that the number of traits or characteristics shared by children and adults in the context of migration indicates that they are indeed in a comparable situation: they are either outside of their country of origin, have family members who are migrants, or are born in migrant families, they may have insecure legal status in the destination country (as in temporary residence permits, tolerated status etc.), they are or have been in a process of applying for asylum and/or residence permit, and so on. These similarities are added to the fact that many of the norms according to which both children and adults

96 Smyth, *supra* note 17, pp. 255–256.

are to be assessed in the context of migration are age-neutral. Thus, children and adults in this context to a large extent share the experience of being 'migrants'. Additionally – which seems almost too obvious a point to make – migrants of all ages share the common experience of being human, and are thus free and equal in dignity and rights. The crucial factor distinguishing the two otherwise similarly situated groups is the number of lived years, and whether the age of majority has been attained or not. A counterargument could be that adults and children in the migration context are not similarly situated because of the many measures taken to ensure that the particular vulnerability of children is considered. As a result, children in the migration context could in fact generally be in a more favourable position than adults. The comparator issue is thus at least as complicated in the migration context as in general – perhaps even more so, due to the emphasis placed in national and international migration law on the best interests-principle, which has no equivalent for adult migrants.

Whether the third criteria – the lack of reasonable and objective justification for the distinction made – is fulfilled depends on whether the reasons for directly or indirectly limiting migrant children's rights compared with those of adult migrants are found legitimate and proportionate. In other words, the question to be asked is whether it can be justified to treat children in the context of migration less favourably, directly or indirectly, than adults in a similar situation due to their young age, even if age is recognised as a prohibited discrimination ground. How one chooses to answer that question is linked to the understandings, attitudes and prejudices towards children, their rights, capabilities and agency that permeate our societies, some of which are displayed in the examples described in the previous section. Differential treatment could on the one hand be considered to be an expression of childism. On the other hand, limiting children's right to be heard in migration proceedings (like in the Swedish case) could be argued to be justified based on concern for the child's interests and a wish to protect him or her. Imposing an integration condition for certain children but not for adults could be legitimised based on concerns regarding the integration of teenagers in the destination country, to protect them from (future) harm. Interpreting children's asylum claims based on adult norms without sufficiently taking into account how children would exercise political agency or manifest their convictions could be explained by traditional views on children's lack of competence and capabilities, resulting in limited understanding of what could constitute child-related persecution. What is considered proportionate and legitimate and thus justified can therefore be argued to depend on the point of departure for the discussion. If that point of departure is that rights limitations are justifiable to a larger extent for children than for adults, then this is also what will happen – even though it would be considered questionable, or even discriminatory, if the involved actors were different.

We sometimes speak of the need of 'calling a spade a spade'. Using the language of non-discrimination in relation to unequal treatment of children in the context of migration compared with adults in the same situation would be to do precisely that. Although not all differential treatment of persons in the context of migration constitutes discrimination, applying a discrimination lens contributes to recognising the existence of unfavourable differential treatment based on childhood, that directly or indirectly allows children to be treated less favourably than adults, and to challenging the justifiability of such treatment. CRC Article 2 is central to this endeavour. As a general principle of the key human rights instrument for children, it serves both as a provision in its own right and as a guiding principle for interpreting other CRC provisions. As discussed earlier, the CRC Committee has opened for including age among the grounds of discrimination covered by Article 2. The CRC Committee has on several occasions emphasised the fundamental importance in the context of international migration of the principle of non-discrimination for children as expressed in Article 2.[97] The Joint General Comment on the general principles regarding the human rights of children in the context of international migration states that "[A]ny differential treatment of migrants shall be lawful and proportionate, in pursuit of a legitimate aim and in line with the child's best interests and international human rights norms and standards".[98] The Joint General Comment also explicitly mentions age as a prohibited discrimination ground under Article 2, thus paving the way for addressing age-based unequal treatment of children compared with adults in this context in discrimination terms.[99]

Using the non-discrimination lens provided by CRC Article 2 in migration contexts, but also in other fields (of law), may serve several different purposes. It can be a valuable tool for identifying and addressing the negative consequences of permitting adult-centred norms to guide the application of seemingly neutral migration law provisions to children. Applying this perspective could contribute to consistently emphasising the status of migrant children as rights holders on an equal footing with adult migrants. It can also contribute to shedding light on an issue that otherwise tends to go under the

---

97 CMW/C/GC/3-CRC/C/GC/22, *supra* note 15, paras. 3, 21–26. *See also* CRC/GC/2005/6, *supra* note 15, para. 18.

98 CMW/C/GC/3-CRC/C/GC/22, *supra* note 15, para. 22.

99 Ibid, para. 21.

radar because of the number of measures taken to accommodate the vulnerable position of persons who are both children and migrants and the prominent position accorded in migration law to the best interests-principle. However, such efforts may, ironically, obscure the fact that there are situations, like the ones described earlier in this chapter, when the safeguards do not function as intended or are not considered applicable, or in practice do not work in favour of the child. One example is the aforementioned limitations to the child's right to express views and have them taken into account in the Swedish Aliens Act.

To summarise, systematically invoking Article 2 to identify unequal treatment based on childhood has the potential to strengthen the rights of children in particularly vulnerable situations, such as migration, and to challenge prevailing assumptions about the legitimacy of in practice according migrant children fewer or more limited rights than adults on the basis of age. This could also contribute to advancing children's rights more broadly and help dismantle the lingering perception of children as "mini human beings with mini human rights".[100] That perception may have particularly negative effects on individuals whose positions as rights holders are already questioned due to their immigration status. In this day and age, when migrants of all ages are subject to increasingly restrictive rules, it is all the more important to ensure that children, the most vulnerable of migrants, are not treated less favourably than adults without objective and reasonable justification, and that age discrimination is not treated differently than any other form of discrimination.

100 Mezmur, *supra* note 7, p. 261.

CHAPTER 10

Children, Age Discrimination Law, and Consent to Surgery

Priscilla Alderson

Abstract

A central human right, most highly valued by adults, is respect for each person's autonomy and bodily integrity. In English law – and also in many other jurisdictions – the body may be touched only after the person concerned has given explicit or at least tacit informed consent; touching should cease if the person objects except in specific cases such as the duties of police and prison officers. Numerous court cases around the world confirm the importance of this legal protection, many involving healthcare. The major exception to this protection is legal minors. For them, parents' or guardians' consent is required but not their own consent.

This chapter considers reasons for discrimination against minors that allows touching without their consent and regardless of their resistance, with the benefits, risks and harms of this exception in relation to medical treatment, specifically surgery. Standards in international law and in bioethics are considered, with reasons and supporting pressures behind the long-held ageist views that undermine respect for children's consent. Examples of recent rethinking of this discrimination are reported, with hopes for future progress.

1 Introduction: Non-discrimination

The aspiring UN human rights Declarations and Conventions, and the 1989 UN Convention on the Rights of the Child (CRC), particularly Article 2, prohibit discrimination or 'distinction of any kind'. Yet age discrimination is notably missing. However, this affects nearly one third of humanity aged under 18-years, and countless older people too. Minority age is the prototype for all discrimination, which is to treat the other as inferior, ignorant, inexperienced, unreliable, immature, foolish, weak or untrustworthy – like a child.

DOI:10.1163/9789004708433_011

The CRC has been criticised for its limitations, especially Article 12 for the power invested in adults to determine the 'weight' of a child's views.[1] This paper is about how all children's views should be respected unless there is significant risk of harm. Autonomy is so highly valued (by and for adults) in liberal democracies because we are "rational beings, deserving of dignity and control over our own destinies" and wellbeing. It is therefore "extraordinary that there has been so little progress in negotiating...the adult/child legal dichotomy [which] denies children any legal control over their own persons."[2]

Calls to reduce age discrimination and to equalise rights, opportunities and responsibilities between all age-groups risk placing undue burdens, responsibilities and, potentially, unfair blame on the very young. This can expose them to harms from which they have the right to be protected. Obviously young children cannot give detailed informed and legally valid consent, for example to surgery, in ways the average adult can. Yet there is a danger when overemphasising adult-centric, over-legalised, informed consent, of neglecting respect for the two other vital aspects of consent, in which children can be deeply involved: physical bodily interactions, and moral emotions.

The active physical expression of consent or refusal involves the child's willing cooperation or frightened resistance, with the accompanying need for force, from which a major purpose of human rights and consent is to protect patients. It is contradictory to ignore and override this embodied aspect of consent when caring for the most vulnerable patients.

Consent to surgery is unusual in that the individual child's needs and rights are much more central than in most other experiences throughout life. In other services – education, social care, urban planning, care of asylum seekers – every individual child matters but they also have to be considered much more as part of a group, a family, a school, a community, than when they have surgery. In healthcare, the needs of other patients and fair use of time and resources are always also vital but the central concern is the patient.

The purpose of this chapter is not to advocate a form of rights as selfish individualism but to show how deeper understanding of the individual child during treatment for surgery can help to illuminate ways to respect children's

1 A. Daly, 'No Weight for "Due Weight"? A Children's Autonomy Principle in 'Best Interest Proceedings', 26:1 *International Journal of Children's Rights* (2018) pp. 61–92; P. Alderson, 'Weight for children's views in medical law', 26:1 *International Journal of Children's Rights* (2018) pp.16–37, doi:10.1163/15718182-02601001.

2 A. Daly, Children, *Autonomy and the Courts: Beyond the Right to be Heard* (Brill, Leiden, 2018) pp. 189–190.

rights in all other contexts. All children can benefit when there is respect for individuals. My research explores consent as an emotional journey, which is relevant to many kinds of interactions and shared decision-making between children and adults.[3] The emotional aspects of voluntary consent develop when patients have time to overcome initial natural fears of painful frightening interventions. With adults' help, young children can move on from instinctive fear and rejection of proposed interventions, through doubt, towards trust in the practitioners, hope that interventions will help to heal their illness or injury, and courage to undergo any harms in order to gain the benefits. Very young children have strong life-preserving instincts and intuitions of fear and trust, of feeling harmed or helped, and healthcare professionals increasingly respect these emotions as an integral, practical part of therapeutic rights-respecting paediatrics.

A review of 56 journal papers about children's participation rights published over 30 years found "a remarkably consistent narrative...[with] far more written about challenges than solutions". The authors recommend expanding the "geographic and intellectual boundaries" and the use of "powerful concepts like agency, competency and autonomy with greater precision" with further exploration of "fresh ideas like child protagonism, activism and children as human rights defenders".[4] With surgery, challenges for the caring adults still include informing children as clearly as possible about the surgical options and hoped-for outcomes, and also offering advice and support while helping children to share in making decisions as much as they are willing and able to do so.

This chapter considers benefits but also problems of increasing over-legalising of consent, how this affects discrimination against children and what it means to be 'treated like a child'. By over-legalising, I am not criticising any measures to legalise consent – to make it more legal, respected and powerful. I am also not criticising further legalisation, when this means the process of removing a legal prohibition against something which is currently not legal. I am concerned with the exaggerated legalising that involves adding unnecessarily complicated and often intimidating quasi-legal procedures and requirements. Then children's rights relating to discrimination are reviewed, the physical reality of rights, nonverbal thought and communication, and ways to increase respect for children's consent to surgery. The dangers of

---

3 P. Alderson, *Children's Consent to Surgery* (Open University Press, Buckingham, 1993).

4 C. McMellon and E.K.M. Tisdall, 'Children and Young People's Participation Rights: Looking Backwards and Moving Forwards', 28:1 *International Journal of Children's Rights* (2020) pp.157–182, doi:10.1163/15718182-02801002.

overriding children's consent to surgery and the benefits of respecting their consent and reducing differences between the treatment of child and adult patients all highlight the importance of two terms that recur through this book: negative adultism and positive childism.[5]

The chapter is informed by my research, 1984–2021, about parents' consent to children's heart surgery,[6] children's consent to orthopaedic surgery,[7] and a recent study with Rosa Mendizabal and Katy Sutcliffe of parents' and children's consent to heart surgery.[8] All these projects involved years of observing[9] and interviewing children, parents and hospital staff. I will not attempt to give details about theses complex projects here but instead will draw on them to illustrate ideas in this chapter and I refer inquiring readers to the reports cited. The conclusion presents hopes for the future.

2 Over-Legalising of Consent

Human rights law tends to be discussed in quite abstract cerebral terms. Rights related to medical ethics mainly concern informed consent. Consent involves whether the patient or parent/guardian has been informed about all the relevant details of the nature, methods and purpose of the treatment, the risks and hoped-for benefits and outcomes, any alternative treatments, and the right to refuse or withdraw from treatment. The person who will

5 M. Liebel, 'Working children: Children without childhood or opponents against age-based discrimination?', This volume (2025); S. Morales and G. Magistris. 'Reinventing politics from a child perspective', In G. Magistris and S. Morales (eds.), *Reinventing the World with Children. From Adultcentrism to Child Perspectives* (Chirimbote and Ternura Revelde, Buenos Aires, 2023) pp. 13–42; M. Bourdillon and R. Carothers. 'Policy on Children's Work and Labour', 33 *Children & Society* (2019) pp. 387–395; M. Marcondes Smith and W. Vandenhole, '"Handle with Care": Addressing Disadvantage based on Childhood through a Non-discrimination Frame', This volume (2025).

6 P. Alderson, *Choosing for Children: Parents' Consent to Surgery* (Oxford University Press, Oxford, 1990).

7 P. Alderson, *Children's Consent to Surgery* (Open University Press, Buckingham, 1993).

8 Children's Consent to Heart Surgery Website (2024) <https://www.ucl.ac.uk/ioe/departments-and-centres/centres/social-science-research-unit/consent-and-shared-decision-making-healthcare/heart-surgery>, visited on 24 January 2024. Open access papers reporting this research are listed on the website.

9 During the 2018–2021 research, the COVID-19 pandemic ended observations in 2020, but interviews and other data collecting continued by 'phone and online group meetings and surveys.

give consent is expected to recall and understand the information, weigh the related risks and benefits, and make a competent rational decision to give or withhold consent.[10]

Children are often assumed to be unable to manage this intellectual process until around 12-years of age. In medical law, the legal status of the person, in being competent to give or withhold consent, is crucial. The need to avoid uncertainties that would not satisfy the court in cases of litigation leads many doctors to be cautious about minors' consent, and to rely mainly on parents' or guardians' consent. This paper is mainly about UK and US law and practices and their global influence, though under-estimation of children is not universal. For example, many indigenous social groups in Brazil believe children live ambiguously in-between this world and the world of spirits, and so children help societies to achieve their shared objectives. Children are respected as most able to mediate with the non-indigenous, the gods, or even, the enemies.[11] Western societies have much to learn from other cultures.

While legal standards of consent to surgery are vital protections for both patients and practitioners, over-legalising or over-concentration on the law of informed consent and the necessary intellectual interactions can divert attention from other crucial elements of consent. These include patients' embodied experiences in their active cooperation or resistance, as well as the emotions within voluntary consent. When these elements are recognised, the discriminatory adultism assumed in human rights law of consent can be more fully questioned. Children's capacities and the routines that 'treat them like a child' can then be reconsidered.

Numerous court cases around the world attest to the importance of legal protection from the tort of battery (or assault) or of negligence (neglecting to request consent). A tort is an act or omission that gives rise to injury or harm to another and amounts to a civil wrong for which courts impose liability. Many of these cases involve healthcare. Yet the major exception to this protection in law is legal minors. Their parents'/guardians' consent is required for healthcare interventions that would otherwise be assaults, and children's own

10 Consent was first defined in detail in relation to medical research in *Nuremberg Code.* (1947) https://media.tghn.org/medialibrary/2011/04/BMJ_No_7070_Volume_313_The_Nuremberg_Code.pdf, visited on 24 November 2024; World Medical Association, Declaration of Helsinki (WMA, Fernay-Voltaire, 1964/2013) https://www.wma.net/policies-post/wma-declaration-of-helsinki/, visited on 24 November 2024.

11 L. Rabello de Castro, 'Decolonizing discrimination against children: alternative generationing and generativities', This volume (2025).

views may be ignored or overridden so that doctors do not routinely inform them about imminent surgery.

Consent has increasingly been seen as a legal contract designed to reduce and prevent the mistreatment and the stress and costs of complaints and litigation. This is in everyone's interests. Yet the consent contract is not always effective. In England, the National Health Service (NHS) Payments on Clinical Negligence Scheme "claims increased by £152.8 million (seven per cent) to £2,213.9 million from 2020/21".[12]

One main problem is insufficient or inadequate information. Ankuda and colleagues found that one third of the adult patients they studied did not know "the procedure being performed or risks and benefits".[13] With other patients, their doctors had not "addressed patient values, preferences and goals", and patients who did not speak English or who had a lower educational level or lower health literacy were most likely to be affected.[14] Many patients tend to feel under pressure to show respect and trust for the surgeon and not to ask as many questions as they would like to.[15]

Another problem is excess information that may confuse and intimidate patients and distract them from checking even basic questions. Patient information leaflets and consent forms may run to pages of details about risks and side effects, particularly in the USA. In English law, doctors must explain all known risks of proposed surgery.[16] Rare or mild risks may not interest most people, but they become highly significant for a few patients. One example is if a professional singer's voice is slightly impaired. This is devastating for the singer, but it is a problem most people would hardly notice when they are grateful that the treatment has effectively cured their problem. Detailed reading of contracts is unusual. When requested to tick the box online to show we have read all the information and we consent to the terms and conditions of the company whose services we are using, how many people actually read the details?

12 NHS England (2023) <www.resolution.nhs.uk/2022/07/20/nhs-resolution-continues-to-drive-down-litigation-annual-report-and-accounts-published-for-2021-22/>, visited on 8 June 2024.

13 M. Falagas et al., 'Informed Consent: How Much and What Do Patients Understand?', 198:3 *American Journal of Surgery* (2009) pp. 420–35.

14 C. Ankuda et al., 'Measuring Critical Deficits in Shared Decision Making Before Elective Surgery', 94 *Patient Education & Counselling* (2014) pp. 328–33.

15 L. Convie et al., 'The Patient and Clinician Experience of Informed Consent for Surgery: A Systematic Review of the Qualitative Evidence', 21:58 *BMC Med Ethics* (2020).

16 *Montgomery* v. *Lanarkshire Health Board* [2015].

Research repeatedly shows that many adults forget or misremember information to which they have consented before surgery.[17] This can reduce their informed cooperation with post-surgical care and may adversely affect their recovery.[18] Many people misunderstand the information.[19] Adults' thinking and memory may be impaired before and for months after major surgery by "anxiety, depression, fatigue, sleep disturbance and other characteristics",[20] burdens that can also affect parents/guardians. Excess information about risks deters many adults from wanting to learn about the dangers, worried that this will increase their pre-surgical anxiety. "High pre-surgical anxiety is associated with a high incidence of post-surgical pain, decreasing the ability to resist infection, delaying wound healing, imposing adverse effects on patients' mood and hospital stay, and reducing patient satisfaction with their treatment".[21] The self-defence of positive thinking, of not attending to negative aspects of their condition, is associated with better recovery after surgery.[22] Yet many adult patients also worry about their unanswered questions.[23] There are further complications in that patients vary, individually and in different countries, in the kinds and amounts of detail they want to know, and in the methods by which they want to be informed. Many prefer spoken to written information, but surgical teams may not be trained, or encouraged, or given quiet space or time, to hold open discussions with patients.[24]

These problems can be still more serious for children than for adults. There is likely to be even greater concern to shield children from worrying complex knowledge, and to deny them information, than there is to protect adult patients. On average, young children are more likely than adults to be confused,

17 D. Hekmatpou et al., 'Pathology of Patient Education: A Qualitative Study', 20 *Iran Journal of Nursing* (2007) pp. 51–60.

18 F. Kim et al., 'Current Issues in Patient Safety in Surgery: A Review', 9 *Patient Safety in Surgery* (2015), doi:10.1186/s13037-015-0067-4.

19 G. De Oliveira et al., 'The Impact of Health Literacy in the Care of Surgical Patients: A Qualitative Systematic Review', 15:86 *BioMedical Central Surgery* (2015), doi:10.1186/s12893-015-0073-6.

20 Y.-Y.Allemann-Su et al., 'Pre-Surgery Demographic, Clinical, and Symptom Characteristics Associated with Different Self-Reported Cognitive Processes in Patients with Breast Cancer', 14 *Cancers* (2022) p. 3281.

21 E. Nasiri et al., 'Health Care Team Understanding of Patients' Desire for Information on Surgery and Anesthesia: A Cross-sectional Study', 21 *Perioperative Care and Operating Room Management* (2020) p. 100134.

22 C. Schwartz et al., 'Cognitive Processes during Recovery: Moving toward Personalized Spine Surgery Outcomes', 12 *Journal of Personalized Medicine* (2022) p. 1545.

23 Nasiri, *supra* note 21.

24 Ibid.

to misunderstand medical information, and to need skilfully explained details. Practitioners may not expect children to understand, and doctors are then likely to assume any problems with communication lie with the child and not with the adults. They may believe that it is kinder not to confuse and worry children with information, or they may accept the parents saying that their child should not be told.

Children can be left very confused. Alice Miller's research found that if adults hurt and frighten them, children tend to assume they are to blame for anything shameful or hurtful that happens to them.[25] She found that many think they are being punished for some unknown wrong they have done but dare not ask about. Lonely guilt and anxiety can increase their pain. From their earliest years, children are meaning makers and attribute motives to others' actions.

Doctors are still less likely to talk about children's own values, preferences and goals with them, than they would with adult patients. Many doctors tend to see only the parents' values as sufficiently formulated to be relevant, or they rely on parents' beliefs about their child's views and needs rather than the child's.[26] These traditional views persist with many adults still believing that only they should decide children's best interests, that children are too ignorant and volatile to be trusted to make wise decisions, and that children's reports of abuse from adults are only phantasies. CRC Article 12 respects adults' assessments ('due weight') about children's views, not children's views directly.

These traditions, which sideline children's views, are based on convictions that children are entirely different from adults, that they need different standards of care, and need 'to be treated like a child'. This includes being excluded from the adult-centric over-legalising of consent that prioritises preventing complaints and litigation by obtaining the legally valid adult's signature on the consent form. Doctors are deterred from risking queries about the child's uncertain legal liability or status or understanding. Children are routinely tested on their abilities if their consent is to be considered, whereas adults are not, although many adults would fail tests of their understanding and recall of the medical information.[27] Clear appropriate information and sensitive support are vital for all age groups.

25 A. Miller, *Thou Shalt not Be Aware: Society's Betrayal of the Child* (Plume, London, 1998).

26 J. Goldstein et al., *The Best Interests of the Child: The Least Detrimental Alternative* (Simon & Schuster, London, 1973/1986).

27 Falagas, *supra* note 13.

3 Rights Related to Consent: Combatting Discrimination

An alternative approach to over-legalising is to relate respectfully to children as persons with inalienable rights during the consent process. Children, especially young, ill or disabled children, tend to be seen as not-yet persons, to the extent of the young child being called "a capacitous person who has not yet existed".[28] In this chapter, the rights to bodily integrity and autonomy of young surgery patients are seen to involve complex mental legal process and also physical realities: the child's impaired body and physical needs; actual corrective surgery; the staff who interact with the child and who handle the child's body; the child's active physical cooperation, or resistance. Understanding that human rights at all ages involve physical realities and nonverbal mental processes and interactions is more inclusive and respectful of the rights of all young and disabled children. This accords with the Preambles of all the UN Human Rights Conventions: that "recognition of the inherent dignity and of the equal and inalienable rights of all members of the human family is the foundation of freedom, justice and peace in the world". 'Inalienable' means that rights cannot be taken away, surrendered or transferred. This implies they are innate, not gradually emergent after the first years. 'Innate' is taken to mean from the moment of birth when the child is independent of the mother's body.[29]

An alternative to the cerebral, institutionalised, over-legalising approach is also to recognise consent as part of the respectful, therapeutic, personal doctor-patient relationship. "A patient's right to autonomy and dignity should today be accorded the highest priority in English law."[30] Respect for each person's autonomy and bodily integrity means that the body should be touched only after the person concerned has given explicit or at least tacit informed consent; touching should cease if the person objects except in specific cases such as the duties of police and prison officers.[31]

---

28 J. Pugh, 'The Child's Right to Bodily Integrity and Autonomy: A Conceptual Analysis', *Clinical Ethics* (2023) <https://journals.sagepub.com/doi/pdf/10.1177/14777509231188817> visited on 24 January 2024.

29 Nation states chose the age when rights begin when they ratified the CRC, and in UK law rights begin when the child is born, in order not to infringe on mothers' rights.

30 Judgment in the law case [2004] *UK* v *HL 16* cited in M. Brazier and E. Cave. *Medicine, Patients and the Law* (University of Manchester, Manchester, 2016), p.123.

31 P. Alderson, 'Bodily Integrity and Autonomy of the Youngest Children and Consent to their Healthcare', 18:4 *Clinical Ethics* (2023), doi:10.1177/14777509231188006.

Yet children are still often constrained and forcibly 'held' during clinical procedures, in the belief that there is not time to inform, prepare and support them to gain their cooperation, or that they are incapable of rational understanding. Increasingly, these views are challenged. Nurse researchers report the moral distress to practitioners and children during such interactions.[32] Research shows that young children can understand and cooperate, when they are carefully informed, far more than used to be believed possible.[33] Practitioners contend that treating young children respectfully, such as when administering anaesthesia before surgery, can prevent suffering including PTSD.[34] Time spent informing and supporting children, especially those with serious long-term conditions, is cost-effective when it can avoid much time being wasted later if they become more scared and resistant during repeated treatment as they grow older. Paediatric cardiology teams are deeply concerned that enforced interventions can cause children to lose mutual trust and respect with their clinical team. When aged about 16, they become responsible for booking their own regular clinic appointments. Some young people have such painful memories that they opt out of the life-long care on which their health and survival depend.[35]

Respectfully listening to children and negotiating with them involves many of the inter-related, indivisible CRC rights. The CRC Preamble recognises that many children need extra protections: "the child, by reason of his or her physical and mental immaturity, needs special safeguards and care, including appropriate legal protection". Yet many adults also have extra needs, and for plenty of mature young people 'special safeguards' can be unnecessary and unwanted oppressions. However, the wording 'special safeguards and care' and 'protection' can suggest flexibility that adapts to each child's needs and avoids coercive control. This involves checking with each child how much they want and need to know before and during their investigations and treatment.

CRC Article 2 states that every child shall be respected

32 L. Bray et al., 'A Qualitative Study of Health Professionals' Views on the Holding of Children for Clinical Procedures: Constructing a Balanced Approach', 23:1 *Journal of Child Health Care* (2019) pp. 160–171.

33 I. Coyne. 'Children Should be Seen and Heard' 6:2 *Children's Research Digest* (2020) pp. 4–8; P. Alderson et al., 'Children's Consent to Medical Treatment', 36 *Hastings Centre Report* (2006) pp. 25–34.

34 H. Wellesley et al., 'When children refuse their anaesthetic - restrain, deceive, or postpone?' 31:9 *Pediatric Anesthesia* (2021) pp. 1016–17.

35 P. Alderson et al., 'Children's Ages of Consent to Non-urgent Heart Surgery: The Views of Two Paediatric Cardiology Teams' 38 *Children & Society* (2023) pp. 487–504.

> without discrimination of any kind, irrespective of the child's or his or her parent's or legal guardian's race, colour, sex, language, religion, political or other opinion, national, ethnic or social origin, property, disability, birth or other status [or] on the basis of the status, activities, expressed opinions, or beliefs of the child's parents, legal guardians, or family members.
>
> Article 2

Age discrimination, the main concern of this chapter, is notably missing. However, Article 2 is vitally important on equal rights to healthy living and to healthcare among all children. This involves extra care and services for all disadvantaged children to bring these up to standards enjoyed by children in secure prosperous families and in wealthier countries, to counteract racism, classism and all other unjust discriminations. Many of these are detailed in the following paragraphs.

Article 3 continues: "The best interests of the child shall be a primary consideration [with] such protection and care as is necessary for his or her well-being, taking into account the rights and duties of his or her parents" or other legally responsible adults. There should also be respect for "the responsibilities, rights and duties of parents to direct and guide the child" (Article 5). During our research interviews about children's consent to heart surgery, a play specialist recounted working respectfully with parents but also persuading some parents, who insisted their child should not be informed before heart surgery, to see how greatly their child needed some explanations and preparation. She described parents' relief and growing confidence when she helped them to find ways to inform and prepare their child.[36] Eileen McPartland, among many authors, shows how the child's best interests are respected through listening to children's own views.[37]

The CRC positions 'states parties' as the key agents that observe and protect human rights, meaning governments, politicians and public servants who legislate and implement state policies and services. "States Parties shall ensure to the maximum extent possible the survival and development of the child" (Article 6). "Survival and development" involve not only the best outcomes for any healthcare intervention for children but also the best processes, through which children are respectfully involved and helped to learn and gain knowl-

36 P. Alderson et al., 'Children's understanding and consent to heart surgery: Multidisciplinary teamwork and moral experiences' 27:2 *Journal of Child Health Care* (2023) pp. 197–211, doi:10.1177/13674935221100419.

37 E. McPartland, *The Best Interests of the Child* (Gill Education, Dublin, 2013/2020).

edge and confidence. The CRC's broad international standards can be interpreted and implemented in numerous local, detailed ways, for example by the whole range of healthcare professionals who care for children from surgeons to chaplains, psychologists to physiotherapists.

> States Parties shall assure to the child who is capable of forming his or her own views the right to express those views freely in all matters affecting the child, the views of the child being given due weight in accordance with the age and maturity of the child.
>
> Article 12

Article 12 continues with the child's right to "be provided the opportunity to be heard in any judicial and administrative proceedings affecting the child". Protection rights to keep children safe have traditionally been contrasted with so-called participation or freedom rights (mainly articles 12–17) as if, when allowed to make choices about their best interests, children will make foolish, ignorant, risky decisions, and are their own worst enemies. Yet although "to respect the rights and duties of the parents and…guardians, to provide direction to the child in the exercise of his or her right in a manner consistent with the evolving capacities of the child" (Article 14.2, repeating Article 5) can be interpreted oppressively to overrule young patients, it can also involve informing, respecting and supporting children's choices. Respect for autonomy therefore involves mutual respect for everyone's dignity and protection and support when needed.

While strongly supporting Article 12, researchers have shown problems associated with the concept of 'due weight', as assessed by adults. It can be an obstacle, allowing adults to dismiss children's views that seem to have insufficient 'weight', to silence and exclude them from discussions. Aoife Daly contends that when the child's best interests are the primary consideration, the child's involvement in decision-making and the child's choices should be supported unless there is risk of significant harm.[38] Kay Tisdall has analysed concepts of competence and capacity to show they have uncertain meanings, interpretations and applications. Too often they are seen as integral to the child's development, whereas poor communication often arises from adults' own limited competencies and capacities. The concepts need to be more precisely and critically defined and the 2006 UN Convention on the Rights of Persons with Disabilities offers fresh ideas on recognising and supporting peo-

---

38 Daly, *supra* note 1.

ple's legal capacities.[39] Centuries of prejudice in philosophy, law and psychology can confuse today's analyses and need to be unravelled.[40] Long-standing research evidence of young children's capacity for profound understanding needs to be much more widely known, such as their realistic knowledge about death.[41] Children should not be tested for their general knowledge but for their understanding of the specific matter, especially ill and disabled children. Their daily lives may be limited but their understanding of their condition may be profound. The UN Committee on the Rights of the Child has also emphasised that children do not need "comprehensive knowledge of all aspects of the matter…but sufficient understanding" to enable them to form their own views on the matter.[42] This begins "in early childhood" and therefore adults should not assume incapacity but "should presume that a child has the capacity" to form and express views; "it is not up to the child to first prove his or her capacity". The Committee offered much useful advice on the stages of consulting with children, avoiding an environment that "is intimidating, hostile, insensitive" or age-inappropriate, and instead providing "child-friendly information, adequate support for self-advocacy, and appropriately trained staff".[43] This firmly puts responsibility on the adults, not the child, to ensure the encounter is effective. There is a slowly growing literature on the benefits of respectfully consulting with children who have serious conditions.[44]

English and Scottish law exceed CRC standards, that the legal right to consent or refuse begins at a fixed age, 16- or 18-years and before then only pa-

39 E.K.M. Tisdall, 'Challenging Concepts of Competence and Capacity?', 26 *International Journal of Children's Rights* (2018) pp. 59–82.

40 R. McDougall et al., *When Doctors and Parents Disagree: Ethics, Paediatrics and the Zone of Parental Discretion* (Federation Press, Sydney, 2016).

41 M. Bluebond-Langner, *The Private Worlds of Dying Children* (Princeton University Press, New Jersey, 1978); C. Clunies-Ross and R. Lansdown, 'Concepts of Death, Illness and Isolation Found in Children with Leukaemia' 14 *Child: Health, Care and Development* (1998) pp. 373–86; Alderson, *supra* note 8.

42 UN Committee on the Rights of the Child, General Comment no. 12 The Right of the Child to be Heard (United Nations, Geneva, 2009) pp. 20–21.

43 Ibid.

44 I. Coyne et al., 'Children's Participation in Shared Decision-Making: Children, Adolescents, Parents and Healthcare Professionals' Perspectives and Experiences' 18:3 *European Journal of Oncology Nursing* (2014) pp. 273–280; E. Beecham et al., 'Children's and Parents' Conceptualization of Quality of Life in Children With Brain Tumors: A Meta-Ethnographic Exploration' 29:1 *Qualitative Health Research* (2019) pp. 55–68, doi: 10.1177/1049732318786484; P. Alderson et al., 'Children as Partners with Adults in their Medical Care', 91 *Archives of Diseases in Childhood* (2006) pp. 300–303; Alderson, *supra* note 8; Children's Consent to Heart Surgery Website, *supra* note 7.

rents/guardians may give consent. Instead, doctors assess and determine the child's Gillick competency and right to consent.[45] They

> take into account the child's age, mental capacity and maturity, their understanding of the issue, the risks, implications and consequences that may arise from their decision, how well they understand any advice or information they have been given, their understanding of any alternative options, and their ability to explain a rationale around their reasoning and decision making.[46]

Some hospitals move on from the legal tradition that only one person may sign the consent form. They provide two spaces and families can choose whether the child's or a parent' signature is written on the first line to show who was the 'main decider'. In the USA, the 'mature minor' is respected on similar terms to the UK, though in the definition there is more emphasis on a lack of supportive involved adults than on the child's capacity.[47] The USA is the only state in the world not to have ratified the CRC. The British NHS respects healthcare as a right, a view that is undermined in countries where healthcare is a profitable commodity mainly on offer to those who can afford it.

CRC Article 12 is valuable in setting out children's rights to be involved and listened to in decision-making that affects them. Yet as noted earlier, the right is qualified by concerns about capacity, and too often depends on adults who, it is assumed, will make the actual decision. The CRC is both more advanced than other Conventions in having an Article that relates to the right to make personal decisions, but less advanced in qualifying this right in mainly adult-centric terms. In other Conventions, such as the Universal Declaration of Human Rights (UDHR) 1948, it is implied this right is too obvious and basic to all other rights, such as privacy or noninterference, even to be worth mentioning. It is referred to most nearly in UDHR Article 19, "Everyone has the right to freedom of opinion and expression; this right includes freedom to hold opinions without interference and to seek, receive and impart information and ideas through any media and regardless of frontiers." Yet everyone's human rights are qualified: by "due recognition and respect for the rights and

45 *Gillick* vs *West Norfolk & Wisbech AHA* [1984] Age of Legal Capacity Scotland Act [1991].

46 R. Griffith, 'What is Gillick competence?', 12 *Human Vaccines Immunotherapeutics* (2016) pp. 244–247, doi:10.1080/21645515.2015.1091548.

47 G. Sigman and C. O'Connor, 'Exploration for Physicians of the Mature Minor Doctrine', 19:4 *Journal of Pediatrics* (1991) pp. 520–5, doi:10.1016/s0022-3476(05)82398-4.

freedoms of others…meeting the just requirements of morality, public order and the general welfare in a democratic society", and in never being "exercised contrary to the purposes and principles of the United Nations".[48]

When doctors began to perform heart transplants for children in the late 1980s, they soon found that they had to listen to young children's views. Doctors were not only mending impaired bodies, they also encountered inquiring minds. A psychologist who worked with the first paediatric cardiac transplant team and is still in practice explained how she had to persuade the doctors to listen and respect the children's views. Children who did not want the transplant literally had their life in their hands. They had to take daily immunosuppressive medication for the rest of their lives. Some children refused to do this and they died.[49] There are too few small donated hearts for all the children who need them, and doctors have to choose their patients very carefully, treating those who have most hope of success. The psychologist explained how she discussed his transplant with a 3-year-old. She compared his heart transplant to a car that gets a new engine. This showed how his body and identity would be unchanged. She told him his new engine would need petrol and that was the daily medicine. She believed the little boy deeply understood what was involved, as he was so ill and in great need of the treatment. He knew what it was like when his 'engine' was not working well and 'might stop'.[50]

Also vital is "freedom to seek, receive and impart information and ideas of all kinds…orally, in writing or in print, in the form of art, or through any other media of the child's choice" (Article 13). This especially helps children who need more than verbal explanations, in images or play with medical equipment or with puppets.

"Freedom of thought, conscience and religion" (Article 14) extends Articles 12 and 13 to imply respect for children's decisions. Freedom of religion is most clearly debated when young Jehovah's Witness patients refuse life-saving blood transfusion and blood products, deeply believing this is vetoed in the Bible. Doctors rely on the courts to authorise treatment that overrules legal minors' choices. However, there is now greater concern to respect children's religious beliefs and to work with them as closely as possible, with early communication and multidisciplinary team planning.[51]

---

48 Universal Declaration of Human Rights (United Nations, New York, 1948) Article 29, 2,3.

49 P. Alderson and M. Goodwin, 'Contradictions within Concepts of Children's Competence', 1:3 *International Journal of Children's Rights* (1993) pp. 303–313.

50 Alderson, *Supra* note 35.

51 E. Murphy and P. McConnell, 'The Perioperative Care of Jehovah's Witnesses', 23(8) *Anaesthesia & Intensive Care Medicine* (2022) pp. 472–476; A. Klein et al., 'Association

Article 16 states, the child's right to be protected by law from "arbitrary or unlawful interference with his or her privacy, family, or correspondence [and] unlawful attacks on his or her honour and reputation". Parents who wish to see their child's medical records should request permission from children aged from about 13,[52] and all healthcare staff should be extremely careful about spreading criticisms of children or parents.

While being protected from 'injurious' information, children have the right to access the mass media and "information and material from a diversity of national and international sources, especially those aimed at the promotion of his or her social, spiritual and moral well-being and physical and mental health" (Article 17). Clear information with images helps children and parents to become highly informed before surgery. A surgeon we interviewed recalled explaining planned heart surgery to a boy aged 7, "who was looking at his iPad and he was watching the operation I was going to do, he'd found it on YouTube, sitting there saying 'Is this what you're going to do?'"

Article 18 recognises that parents have "the primary responsibility for the upbringing and development of the child. The best interests of the child will be their basic concern". Article 19 concerns "measures to protect the child from all forms of physical or mental violence, injury or abuse, neglect or negligent treatment, maltreatment or exploitation". 'Neglect' refers to millions of children around the world who do not have the surgery they need to cure problems from blindness to cancer. Avoiding abuse relates to careful planning and informed negotiation with children and parents, especially before high-risk or experimental surgery. CRC later states more forcefully, "States Parties shall protect the child against all other forms of exploitation prejudicial to any aspects of the child's welfare" (Article 36). "No child shall be subjected to torture or other cruel, inhuman or degrading treatment or punishment" (Article 37). By the uninformed child, surgery can be experienced as torture, another reason for ensuring that children are as fully informed and involved in decisions as possible.

States Parties recognise that "a mentally or physically disabled child should enjoy a full and decent life, in conditions which ensure dignity, promote self-reliance and facilitate the child's active participation in the community". The aim is the child "achieving the fullest possible social integration and individual development" (Article 23). Surgery enables countless children to enjoy better health, mobility and a more 'normal' fulfilled childhood. Ensuring 'dignity'

---

of Anaesthetists: Anaesthesia and Peri-operative Care for Jehovah's Witnesses and Patients Who Refuse Blood', 74 *Anaesthesia* (2019) pp. 74–82.

52 British Medical Association, *Children and Young People Toolkit* (BMA, London, 2021).

involves respecting children's thoughts as well as their bodies when making decisions about surgery. "International cooperation, the exchange of appropriate information in the field of preventive health care and of medical, psychological and functional treatment of disabled children" (Article 23) help to spread surgical research knowledge and technical expertise around the world. Medicine is the most internationally practised and shared profession (perhaps apart from music) and Articles 23 and 24 endorse "the spirit of international cooperation, the exchange of appropriate information" enabling practitioners "to improve their capabilities and skills and to widen their experience...Particular account shall be taken of the needs of developing countries".

All CRC rights contribute to supporting "the right of the child to the enjoyment of the highest attainable standard of health and to facilities for the treatment of illness and rehabilitation of health" (Article 24). There is no right to health because health cannot be willed or enforced. A dying child has no "right to heath", only to the "highest attainable standard of health". "The right of every child to a standard of living adequate for the child's physical, mental, spiritual, moral and social development" includes assistance for families in need "particularly with regard to nutrition, clothing and housing" (Article 27). This involves preventing illness and the need for medical treatment, and it complements education that is directed to "the development of the child's personality, talents and mental and physical abilities to their fullest potential" (Article 29). There are also health-related rights "to rest and leisure, to engage in play and recreational activities appropriate to the age of the child and to participate freely in cultural life and the arts" (Article 31).

Other vital health-related rights that involve children's minds and bodies and informed decision-making and partnership with adults include the rights to protection from: economic exploitation and from performing any work that is likely to be hazardous or to interfere with the child's education, or to be harmful to the child's health" (Article 32); illicit use of narcotic drugs and psychotropic substances (Article 33); "sexual exploitation and sexual abuse" (Article 34); "the abduction of, the sale of or traffic in children" (Article 35); "all other forms of exploitation prejudicial to any aspects of the child's welfare" (Article 36); arbitrary imprisonment and associated mistreatment (Article 37); recruitment into the armed forces (in the UK young people aged over 15 are not protected despite the serious known physical and mental health harms) (Article 38). Healthcare includes 'all appropriate measures to promote physical and psychological recovery and social reintegration' of a child victim recovering from a range of named abuses (Article 39). Article 40 lists health-related dangers of treating children like adult criminals.

"Nothing in the present Convention shall affect any provisions which are more conducive to the realization of the rights of the child and which may be contained in … the law of a State party" (Article 41). This supports USA mature minors law. English Gillick law also exceeds CRC standards in that it respects young children deemed to be competent to consent with no stated age barrier. There is much further valuable information in CRC, the General Comments, and the Committee's Concluding Observations.

4 Conclusion: Hope for Future Progress

As noted earlier, the UN human rights Conventions, especially CRC Article 2 prohibit discrimination or 'distinction of any kind' except for age discrimination. Perhaps the UN will reconsider this omission and declare retrospectively that anti-age discrimination is formally included in all its treaties, with reservations that respect each nation's age-related laws. If adultist, anti-child discrimination were challenged and prohibited more, that is likely to improve attitudes underlying discrimination against all other groups of people.

To replace the present weak "right to be heard" in CRC Article 12, and so to honour non-discrimination standards in Article 2, children need rights, embedded in good systems, to be encouraged and assisted to express themselves. Instead of dismissing children's (and adults') emotions as problems, adults need to understand and support the emotional moral journey that patients have to make from initial fear and possibly rejection of proposed surgery through doubt and trust towards resolve and courage to undergo the treatment hoping for the intended benefits. Very young children can be helped to achieve this. The following view of the future, in an analysis mainly of law on adults' rights, also affects children.

> The next stage in the development of health care law lies in spelling out the scope of our rights as citizens, not as patients awaiting the ministrations of professionals. I have suggested that this will leave the judicial protection of clinical freedom intact, but it will bring it out into the open, and place it in the context of the obligations of health services to give people worthwhile choices.[53]

53 J. Montgomery, 'Patient No Longer? What Next in Health Care Law?' (2017) https://discovery.ucl.ac.uk/id/eprint/1569251/1/Montgomery_Patient_No_Longer.pdf> visited on 23 November 2024.

To relate to children as present and future citizens with rights gives them greater equality with adults. Society depends on having healthy citizens and this involves 'the highest attainable standards' of healthcare. Working *with* children can increase their active cooperation with their treatment and reduce the risk of enforcing interventions that leave some children with long-term trauma. The heart surgery teams were observed to look ahead to the years when young people become responsible for their own care. Practitioners knew that, for children's present and future wellbeing, they must sustain mutual trust and strive to work with the child's informed willing consent.

Finally, this chapter and this book have advocated that children should not be 'treated like a child', which equals negative discrimination. But perhaps we are falling into adultist prejudices. Some great philosophers have imagined a positive world where we are all treated, and treat one another, like young children in preference to being like adults. Jesus said, "Allow [suffer] the little children to come unto me and forbid them not, for as such is the kingdom of heaven".[54] And he warned, "Unless you change and become like little children, you will never enter the kingdom of heaven. Therefore, whoever humbles himself like this child is the greatest in the kingdom of heaven."[55]

Acknowledgements

Thank you to all the children and adults who took part in the research, and to many research colleagues including Rosa Mendizabal-Espinosa and Katy Sutcliffe. Our recent research was funded by The British Heart Foundation, Project code: 546781/award number: 176835, PI Katy Sutcliffe.

54 Matthew 19.14.
55 Matthew 18.3.

CHAPTER 11

Children as Bearers of Rights or of Problems? Non-legitimate and Unfair Treatment of Children in the Context of Combatting Gang Crime in Sweden

Pernilla Leviner

Abstract[1]

This chapter discusses recent shifts and contradictions in the Swedish child protection and welfare system in the context of the fight against gang crime which is an increasing problem in Sweden today. The overall question in this chapter is quite simply – what is happening with children's rights in Sweden in the 2020s? – and the overall aim is to discuss what the legal shift and changes in Sweden can tell us about challenges when it comes to realizing and respecting children's rights in other contexts and jurisdictions more than 30 years after the entry into force CRC. The focus is on how law reforms in Sweden in the 2020's may lead to that children's right are overlooked and the risk of discrimination against groups of children affected by and suspected to be involved in gang crime, but also how such discrimination by extension can be seen as non-legitimate differential treatment of (all) children because they are children, i.e., age discrimination. It is discussed how children, in the context of the fight against gang criminality are, on the one hand subjected to what can be labelled 'adultification' and 'over-responsibilization', making children responsible in the same way as adults, but on the other hand, children are perceived as 'different' and therefor in need of more control than adults – being 'treated like a child'. The hope is that this chapter can broaden the understanding of discrimination against children, both that between different groups of children, and non-legitimate differential treatment of children as a group, i.e. discrimination on the basis of childhood.

---

1 Thank you to co-editors and authors in this anthology and also to professors Mauro Zamboni, Jan Flyghed (both Stockholm University, Sweden) and Bronwyn Naylor (RMIT University, Australia) who have all discussed and given valuable comments on earlier drafts of this chapter. The chapter is written as part of the research project Treated like a child, funded by the Ragnar Söderberg Foundation.

1 Introduction and Aim

Sweden as a state for decades has marketed itself as a world leader when it comes to respecting and fulfilling human rights, not the least children's rights. Reference in this context is made by way of example to being the first country to introduce (in 1979) a ban on corporal punishment of children, to the generous welfare programs aimed at supporting families with children, and also through an overall child-friendly self-image with child-safe Volvos and child-adjusted home environments with IKEA furniture. Another strongly held Swedish self-image is the belief that the Swedish welfare system provides equal treatment and opportunities for everyone, again, not the least for children, by focusing on universal welfare support with free schools, highly subsidized pre-schools, free health and dental care and a child protection system focusing on prevention and parent-voluntary support and services. In this same spirit of being a world leader when it comes to children's rights, Sweden incorporated the UN Convention on the Rights of the Child (CRC) into national law in January 2020, with the express purpose being to strengthen children's rights "even more".[2]

However, a contradiction, and signs of a shift, have appeared in the debate relating to law reforms on children's issues and rights in Sweden. On the one hand, Sweden has never generally discussed and emphasized children's rights more than during the first years of the 2020's, but on the other hand, and at the same time, the rights of (some) children are made invisible or even forgotten in Sweden today. Efforts to strengthen children's rights are to a large extent focused on children in need of protection from abuse and neglect, a field in which we have seen many law reforms in recent years in the wake of a high-profile child protection incident in January 2020 where a four-year-old girl, referred to in media as "Lilla hjärtat" [Little Heart], was killed by her birth-parents. In contrast, children's needs and rights are not at all in focus in the debate and the many recent law reforms enacted with the aim of combatting gang crime and fatal shootings with young perpetrators and victims which has become an increasing and serious problem in Sweden.[3] However, even though

2 Prop. 2017/18:186 *Inkorporering av FN:s konvention om barnets rättigheter.*

3 "Gang crime" (in Swedish *gängkriminalitet*), or criminal networks, is a recurring term now in Sweden. It is not a distinct nor defined type of crime, but often (and in this chapter) is understood to include crimes committed with a connection to a group, often locally based in suburbs, and to a large extent involving drugs. As described further below, in recent years, there has been an increase in fatal shootings and explosions with the intent to kill as a result of conflicts between gangs in Sweden, and often both perpetrators and victims are young men, *see* S. Granath, 'Gäng och skjutningar', In F. Estrada Dörner et al. (eds.), *Den svenska*

children and young people are very much affected by both the consequences of gang crime and the law reforms aiming at combatting the problem, discussions on children's rights is lacking. There are also indications that there is a shift in the way that children are described and how their needs are considered in this context. From emphasizing more and more during the last decades that children are individual *rights bearers* who sometimes are in need of support and protection – also in situations when they are in conflict with the law – there is now an increasing tendency to describe (some) children as *problem bearers* responsible for societal failures and that they should be controlled and punished, without considerations of respecting their fundamental rights.

This demonstrates a clear shift in Sweden in the perception of children and in how children's rights are discussed. Initiatives for reforms in this context can be said to stand in sharp contrast to the ideas behind the Swedish welfare state, with its universal focus on equal treatment and opportunities. The shift is perhaps not surprising bearing in mind how serious the problem with gang crime and fatal shootings are in Sweden today (see further below). It can be reasonable to consider tougher measures and interventions, also targeted against children and young people. However, the invisibility of children's rights and any discussion hereof in this context, and the shift in the perception of children and childhood, is remarkable, not in the least as it is happening only a few years after the Swedish incorporation of the CRC and while at the same time there is a clear political striving to strengthen children's rights in other contexts. In both the context of the fight against gang crime and in the "Little Heart-reforms", children and the powers of the social services to intervene are in focus, but with different and contradicting purposes – in one context the motive is to *protect* children and their rights and in the other to *control* and hold young potential offenders and their families *accountable*.

This chapter addresses this current shift and contradiction. The question is quite simply – what is happening with children's rights in Sweden in the 2020s? The focus is specifically on the Swedish child welfare and protection system and the fight against gang crime. With this question as a backdrop, the overall aim in this chapter is to discuss what the shift and changes in Sweden can tell us about challenges when it comes to realizing and respecting children's rights in other contexts and jurisdictions more than 30 years after the entry into force CRC. The focus is on how law reforms in Sweden in the 2020's may lead to discrimination against *groups of children* affected by and sus-

ungdomsbrottsligheten, 5th ed. (Studentlitteratur, Lund, 2022) pp. 81–83; and J. Sarnecki and C. Carlsson, *Brottsligheten och samhället*, 3rd ed. (Studentlitteratur, Lund, 2022) pp. 100–110.

pected to be involved in gang crime – i.e. the risk that extended mandates for public authorities, aiming to combat gang crime, will in practice target and affect some children because of their immigrant background and where they live. Through such discrimination, there is a risk that (some) children's rights are not realized and respected and that their life opportunities are unfairly restricted. In line with the overall theme of this anthology the aim in this chapter is furthermore to highlight and discuss how such discrimination of some groups of children, by extension can be seen as non-legitimate differential treatment of (all) children because they are children, i.e., age discrimination. The hope is that this chapter can broaden the understanding of discrimination against children, both that between different groups of children, and non-legitimate differential treatment of children as a group, i.e. discrimination on the basis of childhood.

2 Theoretical Starting Points, Method and Outline

The analysis and discussion in this chapter takes as a starting point Article 2 CRC – the non-discrimination principle – which prescribes that states parties shall respect and ensure the rights in the CRC "to each child within their jurisdiction without discrimination of any kind, irrespective of the child's or his or her parent's or legal guardian's race, colour, sex, language religion, political or other opinion, national, ethnic or social origin, property, disability, birth or other status". Discrimination is generally – also in Article 2 of the CRC – understood to mean that a person is not treated equally to others. As discussed by Daly, Thorburn Stern and Leviner as well as Breen and other chapters in this anthology, the non-discrimination principle in the CRC has been interpreted to include not only discrimination against children on the basis that they belong to particular minority groups such as ethnic minorities, disabilities and gender, but also that age – although not explicitly referenced in the article – falls under the heading "other status".[4] It has also been noted that it is important to consider intersectionality, i.e. discrimination on multiple grounds. For example, the UN Committee on the Rights of the Child (the Committee) has, in its General Comment No. 20 from 2016, which deals with

4 *See* A. Daly et al., 'UN Convention on the Rights of the Child, Article 2 and Discrimination on the basis of Childhood – The CRC Paradox?', 91:3 *Nordic Journal of International Law* (2022) pp. 419–452; and W. Vandenhole et al., *Children's Rights: A Commentary on the Convention on the Rights of the Child and its Protocols* (Edward Elgar Publishing, Cheltenham, 2019).

children's rights during adolescence, drawn specific attention to that the risk of discrimination, not least intersectional discrimination, is of particular importance to consider during children's adolescence. It is also noted that adolescence in itself can be a source of discrimination as "adolescents may be treated as dangerous or hostile, incarcerated, exploited or exposed to violence as a direct consequence of their status".[5] In this chapter Article 2 of the CRC, with this broadened interpretation and clarification that it includes a prohibition of differences in treatment on grounds that are arbitrary and objectively unjustifiable, is used as an analytical lens. In line with what Breen argue, it is assumed that every differential treatment of children should be objectively justifiable and proportionate in order not to be discriminatory, and that the failure to identify childhood or age as a site of discrimination can have serious consequences for children.[6]

As described above, focus in this chapter is on the shift and contradictions in the context of the Swedish child welfare and protection system. The shift and contradictions are identified and analysed through a study of political initiatives and law reforms and how these are formulated in legal sources (directives for law reform commissions and preparatory works), but also described in debates in national media and political programs. It is not a comprehensive collection of material, but rather a qualitative overview based on materials that together depict the shift that has taken place, and those contradictions that can be noted when it comes to how children's rights are handled in Sweden today. It is a study of the perception of childhood and children's rights at the intersection of law and politics, with a legal scientific starting point in that the legal content and consequences of political initiatives and law reforms are the focus of the analysis. Those initiatives directly or indirectly focusing on children, adolescents and young people are central to the analysis, both that which is, and is *not* discussed and emphasized in this context.[7] Children – i.e. defined in the CRC as individuals under the age of 18 – and their

---

5 UN Committee on the Rights of the Child, *General comment No. 20 (2016) on the implementation of the rights of the child during adolescence* (CRC/C/GC/20) 6 December 2016, para. 21.

6 C. Breen, *Age Discrimination and Children's Rights: Ensuring Equality and Acknowledging Difference* (Martinus Nijhoff Publishers, Leiden, 2006); C. Breen, 'The Ageing of Article 2(1): The child's right to be free from age-based discrimination', In M. Skivenes and K. H. Sovig (eds.), *Child Rights and International Discrimination Law: Implementing Article 2 of the United Nations Convention on the Rights of the Child* (Routledge, New York, 2019).

7 The importance of also looking at what is not in focus in the political debate about children is discussed for example by G. Theborn, 'Child Politics: Dimensions and Perspectives', 3:1 *Childhood* (1996) pp. 29–44 <https://doi.org/10.1177/0907568296003001003>.

rights are in focus, but in the context analysed and discussed here, reforms and actions are sometimes targeted against 'young people' more broadly and the term 'adolescents' are also used, for example in the above mentioned General Comment by the UN Committee on the Rights of the Child. For that reason, all these terms will be used, although what will be discussed and analysed is how the shift and contradictions are affecting children (as defined in the CRC) as a group and their rights.

Political initiatives and law reforms in this field during the first four years of the 2020's in Sweden are discussed through the above-mentioned 'discrimination lens' and in light of the concept *adultification* which has been used to capture how (some) children, who are not perceived as innocent or worthy of protection, are "denied the privilege of childhood".[8] Relevant here is also scholarly discussions about how children in some contexts are not labelled as children, leading to that the subordinate position of children as a result of their age is not considered, and instead rather equating children with adults, thus making invisible the power imbalance between children and adults.[9] The shifts in political initiatives and law reforms are in this chapter also analysed and understood in the light of the basic (legal) principles on which both the Swedish welfare and child protection systems are based, but also literature and debate about the driving forces behind the exclusionary mechanisms in a universal welfare state like Sweden.[10]

8 *See* for discussion about the term 'adultification' in the context of black children in USA, but also in relation to how children with migrant background are subjected to discrimination in Germany and other European countries, M. Liebel, 'Haben Schwarze Kinder (k)eine Kindheit? Anmerkungen zur Adultification-Debatte in den USA', 20 (1) *Diskurs – Kindheits- und Jugendforschung*, (forthcoming 2025). Liebel describes in this article how the term adultification has been used by researchers in the USA for around twenty years to analyse and explain violence and discrimination experienced by black children. *See also* K. Lainpelto, 'Våra barn och andras (skäggiga) ungar', In D. Hedlund et al. (eds.), *Sammanhållning eller splittring? – Olikgörande av barn och unga i samtidens Sverige* (Jure, Stockholm, 2024) for a discussion, resembling that of Liebel and others, about how adolescents with migrant background are discriminated in the Swedish justice system.

9 J. Sundhall and S. Hillén. 'The Punishable Child in Sweden - The Tidö Agreement from a Children's Rights Perspective', 13:4 *Social Sciences* (2024) <https:// doi.org/10.3390/socsci13040215>.

10 V. Baker, *Nordic Nationalism and Penal Order: Walling the Welfare State* (Routledge, Abingdon, 2018); P. Leviner, 'Våra barn och andras ungar – om solidaritet och (o)likabehandling av barn i det svenska välfärdssystemet', In T. Erhag et al. (eds.), *Socialrätt under omvandling – om solidaritetens och välfärdsstatens gränser* (Liber, Stockholm, 2018); J. Rennerskog, 'Children in coercive care as "Responsibilized Becomings": On rights

This chapter starts with a section (Section 3) that contextualizes and describes the basis of the Swedish welfare state and the Swedish child welfare and protection system, but also the law reforms in the wake of the above-mentioned Little Heart-case, against which the 'gang crime reforms' are contrasted. Thereafter the legal aspects of political initiatives and law reforms with the aim to fight gang criminality are described and analysed. It is a snapshot description of initiatives in the first years of the 2020's and the focus is on that which can be said to represent a shift in the rhetoric, both when it comes to the role of the child welfare and protection system and how children and their rights are discussed. As will be shown, the political initiatives and law reforms are very much targeted against children, but more specifically children and young people living in disadvantaged suburban areas in Sweden, often with a migrant background and in practice affecting boys more than girls.

Based on the analysis of initiatives and reforms, the chapter ends with a concluding discussion on how, at the same time as children are very much in focus in the political debate, and thereby can be said to be 'politicized', there is a tendency to make their rights invisible. This is explained by what can be seen as an overall political understanding that combatting gang crime is more important than respecting the rights of children and young people. In the context of fighting gang criminality, children are, on the one hand, subjected to what can be labelled 'adultification' (see above) and 'over-responsibilization', which clearly risks leading to that some children – especially boys with migrant backgrounds living in disadvantaged areas in Sweden – suffer direct and indirect discrimination. However, on the other hand, by extension and somewhat contradictory, the reforms described and analysed in this chapter can also be seen as an example of children as a group being subjected to non-legitimate differential treatment compared to adults. As interventions are to a large extent are targeted against children without clear justification or assessment of proportionality this can be seen as discrimination on the basis of childhood. Children are in one sense perceived as 'different' than adults and therefor 'in need of control' – being 'treated like a child' – but at the same time, the proposals focus on making children responsible in the same way as, or even harsher than, adults. As a consequence, by this 'adultification' (some) children are denied the privilege of a childhood.

---

and responsibilization in the Swedish welfare state', 4 *Incarceration* (2003) pp. 1–18 https://doi.org/10.1177/26326663231169717

3 Contextualization: The Basis of the Swedish Welfare State and the Child Protection System

By way of background to the overall question of this chapter – what is happening in Sweden in the context of children's rights – the foundation on which the Swedish welfare state and child protection system are, or at least have been, based must be understood. It is also important to understand how this system has been reformed in recent years in the wake of the Little Heart-case described above.

The Swedish welfare state was built and grew primarily in the decades after the Second World War, but when it comes to the child welfare and protection system, the first laws came in the early 1900's. These early child protection regulations were largely focused on children who had been "morally neglected by their parents" and the "serious danger" that threatened the social order through the "moral depravity of some of the growing generation". The motive for intervention and taking children into care was the protection of society. Gradually, during the first decades of the 20th century, the focus became more and more on protecting children from harm due to poor home conditions.[11]

By the 1960's and onwards, mostly under Social Democratic governments, a welfare system emerged that – at least on the surface and in the regulations – increasingly emphasized voluntariness and self-determination, and where trust between the state and its authorities and the individual and families can be said to have been seen as a prerequisite for the ability of welfare measures to create good living conditions for the population.[12] It was not a question of ensuring the rights of individuals, but rather of helping individuals who, "with a little support", should be self-sufficient and able to contribute to society.

In an international comparison and in line with Esping-Andersen's often-cited work, The Three Worlds of Welfare Capitalism, the Swedish welfare state has been classified as "social democratic".[13] This type of welfare system, which differs from liberal systems (found in countries such as the US, Great Britain and Australia) and conservative systems (such as in Germany, France and

---

11 T. Lundström, *Tvångsomhändertagande av barn: en studie av lagarna, professionerna och praktiken under 1900-talet* (Stockholm University, Stockholm, 1993) p. 47.

12 H. Berggren and L. Trädgårdh, *Är svensken människa? – Gemenskap och oberoende i det moderna Sverige*, 2nd ed. (Norstedts, Stockholm, 2015).

13 G. Esping-Andersen, *The Three Worlds of Welfare Capitalism* (Princeton University Press, 1990).

Italy), is characterized by its focus on generous, broad and non-needs tested social support for the country's population. Equality among people is the central theme in the social democratic systems. Overall, effort is put into giving citizens a relatively high degree of independence by limiting their dependence on the family and the market, but as already mentioned, individuals are to a large extent dependent on support from the state and trust has therefore been an important aspect of Swedish society.[14]

In the same spirit with which the welfare system as a whole was built, a new child welfare and protection framework was developed in Sweden in the late 1970's, with legislation (the Social Services Act, 2001:452 and the Care of Young Persons Act, 1990:52) entering into force in the beginning of the 1980's, which still is the basis of the Swedish child welfare and protection system. This system is usually categorized as family and service-oriented, while systems in countries such as Great Britain, Australia and the US are described as risk and protection oriented.[15] In simple terms, the difference lies in the threshold for interventions by child protection authorities: it is higher in risk and protection-oriented systems than in family and service-oriented systems, and in family and service-oriented systems ideally a broader set of voluntary measures with the aim to avoid out-of-home placements to the greatest degree possible is in place and offered.

As already indicated, and described further below, the Swedish child welfare and protection system is currently going through many reforms, but it has for a long time been founded on principles of voluntariness and self-determination, and increasingly rights based in that children's rights are explicitly emphasized in the regulations. The system is also built on a fundamental belief in the notion that with some degree of support from the state, parents can achieve good living conditions for their children. Principles of voluntariness and self-determination apply – or more correctly now, have applied – regardless of what the problem and needs are – whether it is a lack of parental care and control or self-destructive behaviour by children and young

14 Berggren and Trädgårdh, *supra* note 12.

15 N. Gilbert et al. (eds.), *Child Protection Systems: International Trends and Emerging Orientations* (Oxford University Press, New York, 2011). It should be noted that, as is often the case with typologies, even in countries that at first glance seem to have similar systems, differences can be found on deeper levels, and systems with differences can of course also have similarities. The different models have been described as merging and the typology described here has been developed to include that many child protection systems are increasingly focusing on children's rights, *see* J.D. Berrick et al., 'Child Protection Systems: A Global Typology', In J.D. Berrick et al. (eds.) *Oxford Handbook of Child Protection Systems* (Oxford University Press, Oxford, 2023).

people, including criminality.[16] However, the social services have a specific and ultimate responsibility for children and young people that includes the power and obligation to intervene without consent if support and protection cannot be provided voluntarily and if a situation is so serious that there is a risk that the health and development of a child or young person will be seriously harmed (Sections 2 and 3 of the Care of Young Persons Act). Despite this mandate for the child welfare services to intervene, but in line with principles of voluntariness, it can be noted that most out-of-home placements (around 70 per cent) are voluntary, i.e., decided in collaboration with, or at least with the consent from, parents and children over 15 years old.[17] The legislation has also (so far) overall emphasized reunification of children placed outside the home with their biological parents.

When it comes to children and young people with criminal or other destructive behaviours, a basis for the Swedish child welfare services since the introduction of the Social Services Act and the Care of Young Persons Act in the 1980's, has been that interventions in this context always should be focused on meeting the need for support and care of the individual child, *not* to provide protection for society. In line with this, a clear aspiration has been that young offenders, also those who have reached the age of criminal responsibility (15 years), should be given care and support in the first instance by child welfare services rather than being sentenced to prison. As will be discussed further in this chapter this is now changing in line with reforms to combat gang criminality.

As mentioned above, the child welfare and protection system in Sweden became highly debated as a reaction to a high-profile child protection incident in January 2020 where a four-year-old girl, referred to in media as "*Lilla hjärtat*" [Little Heart], was killed by her birth-parents.[18] She had been re-united with her parents after having been placed in a foster family with the support of

16 The Swedish system, which has been described as an almost "ideal" family and service-oriented system, has already before the more recent reforms described here seen a trend during the last decade towards increased protection-oriented thinking, *see* M. Heimer et al., 'Vulnerable children's rights to participation, protection, and provision: The process of defining the problem in Swedish child and family welfare', 23:2 *Child & Family Social Work* (2018) pp. 316–323; and P. Leviner, 'Barns rätt till skydd från att fara illa – ett tydligt uppdrag men komplexa bedömningar', In K. Åhman et al. (eds.), *Barnkonventionen i praktiken – Rättsliga utmaningar och möjligheter* (Norstedts, Stockholm, 2020).

17 Socialstyrelsen, *Statistik om socialtjänstinsatser till barn och unga 2023* (Stockholm, 2024).

18 *See* Dagens Nyheter, 'Hon fick inte fylla fyra', 8 March 2020, <www.dn.se/nyheter/sverige/ hon-fick-inte-fylla-fyra/>, visited on 15 September 2024.

Care of Young Persons Act (i.e. without consent) since she was a newborn. The case gave rise to discussions concerning the entire Swedish child welfare and protection system, and a number of reforms have been implemented under the umbrella name "*Lex Lilla Hjärtat*".[19] These reforms – which to a large extent have been made with reference to the CRC and the need to strengthen children's rights – have meant that the social services have been given expanded opportunities to decide on drug tests prior to contact and reunification, and have also been given extended powers and opportunities for follow-up after placement outside the home. The most significant changes, however, concern the possibility of deciding on continued out-of-home placement and obligations to consider earlier transfer of custody to foster parents.

Overall, the recent reforms in the wake of the Lilla hjärtat case represent a clear shift from focus on voluntary services and support to focus on protection and risk, but also from the pursuit of reunification to stability and permanency for children in out-of-home-care. Thereby there is also a shift towards more control through increased mandate for child welfare services to investigate and intervene. Many aspects of these reforms are needed, but in light of other initiatives and reforms as part of the fight against gang crime discussed and analysed in the next section, it can be questioned whether this shift is proportionate and appropriate. This will be further discussed in the concluding part of the chapter.

4 The Political (and Legal) Fight against Gang Criminality from a Child Rights Perspective

4.1 *Gang Crime in Sweden in Context*

As already mentioned, gang criminality and fatal shootings have increased in Sweden in recent years and as a result, have become one of the most reported problems and debated political issues.[20] An often-raised question is why is this happening, but also, what the reasons for this problem are its increase and to what extent does it differ in Sweden compared to other countries? It is beyond the scope and aim of this chapter to describe and analyse these

19 As many as six law reform investigations have been initiated since the reporting of the case in media in March 2020 and by January 2025, four reforms have already entered into force.

20 As noted above, gang crime is not a distinct or defined type of crime, but is often (and in this chapter) understood to include crimes committed with connection to a group, often being locally based in suburbs, and to a large extent involving drugs.

questions in depth. However, by way of background, it can be concluded that while these problems are not unique to Sweden, reports indicate, and researchers seem to agree, that even though the development of violent crime in Sweden largely follows the overall decreasing trend in other comparable countries with juvenile criminality decreasing during the last two decades, Sweden seems to stand out – also in a Nordic comparison – in terms of the increase in firearm violence in criminal circles with young offenders over the last decade.[21]

Specific to these violent crimes in criminal networks or gangs, apart from the fact that the offenders and victims often are young men, often under 18 years old,[22] is that the shootings often take place in disadvantaged suburbs to Sweden's bigger cities.[23] Furthermore, research indicates, that in line with other types of criminality, those involved in gang crime to a large extent come from households with less social and economic resources, and with parents born in countries outside Europe.[24] The reasons for the development in Sweden, and why Sweden stands out in an international comparison, are (yet) uncertain.[25] Swedish criminological studies discusses situational factors such as increased access to illegal firearms and drug flows, but also segregation, increased class divisions, dismantled welfare, an increasingly unequal school system and large migration from poor countries. All in all, this has been considered to have resulted in larger groups of young men who have grown up in precarious conditions and, have had a weak connection to the labour market with a high risk of developing a criminal lifestyle as a result.[26]

---

21 *See* several chapters in A. Rostami and J. Sarnecki (eds.), *Det svenska tillståndet – en antologi om brottsutvecklingen i Sverige* (Studentlitteratur, Lund, 2022); Granath, *supra* note 3, pp. 79–114. For statistics and analysis of crimes in Sweden see reports from The Swedish National Council for Crime Prevention (in Swedish 'Brottsförebyggande rådet' or 'BRÅ' in short name): BRÅ, *Utredning och uppklaring av dödligt våld i kriminell miljö* (Rapport 2023:4); BRÅ, *Barn och unga i kriminella nätverk. En studie av inträde, brott, villkor och utträde* (Rapport 2023:13); BRÅ, *Konstaterade fall av dödligt våld – En granskning av anmält dödligt våld 2023*.

22 There are no exact numbers, but estimations are that around 1 000–1 500 young people in the age group 15–24 are involved in criminal networks or gangs, of the 1 170 000 individuals in that same age group living in Sweden, *see* Granath, *supra* note 3, pp. 79–114.

23 BRÅ, *Utredning och uppklaring av dödligt våld i kriminell miljö*, *supra* note 21; Granath, *supra* note 3.

24 Granath, *supra* note 3, pp. 79–114.

25 L. Westfelt, 'Den svenska våldsutvecklingen i ett europeiskt perspektiv', in Rostami and Sarnecki (eds.), *supra* note 21.

26 Granath, *supra* note 3, pp. 79–114.

While the reasons for the development and the cause of the problems in Sweden are uncertain, there is an overall political consensus that something must be done. As described further below, there also seem to be an absolute political bottom line – harsher punishment, more coercion and control – also in the child welfare and protection system, as the solution. The focus is also clearly very much on taking action against children and young people, who as mentioned above are over-represented as offenders in these type of crimes compared to other types of violent crimes.[27] This political response can be seen as an example of penal populism that is a trend not only in Sweden, but in many European and other 'Western countries'.[28] What is possibly specific to Sweden is that the shift towards repression and tough-on-crime-agenda, with its strong focus on children and young people, came relatively suddenly, and in such a sharp contrast to the ideology behind the Swedish welfare and child protection system described above.[29]

In the coming section this shift will be described by giving examples of political initiatives and law reforms with a focus on fighting gang crime. It is an overview of what has happened in this context in Sweden in the first years of the 2020's. The focus is not on the details of the initiatives and reforms. The aim is rather to capture that which can be said to represent a change when it comes to how children (and young people's) needs and perspectives and their rights are not on the agenda and part of the debate, but also how the role of the child welfare and protection system has shifted in the effort to combat gang crime. Attention is drawn to the risk for different types of discrimination of children in this context. As noted above, discrimination is defined as treatment of a person that is not equal to that of others, but also that non-discrimination and striving for equality includes a prohibition of differences in treatment on grounds that are arbitrary and objectively unjustifiable. In other words, it is assumed that every differential treatment of children should be proportionate and justifiable. Political initiatives and law reforms are analysed here through this lens. The focus is both on discrimination of children based on childhood, i.e. non legitimate differential treatment against children as a group, and in relation to other intersecting identities, such as

27 BRÅ, *Barn och unga i kriminella nätverk – En studie av inträde, brott, villkor och utträde* (Rapport 2023:13), *supra* note 21.

28 H. Tham, *Kriminalpolitik*, 2nd ed. (Norstedts, Stockholm, 2022). Tham refers further to Y. Monk, *The People vs. Democracy: Why Our Freedom Is in Danger and How to Save It* (Harvard University Press, Cambridge, 2018).

29 *See* for a discussion about the development in Swedish criminal politics in Tham, *supra* note 28, pp. 69–88.

socio-economic factors, living in disadvantaged areas, being first- or second-generation migrants and also being male.

4.2 *The Political Scene in Sweden in the 2020s: An Overall Tough on Crime Agenda and a New Meaning of Early Intervention*

By way of background, Sweden holds parliamentary elections every fourth year with the most recent election held in September 2022. Before this election, the Social democrats (*Socialdemokraterna*), a middle to left wing party had governed for four years, and in October 2022, three right-wing parties – the Moderate Party (*Moderaterna*), the Liberals (*Liberalerna*) and the Christian Democrats (*Kristdemokraterna*) – formed a new government with support from a right-wing populist party, the Swedish Democrats (*Sverigedemokraterna*). At a press conference in October 2022, these parties presented their political agreement, the Tidö agreement, under which they were to govern and conduct policy during their current (2022–2026) mandate period.[30] The Tidö agreement contains proposals and agreements in different areas such as healthcare, climate and energy, schools, growth, etc. and two specific sections on migration and crime.[31] With regards to the crime section of the agreement, several of the proposals relate to the fight against gang crime with heavy focus on children and young people, "Tackling youth crime" being a separate heading. Although not explicitly noted, the undertone is that the proposals target people with migrant background, living in disadvantaged areas.

Combatting gang criminality was a key issue already in the run up to the 2022 election.[32] All political parties – not only the right-wing parties that formed the basis for government in October 2022, but also the Social Democrats – came up with one proposal after the other – in an overall political consensus with a 'getting tough agenda'. Some proposals focused on tougher sentencing and increased powers for law enforcement agencies, but many initiatives were concerned with what has been labelled as 'early intervention'. However, in sharp contrast to the focus of the Swedish welfare state's voluntary measures and proactive support described above, in this setting early intervention comprises prompt repressive reactions with control and coercion. Furthermore, as will be described, the interventions are to a large extent

30 Tidö is the name of the castle where the post-election negotiations between these parties took place in October 2022.

31 The Tidö Agreement <https://moderaterna.se/app/uploads/2022/10/Tidoavtalet-Overenskommelse-for-Sverige.pdf>, visited on 15 September 2024.

32 *See further* in Tham, *supra* note 28, pp. 168–185 for a discussion and description of the specific political dimension of criminal politics in Sweden during the last 50 years.

focused on children and young people, but lack considerations in relation to how these could affect children and the respect for their rights.

4.3 *An Overview of the Shift: A New Rhetoric and Political Agenda in the Beginning of the 2020s*

A distinct beginning of the rhetorical shift when it comes to both children's rights and the role of the child welfare and protection system in the efforts to combat gang crime can be detected in September 2020 when the Moderate Party leader (who later became prime minister in the current (2025) conservative government) was interviewed on Swedish radio. In this interview, he presented a proposal that children of gang criminals should be forcibly taken into care more often and that the police and prosecutors, as a complement to the social services, should be empowered to intervene within the framework of the child protection regulations.[33] He stated the following: "If you do not ensure that your children do not grow up in serious criminality or if you do not ensure that your children do not commit crimes, then we must take over that task. I would say this is a signal that would be quite crystal clear to quite a few families".[34] This denotes a clear change in tone that led to reactions from among other researchers who responded against such a shift, noting that children would pay the price for their families' offending.[35]

Closer to the election, in August 2022, the Moderate Party also made political statements in media that all five-year-olds in disadvantaged areas should be tested for ADHD, with the aim of preventing recruitment to criminal gangs. The basis for the proposals, as it must be interpreted from statements by party representatives, is that there is a clear link between ADHD in childhood and later violent crime, and the fact that children with migrant backgrounds consume ADHD medication to a lesser extent than other children in Sweden (i.e. not 'treating' the symptoms) is a problem. The party's legal policy spokesperson stated: "There is no single reason why a person becomes a criminal, but there is a large representation of people with ADHD in the country's prisons. We need to get into this field if we are serious about breaking the cycle of gang

---

33 There is now an on-going governmental committee preparing concrete law reform in line with this proposal – *see* Government Committee Directive, Dir. 2023:160, *Stärkt barnrättsperspektiv i LVU och en översyn av grunderna för vård.*

34 Swedish Radio, 'Gör det lättare att omhänderta gängkriminellas barn', 12 September 2020, <https://sverigesradio.se/artikel/7552424>, visited on 15 September 2024.

35 *See* for example, Svenska Dagbladet, 'Risk med förslaget: barnen får betala priset', 12 September 2020, <https://www.svd.se/a/1Bk5GK/kritik-mot-m-forslag-barnen-betalar-priset>, visited on 15 September 2024.

recruitment. We need to find these children, and it will also prevent crime."[36] This proposal was also criticized by researchers, questioning among other things its effectiveness and the risk of discrimination.[37]

Around the same time, in August 2022, the Liberals proposed that all two-year-olds should have their language development assessed by the Child Health Services, and that this test should be made mandatory for parents whose children are not enrolled in preschool.[38] The idea as it was presented was that this would allow children with language difficulties to be detected earlier and the aim was said to be to prevent the recruitment of young people into gang criminality. The proposal was combined with the suggestion that where children have language difficulties and do not attend preschool, "social services should be involved".[39] In line with the reactions against the ADHD-proposals, this initiative was also criticized for lacking scientific ground and reasonability.[40]

During the election campaign in 2022 the right-wing populist party the Swedish Democrats (part of the Tidö agreement described above) put forward a proposal that children – as young as nine years old – who commit crimes could be given what was called "shameful community service". The proposal appeared to be aimed at gang criminality and the purpose was stated to be "status degradation" through the idea that children and young people in a criminal environment will have their status reduced within their circle as a result of the sanction. The legal policy spokesperson for the party explained that it should be a form of community service with a "status degrading purpose", the meaning of which was not further explained. In the same statement,

36 *See* article in the evening newspaper Expressen, 'M: ADHD-testa alla barn i utsatta områden', 11 August 2022, <https://www.expressen.se/nyheter/m-adhd-utred-alla-barn-i-utsatta-omraden/>, visited on 15 September 2024.

37 *See* interview with Lisa Thorell, Karolinska Institute in Swedish Radio, 'Forskare på ADHD: Jag tror inte att det här är lösningen', 12 August 2022, <https://sverigesradio.se/artikel/forskare-pa-adhd-jag-tror-inte-att-det-har-ar-losningen>, visited on 15 September 2024.

38 *See* the Liberal Party website and election manifestation, 'Förskoleplikt för barn som ligger efter i svenska', 9 August 2022, <https://www.liberalerna.se/nyheter/l-forskoleplikt-for-barn-som-ligger-efter-i-svenska>, visited on 15 September 2024.

39 *See* debate in Swedish Television, 'Debatt mellan Pehrson och Stenevi om förskoleplikt för barn med bristfällig svenska', 12 August 2022, <https://www.svt.se/nyheter/inrikes/debatt-mellan-pehrson-och-stenevi-om-forskoleplikt-for-barn-med-bristfallig-svenska>, visited on 15 September 2024.

40 *See* debate article in Dagens Nyheter, Signe Tonér et al., 'Obligatoriskt språktest saknar vetenskapligt stöd', 18 August 2022, <https://www.dn.se/debatt/obligatoriskt-spraktest-saknar-vetenskapligt-stod>, visited on 15 September 2024.

the party proposed that the age of criminal responsibility be lowered from 15 to 13 years.[41]

These proposals from the first years of the 2020's focused mostly on younger children, but both the previous and current government under the Tidö-agreement have also proposed several legal reforms focusing more on, and definitely affecting, how children and young people can be controlled 'preventively' through among other things curfews controlled by electronic monitoring, security zones, and secret coercive measures such as wiretapping.[42] These preventive measures would under some circumstances be allowed on the basis of mere abstract suspicion of crime, and against children under 15.[43] Overall, it can be concluded that during the first years of the 2020s there was a clear shift in rhetoric, and the tough on crime agenda with a focus on children and young people now appears to be a 'new normal'. Restrictions on fundamental rights and freedoms are being legitimized by reference to the fight against gang crime. This new agenda will be described in a bit more detail in the next section.

4.4 *From Shift to 'New Normal': The Agenda in Tidö-Agreement*

As described above, the Government in power since October 2022 has, together with the Swedish Democrats, presented the political agreement and program, the Tidö-agreement, under which they govern and conduct policy during the current (2022–2026) mandate period. Several of the proposals in the section concerning crime relate to the fight against gang crime and youth crime generally, and it can be seen that a fast pace of reform is intended. Even though there are critical reactions from for example the Swedish Bar Association and civil rights organizations,[44] the Tidö-agenda can be described as a 'new normal' in the debate and media coverage. Examples of proposed reforms in the Tidö-agreement are to establish youth prisons to re-

---

41 See *for example*, Omni, 'SD vill kunna ge nioåringar skamfull samhällstjänst', 17 August 2022, <https://omni.se/sd-vill-kunna-ge-nioaringar-skamfull-samhallstjanst/a/Qyn9dQ>, visited on 15 September 2024. As will be described below, by January 2025 a committee has put forward a proposal to lower the age of criminal responsibility from 15 to 14, See SOU 2025:11 *Straffbarhetsåldern.*

42 Prop. 2019/20:118 *Ungdomsövervakning*, Ds 2022:12, *Vistelseförbud för barn,* and Prop. 2023/24:84 *Säkerhetszoner.*

43 Prop. 2022/23:126 *Hemliga tvångsmedel – effektiva verktyg för att förhindra och utreda allvarliga brott* and Dir. 2023:102 *Utökade möjligheter att använda tvångsmedel mot barn och unga.*

44 *See e.g.* Statement of Opinion from the Swedish Bar Association, Advokatsamfundet, R-2022/2284 (Stockholm, 2023) and Civil Rights Defenders, *As a whole, it is worrying – One year with the Tidö Agreement* (Stockholm, 2023).

place special youth homes,[45] the extension of sentences for young people including lowering the age of criminal responsibility,[46] and an expansion of youth supervision with, as already mentioned above, expanded possibilities for strip searches, house searches and secret coercive measures also targeted against children. At the time of writing, begining of 2025, all of these proposals seem likely to be introduced.

As to the specific question of lowering the age of criminal responsibility, the government, in July 2023 initiated a law reform committee that was to consider stricter rules on punishment for young offenders. In the directives to this committee, it was first pointed out that "there is an exceptional situation in Sweden when it comes to the development of young offenders with connection to gang criminality and serious violence to which this leads". It is also emphasized that this situation is a result of the failure of society to react in time with sufficient interventions and preventive actions.[47] The directives for the committee further specifically emphasizes that the CRC and its article 40 do not pose a problem to lowering the age of criminal responsibility, that the age in Sweden must be adjusted to "Swedish conditions" and that the recommendations from the UN Committee on the Rights of the child "are not binding".[48] As will be further discussed, these statements by the Government are surprising in light of its strong commitment to the CRC in other contexts and as these proposals stand in sharp contrast to the long tradition of diverting children and young people out of the criminal law system. By the time of proof reading this chapter the committee has, in line with the directives from the Government, proposed to lower the age of criminal responsibility from 15 to 14 in cases with certain serious crimes.[49]

A shift in the role of the social services and the child welfare and protection system can also be found in the Tidö agreement. For example, it is proposed that social services would be more frequently co-located with the police. It is

---

45 A law reform proposal has already been presented, *see* SOU 2023:44, *En översyn av regleringen om frihetsberövande påföljder för unga*, which will likely enter into force in the near future.

46 A law reform committee has been established to give proposals as to both removing penalty discounts for young offenders and lowering the age of criminal responsibility, *see* Dir. 2023:112, *Skärpta regler för unga lagöverträdare*. By the time of proof reading this chapter this committee has put forward a proposal to lower the age from 15 to 14 for some specific and severe offences. *See* SOU 2025:11 *Straffbarhetsåldern*.

47 Ibid, p. 4.

48 Ibid, 2023:112, p. 6.

49 It is also proposed that the reform should be evaluated after five years of entering into force. *See* SOU 2025:11 *Straffbarhetsåldern*.

explicitly stated that the Care of Young Persons Act, the law that permits out-of-home placements of children and young people, "should be used more often" and that the child welfare and protection regulation is to be reformed with a view to extending the mandate to take children into care in order to keep them from organized crime or other criminal activities.[50] In line with the Tidö-agreement, a law reform has also been proposed to give authorities the mandate to evict parents from housing whose children are involved in gang crime.[51]

The aim of this description of Swedish law reform proposals in the 2020's is to illustrate the shift in the rhetoric and political agenda, both when it comes to the role of the child welfare and protection system and how children and their rights are discussed (and not). How the initiatives and proposals can be understood and what the risk of negative consequences are from a child rights perspective, are discussed below. The challenges in realizing and respecting children's rights 'even' in a country such as Sweden, having marketed itself as the most child-friendly country in the world, will be discussed, and the initiatives and proposals will be contrasted and analysed against the back-drop of the ideas behind and challenges in the Swedish universal welfare system.

5 Politicized Children, Invisible Rights and Discrimination against Groups of Children and Children as a Group

So, what is happening with children's rights in Sweden in the 2020s? As shown above, children's rights have never before been so widely discussed, not least in relation to the incorporation of the CRC in January 2020. At the same time, reforms entailing limitations of children's fundamental rights and discrimination against (some) children are proposed in the context of the political frenzy to combat gang crime. The recent political reforms outlined above are very repressive in character, and focussed largely on children and young people. The social services are to be given a new controlling and reactive role, which is in sharp contrast to the basic principles of the Swedish welfare state and those that the child welfare and protection system have been based on. The pro-

50 *See* the Tidö Agreement, *supra* note 31, pp. 21–22; *See also* directives to yet another law reform committee established in December 2023 with the task of proposing reforms of the Care of Young Persons Act, Dir. 2023:160, *Stärkt barnrättsperspektiv i LVU och en översyn av grunderna för vård.*

51 Prop. 2023/24:112 *Åtgärder för tryggare bostadsområden.*

posals also imply a shift in the approach to young offenders in the Swedish welfare and child protection system. This concluding section of the chapter will address how the shift and changes can be understood and challenged from a child rights perspective, and more specifically, how the recent political initiatives and law reforms may lead to discrimination of groups of children affected by and involved in gang crime, but also, by extension, how this can be seen as an example of non-legitimate differential treatment of children because they are children.

5.1 *'Adultification' and 'Over-Responsibilizing' Children for Society's Failure*

As has been described focus in the political debate is to a large extent on how to handle children and young people and thereby to combat gang crime. Children in this way have become 'politicized', but with a tendency to make children's rights invisible. In other words, it can be described as politicians being tough on crime but soft on children's rights. This is happening at the same time as children's rights and the need to strengthen these rights are very much in focus in the wake of the Little Heart case with reforms enacted to make sure children are protected from abuse and neglect.

It is easy to see that a child rights perspective is to a large extent absent in the political debate and in the discussion about the proposed law reforms to combat gang crime. In fact, not even the risk that children themselves face being in unsafe environments and becoming potential victims of crime, or drawn into criminality, is being discussed. Instead, children and young people who are perceived to be, or who are at risk of being, connected to criminal circles are to a large extent portrayed as 'adult criminals' even without suspicions of them having committed crimes. This can be compared to what has been noted in the migration context and the discussion about the "migrant child-paradox" with children being seen as migrants first and only children (with specific rights) second.[52] In the context here, children are to a large extent viewed and portrayed as 'just criminals', not even secondly as children. This is in line with what the UN Committee has warned against in the above referred General Comment on adolescence, noting that children in this age

52 *See* for discussion about this in Rebecca Thorburn Stern in this anthology and also, *e.g.* J. Bhabha, 'Arendt's children: Do today's migrant children have a right to have rights?', 31:2 *Human Rights Quarterly* (2009), pp. 410–451; and J. Josefsson, *Children at the Borders*, Tema Barn, Department of Philosophy, Linköping University, Diss. (Linköping, 2016).

group can be seen and treated as dangerous or hostile as a direct consequence of their age.[53]

From an overall emphasis in Swedish child protection and welfare policies on the need to support children at risk and to deal with young offenders in a child-friendly way, we now see a tendency towards holding problematic children accountable for societal failures. This can be described and understood as an over-responsiblization of children as a group. From a historical perspective, there are similarities between the current rhetoric and that which was formulated in the legislative preparatory work for the 1902 child welfare legislation in Sweden mentioned above in section 3. As was the case more than 120 years ago, the priority is now to protect society from the serious danger posed by children and young people. Children in the context of gang crime in Sweden in the 2020's are in this sense seen as children *as* danger, not children *in* danger, and are not being seen as bearers of rights (in need of protection), but instead bearers of problems.

Society's failure to counteract crime and unrest is to a large extent blamed on children and young people, and their involvement is used as an argument for more control and out-of-home care. In sharp contrast to the principles of the Swedish child welfare and protection system, law reforms and initiatives now focus on harsher punishments, the removal of penalty discounts for young offenders and even lowering of the age of criminal responsibility. Apart from this being an example of how children are held collectively responsible for societal failures, this can also be seen as an 'adultification' of those children who are drawn into criminal activities. They are not seen as children and are thereby denied a childhood which there are strong political emphasis on guaranteeing for 'other' children. With the proposed interventions children who are associated with gang criminality are targeted and controlled *more than adults*, but at the same time at the same time to be punished in the *same way as adults.*

This is in sharp contrast to the policies that the UN Committee on the Rights of the Child urge state parties to introduce, the emphasis is here on the need for comprehensive juvenile justice policies that emphasize restorative justice, diversion from judicial proceedings, alternative measures to detention and preventive interventions with a focus on rehabilitation and reintegration, and that state parties should tackle social factors and root causes

53 UN Committee on the Rights of the Child, *General comment No. 20 (2016) on the implementation of the rights of the child during adolescence* (CRC/C/GC/20) 6 December 2016, para. 21.

to youth criminality.[54] As described above, the Committee has specifically, in the Concluding Observations issued after the sixth review of Sweden in 2023, criticized the plans to lower the age of criminal responsibility.[55] However, as described above, the Swedish Government has clearly stated that such remarks and recommendations from the Committee are not binding.[56] Regardless of how such recommendations are to be viewed – they are not binding as such, but provide guidance on how the CRC is to be interpreted and applied – it is of course important that state parties respect them. This leads further to questions about the legality and proportionality of the proposed interventions described above, which, together with the risk of discrimination against some children and by extension, non-legitimate and unfair treatment of children as a group, are discussed in the next and last section of this chapter.

5.2 *Discrimination and Proportionality: 'Our Children vs. Other People's Kids' and the Non-legitimate and Unfair Treatment of Children as a Group*

Most people in Sweden would probably agree that the situation with gang crime and fatal shootings is unsustainable and that something must be done. The purpose of this chapter is not to assess or propose which measures to be taken, nor does it claim that reactive measures are never to be used or that interventions should not target children and young people. No perfect solution to the problem exists, and human rights and fundamental freedoms of individuals must sometimes be limited in order to fight criminality or other threats to society. However, interventions must respect human rights, also those of children, and always be both objectively justifiable and proportionate, i.e. fair, necessary and in balance with the goal to be achieved.

What we are seeing in Sweden today can be described as a slippage in purpose, where there is a normalization of acting repressively and a tough-on-crime agenda is considered necessary in circumstances which are in fact not widespread but exceptional. Here it is worth noting what the UN Committee on the Rights of the Child noted in the above-mentioned Concluding Ob-

54 Ibid., para. 88.

55 UN Committee on the Rights of the Child, *Concluding observations on the combined sixth and seventh periodic reports of Sweden* (CRC/C/SWE/CO/6–7) 6 February 2023, para. 45 a). The Committee has made such remarks in several Concluding observations and also in the above-mentioned General Comment on adolescence, *supra* note 52, para. 88.

56 Dir. 2023:112, *Skärpta regler för unga lagöverträdare*, p. 6.

servations to Sweden in 2023, as an indication of what, in their opinion, should be done in Sweden regarding gang crime:

> Develop a strategy for the prevention of child offending, based on research and analysis of the root causes of children's involvement in crime, in particular organized crime, and ensure that it includes early intervention directed at children at risk or in vulnerable situations and support for their families.[57]

The Committee highlights an important problem – that children in Sweden are made responsible for a societal failure in the absence of an analysis of the reasons behind the problems of gang crime or any deeper understanding of what measures are likely to succeed. There is a risk that the causes of the problem will be lost in favour of dealing with the 'symptoms', and that the measures introduced will be inadequate or, worse, counterproductive, not least for those children and young people being targeted. The fact that reforms are focused on children, and more specifically children in disadvantaged areas, means that the consequences for this group must be monitored and acknowledged.

It is important to emphasize that gang crime and the measures to combat it are closely linked to children's different living conditions in Sweden. It is clear that the measures to curb gang crime particularly affect children in what are usually called disadvantaged suburban areas. As noted in the criminology research referenced above, it is also in such areas that gangs are primarily established and recruit children and young people, and where many of the fatal shootings take place. The risk of exposure to criminal environments is thus unequally distributed across the country and some groups of children are at significantly greater risk than others – both because of gang criminality creating unsafe environments and because they are themselves being targeted in the measures to combat gang crime. There is a clear risk in this context that children are discriminated against, both directly and indirectly, because of belonging to socio-economically disadvantaged groups, often with migrant backgrounds. To put it bluntly, it is not our politicians' 'own children', but rather 'other people's kids' who are affected.[58]

57 UN Committee on the Rights of the Child, *Concluding observations on the combined sixth and seventh periodic reports of Sweden, supra* note 54, p. 45 c).

58 It is worth thinking about the song by Manic Street Preachers – "If you tolerate this, your children will be next".

This can be described as an exclusionary mechanism of the welfare state,[59] where some children, often second-generation migrants in disadvantaged areas, are 'over-responsibilized' and 'adultified', but through law reforms that (at least on the surface) appear to apply equally to *all* children. There is then also a risk that children *as a group* suffer non-legitimate and unfair differential treatment compared to adults, i.e. age-discrimination. Again, it can be concluded that children at the same time are both 'over-responsibilized' and treated like adults in that they are to be sentenced and punished as if they were over 18, but yet in other aspects and settings, treated like children, in that they are to be controlled and disciplined. This is especially true for some children in an intersectional toxic combination of discrimination.

In conclusion, interventions and measures with the aim of combatting gang crime must be proportionate, i.e. balanced against that which can be achieved. This means that there has to be more certainty about the effectiveness of that which is proposed, and interventions should be specifically analysed from a child's rights perspective. The political debate in Sweden today creates a risk that children who for some reason are connected to gangs or criminal circles are not only seen as criminals and problem bearers, rather than children with rights, but are politicized and used in a 'tough-on-crime race'. In times of stress, fear and crisis, it is more important than ever to respect and consider the basic rule of law principles and human rights. When it comes to the human rights of children, it is important to point out that the rights in the CRC apply fully to *all* children, even those who commit crimes or who are at risk of being drawn into criminality. Rights are not to be earned and the status of children as children must always be respected. Also in Sweden.

59 *See* discussion by both Barker and Rennerskog, *Supra* note 10.

Index

www.ingramcontent.com/pod-product-compliance
Lightning Source LLC
LaVergne TN
LVHW020653300926
849161LV00004B/934
9789004708426